W9-DBS-358

Dark Night, Early Dawn

Suny series in
Transpersonal and Humanistic Psychology

Richard D. Mann, editor

Dark Night, Early Dawn
Steps to a Deep Ecology of Mind

Christopher M. Bache

Foreword by
Stanislav Grof

CABRINI COLLEGE LIBRARY
610 KING OF PRUSSIA ROAD
RADNOR, PA 19087

STATE UNIVERSITY OF NEW YORK PRESS

BF
204.7
.B33
2000

#42603193

Published by
State University of New York Press, Albany

© 2000 State University of New York

All rights reserved

Printed in the United States of America

No part of this book may be used or reproduced in any manner
whatsoever without written permission. No part of this
book may be stored in a retrieval system or transmitted
in any form or by any means including electronic,
electrostatic, magnetic tape, mechanical, photocopying,
recording, or otherwise without the prior permission in
writing of the publisher.

For information, address the State University of New York Press,
90 State Street, Suite 700, Albany, NY 12246

Cover Image : *The Earth and Moon* courtesy of the Galileo Project and
NASA

Production by Kristin Milavec
Marketing by Fran Keneston

Library of Congress Cataloging-in-Publication Data

Bache, Christopher Martin.
    Dark night, early dawn : steps to a deep ecology of mind /
Christopher M. Bache; forword by Stanislav Grof.
        p.   cm.—(SUNY series in transpersonal and humanistic psychology)
    Includes bibliographical references and index.
    ISBN 0-7914-4605-0 (hardcover : alk. paper)—ISBN 0-7914-4606-9
(pbk. : alk. paper)
        1. Transpersonal psychology.   2. Psychology—Philosophy.
3. Altered states of consciousness.   4. Reincarnation. I. Title. I. Series
    BF204.7 B33   2000
    150.19'8—dc21   99-049013

10 9 8 7 6 5 4 3 2

To Carol

A new order on earth will not begin, I believe, until we all learn to see the pollution in our own hearts. And that will not happen until many of us, a critical mass, experience with remorse a real change of consciousness.

—James George, *Asking for the Earth*

Contents

Foreword

The second half of the twentieth century has seen an extraordinary renaissance of interest in the exploration of human consciousness. Its most dramatic and widely publicized expressions were clinical research with psychedelics, conducted during the 1950s and 1960s in many countries of the world, and unsupervised self-experimentation with these remarkable agents. After drastic administrative and legal restrictions terminated scientific experimentation with psychedelics, deep self-exploration has continued in the form of powerful new forms of nondrug experiential psychotherapy, such as various neo-Reichian approaches, hypnosis, primal therapy, rebirthing, and Holotropic Breathwork.

Laboratory research contributed the methods of sensory deprivation, biofeedback, lucid dreaming, and the use of various electronic entrainment devices. The work with patients dying of terminal diseases and the study of the states of consciousness emerging in near-death situations gave birth to a new scientific discipline—thanatology. Careful systematic investigation of spontaneous past-life experiences in children and of past-life experiences induced in adults by a variety of methods made it possible to subject to scientific scrutiny the concept of reincarnation and karma. The zeitgeist of this era also brought great enthusiasm for the study of shamanism, the ritual life of aboriginal cultures, the spiritual philosophies of the East, and the mysticism of all countries and ages.

The empirical interest in consciousness and spirituality characterizing this exciting period has been accompanied by systematic efforts to find expanded theoretical frameworks for the wide range of revolutionary discoveries concerning the nature of the human psyche that this work had produced. These challenging observations inspired transpersonal psychology, a discipline that studies the entire range of human experience, including nonordinary states of consciousness, and that attempts to bring together the best of spirituality and the best of science.

Christopher Bache—philosopher, religious scholar, and inspired educator—has made important contributions to this endeavor and has established himself as one of the most creative and original transpersonal thinkers. In a series of articles, presentations at international transpersonal conferences, and his earlier book *Lifecycles*, he has addressed some of the most important and urgent theoretical issues that have emerged in modern consciousness research. *Dark Night, Early Dawn* represents a culmination and synopsis of years of his explorations and is his most mature work to date.

What makes Bache's contribution invaluable is a rare combination of rigorous spiritual discipline, profound personal experience with nonordinary states of consciousness, incisive analytical thinking, and impeccable scholarship. All these qualities are absolutely indispensable for the important task he has set for himself—to seek the greatest possible clarity in a highly controversial area that has the potential to change the entire philosophical paradigm of Western science. As Bache himself convincingly demonstrates in the introductory chapter of his book, what is at stake is nothing less than our understanding of consciousness, our identity, and the nature of reality itself.

It is astonishing that the academic circles in their deep commitment to materialistic philosophy and linear determinism have thus far refused to critically examine the extraordinary and startling observations amassed by several decades of consciousness research and transpersonal psychology. Had that happened, it would have led to an inevitable conclusion—the urgent need for a radical revision of our understanding of human nature and the nature of reality. Bache justly compares the academic community to a culture that in its search for truth has denied itself access to the night sky with its deep secrets and bases its worldview entirely on daytime observations.

A salient example of this deep reluctance to face observations that undermine and challenge the leading paradigm is the repeatedly confirmed fact of out-of-body experiences, during which disembodied consciousness, even that of congenitally blind persons, is capable of perceiving events in the immediate environment and in various remote locations. This observation, in and of itself, should be sufficient to raise serious doubts about our current beliefs concerning the relationship between consciousness and matter. And yet, educators in our universities continue to teach with unshaken authority that consciousness is an epiphenomenon of matter and that it somehow mysteriously emerges out of the complexity of neurophysiological processes in the central nervous system.

Christopher Bache does much more than bring a convincing argument for the critical epistemological and ontological importance of the study of nonordinary states of consciousness. Using his intimate knowledge of the deepest recesses of the human psyche, he brings extraordinary clarity into theoretically important areas in transpersonal psychology, particularly psychedelic states, near-death experiences, and out-of-body episodes.

Bache often reveals impartially both the strength and the weakness of a particular set of data or theoretical position. In the chapter discussing reincarnation, for example, he clearly indicates the impeccability of Ian Stevenson's research of the past-life experiences in children and the defective reasoning of his critics. At the same time, he demonstrates that the very aspects of Stevenson's material that make it compelling evidence for rebirth also create a bias that tends to prevent us from appreciating the profound implications of reincarnation for our understanding of our true identity.

Bache's search for our deeper identity takes him to psychedelic research, where he explores numerous examples of a much more extensive dissolution of personal boundaries than those found in Stevenson's material. Besides the temporal dissolution of boundaries, psychedelic states often involve various degrees of transcendence of spatial limitations. Here Bache focuses on a problem that has intrigued me from the very beginning of my psychedelic research. When the transformational process reaches beyond postnatal biography, one's experiences typically make a quantum leap and become distinctly transpersonal. Instead of identifying with our body and ego in different stages of personal development, we can become the consciousness of entire human groups or even humanity as a whole.

As Bache graphically demonstrates, using examples from his own experience, in many instances this involves re-experiencing unimaginable suffering from various periods of human history. The question arises: is it conceivable that suffering of this scope and depth can be seen as being merely part of the healing process of just one individual? Bache convincingly argues that it is not, that at this point, the therapeutic process transcends the boundaries of the individual and begins to affect the healing of the field of human consciousness as a whole. The archetypal images of Jesus, whose suffering redeems the sins of humanity, or of a Bodhisattva, who sacrifices his or her own spiritual liberation to help other sentient beings, are very appropriate symbols for this phase of the process.

Applying his expanded understanding of the perinatal level to the field of thanatology, Bache focuses on the enigma of terrifying near-death experiences and extends this discussion to the problem of hell. The early reports of near-death experiences all emphasized the transcendental and heavenly nature of these episode and the possibility of hellish NDEs was long denied by most thanatologists. Although their existence has now been proven beyond any reasonable doubt, no one before Bache had offered a convincing explanation of them.

Bache argues that the passage to light that is a common part of the near-death experience represents a condensed and accelerated traversing of what I have called the perinatal realm. Viewed from this perspective, the hellish near-death experience can be seen as an incomplete NDE that did not carry the individual all the way through to the encounter with the divine light. In the same vein, Bache suggests that hell, rather than being the abode of eternal damnation, is an extremely difficult stage of the journey of spiritual opening, a stage of deep and accelerated purification.

Bache then turns to Robert Monroe's soul-centered accounts of his out-of-body experiences and ponders their seeming differences from those encountered in psychedelic sessions, which have a much more holistic character. He argues that these differences reflect the different techniques used to induce these experiences, with psychedelic states dissolving the egoic boundaries more aggressively than out-of-body states, thus allowing broader transpersonal patterns of reality to surface in awareness. Accordingly, he emphasizes the need for transpersonal theorists to pay greater attention to how one's experiential method influences the shape and texture of transpersonal disclosure.

The conclusions of Bache's critical analysis of selected observations from transpersonal psychology and consciousness research, startling and shocking as they might appear to the mind of an average Western scientist, are fully congruent with the great Eastern spiritual philosophies and mystical traditions of the world, which Aldous Huxley referred to as the perennial philosophy. They show that human beings do not have a fixed identity and that the temporal as well as spatial boundaries of our individual self are relative and ultimately illusory.

When we transcend all these boundaries in deep experiential self-exporation, we realize that all of existence is a manifestation of one Being that has been known throughout the ages by many different names—Atman, the Tao, Buddha, the Great Spirit, Allah, Keter, the Cosmic Christ, and many others. The ultimate identity of each of us with this principle, whom Bache chooses to call the Sacred Mind, is the deepest secret of all great spiritual traditions.

While earlier chapters of the book represent primarily original theoretical contributions to transpersonal psychology, its closing chapters also have important practical implications. By discussing at some length and with practical examples how his inner search influenced the nature and quality of his teaching, Bache reveals the existence of mechanisms that are of great interest for educators. His analysis of the emergence of transpersonal fields in the classroom setting has the potential to revolutionize the educational process.

Even more far-reaching are Bache's reflections on the current global crisis. Many authors have suggested that humanity is approaching an evolutionary crossroads, but Bache goes further to explore the role that the impending eco-crisis may play in this transition and outlines specific dynamics operating in the collective unconscious that he believes might be responsible for changing the baseline of human consciousness in an unexpectedly short period of time.

Furthermore, if he is right that the transformational work of an individual can generate a therapeutic effect in the field of species consciousness, then each of us has the potential to contribute to a more harmonious future for the planet by complementing our social activism with deep inner work. Considering the consistent failure of all economic, military, political, and diplomatic interventions, such a mass inner transformation might be humanity's only real hope for survival.

Dark Night, Early Dawn is a unique contribution to transpersonal psychology. It is a product of creative imagination inspired by inner journeys to the farthest frontiers of the psyche and yet a work forged by a rigorous intellect and impeccable scholarship. A fine example of a courageous pioneering venture into rarely traveled territories of the human psyche, it will remain a classic in the transpersonal field.

STANISLAV GROF

Preface

Because the world of nonordinary states of consciousness is unfamiliar territory to most academics even today, many may find the line of thought presented in this volume unacceptably radical. When I finished graduate school in 1978, however, with degrees in theology, New Testament, and philosophy of religion, few would have accused me of being radical. Beginning my academic training as a Roman Catholic and finishing it as an atheistically inclined agnostic, I had recapitulated five hundred years of cultural evolution in my education—moving from medieval theology to the Reformation with its scriptural emphasis, to the revolution of historicocritical scholarship and the eclipsing of the biblical tradition, to the breakthrough of science and self-critical reason, and finally to analytic philosophy, phenomenology, and the enlightened critique of religion. I finished my schooling well versed in the many stages of reason's ascent and religion's decline in the modern mind.

Shortly after beginning my teaching career, however, I encountered the work of Stanislav Grof. In *Realms of the Human Unconscious* Grof convinced me that the entire intellectual tradition I had absorbed was based upon a superficial experience of the human psyche. Through my earlier reading of Jung, I had already become convinced that depth psychology held the key to the modern mind's quest to know itself, and here was a deeper and more comprehensive psychology than any I had seen before. More importantly, Grof outlined a methodology through which one could actually extend one's experience of one's mind and come to have firsthand knowledge of these domains. I could not turn down the invitation.

In time, however, I came to learn that many of my university colleagues did not share my enthusiasm for Grof's research. His observations were so radical, his conclusions so incompatible with their intellectual traditions that it would require enormous evidence to convince them of the legitimacy of his findings. The fact that his results were replicable across large populations and coherent both with recent breakthroughs in science and with philosophical systems of great antiquity coming from the East did not sway them. I came to recognize that it was not just that they viewed psychedelics with suspicion but that nonordinary states of consciousness themselves were not deemed an appropriate source of genuine knowledge, let alone as capable of providing us with information that might actually advance our attempt to solve long-standing problems in epistemology, philosophy of mind, and philosophy of religion. The reigning materialist paradigm stipulated that the keys to the kingdom lay in the continued dissection of ordinary states of consciousness, not in immersing oneself in the uncertain waters of the deep psyche. Once the door had been opened, however, there was no turning back.

This volume springs from a deep engagement of Grof's therapeutic regimen stretching across twenty years, an engagement that has carried me beyond the limits of what I had thought was humanly possible, beyond time and space, and beyond identity as I had known it. It represents an attempt to begin speaking about matters that I started to comprehend only after many years of inner exploration and reflects themes that surfaced during approximately the first half of my journey within.

Whatever I have come to understand from working in nonordinary states is still unfolding, and therefore what follows is necessarily incomplete. Incompleteness is the cost we pay for beginning to appreciate the true dimensions of our existence. Everything we know tends to be reconfigured as deeper levels of mind open. This happens again and again until one eventually realizes that the need for completeness must be set aside. I hope the reader will be able to feel this commitment to openendedness and my willingness to revise anything as still deeper layers reveal themselves.

May all beings be free of suffering and the causes of suffering.
May all beings have happiness and the causes of happiness.

Acknowledgments

I would like to thank my students at Youngstown State University and the California Institute of Integral Studies who worked through earlier drafts of the manuscript and generously shared their reflections with me. I especially want to thank a group of students who met with me on their own time during the winter of 1996 to help me give voice to these ideas when they were at their most vulnerable stage. This includes Janine Copp, Steve Ilko, Rob McBride, Randi Pappa, Marjorie Napoli, Skip Slavik, and Chuck Underwood. Numerous colleagues from several institutions were kind enough to read the manuscript in whole or in part and give me the benefit of their counsel including Duane Elgin, Jorge Ferrer, Stanislav Grof, Sean Kelly, Robert McDermott, David Quinby, Peter Reason, Kenneth Ring, Thomas Shipka, Brian Swimme, Richard Tarnas, Jenny Wade, and Michael Zimmerman. Their enthusiasm for the project made the work lighter, and their many suggestions greatly improved the text. I particulary wish to thank Richard Tarnas for our long conversations on the ideas contained here, for the clarity of his constructive criticism, and for his valued companionship on a road less traveled.

What I owe Stanislav Grof is more than can be put into words. His powerful synthesis of clinical and spiritual psychology has defined the framework of much of my professional and personal life. I would not have had the courage to enter some of these interior regions had I not known that he had entered before me and survived. He gave me the means to see the hidden splendor of the universe from a unique perspective at a critical time in human history, and I am eternally grateful.

The core of this book was written while I was on sabbatical leave from Youngstown State University, and I would like to thank my department chair, Thomas Shipka, and the university community for their support. I would especially like to thank Linda "Tess" Tessier for her partnership in pioneering scholarship that goes against the mainstream.

I want express my deep gratitude to Tsultrim Allione, founder of Tara Mandala, a Buddhist meditation retreat in southern Colorado, for the gift of the living dharma and for her support in helping me integrate two spiritual traditions. In the same vein, I wish to thank the members of the Youngstown Valley Sangha for their friendship and spiritual companionship. I want to thank my children, Jason, Kevin, and Lara, for the joy and support they have given me at every stage of this project, for their patience with my many absences on the weekends, and for their pride in our collective accomplishment. Lastly, I want to thank my wife, who is also my sitter and my best friend. Her participation and support made the work possible, and her hand is on every page.

Grateful acknowledgment is made to the following for permission to quote previously published material:

Chelsea Green Publishing Co. for permission to quote from *Beyond the Limits*, copyright © 1992 by Meadows, Meadows and Randers. To order call toll free 1-800-639-4099. Web site: www.chelseagreen.com; Doubleday, a division of Random House, Inc. and Eleanor Friede for permission to quote from *The Ultimate Journey*, by Robert Monroe, copyright © 1994 by Robert Monroe; Duane Elgin for permission to quote from *Awakening Earth* by Duane Elgin, Morrow Publishers, copyright © 1993; Element Books, Ltd., for permission to quote from *Asking for the Earth*, by James George, copyright © 1995 by James George; Princeton University Press for permission to quote from *Synchronicity*, by Carl G. Jung, copyright © 1973, and *Letters, Vol. 1*, by Carl G. Jung, copyright © 1976; Putnam Berkley, a division of Penguin Putnam Inc. for permission to quote from *The Choice* by Ervin Laszlo, copyright © 1994 by Ervin Laszlo.

Part 1

Introduction

Chapter One

The Pivot to Nonordinary States

The main difficulty here is to procure empirical material from which we can draw reasonably certain conclusions, and unfortunately this difficulty is not an easy one to solve. The experiences in question are not ready to hand. We must therefore look in the obscurest corners and summon up courage to shock the prejudices of our age if we want to broaden the basis of our understanding of nature.

—C. G. Jung, *Synchronicity*

My oldest son went on his first vision quest while I was working on this manuscript. As part of his preparation for this rite of passage, he met with the Native American elders who were overseeing his quest to be "talked out into spirit." Being "talked out" involved making a deep inventory of his life to prepare himself mentally and emotionally for the experiences that might surface during his quest. After his stay in the wilderness was over and before any contact with his family or friends was permitted, he was "talked in from spirit" by the same elders, sharing his experiences with them and receiving their advice on how to integrate them into his daily life.

In some respects this entire book is an exercise in "talking myself in from spirit," as it reflects my attempt to comprehend years of experiences in nonordinary states of consciousness and to integrate their insights into our understanding of human existence. Along the way I have come to believe, together with many others who have explored these states in a systematic manner, that these states are not only powerful agents of personal transformation but also important sources of information about the universe we live in. They offer us

3

insights into not just our personal mind but the deep ecology of mind itself. As the restrictions of the physically grounded mind are lifted, one begins to gain access to what could be described as the universe's inner experience of itself.

It is difficult to overestimate the significance of this development coming when it has at this time in human history. Just when Western culture had convinced itself that the entire universe was a machine, that it moves with a machine's precision and a machine's blindness, the ability to experience the inner life of the universe is being given back to us. Because machines are not conscious, the appearance of consciousness in the universe has been interpreted as a cosmic accident. The entire human endeavor has been emptied of existential purpose and significance because it has been judged to be a product of blind chance. When one gains access to the inner experience of the universe, however, one learns that, far from being an accident, our conscious presence here is the result of a supreme and heroic effort. Far from living our lives unnoticed in a distant corner of an insentient universe, we are everywhere surrounded by orders of intelligence beyond reckoning.[1]

There is a parallel, I believe, between how the academic community has been responding to research on nonordinary states and how it initially responded to the feminist critique of patriarchal culture. Centuries of custom first led scholars to deny that there was anything unique to women's experience that might revolutionize our intellectual and social institutions, and only slowly did feminists convince us that we had been missing half the picture. A similar battle is now being fought over nonordinary states. The mainstream voices that previously marginalized the testimony of women are now attempting to marginalize the testimony coming from these states, resulting in a continued skewing of our philosophical and psychological models in the direction of physical reality.[2] And yet, as with the gender issue, this resistance is misguided, because the kind of knowledge one acquires in nonordinary states of consciousness does not negate but complements and extends the knowledge gained in ordinary states.

When I am making this point with my students, I sometimes draw an analogy with the daytime and nighttime skies. In the bright light of the daytime sky, our immediate surroundings are illumined with great clarity. This clarity is useful for carrying out the pragmatic chores of daily existence, but it overwhelms our more subtle vision and hides the stars that are always present. When the glare of the sun retreats and the night sky shows itself again, we exchange the experience of the close at hand for the experience of the far away. As the stars return, our vision expands to take in the larger rhythms of the cosmos. The night sky does not negate the daytime sky, but gives us a larger frame of reference from which to understand the trajectory of life.

Imagine for a moment a civilization that denied itself the vision of the night sky, a society where by custom no one dared leave their homes after sundown. Trapped within the sun-drenched world, they would have intimate knowledge of the things that lie near at hand but be unaware of these distant realities. Without knowledge of the night sky, they would have a deeply incomplete understanding of the larger cosmos within which they lived. They would not be able to answer the question, "Where did we come from?" with any accuracy. Cut off from the vision of the stars, they would be restricted to the relative immediacy of here and now, stranded in near-time and near-space. They would never discover our celestial lineage, never place our solar system in the Milky Way or the Milky Way in a cosmos almost too large to be imagined.

We are this civilization, of course. Taken as a whole, Western thought has committed itself to a vision of reality that is based almost entirely on the daylight world of ordinary states of consciousness while systematically ignoring the knowledge that can be gained from the nighttime sky of nonordinary states. As the anthropologist Michael Harner puts it, we are "cogni-centric." Trapped within the horizon of the near-at-hand mind, our culture creates myths about the unreliability and irrelevance of nonordinary states. Meanwhile, our social fragmentation continues to deepen, reflecting in part our inability to answer the most basic existential questions. As long as we restrict ourselves to knowledge gained in ordinary states, we will not be able provide satisfactory answers to questions about meaning or value, because neither meaning nor value exist in mere sensation nor in the compounds of sensation. Similarly, we will not be able to explain where we came from or why our lives have the shape they do as long as we systematically avoid contact with the deeper dimensions of mind that contain the larger patterns that structure our existence.[3]

Though of enormous importance, the victories of the age of enlightenment were purchased at the terrible cost of systematically disparaging the depths of human experience and of prematurely dismissing our ability to penetrate these depths. In the modern university, being "rational" or "logical" includes the rider of not straying too far from sensate experience and its derivatives, and "critical thinking" is marked by its epistemological commitment to ordinary states of consciousness. Meanwhile, nonordinary states are little explored or understood, and their relevance to basic questions being raised in epistemology, philosophy of mind, or even ethics is seldom acknowledged. But this is changing. As the twentieth-first century opens, new evidence is challenging old assumptions in practically every department. Seldom have so many axioms been questioned on so many fronts at the same time. The historian of ideas can barely keep up with the revolutions brewing, and one of these revolutions, a major one I believe, centers on nonordinary states of consciousness.

The starting point of this book in the broadest sense, then, is the simple premise that philosophical reflection must today include the findings of depth psychology and the critical study of nonordinary states. Any philosophical system that excludes these states will produce a vision of reality that is profoundly limited in scope. Its refinements in one direction will be continually undermined by its inadequacies in the other, and the resulting system will be hopelessly imbalanced.

The Autobiographical Element in Transpersonal Philosophy

The philosophical discussion of nonordinary states cannot be done well from a distance but requires the commitment of personal experience. As Ken Wilber explains in *Sex, Ecology, Spirituality*, to do philosophy in the transpersonal mode requires training in the spiritual disciplines. First must come years of transformative practice that push back the boundaries of experience. As these practices are mastered, one is gradually "ushered into a worldspace in which new data disclose themselves."[4] With repetition, new levels of experience and understanding open and eventually stabilize, leading to the third stage of checking one's experiences against the experiences of others within the spiritual community.

There is a kind of knowledge that comes from digesting other people's experiences and a another kind entirely that comes from taking the inner journey oneself. If one has only secondhand knowledge of these states, one labors under a great disadvantage. Verbal accounts in books hint at but never capture the extraordinary depth and texture of the experiences that open in them. Only if you have first-hand knowledge of the territory can you appreciate how hard language has been pushed before it falls silent, unable to say more yet with so much more needing to be said. Only if you have personally entered these waters can you understand the strength and scope of the currents that flow here. Without this personal knowledge, you can quickly lose control of the material. You may miss connections that are obvious to the experienced eye and see correlations where there are none. By the same token, one's transpersonal reflections necessarily reflect the limits of one's experience. The experiences of others can help extend one's intuitions but are no substitute for experience itself. Because there is no getting around this basic restriction, the best one can do is own it, even take refuge in it. This means abandoning the goal of trying to give a definitive account of the entire transpersonal domain and instead simply bringing forward a perspective based on one's experience and placing it in respectful dialogue with the perspectives brought by other explorers.[5]

The conflict of philosophical paradigms begins with an argument over what experiences it is possible for human beings to have. Only if we are convinced that certain experiences actually occur will we then begin to ask about the implications of these experiences for human existence. I have had articles rejected by professional journals because cautious editors simply could not believe that the experiences I was analyzing were possible, in this case not my own experiences but ones previously published by others. Incredulous referees penciled in the margins comments like: "How is it possible for a human being to actually experience this?" or "How do you mean this? Metaphorically?" Mainstream philosophy and psychology is based almost exclusively on ordinary states of consciousness. Lacking personal experience of nonordinary states, these editors naturally could not comprehend how the boundaries of experience could be stretched to such seemingly impossible limits.

Over time I began to realize that if the transpersonal paradigm was going to make inroads in mainstream thought, individuals were going to have to be willing to incorporate into their analysis the actual experiences on which their proposals were based. *The more radical or aparadigmatic the concepts one is proposing, the more important it is to provide the experiential evidence for the claims being made.* In transpersonal philosophy, where the experiences in question are not shared by the population at large, it is particularly important to own the experiences that underpin one's theoretical analysis. The situation parallels the difficulty survivors of near-death episodes (NDEs) have had getting their observations to be taken seriously by the medical community. It was only after thousands of NDEers were willing to make their experiences part of the public record that resistance began to soften, and we began to move to the next stage of asking what these experiences were revealing to us about the cosmos we inhabit.

For all these reasons there is no escaping the necessity of writing from a basis in personal experience when addressing the questions raised in this volume. Thus, the chapters that follow weave together theoretical discussion and my own session experiences. I hope this autobiographical element will rest lightly on the project, however, and will not distract attention from the true focus of inquiry. Furthermore, this is not autobiography in the usual sense, for the levels of consciousness discussed here are universal and, as we will see, show up in contexts as divergent as contemplative monasteries and hospital emergency rooms.[6] Let me now describe the investigative discipline used in this study.

Stanislav Grof and Nonordinary States of Consciousness

While meditation has been an important part of my life for many years, the methods of exploring consciousness that lie at the heart of this book are those pioneered by Stanislav Grof. I encountered Grof's work shortly after completing graduate school in 1978 and since that time my self-exploration and philosophical reflection have unfolded in dialogue with his research, together with the great wisdom traditions of the world, especially Christianity and Buddhism. In *Realms of the Human Unconscious* (1976) and *LSD Psychotherapy* (1980), Grof summarized sixteen years of clinical experience exploring the therapeutic potential of psychedelic substances, particularly LSD-25, ten years at the Psychiatric Research Institute of Prague and six as chief of psychiatric research at the Maryland Psychiatric Research Center in Baltimore, Maryland. Although the therapeutic use of psychedelics was no longer legal in the United States when he wrote these books, Grof believed that our society would eventually find the wisdom to reappropriate this extraordinary family of drugs that had demonstrated their safety and therapeutic effectiveness in carefully structured clinical settings for many years.[7] In *The Adventure of Self-Discovery* (1985), Grof drew upon twelve years of work as scholar-in-residence at the Esalen Institute in Big Sur, California, during which he and his wife Christina created a therapeutic method called "Holotropic Breathwork" that evoked powerful nonordinary states of consciousness without the use of psychoactive substances. Holotropic Breathwork uses long periods of faster breathing, evocative music, and body work to activate and engage the deep psyche. *Holotropic* means "aiming for wholeness," and refers, says Grof, to states of consciousness that are oriented toward the whole of existence. It contrasts with *hylotropic* states of consciousness, which are states that are "oriented toward the world of matter," or ordinary sensory awareness.

In both methods the aim is to powerfully stimulate the unconscious, to amplify its patterns bringing them into conscious awareness, and then to engage them fully, experiencing completely whatever the patterns are.[8] Through the unrestricted engagement of one's inner experience (lying down, eyes closed, inwardly focused), the patterns build in intensity until they come to a critical threshold. The same patterns will keep showing up in a variety of forms until a climax of expression is reached—some inner gestalt is consciously realized or some reservoir of pain drained—and then the pattern dissolves. The energy trapped in this pattern is released or integrated, and the psyche is then free to flow into more expansive forms of awareness. If the process is repeated many times, deeper and more elemental patterns begin to emerge. However basic or irreducible these patterns may seem at the time, they can be dissolved by undefended engagement. Once they are dissolved, new worlds of experience will open.

Grof has demonstrated at considerable length that the experiences that emerge in LSD-assisted psychotherapy and Holotropic Breathwork are essentially identical. The triggers used to activate the deep psyche differ, but the dynamics and potentials that emerge are the same and reflect, he thinks, the innate structures and capacities of consciousness itself. Because of this overlap in experiential content, I propose for simplicity's sake to collapse these two methods and to refer to the states of consciousness that emerge using *either* of Grof's therapeutic regimens as "psychedelic states," intending the term in its generic sense of "mind-opening," not its narrow sense of "involving the use of psychoactive agents." While this usage is not ideal, the alternative, calling them "holotropic states," is worse because "holotropic" is an awkward term that is familiar only to a very specialized audience. We need a third term here, something user-friendly and neutral with respect to method, but I've not been able to come up with a good one. Until someone does, I will go with "psychedelic."

The longer I have worked with psychedelic states and spoken with others who have undertaken similar work, the more I have come to appreciate how deeply the therapeutic use of these states differs from their recreational use. Because this distinction is often lost on even an educated public, let me emphasize it here. For deep change to take place in the psyche, it is not enough simply to awaken extraordinary experiences. Powerful experiences come and go and may amount to very little in the long run. For enduring change to take place, there must be a container for holding these experiences in conscious awareness and for engaging them completely until they exhaust themselves—both during the session itself *and* in one's life between sessions. If powerful experiences are brought forward from the unconscious but are not held in this manner, they will give but a temporary release from the patterns that bind, a passing transpersonal distraction from our aching condition of psychospiritual imprisonment. The therapeutic use of these states, therefore, aims at the complete engagement of one's inner patterns until those patterns dissolve themselves, and this takes many years.

The patterns that emerge in this work come from many layers of our being, most of which were not even recognized in the West until recently. Grof has shown that beyond those mapped in conventional psychodynamic theory are patterns that come from the womb, from previous incarnations, and from beyond individual human existence altogether. The patterns that bind may come from what Carl Jung called the collective unconscious or from even deeper in the evolutionary web. In this work we confront barriers to experience that are so foreign to our everyday consciousness that we cannot see how they are restricting us until *after* we have worked through them and broken through to what lies beyond.

Psychotherapists working with patients who are recovering a traumatic episode from their past know that beyond the pain of remembering exists a state of health and wholeness that will be realized only if the trauma is allowed to surface and be consciously reappropriated. The trauma has trapped their patients' awareness, holding it in a narrow orbit of pain or disfunction until the memory of the original event can finally be brought back into awareness and digested. Only then will they really be free to move on to new life adventures. Work in psychedelic states follows much the same pattern except that the "trauma" one engages often seems intent on unraveling not some problematic piece of one's life but the basic structure of one's entire existence. The patterns that eventually emerge as problematic are not just patterns of pain in any conventional sense but patterns that appear to compose our existence in its entirety.

One can imagine one's life without some specific pain or without this or that fixation, but it is considerably more difficult to imagine one's life without one's life. This extreme way of putting it dramatizes the dilemma that one confronts again and again in therapeutically focused psychedelic states. If you open deeply to the process, you engage the patterns that comprise your existence as you have known it. There is no imagining your existence apart from these forms, and yet they are being torn away from you. It is only after these patterns have exhausted themselves and you have been released into a new order of experience that you can begin to recognize the wholeness which they had been denying you. Piece by piece, layer by layer, patterns of conditioning are brought forward, crystallized, and dissolved, and as they are, new orders of inherent being emerge. A level that one is liberated *into* at one stage may become that which one must be liberated *from* at a later stage.

For this successive opening to take place in a productive, safe, and healthy manner, there must be a container for directly engaging the patterns of one's existence from whatever unknown depths they come and for following the experience wherever it takes you, however frightening or incomprehensible it is at the time. Creating this container requires something more comprehensive than what is usually meant by creating a good "set and setting." As with any sustained spiritual practice, this work needs to be grounded in the ethical discipline of right relationship, the physical discipline of caring for the body, and the mental discipline of critical self-inquiry.

In summary, then, this is what I think is distinctive about the therapeutic use of psychedelic states—the completely internalized set, free of outward distractions and totally focused within; conditions that intensify the unconscious and encourage the unrestricted experience of whatever surfaces; holding that point of engagement long enough and frequently enough for the patterns to come completely into awareness, reach a critical threshold, and then dissolve entirely; and finally, the systematic integration of these experiences into one's physical, mental, emotional, and social existence.

Like all long-term projects, this work has a rhythm to it. No one experience is as important as the trajectory of development that unfolds across many sessions. Any experience that emerges in one session has been prepared in the sessions that precede it and is simultaneously laying the foundation for what will emerge in subsequent sessions. Some sessions seem to be spent doing laborious spadework while others harvest the work of many months or years, carrying you forward into entirely new dimensions of consciousness. This pattern of intense cleansing followed by a breakthrough into a new level then followed by stabilization of insight and experience at that level repeats itself over and over again. No matter how extraordinary or clear the level, it seems that there are always levels beyond even that. At whatever level one is working, this cycle of purification will be part of the rhythm of one's work.

Because each session experience is deeply embedded in a larger process, lifting a session out of its context isolates it from the larger pattern that grounds its meaning. *It is always the trajectory of the work that matters most, not individual experiences.* And yet in a book such as this, one cannot realistically include the entire sequence of session experiences but must pick and choose representative examples. This makes the task of using transcripts from actual sessions to illustrate specific dynamics difficult, and I will try to navigate this difficulty in several ways. First, in the chapters that follow I will be drawing primarily from my own experiences to illustrate the dynamics under discussion. Though less than ideal in some respects, following one subject through many layers of the psyche will itself provide a certain continuity of context. In this respect I see this volume as providing something of a methodological complement to Grof's comprehensive description of psychedelic experiences drawn from thousands of subjects. Second, I will be selective and introduce only those experiences that embody in a particularly clear way the dynamic under discussion. This will tend to give the impression that these processes are clearer than they in fact are, for we will be skipping over those sessions where the gestalts emerged in more fragmented and incomplete forms. Nevertheless, if the reader keeps this distortion in mind, the misrepresentation will not be serious.

The third strategy will be to allow a certain repetition into the narrative of session experiences. Repetition of the same theme unfolding at deeper and deeper levels across several sessions is an essential part of this work and must be part of the telling of its story. If we eliminate this repetition from our narrative entirely, we will tend to underestimate the depths one eventually reaches through this circuitous route. One of my concerns in this book is to expose some of the inner workings of these processes in order to allow others to better understand and assess the philosophical implications of these states. For this to be done, a certain amount of repetition must be allowed to enter the narrative. Finally, in a few instances I will take a different approach and consolidate insights gathered from many sessions into a single metanarrative, condensing an often circuitous journey into a shortened travelogue. Where the contents of the ideas themselves are more important that the details of psychological excavation, clinical context will be sacrificed in the interest in creating an overview of some of the territory covered.[9]

Just as there is a rhythm to the work that arches across many sessions, there is also a rhythm that characterizes each individual session if it is well managed. As in any therapeutic progression, there is only so much that can be accomplished in one day, even a good day. Accordingly, there is a rhythm of engagement that allows each individual session to be complete within itself while simultaneously being part of these larger cycles of unfolding. The same cycle of cleansing, breakthrough, and stabilization that characterizes the larger trajectory of many sessions also defines the curve of each individual session if it is well managed. As long as one is working at what Grof calls the psychodynamic and perinatal levels, the early hours of a session will be spent in painful confrontation. This purgatorial cleansing usually builds to a climax that, if successfully negotiated, culminates in a mini-death-rebirth experience followed by a breakthrough to positive transpersonal vistas. The remainder of the session will be spent in these spaces as one's education continues against an often ecstatic background.

In my experience, the nature of one's experience during the ecstatic phase of a session is shaped primarily by two things—the depth of cleansing achieved during the first phase of the session and the depth of the cleansing that has been realized in the whole of one's work to date. These two interact in a sometimes complex fashion to create the conditions of discovery that govern what unfolds during this phase. However profound the space one enters here, the next session will resume the cleansing process approximately where it stopped in the previous session, and the cycle will repeat itself. Deeper cleansing will result in a deeper death-rebirth surrender followed by a resumption of transpersonal instruction and initiation. What you see is always a function of what you are, or what in your heart you still believe you are. The more conditioning one has been able to let go of, the more open-ended are the possibilities that present themselves.[10]

The peak states of consciousness one enters during these precious hours obviously do not become one's new baseline consciousness in any simple or linear fashion. With persistence one's baseline does change over time, but far more slowly than one would wish. From a spiritual perspective, the final measure of the value of this work will be its capacity to bring about a *permanent* shift in consciousness, to free us forever from the prison of self-centered existence. If this is what one seeks, the emphasis in one's sessions will always be on purification until the mind can finally rest at peace in its "natural condition" months *after* a session has concluded.

Temporary immersion in powerful, revelatory states is part of the therapeutic cycle, however, and from a philosophical perspective the fact that these states are temporary does not diminish the truth of the insights that arise there.[11]

Though I have been speaking of psychedelic states as states of *consciousness*, it is important to emphasize that they are also states of *body*. These states profoundly impact one's physical and subtle energy systems, for wherever one's mind goes, the body necessarily follows. Furthermore, to give the mind primacy here may be putting the cart before the horse, for these states are being elicited through physical mechanisms—either ingesting a psychoactive substance or hyperventilating for a long period of time. In both instances it is the body which holds the key that opens the treasure chest of the mind. Therefore, one could say that for these methods the rule is—where one's body goes, one's mind necessarily follows. While I will continue to use the vocabulary of consciousness in the chapters that follow, I want to acknowledge in the beginning that this is not a balanced description of these states. A more complete account would give greater attention to the fact that these states at every stage are being negotiated and integrated somatically as well as mentally. It is important to keep this fact in front of us at all times if we are to avoid interpreting psychedelic therapy in terms that emphasize the dynamics of ascent over descent, of leaving the body behind and fleeing into the transcendent divine rather than waking up inside the immanent divine.

The Project of This Book

This book explores the ancient mystery of death and rebirth, but in a way that expands the conventional categories. Usually this story is told as the tale of individual enlightenment. The spiritual practitioner withdraws from the world, turns his or her mind back upon itself and plunges toward its center. Sooner or later he or she arrives at the Divine within. But as Buddhism and many other spiritual traditions have pointed out, the story of individual enlightenment is saturated with paradox. On the one hand, who can deny that individual awakening occurs? The student who practices diligently makes progress while the one who doesn't flounders. And yet the cry of the awakened is that none of us is isolated from each other, that existential separation is an illusion created by our physical senses, that the world is marked by interpenetration at all levels. The paradox, then, is this. If all existence is ultimately united in the One, no one can awaken alone. The very structure of our being does not allow such a possibility.

In order to awaken to our true and essential condition, we must let fall from us everything that we thought we were or thought we needed in the most fundamental sense. In order to reach this naked condition, one must go through a transformational process that the Christian tradition calls the "dark night of the soul." The dark night is an arduous stage of spiritual purification in which the aspirant endures a variety of physical and psychological purifications, eventually undergoing a profound spiritual death and rebirth (appendix A). The starting point of this book is here, in the middle of the dark night. There are no shortcuts through this night but there are more and less efficient ways of moving through it. Some methods intensify and accelerate the ordeal while others proceed at a gentler, more gradual pace. Psychedelic therapy is an example of the former; it intensifies the purification process and thus concentrates the dark night. However, in ways that I did not understand when I began this work, it also has the potential to greatly expand the scope of the process as well.

As I was making my way through this night, undergoing the various trials that everyone faces here, my journey took an unexpected turn. Over the course of several years, I began to realize that my process was not being allowed to complete itself. Instead of continuing through to its conclusion, my death-rebirth process began to expand exponentially, to take in the experience of tens of thousands, even hundreds of thousands of human beings. Through mechanisms that I did not comprehend at the time, my individual death-rebirth seemed to become a catalyst for a collective transformation that was focused beyond my individual existence. Unable to control what was happening, I had no choice but to follow the process wherever it was taking me.

Where it eventually led me was into a completely new understanding of the interplay of the life of the individual and the life of the species. The explosion of my personal death-rebirth process into a metaprocess aimed at the collective unconscious shattered my frame of reference for understanding the dynamics of spiritual transformation. It took me years to assimilate these experiences and to comprehend their implications, years to surrender the assumptions that my Western education had instilled in me. Because I was a philosopher of religion and reasonably well read in the spiritual traditions, I had the assistance of many wise voices to help me make this transition, but the words of another can only partially prepare one for the profound reversal of perspectives I was being forced to make. I am still finding my way about in this new territory.

This book explores the deep ecology of mind as it reveals itself in nonordinary states, particularly in psychedelic states. It attempts to describe certain dynamics of the death-rebirth process from a transindividual perspective, that is, with the emphasis placed on the dynamics of the species-mind rather than the personal mind, and by extension on that which cradles the species-mind. Deep ecology is a school of environmental thought that developed in the 1970s around the thought of the Norwegian philosopher Arne Naess. Its central premise is that there is no absolute divide between humanity and everything else. Thus it seeks to de-anthropomorphize our view of nature and to draw us away from making human beings the ultimate reference point in debates about the environment. Deep ecology sees a human being not as a social atom independent of other life forms but rather as a node in a web of relationships that reaches out into and includes everything.[12]

By speaking of the deep ecology of mind, I want to bring this profound sense of the interconnectedness of all life to the center of psychological reflection. My core contention is that *in order to understand the transformative dynamics that sometimes surface in nonordinary states, we need to expand our frame of reference beyond the individual human being and look to the living systems the individual is part of.* Thus, I intend the title, *Dark Night, Early Dawn,* to point beyond the individual to the collective dark night that I believe humanity as a whole has entered, and to the interaction of the personal and collective nights. I believe that we cannot fully understand the exceptionally powerful experiences that many spiritual practitioners are undergoing today without understanding the larger historical context within which these experiences are taking place. As we approach what many believe is a critical stage in our collective evolution, our fates are increasingly linked.

One has only to look around to see that our situation is becoming increasingly perilous. Apocalyptic hopes and political denials cannot much longer mask the catastrophic environmental and social cost of our industrial triumph. Any clear-thinking assessment of the ecological facts should convince us that we have entered a time of unprecedented disruption of life at fundamental levels that will soon reach catastrophic proportions. While there is probably no avoiding this painful confrontation with our planetary limits, I think there is also an exquisite beauty to the opportunity we are being given. The more clearly we understand the deep structure of the events that are overtaking our lives, the more we may be able ease the pain of the transition humanity is being called upon to make. The sooner we have the wisdom to begin making the right choices, the less pain humanity will have to endure, and what suffering is inevitable can be softened by at least understanding the significance of the historical pivot we are making.

Because I am an academic, talking myself in from spirit has meant trying to integrate the insights that arise in nonordinary states into a number of discussions. Each chapter that follows addresses a different area of research and reflection. In order to prevent the larger story from getting lost in the details, let me briefly outline the territory we will be covering and indicate how I see the pieces fitting together into in the larger project.

Chapter 2 is a short chapter that builds a bridge between my earlier work on reincarnation and the present book, using the concept of rebirth as a point of departure from which to make the pivot to the study of nonordinary states. My primary objective in this chapter is to show that Ian Stevenson's evidence for reincarnation, while being essential to establish the validity of rebirth in our current intellectual climate, is ironically both liberating and constricting our understanding of the spiritual domain and the nature of identity. I try to show why, in order to answer some of the deeper questions raised by reincarnation, we need go beyond his provocative cases and explore the deep psyche directly.

After the introduction provided in part I, the main body of the book is divided into two sections. Part II explores the deep ecology of death and rebirth as it shows itself in three different nonordinary states of consciousness—psychedelic states, near-death episodes, and out-of-body states. The overarching agenda is to achieve a synthesis of these three areas of research around an expanded understanding of the death-rebirth process. Part III builds upon this foundation to explore various aspects of what I am calling the field dynamics of mind.

Chapter 3 begins the pivot to nonordinary states by critically examining Stan Grof's concept of the "perinatal" level of consciousness. In Grof's model, the perinatal dimension is a level of consciousness that lies between the personal and transpersonal levels. I describe my experience of this domain and my inability to reconcile my experience with Grof's account. This impasse forced me to rethink some of the fundamental assumptions of Grof's model and to propose an expansion of perinatal theory that systematically incorporates Rupert Sheldrake's concept of morphic fields into his paradigm. This exercise lays the intellectual foundation for everything that follows in the book.

Chapter 4 deepens the study of the perinatal dimension by taking up the most terrible nightmare humanity has ever dreamed, the nightmare of eternal hell. It examines the experiences of some persons who have nearly died whose near-death experiences took them not into the heavenly light that many have reported but into the depths of hell instead. Much less common than ecstatic NDEs, these "hellish NDEs" have recently emerged as an important problem in near-death studies, in part because hell is such an abhorrent concept to the modern mind. Hell is the greatest obstacle to seeing the life process as deriving from a loving and benign source. The specter of billions of souls plunged into extreme agony for all eternity is so horrible a vision that many contemporary theologians have simply rejected the concept altogether, and yet on the face of it, these NDEs seem to provide experiential support for the idea. In this chapter I set out an alternative understanding of these hellish NDEs based upon psychedelic experience.

This discussion of hell has implications that extend far beyond the narrow problem of how to interpret certain rare near-death episodes. Our cultural convictions about hell are a distillation of our broader beliefs about the role suffering plays in human existence, and I believe we are entering a period of history that will be possibly marked by profound human suffering. If the crisis of sustainability predicted by many ecological thinkers for the twenty-first century disrupts the world economy to the degree expected, humanity will soon be wracked by social convulsions that are historically unprecedented. Already some social theorists are describing these impending events as a "descent into hell."[13] If such a descent takes place, humanity will cry out en masse to comprehend the suffering that has overtaken it. If we can respond with only a technological answer that strips our pain of any deeper existential significance or offer only regressive theologies of divine retribution, we will deepen the crisis by rubbing the salt of inscrutability into our wounds. In order to maximize our chances for coming through this critical period of history successfully, it is important that we understand as best we can the underlying structure of these events, and part of this means understanding what this acute and terrible suffering may represent in the life of the larger being that we collectively are and the opportunity that it and we are being given to radically transcend our present condition. In short, if the human family is entering a collective descent into hell, then it is critical that we understand what hell truly is.

Chapter 4 brings Grof's paradigm into dialogue with the work of Robert Monroe, founder of the Monroe Institute and author of three books on the out-of-body experience. In this chapter I attempt to reconcile Monroe's cosmology with the cosmology that emerges from psychedelic work. Essentially, Monroe's portrait of extraphysical reality is a soul-centered vision, an atomistic, "Newtonian" vision of a spiritual universe populated by discrete souls. As such it is fundamentally at odds with the more holistic vision that emerges in extended psychedelic work. Because this transition beyond the individual soul is in some respects the fundamental pivot this book is trying to describe, let me say a little more about it here.

When consciousness is systematically explored in psychedelic states, the conditioning of mind tends to fall away in clusters. Some of these clusters concern time and our tendency to take our *present* life as our true identity. Other clusters concern space and our tendency to take our *local* experience as our true identity. My earlier book on reincarnation, *Lifecycles*, addressed the limits that time imposes on our sense of identity by exploring the causal patterns that stretch across multiple lifetimes. This present book primarily addresses the limits imposed by space. It explores that dimension of our being which we share with every life form that is alive at this very moment. While reincarnation is a demanding concept in its own right, I think that by itself it actually poses less of a challenge to the ego than confronting the true breadth of our being. Because it preserves our sense of existential privacy, it allows us the privacy of our individual evolution as we climb whatever spiritual ladder we find credible. When we open to the spatial breadth of our being, however, this privacy is shattered. In this reality, the world moves as one, and it is God's bliss to do so.

When one lets go of the separate self in time *and space*, there is no logical place where one can grab on to it again. From here it is a free-fall into the Divine. Some writers call this metareality the transpersonal mind, because it transcends our personal, autobiographical mind. When Grof calls it the holotropic mind, he is drawing attention to its inclusiveness, to the natural tendency of awareness to be whole within itself. Both these terms are semantically fresh and have the advantage of lacking prior associations that might distort their meaning. Their novelty, however, deprives them of a certain semantic power that words with a longer history possess. Because I want to use language that draws upon our long history with the numinous, I will call this reality the Sacred Mind. To experience Sacred Mind even briefly profoundly shifts one's sense of identity because it gives one an entirely new reference point from which to experience the life process. Instead of experiencing life operating in pieces, here one experiences it operating in its wholeness, our many lives moving as one Life. From this perspective, Sacred Mind is the only mind in town. To awaken in any part of it is to begin to feel its presence in every part.[14]

Bringing these observations back to bear on Robert Monroe, when one's inner work deepens to the point where one begins to experience Sacred Mind, the working identity of the private soul is challenged and eventually shattered. Even a soul that integrates many incarnations is too small a construct to describe the expanded sense of identity that opens at this level. The task, therefore, of trying to reconcile Monroe's soul-centered vision of the universe with Grof's more holistic vision grew out of my struggle to navigate this particular experiential interface. It reflects my attempt to integrate a vision of the universe in which reincarnation is a fact of life with one in which the identity of the reincarnating soul is yielding to a spiritual identity that excludes nothing.

As one falls into the Divine, it is not just the private soul that is left behind, of course, but eventually all other dualities as well. This fall into increasing simplicity, luminosity and transparency has been described by many writers, who sometimes mark its stages by differentiating between the psychic level of transpersonal experience, the subtle level, the causal level, and the nondual level.[15] I will not attempt to describe this entire journey and thus will not reproduce the full range of transpersonal experiences that emerge in psychedelic states. Rather, what I am concerned to explore is the inherent wholeness of life that prevents this journey into the Divine from ever being a solitary journey. If this book has a central theme, it is that *wherever one of us goes, to some degree we all go.*

After exploring the deep ecology of death and rebirth as it is enacted in these three nonordinary states, part III turns to explore the field dynamics of mind from several different perspectives. Chapter 6 takes up a concept central to many spiritual systems, the concept of karma, and proposes an expansion of karmic theory. Usually karma is described as the set of causal processes that operate through time to create the learning conditions of our present lifetime. Psychedelic experience, however, suggests that there is a second, less appreciated dimension of karma that operates through space. This simple but basic distinction will better help us distinguish patterns of collective karma from personal karma in the deep psyche and describe more precisely their subtle interplay in our lives.

Chapter 7 explores the field dynamics of mind as they manifest in the university classroom, of all places. As my inner work slowly deepened through the years, I began to recognize patterns of collective mental functioning operating in daily life around me. Because I am a teacher, one of the places I frequently saw these patterns was in my classroom. In this chapter I describe a variety of transpersonal phenomena that surfaced in my classes over twenty years and draw out what I think are some of the theoretical and practical implications of these phenomena.

In chapter 8 I expand the frame of reference to the species-mind as a whole and develop a line of thought on how the growing ecological crisis may impact the evolution of human consciousness. Combining insights from chaos theory, the study of nonequilibrium systems, and psychedelic experience, I consider how this global crisis may affect the collective unconscious and explore the possible mechanisms through which it may trigger a profound shift in the baseline of human consciousness. In many ways, this chapter represents the culmination of the book, for it outlines the larger evolutionary project that I believe all our individual efforts at self-transformation are part of.

After exploring the field dynamics of mind from these three perspectives, chapter 9 brings the book to a close by considering the fate of the individual in psychedelic therapy, or more pointedly, the fate of individuality itself. As one's experience of the seamlessness of Sacred Mind deepens, the ground that our individuality rests upon seems to become increasingly precarious and uncertain. The more we appreciate the many threads that are woven into the being that we are, the more one cannot but wonder whether there will be anything left of our uniqueness when these threads are completely unraveled. Thus I end the book asking, Does the death-rebirth process dissolve us entirely back into the Divine as some idealist philosophies have contended? Exactly what dies and what is reborn in this transformation? What is the fate of individuality in Sacred Mind?

The Philosophical Context of the Study of Psychedelic States

The proposal that nonordinary states of consciousness are an important source of insight into the nature of mind and one's identity is not new, of course, as it has been an axiom of Eastern and indigenous thought for thousands of years, together with the mystical traditions of the West. Modern Western philosophy has not accepted

this premise and has instead placed all its confidence in an epistemology based almost exclusively on ordinary states of consciousness.
The ascendancy of science in the seventeenth century consolidated a
long historical tradition, going back at least as far as Aristotle,
which established the daylight world of sensate consciousness as the
epistemological norm and the only true source of knowledge. And yet
the legacy of science has been two-edged in this respect, for while it
has encouraged an epistemology based almost exclusively on sensate
states, its relentless self-criticism has also mercilessly exposed the
weaknesses of such an epistemology, thus slowly drawing Western
philosophy toward an encounter with the nighttime sky of the deep
psyche.

Because the pivot to nonordinary states, and psychedelic states in
particular, represents such an important shift in our epistemological
commitments, I would like to briefly review some of the larger philosophical and cultural developments that have been moving us in this
direction. It is beyond the scope of this chapter to describe these developments in any detail, but it would also be a mistake to say nothing
about them. The turn to psychedelic states represents such an important realignment of our philosophical priorities that we must place it
in its larger historical context if its true significance is to be grasped.
Unless we do so, we will fail to appreciate the historical and cultural
pressures that have been building in Western thought for many centuries and that are driving this initiation. I know of no source where
this story is better told than Richard Tarnas's excellent book *The
Passion of the Western Mind*. Widely regarded as one of the most dis-
cerning overviews of Western philosophy from the ancient Greeks to
postmodern thought, it tells the story of the shaping of our intellectual
moment in history with exceptional clarity and insight. In chapter 6,
"The Transformation of the Modern Era," Tarnas weaves together the
philosophical strands of the last four hundred years and illumines
with compelling force the many layers of the intellectual crisis we
have come to in history. Moreover, his personal familiarity with Grof's
research allows him in the "Epilogue" to deftly situate Grof's work in
this larger intellectual context.

The fundamental intellectual crisis of the contemporary mind,
asserts Tarnas, is a crisis of epistemology. It is a crisis in our ability
to know anything reliable about the world. Now aware of our marginal placement in an evolving universe of immense scope and age,
of the inescapably interpretive nature of all human knowledge, and
of the bewitching effect of all culturally embedded metanarratives,
the postmodern mind experiences itself to be profoundly adrift in

space and time. Knowing ourselves to be a conscious and purposeful species, we confront the paradox of having been spawned by a seemingly unconscious, mechanical universe and have concluded that our existence is a mere accident, devoid of purpose or intent. Moreover, ever since Kant, we have been deprived of the luxury of direct knowledge of the world, and now live painfully aware that all knowledge is mediated by mind. As Tarnas puts it:

> We have the post-Copernican dilemma of being a peripheral and insignificant inhabitant of a vast cosmos, and the post-Cartesian dilemma of being a conscious, purposeful, and personal subject confronting an unconscious, purposeless, and impersonal universe, with these compounded by the post-Kantian dilemma of there being no possible means by which the human subject can know the universe in its essence. We are evolved from, embedded in, and defined by a reality that is radically alien to our own, and moreover cannot ever be directly contacted in cognition.[16]

Our situation might be tolerable if we felt we could trust the lens through which we experienced the universe, but the direction of modern thought has been to deeply erode our confidence in our mind's neutrality. "From Hume and Kant through Darwin, Marx, Freud and beyond," writes Tarnas,

> an unsettling conclusion was becoming inescapable: Human thought was determined, structured, and very probably distorted by a multitude of overlapping factors—innate but non-absolute mental categories, habit, history, culture, social class, biology, language, imagination, emotion, the personal unconscious, the collective unconscious. In the end, the human mind could not be relied upon as an accurate judge of reality.[17]

The critique of our inherited mind is simultaneously a critique of the culture that produced that mind, and for decades we have been confronting the darker side of our cultural heritage, further weakening our confidence in our capacity for disinterested truth. The list of our sins is cumulatively staggering:

> the rapacity of its elites from ancient times to modern, its systematic thriving at the expense of others, its colonialism

and imperialism, its slavery and genocide, its anti-Semitism, its oppression of women, people of color, minorities, homosexuals, the working classes, the poor, its destruction of indigenous societies throughout the world, its arrogant insensitivity to other cultural traditions and values, its cruel abuse of other forms of life, its blind ravaging of virtually the entire planet.[18]

The crux of the postmodern epistemological crisis, therefore, is that we are trapped within our minds, and our minds appear to be hopelessly embedded in layers of arbitrary historical and cultural distortions. Given the ontological gap that distances us from the surrounding universe, the psychological filters that mediate our experience of the world, and the embeddedness of those filters in cultural contexts that hide them from our critical awareness, how are we ever to obtain reliable knowledge?

Despite the mounting epistemological pessimism in intellectual circles fueled by the relentless "hermeneutics of suspicion," our public confidence in the fundamental soundness of our intellectual heritage was for a long time secured by the practical and theoretical successes of the scientific enterprise. Regardless of what the philosophers were saying, it seemed undeniable to most people that we were in fact able to know the world accurately through scientific research. Moreover, the technology generated by science that was swiftly reshaping our lives for the better confirmed this optimism and seemed to justify our expectation that the skeptical philosophers would eventually figure out where they went wrong. Science's claim to valid knowledge seemed unquestionable. Two developments, however, have shattered this confidence.

The first was the complete collapse of the classical Cartesian-Newtonian cosmology in the 1930s. The revolution in physics (relativity and quantum mechanics) shattered virtually every major postulate of the Newtonian worldview. While Newton's universe was coherent with our daily sensory experience, the world the new physics seemed to be describing was strange beyond belief: matter that was largely empty and interchangeable with energy, time that flowed at different rates around different gravitational fields and for observers moving at different speeds, particles that were free to move backward or forward in time, space that was curved, a world that existed both as particles and waves, and nonlocal connections that contradicted mechanistic causality. The list of contradictions to our daily experience seemed endless. So counterintuitive were its findings that while scientists largely agree on the mathematics of quantum mechanics, there has been no consensus on its implications for our understanding of the nature of reality. Sixty years after the quantum revolution, most academic disciplines have not fully appropriated its significance and continue to conduct their business as if the world of the rationalist enlightenment were still intact.

While the theoretical collapse of Newton's universe may have shaken the intellectual foundation of our culture to its core, this fact registered for the most part only on the intellectual elite and filtered out to the masses slowly and in small pieces. Such was not the case, however, for the environmental and industrial disasters that soon began to touch the lives of millions and signaled the beginning of the collapse of the public's confidence in scientific technology. Starting with the noble aspiration to raise the human condition to new heights of health and well being, our industrial culture has come in just two centuries to be recognized as the greatest threat to human survival in the history of our species. Its capacity and willingness to contaminate the planet's air, water and soil, to deplete its irreplaceable natural resources, to change the baseline temperature of the planet, to permanently erase species from existence at the rate of one per hour, and to create weapons of such destructive capacity that they cannot be used are increasingly recognized as symptoms of a deeply disturbed, even pathological enterprise. Furthermore, the close association of scientific research with the military and corporate establishments has eroded science's implicit promise to be conducting "pure" research. We are increasingly recognizing that science has been serving, "either consciously or unconsciously, specific political and economic agenda, often allowing vast resources and intelligence to be commandeered for programs of social and ecological domination."[19]

As science's prestigious position as the anchor of the enlightenment continues to erode even into the present day, the epistemological crisis of the postmodern era continues to gather momentum. If the legacy of the modern era is the insight that the primary datum in human experience is not the material world but human experience itself, then *the ultimate challenge facing us is to explore the seat of all human experience, the human psyche.* Our task becomes scrutinizing that through which we know anything at all, to sound its depths and chart its reefs. Thus, the line of philosophical inquiry into the role of the human mind in cognition that extends from Descartes to Locke, Hume, Kant, and Nietzsche leads inevitably, argues Tarnas, to Freud and depth psychology. The epistemological crisis of the modern and postmodern mind draws us inevitably into the depths of the unconscious.[20]

We turn to depth psychology today, therefore, not merely to heal the various forms of psychopathology that plague modern society, but for basic insights into the nature of mind itself. Cut off from knowing the world directly, we have no other recourse than to turn our critical eye back upon itself. Because there is no making contact with the world or each other except through our minds, *the discipline that can unlock the mind's deepest secrets holds the key to this moment in history*. Mind is the context within which all knowing arises; it is the frontier which comes before all other frontiers. "The pivot of the modern predicament is epistemological," says Tarnas, "and it is here that we should look for an opening."[21] It is against this background of intellectual impasse, profound existential confusion, and darkening ecological horizons that Tarnas locates Grof's research. Describing it as the "most epistemologically significant development" in the history of depth psychology, he believes it to be the most important advance in the field since Freud and Jung.[22]

The Epistemic Warrant of Psychedelic Experience

In today's intellectual environment where consensus is rapidly breaking down and so many disagreements can be traced to differences of starting point, an author has to make countless choices about what to defend and what to assume. In choosing to dialogue with thinkers already committed to the transpersonal paradigm, I know that I have not built as many bridges to the established paradigm as could be built. Nor have I tried to answer all the possible kinds of objections that I anticipate may be raised to the some of the ideas present here. Instead, what I have tried to do is to articulate as clearly as I can certain features of a new vision of human existence that I believe is surfacing in research on nonordinary states. This vision is grounded in experience, but because the experiences are somewhat rare and not shared by the general population, the question of whether we should trust them naturally arises. Because I will not be able to prove the truth of these experiences in any conventional manner, certainly not by referring back to data in physical reality, how can the reader decide whether they are valid or merely interesting hallucinations?

The question of the epistemic warrant of psychedelic experience is a subset of the larger question of the epistemic warrant of transpersonal experience in general, and the answer to this question will ultimately reflect one's assessment of the legitimacy of the entire transpersonal enterprise. This would require a careful evaluation of the many intellectual and cultural streams that have converged to form this movement, which is obviously beyond the scope of this chapter. Fortunately, however, it has already been formulated in the work of Ken Wilber. Through his many books, Wilber has done more to establish the philosophical credentials of the transpersonal movement than any other one person. His identification of the underlying deep structure of Eastern models of consciousness, his articulation of a vision of psychospiritual development that integrates a vast range of Eastern and Western insights into a comprehensive synthesis, his penetrating critique of a culture that has allowed itself to become tone-deaf to the transcendent, and his revitalization of the concept of the Great Chain of Being are but a few of his many accomplishments. If I have not built many bridges to the mainstream philosophical tradition, it is because I have assumed the bridges Wilber has already built.[23]

As for the epistemic warrant of psychedelic experiences in particular, I would offer three general observations. First, I would point to the fundamental agreement between the vision of reality that surfaces in psychedelic states and the perennial philosophy articulated in the world's wisdom traditions. This important correspondence has been demonstrated in numerous places, most compellingly in Grof's recent book, *The Cosmic Game.*

Second, while many of the ideas that I will present in the following chapters have not been empirically verified, and perhaps by their very nature cannot be verified for the foreseeable future, many unusual insights that have surfaced in psychedelic states *have* been verified. These verifications establish a certain epistemic collateral, a certain confidence in the method, which is relevant to the question of whether we should trust those insights that cannot be verified in this manner. The situation is similar to the problem that Michael Sabom faced in his attempt to critically assess the accuracy of observations that persons had while in the out-of-body state during a near-death episode. In his book, *Recollections of Death*, he distinguished between the "local" phase and the "transcendent" phase of near-death experiences. He argued that while it was impossible to verify the transcendent phase of the experience, it should be possible to verify or falsify the local phase, because one could check the accuracy of the subject's perception of events against their medical records and the accounts of eye-witnesses. Much to his surprise, he was able to confirm the "local"observations of many subjects. This did not prove the validity of the transcendent phase of their experiences, of course, but it clearly increased their epistemic warrant to some degree.

The same argument can be made for many of the experiences that arise in psychedelic therapy. The fact that some of these unusual experiences have been empirically verified increases the credibility of those experiences which by their very nature cannot be verified in this manner, but which were generated using the same therapeutic method. In this context, I would draw attention to Grof's successful verification of the following items: the details of many persons' intrauterine experience and biological birth,[24] the historical details of a remembered former life,[25] experiences from the lives of one's parents or ancestors,[26] the identity of deceased persons encountered in spirit form during a session,[27] unexpected insights into the physiology of particular animals,[28] and insights into some aspect of a culture with whom the subject was not previously familiar.[29]

Third, I would like to take the question of verification one step further by drawing upon Wilber's work. Wilber has argued in numerous places that there is a spectrum of different modes of knowing, each with its own set of instrumental injunctions for gathering information, its own modality of experiential disclosure, and its own form of evaluation. He divides this spectrum into three broad categories, which he calls the eye of flesh (empiricism), the eye of mind (rationalism), and the eye of spirit (mysticism). While agreeing with empiricism that all genuine knowledge must be grounded in experience, he has criticized empiricism's reduction of experience to sensory experience, arguing that the eye of mind and spirit are equally legitimate modalities of experience that produce equally legitimate forms of knowledge. He emphasizes Thomas Kuhn's insight that all knowledge claims are ultimately grounded in paradigms or exemplars that include a set of injunctions that tell one how to go about finding the knowledge that one is seeking. If one wants to have knowledge of spirit, he argues, one must follow the methodological injunctions of spirit. Furthermore, it is a mistake to hold this knowledge hostage to the methods of verification appropriate to the other levels. He writes:

> Both the rationalist and the empiricist press us: they want us to state our contemplative conclusions and let them check these conclusions *against their own injunctions*. That is, they want our words stripped from and divorced from the actual and specific injunctions. They want to try to follow our

words without the pain of having to follow our exemplars. And so we must remind them: Words without injunctions are meaningless. . . . Our words and our conclusions can indeed be carefully justified—verified or rejected—but only if the injunctions are engaged.[30]

Wilber champions meditation as the instrumental injunction that he believes should guide our search for spiritual knowledge, but this strikes me as unnecessarily narrow. There are a wealth of spiritual methods practiced around the globe that offer training in opening the eye of spirit, and it would be premature to exalt one over all the others. The essential injunctive principle that Wilber sets out, however, applies to all these methods—if you want to gain access to spiritual knowledge, you must first undertake spiritual training. From this perspective, the validity of many of the proposals presented in this volume will rest upon not whether they can be confirmed by empirical research but whether they can be experientially corroborated by other spiritual explorers. That is, they reflect a *kind of knowledge* that can only be assessed, or perhaps that is best assessed, by persons who have undertaken the training designed to awaken this knowledge. This condition is not intended to exclude anyone and certainly not to insulate any of the ideas presented from critical review, but rather to ensure that all the conditions of critical evaluation have been fairly met. History reminds us that those who were not willing to look through Galileo's telescope were not in a position to evaluate his evidence.

In the long run, therefore, the adequacy of many of the concepts presented in this book will depend upon whether the experiences on which they are based can be replicated and whether other persons who have these experiences concur with the interpretations offered here. With this in mind, I would point out that my psychedelic experiences fall within the wide range of experiences that Grof has been reporting in his books for years, even if pushing the edges of those experiences in a certain direction. As far as the future replication of these experiences is concerned, this will take years to establish and perhaps a different political and legal climate, and I look forward to when the discussion has progressed to this stage.

None of this means, of course, that everything which one perceives in these states is veridical. It does not mean that there cannot be distortions, projections, or misinterpretations. Indeed, one of the things that makes transpersonal experience so complex is how multidimensional it is, how many "layers" there are to the reality being explored, and therefore how many half-truths one must contend with. Error and misjudgment is always possible and must be acknowledged from the start. Controlling for these errors requires presenting one's claims as carefully as possible and exposing the experiences on which they are based to the scrutiny of other explorers in the transpersonal community, which is what I am doing in this volume. I would take much more seriously a response from someone who said, "I have worked in transpersonal states of consciousness for many years using this or that methodology and have not had any of the experiences you are describing or do not interpret them the same way you do" than one that simply criticized my findings for not having yet been empirically verified. That would be analogous to criticizing a modern astronomer's observations because they cannot be verified by the naked eye.

In conclusion, I think that Grof has actually given the postmodern mind two things of lasting importance. First, he has given us a new clinical method for engaging the deep psyche and, second, he has given us a model of consciousness that synthesizes a vast range of experiences that emerge when this method is used. To give the modern mind a new method for exploring itself at this critical point in its history allows others to enter these interior regions themselves, to experience them firsthand, and to undergo the transformation that frequent contact with these domains initiates. In this way, the gift of method makes inevitable the continued expansion of the gift of paradigm. By inviting others to join him in the systematic exploration of the deep psyche using the amplifying lens of psychedelic states, Grof has virtually guaranteed the perpetual revision of his paradigm. It is a new continent that beckons us, and no paradigm will soon plot all its secret coves.

It is not only the vast expanse of the psyche that ensures the ongoing revision of our maps but a more subtle dynamic operating in transpersonal disclosure as well. When we explore the deep psyche, we must use mind to explore mind. Transpersonal experiences are not simply "given" to a subject who exists separate from and independent of what is being experienced, but rather arise from a complex interaction between the mind doing the exploring and the larger Mind being explored, even as this distinction is being slowly dissolved. The fact that Nature has made each of us unique guarantees that different explorers of the deep psyche will see different aspects of her complex being.

The archetypal energies that were locked into each of us at birth give a distinct inflection to each of our minds. Like gems cut with different facets, we seem designed to catch and reflect light differently. As we detach ourselves from the common ground of physical existence and move into the interactive arena of the deep psyche, therefore, it is inevitable that each of us will draw forth different experiences from her treasure chest. From this perspective, our differences are perhaps our greatest gift to each other, for it is through the unique prism of each other's mind that we discover yet another facet of the workings of Sacred Mind. It is with a deep sense of collaboration, therefore, that I undertake the current project. In the end, we are all pilgrims making maps at the edges of the world.

Chapter Two

Beyond Reincarnation

I believe there is no source of deception in the investigation of nature which can compare with a fixed belief that certain kinds of phenomenon are *impossible*.

—William James, Letter

For a large part of the world, including one-quarter of the adults in the United States, reincarnation and karma are the starting point of a true understanding of the human condition. From ancient times to the present, there have been voices saying quietly but firmly that if one does not grasp these basic principles, one's perception of human existence will necessarily be stunted and artificially constrained. Until we understand the simple fact that our minds are not the product of the few years that our current bodies have existed but draw their shape instead from a much longer history, we will always be a mystery to ourselves and life will appear more inscrutable than it need be. But while reincarnation and karma may be essential elements in any adequate understanding of human existence, they are not the whole story, and sooner or later we must reach beyond them.

Reincarnation grounds the insight that we have unlimited time to discover and develop the being that we are, and karma establishes the causal lawfulness that guides all such self-actualization. Together they constitute the framework within which human consciousness evolves, but the potentials that are activated through this long evolutionary development are not explained by either of these principles alone. Reincarnation and karma define the caldron within which human experience cooks, but what is cooking comes from the

33

nature of mind itself. To see that our mind survives the death of this body and that it carries forward the lessons of its experience is to begin to recognize the true depth of the mind, but this is just the first movement of the symphony. It does not tell us what other capacities the mind has. It does not tell us what inherent potentials will reveal themselves as we press against our evolutionary limits.

In this chapter I want to build a bridge between my earlier work on reincarnation and this study by using the concept of rebirth as a point of reference from which to make the transition to the study of nonordinary states of consciousness. In my book *Lifecycles,* I took the position that the critical evidence for rebirth was already very strong and getting stronger. I placed greatest emphasis on Ian Stevenson's research with small children who have spontaneous, detailed knowledge of their immediately previous life. The Carlson Professor at the University of Virginia, Stevenson studies children from around the world who when they are three or four years old begin to speak matter-of-factly about their "other" life which they can describe in considerable detail, often recognizing people from that life, calling them by name and showing the appropriate emotional response given their previous relationship. As a first step in constructing this bridge, therefore, I want to ask: How has Stevenson's research held up among professional philosophers? (In the interest of efficiency, I am going to assume a familiarity with Stevenson's work.) After summarizing where the debate on the evidence for reincarnation currently stands, I will then explain how Stevenson's data is both advancing *and inhibiting* our understanding of human identity. I will suggest that while his evidence is absolutely essential to establish the validity of reincarnation in our current intellectual climate, it also has within it certain limitations that are constricting our ability to comprehend some of the broader implications of rebirth. In order to understand the deeper dynamics of the mind that reincarnation points us toward, we must move beyond Stevenson's evidence. In fact, we must eventually move beyond the atomistic vision of separate souls reincarnating for their individual evolution and begin to grasp the larger intentional fabric that our lives collectively express.

Assessing Stevenson's Evidence for Reincarnation

Because reincarnation is the beginning point of a true spiritual understanding of ourselves, it is exciting that it has become a topic of heated academic exchange. Philosophers accustomed to operating within the landscape of secular humanism are understandably outraged that what many had taken to be an old-fashioned superstition should now be claiming the high ground of empirical verification. These fights are symptomatic of the larger paradigm shift that is marking the collapse of the materialist worldview we have lived within for the last three hundred years. While the revolutionary nature of Stevenson's research has caused him to be heralded by some as a modern-day Galileo, to others he is just another false messiah calling us away from the cold facts of a truly scientific understanding of ourselves. One who takes the latter view is Paul Edwards, editor of the monumental *Encyclopedia of Philosophy* and professor of philosophy at the New School for Social Research in New York City.

In 1986–87, Paul Edwards published a lengthy, four-part article in *Free Inquiry* entitled "The Case against Reincarnation" in which he argued that reincarnation is a conceptually incoherent and intellectually irresponsible belief given the best scientific information available today. He later published a more complete formulation of his argument in his introduction to an anthology entitled *Immortality*, followed later by a book on the subject entitled *Reincarnation: A Critical Examination*. Edwards's critique of reincarnation is regarded by some as the most powerful refutation of the concept ever formulated, and he has emerged as Ian Stevenson's most formidable critic. His rejection of Stevenson's data is absolute and unqualified, for to accept it, he says, would amount to nothing less than a " 'crucifixion' of our understanding."[1]

When the editor-in-chief of the *Encyclopedia of Philosophy*, a highly regarded philosopher and author of several important books, tells us that reincarnation represents a "crucifixion of our understanding," we can trust that what he says is true. If reincarnation can be proven to be true, then the modern Western philosophical paradigm will crumble because rebirth contradicts the core assumptions of that worldview. Reincarnation is a thread that when pulled unravels not just individual concepts but whole disciplines. The modern western worldview has been two thousand years in the making, and Edwards is not going to give it up without a fight. In this respect, he has shown that his philosophical instinct is sharper and his horizons larger than many of his colleagues, who have not given reincarnation the attention it deserves. To his credit, Edwards recognizes exactly what is at stake.

By drawing a line in the sand and forcing the confrontation, Edwards has done us a great service, though not necessarily the one he intended. His blistering criticisms will force reincarnationists to formulate their proposals more carefully and with greater precision. More importantly, by identifying those assumptions of the modern worldview that are incompatible with the reincarnation hypothesis, he has created a list of the premises that will have to be either dropped or deeply revised if the evidence for reincarnation should hold up in court. While Edwards believes that the current weight of intellectual opinion is sufficient to rule out this possibility, the logic of his analysis cuts both ways. If Stevenson's children turn out to be credible witnesses for rebirth, then Edwards has shown us exactly where the modern paradigm will have to be adjusted, and the adjustments are so deep as to represent nothing less than a collapse of that worldview.

If Stevenson's data holds up, for example, we would have to conclude at the very least:

1. That materialism in its many forms is false.

2. That mind is not reducible to the brain but retains its coherence and integrity without its biological substrate.

3. That our identity is more than our conscious (and unconscious) personality.

4. That there must be a domain other than spacetime in which we exist in an organized fashion between death and birth. Hence, the cosmos is multidimensional and populated by more types of beings than we had previously imagined.

5. That death is an illusion, a trick of the senses.

6. That there may be a deeper logic to the existential predicaments that we find ourselves in.

If we are forced to accepted these premises, truly our modern understanding of existence will have been "crucified," that is, painfully sacrificed for a higher good.

Because of Paul Edwards's stature in the academic community and because he is held by many philosophers to have dealt a fatal blow to reincarnation, it is important that his criticism of Stevenson's research be given careful attention. Fortunately, this has been done by Robert Almeder in his excellent book *Death and Personal Survival: The Evidence for Life After Death*. Almeder's examination of Edwards's position does not include his most recent book, but because the core of Edwards's position was clearly articulated in his earlier writings and has remained unchanged since then, Almeder's analysis is still relevant. Here I will simply report Almeder's conclusions while recommending that the interested reader consult the original for the details.

Almeder teaches philosophy at Georgia State University and has published or copublished seventeen books. His project in this volume is to give a comprehensive evaluation of the best available evidence for the personal survival of death. Toward that end he studies five types of cases: reincarnation, apparitions of the dead, possession, out-of-body-experiences, and communications from the dead. Fully one-third of his book is devoted to the evidence for reincarnation. Wisely bypassing the weaker evidence from past-lives therapy, Almeder focuses on Stevenson's research and scrutinizes the arguments put forward by his critics, especially Paul Edwards. He meticulously unpacks the arguments layer by layer, exposing the assumptions and implications of each position taken. In my opinion, his is the most comprehensive and fair-minded analysis of the reincarnation debate published thus far by a professional philosopher.

Jumping to the bottom line, Almeder's critique of Edwards—and through him Stevenson's other critics: Ian Wilson, William Roll, and C. T. K. Chari—is devastating. Almeder shows that time and again Edwards's arguments amount to, as he puts it, "a blatant bit of question begging" because he repeatedly and dogmatically assumes what is in contention, namely, that consciousness cannot exist without a brain. Time and again at critical points Edwards claims that the fatal objection to reincarnation is the fact that there is simply no conceivable way that one life can influence another in the absence of a physical link. This is what Edwards calls the *modus operandi* problem.[2] But this assumption is precisely what Stevenson's cases call into question. Edwards does not refute Stevenson's evidence so much as refuse to look at it seriously. Because he is convinced that science has proven beyond question that mind is reducible to brain, Edwards believes we are safe in assuming that Stevenson's cases *must* be flawed in some way and is quick to exploit any opinion which supports his position, no matter how unsubstantiated it may be.

The usual litany of mistakes Stevenson is accused of making is that he is insensitive to the possibility of fraud, that he underestimates the likelihood of alternative explanations for the transmission of information between lives, that he is sloppy in collecting his data and prejudicial in interpreting it, and that he underestimates the likelihood that his witnesses have unconsciously distorted their testimony in order to make it conform to their preexisting cultural beliefs concerning rebirth. Almeder's painstakingly thorough analysis, however, conclusively demonstrates that neither Edwards nor those on whom he depends have proven any of these charges. Despite their repeated allegations, none of them have actually made good on their claim to have uncovered either Stevenson's incompetence or misconduct. On the contrary, Almeder finds that Stevenson has been scrupulously sensitive to each of these issues and that he has employed every reasonable means to guard against drawing either premature or unwarranted conclusions.

I'm told that there is a saying in legal circles: "When the law is against you, argue the evidence; when the evidence is against you, argue the law." What Almeder demonstrates is that Edwards is really arguing the law, not the evidence, and in this case the "law" is simply the network of epistemological, metaphysical, and scientific assumptions that comprise the materialist worldview. In a key passage, Edwards clearly states that the burden of his refutation rests less on actually proving that Stevenson's research is methodologically flawed than on demonstrating the unacceptability of the concept of reincarnation itself, for he writes: "even in the absence of a demonstration of specific flaws, a rational person will conclude either that Stevenson's reports are seriously defective or that his alleged facts can be explained without bringing in reincarnation." [3] To accept the evidence for rebirth would require that we accept a number of "collateral assumptions" accepted by most reincarnationists (such as the six propositions listed above), and these would bring about the previously mentioned crucifixion of Western thought. Given this orientation, Edwards can dispense with seven volumes of detailed case studies in just four pages in his original study.[4]

In essence, Edwards's position is that if we accepted Stevenson's cases, we would have to admit that we understand much less about reality than we currently think we do. But is this such a terrible thing to have to concede? Is it so terrible to admit that just three hundred years after Newton and one hundred years after Darwin, we have not discovered all the important secrets of a universe that has been evolving for 15 billion years? In the century that gave us relativity theory, quantum theory, superstring theory, and chaos theory, is it preposterous to think that there are major surprises also waiting for us in the human mind? When mathematicians are debating whether there are seven, eleven, or thirteen dimensions to our universe, when astrophysicists are considering whether black holes might be portals to other dimensions and quantum physicists are mapping particles that pop in and out of physical existence, coming from and returning to we know not where, is it really as absurd as Edwards thinks to consider the possibility that our minds may not be restricted to the simple four-dimensional spacetime world we can touch with our fingers and toes?

One could use the same general observations, of course, to recommend any outrageous notion, and that is obviously not my intention. My point is that when Edwards sets aside carefully gathered and well-documented research simply because it violates our conventional thinking about the relationship of mind to matter, he underestimates the revolutionary temper of the times we live in. The rapid pace at which knowledge is expanding and the paradigm-breaking nature of much of that expansion should not cause us to cavalierly set aside the past whenever we choose, but it should cause us to be more sensitive to the limits of human understanding and more open to the unknown than Edwards is. It should lead us to be willing to carefully consider even controversial data if that data has been gathered according to the same methodological standards accepted in other contexts. To do anything less is prejudicial and out of keeping with the critical standards that Edwards claims to represent.

In *Death and Personal Survival* Almeder demonstrates that Edwards has failed to prove his case, but he goes further to argue that Stevenson's evidence for reincarnation is actually stronger than Stevenson himself has claimed. Almeder believes that Stevenson has underestimated or at least understated the cumulative evidentiary value of his research. Stevenson has been content to argue only that the evidence supports the conclusion that it is not unreasonable to believe in reincarnation, but Almeder believes that Stevenson's evidence justifies the much stronger position that *"it is unreasonable to reject belief in reincarnation."* These children who know more they ought to know confront us with a body of data that "outstrips philosophical biases and theological dogmas" and forces a fundamental revision of our thinking. As the twentieth century closes, he concludes, reincarnation must be the starting point of any truly critical and informed philosophical reflection.

Almeder's book sets a new standard of critical excellence in the philosophical assessment of the evidence for rebirth, and any subsequent discussion of these matters must take his contribution into account. His evenhanded treatment tells us that the evidence for reincarnation is thus far holding its own in the debate. But as the appearance of Edwards's book *Reincarnation* makes clear, the debate is far from over. It would take us too far from our current project to respond to this volume, nor do I think it would be productive. The arguments found there are in the main the same as in his earlier publications, though they are more fully developed and deserve careful study. Edwards does not respond to Almeder's criticisms, whom he dismisses as a "loyal disciple" of Stevenson, and he continues to hold that only "ignorant and superstitious people" will believe that Stevenson has provided compelling evidence of rebirth.

Edwards is a formidable opponent and readers will have to weigh his arguments for themselves. I myself find them unconvincing for many of the same reasons Almeder has identified. No doubt some philosophers will applaud Edwards's stirring defense of materialism, but I do not think that history will be so kind. For all its scholarship and erudition, this is a caustic book that indulges too freely in condescension and personal attack and badly misrepresents many of its adversaries. This failing is symptomatic, I think, of a worldview that is finding it increasingly difficult to defend itself on the basis of the evidence alone.[5]

Despite Edwards's best efforts to destroy Stevenson's credibility, this evidence just won't go away. In fact, Stevenson has recently raised the ante by publishing what he considers to be his strongest evidence for rebirth to date in *Reincarnation and Biology*. This massive two-volume study (2,200 pages) focuses on cases in which children not only have memories of a previous life but also show birthmarks and birth defects that correspond to wounds, lesions, or marks on the previous incarnation's body. In addition, Stevenson examines the existence of internal diseases in children that correspond to conditions that afflicted the previous personality, as well as correlations of abnormal pigmentation. Stevenson is not suggesting that all birthmarks and birth defects are rooted in previous lives or that reincarnation subverts biological etiology, but rather that a multifactorial approach that makes room for a psychogenic component for some birthmarks and birth defects will have greater explanatory power and fit more of the data than a purely physiological approach. Drawing upon psycho-neurophysiology's deepening understanding of psychosomatic disorders, which not long ago challenged all our assumptions about the body/mind relationship, Stevenson argues that in some cases one's previous life experience registers not only in the mindstream of one's subsequent incarnation but also in its body as well.[6] It will be years before we learn whether *Reincarnation and Biology* stands up to critical review as well as

Stevenson's earlier books have. His track record thus far leads me to be optimistic, and I suspect that this work will be the culmination of his long and distinguished career.[7]

Moving Beyond Stevenson's Evidence

By establishing rebirth as a fact of nature, Stevenson has opened the door to a expanded understanding of human existence. He has helped begin write a new chapter in Western thought by removing a key restriction in our understanding of ourselves. The restriction he has lifted is the restriction of time. After Stevenson, we no longer have to try to understand the qualities of our hearts and minds solely in terms of a developmental process that has taken place during the few years that our present body has existed. Now we have intellectual permission to grasp the fact that the distinct shape of our person has been developing across untold vistas of time. We have permission to see that evolution has been patiently shaping not only whole species but also individuals within the species. Whether human beings are the first species to be capable of individual evolution or whether this trait begins farther down the evolutionary ladder is less important than recognizing that somehow Nature has found a way of preserving and carrying forward the life experience of the individual. Now we see that our unique way of experiencing life, our singular individuality has emerged out of a ocean of time so vast as to be almost immeasurable and that it can continue to develop for as long again still. Death is but a pause that punctuates the seasons of our life, nothing more. This insight brings us to the threshold of a new understanding of human existence.

And yet, by itself, Stevenson's research cannot take us very far across this threshold, and this brings us to a paradoxical twist in the story. There is a certain irony that surrounds Stevenson's evidence, namely, that it simultaneously liberates and constricts our thinking about ourselves. In order to prove the existence of reincarnation in a hostile intellectual environment, we have needed verifiable cases in which one life imprints a subsequent life in a strong and demonstrable way. Stevenson has found these cases and collectively they are freeing us from the self-imprisonment of the one-timer's worldview. But what have these cases liberated us into? How far do they allow us to see into the life of the larger being that we must be if reincarnation is true? I want to suggest that they do not allow us to see very far at all. In them we can see the causal connection between some historically adjacent lives, but this is just the tip of the iceberg. If we focus on just these cases as we begin the process of rethinking our identity, we will tend to draw conclusions about what we are and how we function that are far too modest. *The task at this point, therefore, is to detach the project of understanding human identity in light of reincarnation from the evidence that convinced us of the truth of reincarnation in the first place.*

We can begin this process by first recognizing that the concept of reincarnation completely explodes our conventional reference points for discussing identity. It does so not only because it overturns the requirement of a continuous physical substrate (the brain) to anchor a continuous mindstream, but more importantly because it shatters the concept of *personal* survival. The significance of this basic fact is missed by even some astute students of rebirth. To illustrate this point let me return to Robert Almeder.

As already pointed out, Almeder believes that the evidence from a variety of sources can be used to build a strong case for personal survival after death. He does not fully appreciate, however, that there is an inherent tension between reincarnation and the other types of evidence for survival he examines. In addition to reincarnation Almeder studies apparitions of the dead, possession, out-of-body (OOB) experiences, and communications from the dead. All the cases other than reincarnation support a somewhat straightforward concept of personal survival. The apparitions he examines are apparitions of an individual discarnate person; in mediumship one communicates with an historically specific person; what possesses in cases of possession and goes out-of-body in OOB cases is some psychological core of an individual person, however we conceive it. Taken by themselves, this evidence could be interpreted to support a worldview that simply multiplies the number of dimensions in which individual persons can exist. The working unit of reality would still be the personal identity; the only difference is that now this individual identity can exist in a number of ontological environments other than spacetime. Almeder misses the fact, however, that the concept of reincarnation actually challenges the notion of personal survival because *it ruptures the category of personal identity itself*. By expanding exponentially the parameters of one's existence across an unlimited series of incarnations, reincarnation expands one's sense of identity far beyond mere "personal survival." If reincarnation is true, then personal survival is a rudimentary approximation of what continued existence actually involves. The stronger the evidence for rebirth, the less we ought to be preoccupied with personal survival at all except as a preliminary first step in speaking about the larger life process that manifests as personal existence.[8]

The Atypical Nature of Stevenson's Cases

The degree to which reincarnation forces a drastic revision of our concept of personal identity is partially obscured, I think, by the nature of the cases Stevenson uses to document the reincarnation hypothesis. It might be useful at this point, therefore, to remind ourselves that Stevenson's cases represent somewhat *atypical* examples of reincarnation that may not necessarily reflect reincarnational patterns in the population at large. Because this body of data is slanted in a particular direction, it has a tendency to give us a restricted impression of how reincarnation actually works. In a universe where the vast majority of people don't consciously remember their previous life, these children's ability to do so is the exception. The first question we should ask, therefore, is why do these children remember what, judging from the numbers alone, nature has seemingly "intended" that we forget?

In a comprehensive review of his cases, Stevenson found that approximately 61 percent of these children had died violently in their previous life. The associated characteristics of violent deaths are that they tend to be sudden and unexpected, they often involve acute physical suffering, and they happen more frequently to younger persons. The remaining 39 percent who died naturally were persons who died either suddenly (within twenty-four hours after the onset of an illness, for example), who died young (under the age of twelve), or who died with an acute sense of "unfinished business" (such as mothers with young children). What these latter groups have in common is the fact that their previous life ended with an acute sense of incompleteness. Those who die suddenly do not have time to come to terms with their death and the disruption to their relationships; similarly, persons who die young naturally feel that they had been denied the opportunity to complete what they have started. Thus Stevenson's cases suggest that the trauma of dying either violently or with an acute sense of incompleteness might be creating the conditions that cause the themes of one life to become so deeply woven into the fabric of the immediately following life that the usual amnesia concerning one's previous incarnation is overridden.[9]

But most of us don't die violently, of course, nor do most of us leave this world with such an acute sense of unfinished business. It is important to constantly remind ourselves that Stevenson's children are the exception to the rule—exceptions to the rule of forgetfulness and perhaps exceptions to other "rules" as well. For example, Stevenson reports that these children tend to be reborn relatively quickly and close to the life place of the previous personality. The average time interval between the death of the previous life and the birth of the present life is two and a half years, and most births take place within approximately fifty miles of the life place of the previous incarnation. In contrast to this, in two large studies of over 750 subjects hypnotically regressed to recover memories of their former lives, Helen Wambach found a much longer time interval between lives—an average of fifty-two years.[10] Other past-life therapists have observed a similar pattern. Joel Whitton, a Canadian psychiatrist and coauthor of *Life Between Life*, found an average interval of about forty years among his patients.[11] Both authors also reported a more generous geographic range between incarnations.

Now, cases of evoked past-life recall, which are often unverified, do not have the same evidentiary value as verified cases of spontaneous recall, but so many past-life therapists have reported similar findings that their cumulative testimony ought not to be dismissed out of hand. Once we have accepted reincarnation as a fact of life on the basis of Stevenson's evidence, there is no reason for not looking at what this second body of data might contribute to our understanding of reincarnational *patterns* in the population at large. If we do so, it appears that Stevenson's children are reincarnating *much faster* than the population at large and *much closer* to home.

There may be an even subtler bias operating in Stevenson's population. Taken as a group, Stevenson's cases suggest that one's immediate prior life will be the strongest conditioning influence on one's present life. While this may be the case for many people, we should not assume that it is the norm for everyone. While some patients in past-life therapy also show this pattern, particularly those whose immediate previous life ended traumatically, many others find that there is a much more complex relationship between their past and present lives, with not just one but many previous lives contributing significantly to the conditions of their present existence. Taken as a whole, the evidence coming from past-life therapy suggests that the causal web that weaves our past into our present is less linear than Stevenson's cases alone would suggest. Past-life therapy points us in the direction of a deeper center of integration in the psyche where the liabilities and deficits of our many lifetimes are brought into dialogue and out of this dialogue emerge the conditions of our present life.[12]

In summary, then, the very tightness of the connection between lives that makes Stevenson's data so compelling as evidence *that* reincarnation occurs tends to obscure the subtlety and complexity of *how* the process operates in the population at large. The connection between lives is so strong in these children that it tends to stretch rather than rupture our sense of personhood. If we restrict ourselves to this database alone, we will underestimate the true scope and depth of the being that reincarnation allows us to glimpse.

This tendency to underestimate the true parameters of the being that lies behind the incarnated presence is reflected in the modesty of Stevenson's description of the conditions of postmortem existence. In *Children Who Remember Previous Lives*, for example, he writes:

> The postmortem world that I envisage would, therefore, derive much of its content from the premortem thoughts of a person inhabiting it. It would reflect both the culture in which he had lived and the personal experiences and attitudes that he had had. It would be pleasant or painful according to the kind of life that the inhabitant had lived before dying.[13]

Stevenson's vision of our existence after death is of a world populated by discarnate *persons* who closely resemble their previously incarnate personalities except for the fact that they no longer have material bodies. These persons live for a while in familiar circumstances derived from their most immediate previous life before re-immersing themselves into physical existence. Clearly there is evidence that supports Stevenson's vision, as Almeder has shown us. The problem with this evidence, however, is not that it is false but that it is *superficial*. It underestimates the variety and complexity of postmortem existence. This brings us to the larger problem of what we are actually seeing when we look at the evidence for life after death.

Looking in the Astral Mirror

There has been a increase recently in the number of books (and movies) attempting to describe the nature of our existence after death on the basis of information derived from a variety of sources including near-death experiences, mediumistic communication, meditative intuition, and so on. Many if not most of these books, however, are marred by a failure to recognize subtle restrictions that are influencing their information. If we were to use the vocabulary of the occult tradition, we could say that much of the evidence concerning postmortem existence is coming from the lower astral planes (corresponding to Wilber's psychic level of transpersonal experience). As we will see in chapter 5, these are the planes "closest" to the physical plane, meaning that they are the most heavily imprinted by spacetime reality. The beings who populate these planes live in conditions that are strongly shaped by their recent experiences on Earth. Thus, to various degrees all we are doing when we look at information from this level is *looking at ourselves in an astral mirror.*

There is an unfortunate catch-22 operating here. The most careful investigations of postmortem existence naturally focus on cases that lend themselves to some degree of empirical verification, because without verification no case will be taken seriously by the academic community. What is often overlooked, however, is the fact that the demand for verification, while entirely appropriate in its own right, tends to restrict the cases we are studying to those in which the conditions of postmortem existence sufficiently parallel the conditions of spacetime to generate information that can be verified back in spacetime. For there to be a case of continued existence to investigate, there must be a deceased party that "matches" a prior human existence and that is interested in communicating with researchers. To put this simple fact in perspective, most advanced spiritual traditions (such as Kashmir Shaivism, HuaYen Buddhism, or Vajrayana Buddhism) have long held that a sustained interest in communicating with human beings after one's death is usually a sign of lower spiritual development. More developed beings are simply less interested in these matters because they now know themselves to be much more than their last incarnation and are absorbed in realities far removed from their spacetime identity and its concerns.

The demand for verification, therefore, restricts researchers to studying cases which come from planes where the mode of postmortem survival is personal survival. This restriction will produce an abridged and distorted portrait of postmortem existence because many of its subtler dimensions will simply not show up on this screen. In short, this "paranormal" information is much less "para" and much more "normal" than we might at first think. Until we realize that much parapsychological investigation of postmortem existence is simply looking at spacetime in an astral mirror, we will continue to trap ourselves in mythologies that are simply feeding back to us our spacetime experience with a few extra bells and whistles thrown in. We will tend to miss holographic capacities that are inherent in the nature of mind but that are being obscured by the self-referential habits of our physical conditioning. As I see it, this is the dangerous potential of much parapsychological research on post-mortem existence—*the actual deepening of spacetime conditioning by feeding back into ourselves the testimony coming from the mirror of the lower astral planes*. We can waste a lot of time looking in the astral mirror thinking we are learning more about the "deeper" workings of the universe than we actually are.

Let me now focus these observations on the subject of reincarnation. By itself, the evidence for rebirth shifts our thinking about identity from the level of egoic identity to the soul. It dramatically expands our sense of self by allowing us to recognize that our present life is an integral part of a larger being that lives across vast stretches of time. As we turn to try to understand what the life of this being might be like, however, we inevitably tend to import into our calculations subtle assumptions derived from our current reference point in spacetime. We tend to think about the soul's experience in ways that reflect our present experience, specifically our experience of being a separate, private self. To the extent that we fall into this trap, we will tend to underestimate the degree to which the life of the soul may in some respects be radically *unlike* life as we ordinarily know it here. We will miss holographic concerns and capacities that reflect realities that are invisible to dualistic spacetime vision.

In saying this I am criticizing my own work in this area. Though the concept of the Oversoul developed in *Lifecycles* was expansive, it was not expansive enough. It honored the temporal depth of our lives but it did not sufficiently honor our spatial breadth. I did what so many writers before me had done and transferred pieces of the myth of atomistic individuality from the physical domain to the spiritual domain. It was only as my inner work deepened that I began to see the necessity of revising this picture. The core of this revision lies in recognizing the inherent holistic functioning of mind. It lies in dropping the atomistic categories of a Newtonian psychology and adopting an eco-centric vocabulary, a "quantum" vocabulary better suited to describing the field dynamics of mind.

As I said in the previous chapter, the confusions about what we are tend to fall away in clusters. Some of these clusters concern time and our tendency to take our present life as our real identity. Other clusters concern space and our tendency to take our local experience as our real identity. Systematic spiritual practice eventually shatters both these assumptions en route to the recovery of a more essential identity which is a divine identity. Along the way we are brought face to face with an ancient truth articulated by many spiritual traditions. The certainty of surviving death and the continuity of learning across many lifetimes is the entry point of spiritual wisdom, but not even death can be counted on to shatter the deepest illusions and in the end the *bardo* only gets in the way. We must penetrate beyond these dreamy astral reflections until we shatter the hidden assumptions they perpetuate. With this discovery we make the pivot to pursuing the question of identity beyond Stevenson's evidence and beyond the parapsychological evidence from the lower astral levels. We turn to the study of the deep psyche and the work of Stanislav Grof.

Part II

The Deep Ecology of Nonordinary States

Chapter Three

Expanding the Concept of the Perinatal

Mental facts do function both singly and together, at once, and we finite minds may simultaneously be coconscious with one another in a superhuman intelligence.

—William James, *A Pluralistic Universe*

P sychedelic therapy dissolves the glue that holds consciousness in its customary, personal configuration. When its powerful evocative techniques are used to hyperstimulate the psyche, our mind opens to reveal its underlying processes. Through a long series of trials, one is eventually forced to question everything one had previously believed to be true about life, death, and the nature of one's identity. Because we must shed many layers to discover the deeper truths about ourselves, this process has many stages, and it would be a mistake to emphasize any one at the expense of the others. Nevertheless, one transition stands out as particularly important—the collapse of our fundamental sense of ourselves as separate, independent, autonomous beings, what Buddhism calls the "inherently existing self." Making this transition requires shedding everything that physical sensation has told us that we are—discrete, self-contained beings consisting entirely of our physical experience. To let go of ourselves here is truly to undergo a great death.

This spiritual death takes place at what Stanislav Grof calls the perinatal level of consciousness, and therefore the project of this chapter is to look deeply into this domain. After summarizing Grof's description of the perinatal dimension, I will introduce a series of perinatal experiences that I could not reconcile with Grof's theory in its current form and that forced me to rethink some of the fundamental assumptions of Grof's model. In time I began to recognize the possibility of expanding Grof's account in a way that extended its explanatory power while making it more internally self-consistent. I believe the interpretation of the perinatal domain that follows clarifies Grof's original intent by lifting from his theory some of the concessions he made to the intellectual temper of the times in which he first formulated his paradigm.

The Perinatal Dimension in Psychedelic Psychotherapy

Grof's model of consciousness divides consciousness into three broad experiential realms: the psychodynamic, the perinatal, and the transpersonal. The psychodynamic realm reflects our life experience since birth and is addressed by the various schools of psychodynamic theory. Perinatal experience ("concerning birth") focuses on problems relating to biological birth, physical pain, disease and aging, the meaningfulness of existence, death and spiritual rebirth. The transpersonal realm is a highly diversified set of experiences in which consciousness expands far beyond one's ego boundaries. Typical transpersonal experiences may include unitive states of consciousness with other life forms; exploring one's cultural, racial, and even evolutionary past; recalling past incarnations; and various ESP or out-of-body experiences. In some transpersonal experiences, spacetime is transcended altogether as one moves into experiential realms traditionally the exclusive domain of shamans, mystics, and advanced meditators.

Perinatal experience represents the experiential frontier between the personal and transpersonal realms and combines both in a complex manner that makes it difficult to summarize concisely. I will therefore highlight only the most relevant portions of Grof's findings here.

The dominant motif of the perinatal level is the confrontation with death, a confrontation that is so realistic that subjects often lose awareness that they are in a therapeutic session and come to believe that they are actually dying. This ordeal forces them to experience all the fears and resistances that surround dying and to confront the frailty, impermanence, and suffering inherent in human existence. The resulting existential crisis can become so extreme that persons transcend the boundaries of their individual lives and begin to experience the suffering of entire groups of people, in some cases even reaching beyond human experience. Paradoxically, this confrontation with death is often intertwined with an equally vivid reliving of one's birth, specific aspects of which have sometimes been verified by family members or attending physicians (twisted cord, breech birth, forceps, resuscitation maneuvers, odors, sounds, and lighting).

The perinatal level thus combines birth and death, personal and transpersonal experiences in a complex fashion that is difficult to dissect. The exact relation of perinatal experience to biological birth is still uncertain. On the one hand, the content of these experiences cannot be reduced to the memory of biological birth, while on the other hand many of the physical symptoms that manifest in this context appear to derive from biological birth. In addition, both the physical symptoms and their corresponding experiential content seem to form four experiential clusters that can be modeled on the four consecutive stages of biological birth.

To explain these patterns in his data, Grof introduced the concepts of COEX system and Basic Perinatal Matrix (BPM). A COEX system, short for "system of condensed experience," is a specific constellation of memories (and fantasies) from many periods of an individual's life that share a common theme and are marked by a common emotional charge. For a simple analogy, imagine taking a novel and highlighting the protagonist's many experiences in different colors according to their emotional content—red for anger, green for jealousy, yellow for fear, and so on. If you were then to cut up the entire book and gather all the cuttings of each color into separate piles, each pile would represent a single COEX system. The surface layers of a COEX system are made up of more recent or superficial experiences of that particular emotion. As you move deeper into the system, the experiences tend to become older and more basic. At the center of each system, says Grof, is a core experience or set of experiences that represents the primary disturbance, the seed experience around which later experiences cluster.

A Basic Perinatal Matrix is a COEX system whose core is anchored in fetal experience, especially the experience of birth. According to Grof, the four phases of birth come to constitute four basic matrices in which are stored subsequent memories of psychologically similar experiences. Our unresolved and unintegrated birth experience is carried in these matrices. It is always there, below the surface and out of view but shaping in subtle and pervasive ways how we experience the world, even influencing what parts of the world we are drawn to experience. In addition, when one reconnects with the memory of one's birth as preserved in these matrices, one also gains experiential access to the collective unconscious and other transpersonal realms that contain similar material. When one of the perinatal matrices emerges in a psychedelic session, therefore, it manifests as a multilevel repository of experience and insight, and always with an overwhelming emotional charge.

Turning to specifics, Grof defines the four stages of biological birth as:

1. Intrauterine existence before the onset of delivery;

2. Labor before dilation of the cervix;

3. Labor after dilation of the cervix;

4. Final propulsion through the birth canal and separation from the mother.

Before delivery the fetus has "good womb" or "bad womb" experiences depending on the quality of prenatal support given by the mother. In the first phase of labor, the fetus experiences a biochemical and physical assault; but because the cervix is not open, it has no place to escape to, experiencing a literal "no-exit" situation. In the second phase, the cervix is open, thus creating a possible way out of the dilemma, and a heroic struggle to navigate the birth canal begins. In the final phase, the labor agonies culminate, followed by sudden release and separation from the mother.

The prototypical themes of the four stages of birth as matrices for storing subsequent memories include the following: (This is not an exhaustive list.)

1. Good womb: satisfaction of important needs, fulfilling love, dissolution of boundaries, unitive, oceanic bliss. Bad womb: experiences of malaise, disgust, anxiety, paranoia, unreality.

2. Unwarranted, violent aggression against the helpless innocent; hopelessness, guilt, unspeakable aloneness, the absurdity of human existence, entrapment without escape, the sovereignty of death.

3. Titanic struggle, life-death crisis but not absolutely hopeless, high energy experiences of various sorts—murderous rage, volcanic ecstasy, sexual excitement, sadomasochism.

4. Death-rebirth experience: total annihilation of the individual followed by breaking through to a new level of existence, sudden liberation, profound love, spiritual illumination.

Infant, child, and adult experiences (and fantasies) that approximate these themes cluster around the relevant perinatal core in our memory, with the result that each constellation gathers energy through time and comes to influence behavior.

When a subject in a psychedelic session engages a perinatal matrix, then, the experience will be multidimensional but thematically coherent. He or she may experience simultaneously one or more phases of the original birth trauma, similar real or imagined traumas from later life of both a physical and psychological nature, and, in addition, thematically congruent spiritual and philosophical conflicts and insights. Following Grof, let us distinguish the physical component of the matrices from the psychospiritual component and discuss each in the order in which the matrices often emerge in one's sessions—BPM II, III, IV, and I.[1]

Typical among the *physical symptoms* associated with engaging these matrices are enormous pressures on the head and body, excruciating pains in various parts of the body, tremors, jerks, twitches, twisting movements, chills and hot flashes, and ringing in the ears. Perinatal seizures can be quite severe and mimic full-blown seizures. As Grof summarizes it:

> Subjects may spend hours in agonizing pain, with facial contortions, gasping for breath and discharging enormous amounts of tension in tremors, twitches, violent shaking and complex twisting movements. The face may turn dark purple or dead pale, and the pulse show considerable acceleration. The body temperature usually oscillates in a wide range, sweating may be profuse, and nausea with projectile vomiting is a frequent occurrence.[2]

These symptoms characterize BPM II, III, and IV, often becoming more intense as the third and fourth matrices are activated. Eventually the physical torments peak and end as the subject moves from intense constriction and confinement to sudden decompression and spaciousness in the death-rebirth experience. While not all subjects experience these symptoms as a self-conscious reliving of their actual birth trauma, many of the physical symptoms themselves seem to be best interpreted as deriving from biological birth.

Subjects often assume fetal postures and move in ways that resemble the movements of a child during biological delivery. This is sometimes true even for those subjects who psychologically experience their perinatal encounter in purely philosophical or spiritual terms.

The *psychospiritual dimension* of perinatal experience is difficult to summarize because of the extreme multidimensionality of psychedelic states. In BPM II, III, and IV, the individual must face the deepest roots of existential despair and metaphysical crisis, but the nature of the crisis differs with each matrix and follows an overarching developmental sequence. (It would be a mistake, however, to overemphasize the sequential nature of this encounter, as the perinatal matrices often manifest in different sequences and in combinations.)

In BPM II the subject typically experiences an overwhelming assault against which he or she is utterly helpless. Tortured without chance of escape, one is plunged into extreme metaphysical despair and loneliness. Existence appears to be completely meaningless, and feelings of guilt, inferiority, and alienation have a distinctly hopeless and endless quality to them.

In BPM III many of the above themes are continued but with an essential difference. Because there is now a slight possibility of escape—the cervix is dilated—a titanic struggle for survival takes place that Grof calls the *death-rebirth struggle*. Amid crushing mechanical pressures and often a high degree of anoxia and suffocation, the subject typically experiences powerful currents of energy building in his or her entire body and then releasing themselves in explosive discharges. A frequent experience related to this matrix is the encounter with purifying fire that destroys all that is disgusting or corrupt in the individual.

In BPM IV the subject eventually loses the struggle for survival and is completely annihilated:

> Suffering and agony culminate in an experience of total annihilation on all levels—physical, emotional, intellectual, ethical, and transcendental. The individual experiences final biological destruction, emotional defeat, intellectual debacle, and utmost moral humiliation. . . . He feels that he is an absolute failure from any imaginable point of view; his entire world seems to be collapsing, and he is losing all previously meaningful reference points. This experience is usually referred to as *ego-death*.[3]

After the subject has died as an ego, he or she experiences rebirth into a more holistic, transindividual mode of consciousness. All torment suddenly ceases and is followed by experiences of physical and psychological redemption, forgiveness, and profound love. "The individual feels cleansed and purged, as if he has disposed of an incredible amount of 'garbage,' guilt, aggression, and anxiety. He experiences overwhelming love for his fellow [human beings], appreciation of warm human relationships, solidarity, and friendship."[4] These experiences are subsequently deepened in a mystical direction as the subject becomes absorbed into fully developed experiences of cosmic unity associated with BPM I.

One experiences this perinatal descent, death, and rebirth at many transpersonal as well as personal levels. The entire history of the human race seems to be potentially available to one, together with all its myths, symbols, and historical rituals. In BPM II, for example, one may experience archetypal sequences of the primal fall from grace or become various tragic figures from Greek or Roman mythology tortured endlessly in Hades for their offenses. Alternatively, one may expand to encompass the experience of thousands of persons caught in tragic historical dramas of victimization. At its deepest level, BPM II takes the form of an absolutely realistic descent into hell as described in the world's major religions. In BPM III, scenarios of hopeless despair are replaced with mythic and historical dramas of heroic struggle, often with pronounced sadomasochistic, sexual, scatological, satanic, purgatorial, and pyrocathartic features. One might experience in vivid detail bloody Pre-Columbian sacrifices, the bacchanalian rites of ancient Greece, the Satanic Mass, or even the crucifixion of Christ. When one's process shifts to BPM IV, one might experience the death-rebirth experience in the mythological dress of any historical peoples, including those one is completely unfamiliar with. One can experience the gods and goddesses of ancient pantheons as living forces crushing one's existence into dust and then bringing that dust back to life in spiritual rebirth. BPM I often mediates profound experiences of cosmic unity in which the dualities of historical existence are dissolved into the seamless flux of divinity that all existence is at a deeper level. Like the previous stages, this divine reunion may express itself in the archetypal form of any mythology that describes this level of existence.

Whether it is experienced in primarily fetal or cosmological modalities, the death-rebirth process is never fully completed in a

single session. Many sessions of repeatedly engaging the same issues are required before one has exhausted them. The usual pattern
is that a subject working at this level will eventually experience a
major perinatal crisis centering on one of the phases described
above. Yielding to and resolving the crisis will usually shift the person into positive transpersonal experiences for the remainder of the
session even though perinatal content may remain for future sessions. If the process is continued through serial sessions, a final
death-rebirth experience eventually will completely exhaust all perinatal content. Making copious use of case histories, Grof has demonstrated that systematically engaging this traumatic material can
actually dissolve the perinatal matrices, thus permanently removing
their influence from the individual's behavior. In subsequent sessions the subject moves directly into transpersonal experience as the
journey in consciousness continues. Grof has found that *every single
person who reaches this level in their work adopts a spiritual interpretation of existence, regardless of their prior psychosocial conditioning.* This includes such unmystical types as staunch atheists,
skeptics, Marxists, and positivistically oriented scientists.

This brief overview does not do justice to the complexity and subtlety of Grof's account. His articulation of the stages of the birth
process and their pervasive influence on subsequent character development, his demonstration of the psychic conflation of birth and
death and of the intimate correspondence between our struggle to be
spiritually reborn and our struggle to be physically born stand as
lasting contributions to the field. Furthermore, his account of the
transpersonal components of the death-rebirth experience is comprehensive. And yet, as deep and subtle as Grof's account of the perinatal dimension is, it contains an unsolved puzzle that signals the
need to take his analysis one step further.

The Paradox in Grof's Description of the Perinatal

There is a subtle paradox in Grof's account of the perinatal that runs
throughout his many books. On the one hand, perinatal experience
is defined as being a category of experience that is sui generis and
not reducible to personal categories, while on the other hand the
burden of Grof's explanation of the inner logic of perinatal experience tilts decidedly in the direction of personal psychology. He has
demonstrated that perinatal experience intertwines biographical
and trans-biographical experience and represents a dynamic inter-

penetration of these two levels of consciousness. We would expect, therefore, that a complete explanation of perinatal experience would be equally balanced between these two modes, that it would explain as much in one direction as it does in the other. What we find, however, is an explanation that works out the logic of the personal side of perinatal experience in considerably greater detail than the transpersonal side. No matter how many times Grof reminds us that perinatal experience cannot be reduced to the birth trauma, the sheer volume of explanation that he provides in that direction cannot help but leave the reader thinking of the perinatal disproportionately in terms of biological birth. The very name "perinatal" reinforces this tendency, as does his calling it the Rankian level of the unconscious.[5]

Grof's presentation of the range of experiences that can occur at the perinatal level is comprehensive, but this very richness, I think, has obscured the fact that an important problem has been overlooked; namely, *why should persons who are engaging unresolved fetal trauma be drawn into torturous experiences of collective suffering or excruciatingly painful archetypal sequences in the first place?* If connecting with the birth trauma acts as a stencil providing access to various experiences of collective suffering, what therapeutic role do these experiences have? Grof's explanation that persons are drawn into them through the similarity of emotional content or physical sensations may help us understand *how* this happens, but not *why*. He documents that these painful encounters are extremely beneficial for the individuals involved, as they are part of the death-rebirth experience, but this by itself is not a sufficient explanation of the phenomenon.[6]

The pressure to answer this question comes from the fact that the levels of suffering reached in these collective perinatal episodes are many times greater than anything deriving from the personal side of perinatal experience. In *Realms of the Human Unconscious,* Grof indicates the scope of these ordeals when he writes:

A subject can experience himself as thousands of soldiers who have died on the battlefields of the whole world from the beginning of time, as the tortured victims of the Spanish Inquisition, as prisoners of concentration camps, as patients dying of terminal diseases, as aging individuals who are decrepit and senile, as mothers and children dying during delivery, or as inmates maltreated in chronic wards of insane asylums.[7]

If a person is repeatedly immersed in torment such as this, he or she must eventually try to answer the question, How is this a meaningful part of my therapy? Where is its therapeutic effect focused and to what end? The absence of an answer to these questions—indeed, the absence of the questions themselves—stands in stark contrast to the depth of explanation Grof provides for the personal roots of the perinatal ordeal. On this side of the ledger, his analysis is subtle and penetrating. It is on the transpersonal side that his presentation, as rich and detailed as it is, is incomplete.

To anticipate somewhat, I will suggest below that in order to answer these questions we must look beyond the individual subject who is having these experiences to the collective group that he or she is part of. We must enlarge our definition of the patient to include the entire human species. By way of contrast, Grof always discusses the therapeutic impact of the death-rebirth experience solely in terms of the individual patient. He consistently focuses our attention on the psychospiritual transformation of the individual undergoing the experience (and in a few instances on the transformation of the subject's karmic antagonist). This focus on the spiritual evolution of the individual is another indication of Grof's tilt toward the personal and sharpens the paradox in his account. The death-rebirth sequence culminates in the discovery that one is, at deeper levels, much more than the body-mind self, yet Grof's discussion of the impact of this discovery consistently focuses our attention on the individual subject alone.[8]

As I came to identify this lacuna in his formulation and began to write about these matters, I shared my thinking with Stan. He confirmed my observations and supported the proposals I was making for extending the concept of the perinatal. He explained that he had slanted his original interpretation of the perinatal domain toward the personal in part for political reasons, to build a bridge to the psychiatric community that at the time was much more wedded to a personal psychology than it is today twenty-five years later. In order to prevent his findings from being rejected out of hand and to make it easier for clinicians to accept the evidence for a transpersonal dimension, he had emphasized the fetal side of perinatal experience as a logical extension of personal psychology. His presentation of transpersonal experiences is abbreviated in his early books for the same reason. Similarly, in a recent exchange with Ken Wilber, he has acknowledged that when he first formulated his paradigm, his medical and psychiatric training had inclined him to explain perinatal experience in terms of the birth experience.[9]

Grof's decision to model the complex phenomenology of perinatal experience in terms of a birth hermeneutic was understandable given his historical context and represented an important break-through that opened new horizons in clinical theory. Its very productivity, however, hid for a time its incompleteness. While Grof has moved on to present a richer and more complete exposition of transpersonal experience in his later books, challenging his audience to follow him into increasingly radical ways of thinking, he has not doubled back to revise his original account of the perinatal dimension. The most complete analysis he has given continues to be that found his first book, *Realms of the Human Unconscious*, published in 1976. This being the case, it is time to attempt a more rounded explanation of perinatal experience that strikes a better balance between its personal and transpersonal aspects. Such an expansion of perinatal theory will not subtract anything from Grof's account, and because it will more fully integrate insights that come from transpersonal experience, it will make Grof's model more coherent with itself.

A Different Experience of the Perinatal Dimension

The questions posed above did not originate in an academic's fascination with intellectual puzzles but in a practitioner's desperate attempt to make sense of his experience. At a certain point in my inner work, my experiences began to diverge from Grof's model. At first the shift was subtle, but it became more pronounced as the work progressed. What was "supposed" to happen did not seem to be happening, and what was happening did not seem to be explained by his paradigm. Because his model for the stages of therapeutic engagement was derived from such a large data base—now over four thousand psychedelic sessions and twenty-thousand breathwork sessions with a highly diversified population—I kept trying to fit my experiences into it, but I kept failing. In the end, I had no alternative but to follow my process wherever it was leading and hope that it would eventually make sense.

The problem was the shape and scope of the suffering. In all other respects, my experiences seemed to fall within the wide boundaries of Grof's paradigm, but when it came to the suffering, something was different. Here my experiences did not reflect his description of perinatal engagement but seemed to take on a life of their own. They developed in a methodical and orderly manner, if one can ever call perinatal experiences orderly, but their logic was not the logic of the womb.

As we saw above, Grof tends to see the birth experience as providing the fundamental organization to perinatal experience. While never reducing the perinatal to the fetal, the logic of perinatal experience is described as being at core the logic of the fetus being born. Resonances with the collective unconscious of humanity, archetypal sequences, and religious myths are acknowledged and described in detail, but these resonances are in the end presented as being governed by the deeper logic of birth and a corollary of the individual's death-rebirth process. Not being given any further explanation in Grof's system, they appear by default to be almost byproducts of the cleansing of the individual psyche. In my perinatal work, however, the balance of individual and collective suffering was eventually turned on its head. What appeared to be a transpersonal byproduct for some people became primary for me.

Fetal experiences surfaced early in my work with pronounced physical distress and perinatal spasms combined with a variety of existential ordeals. The fetal sensations and physical symptoms intensified for about ten sessions at which point something larger and darker began to open underneath them. Eventually I began to realize that staying with the physically saturated ordeal was actually less threatening than turning to explore this frightening abyss, that in some subtle way I was holding on to a storyline at one level in order to avoid confronting something even more frightening. As I surrendered to this deeper unknown, the physical convulsions began to subside and I found myself entering regions of profound collective suffering. The fetal themes receded with the physical symptoms. They were present but in a diminishing minor role while the major role was taken over by collective anguish. This ordeal grew to such proportions and lasted for so many years that eventually I began to recognize that it was being driven by something larger than fetal logic and larger even than the death-rebirth of an individual. The story of collective pain took over my sessions, and this story had a life of its own, a life that I did not understand.

I would prefer at this point to be able to introduce sessions other than my own to illustrate this dynamic, but with the exception of one case quoted later in this chapter, suitable examples have not yet appeared in print. The only published cases of perinatal experience deriving from psychedelic work that I am aware of have appeared in Grof's books. I have combed his corpus carefully, and while experiences of this sort are acknowledged, the cases that are presented reflect, from my frame of reference at least, perinatal experiences that are more personal than transpersonal in orientation. Not being a clinician, I do not have access to a large sampling of other people's sessions. In order to provide the evidence for the expansion of perinatal theory that follows, therefore, I have no alternative but to draw upon my own experiences, however less than ideal that may be.

What follows is the perinatal portion of two sessions that date from the early 1980s. These accounts are excerpts taken from the records I have kept of my work and were not originally written for public distribution. My initial purpose in making this record was entirely personal, to help me retain and integrate as much of each session as possible. This often forced me to write at the limits of my understanding as I struggled to put into words experiences that I could not always comprehend at the time. In order not to distract attention from our primary objective, I have included only the cleansing portion of each session, omitting the subsequent ecstatic portion. This arrangement of material, therefore, does not represent the true balance of negative and positive experiences that occur in each session.

Session 13

Thirty-five minutes into the session, the stomach-jerking spasms began. The physical discomfort was not as bad as previously, but the psychological discomfort was worse. It grew until it was swirling around me in dark clouds. Waves of increasingly intense pain—multidimensional anguish, elemental and on a vast social scale.

When the music shifted to primal chanting one hour later, the anguish thickened into a terrible horror acted out around me on all sides. The forms of the horror were so many that there is no way to describe it. Disembowelings by the score, the mauling of lives, deaths in the thousands. Swirling forms so complex, multidimensional, and multithematic that isolated images do not stand out. It was war, savagery, destruction, killing, anguish. Trying to articulate it I am reminded of Dante's Inferno but sped up incredibly fast and overlaid many times. It lasted hours. Eventually I asked my sitter to change the tape.

Hoping to find some respite in gentler music, instead I was hit with more chanting. I was in agony. . . . The chanting kept pulling

more pain from me. . . . I don't know what happened next. . . . After an
eternity, the pain somehow ended. . . . Amid soft strains of gentle
Indian music, my pain lay down and I moved on to the ecstatic phase
of the session.

Session 15

I don't know how to describe today, the places I was in, the destruc-
tion I was part of, the searing pain and torment of thousands of be-
ings tortured to their breaking point and then beyond. Not
individuals but waves of people. The tortures not specific but legion.
Driving sitar and drums tearing me apart, plunging me into more
and more primitive levels of anguish. Passing through previous lev-
els, I eventually reached a new one I can only liken to hell itself.
Unspeakable horror beyond any imaginings. I was lost in a rampag-
ing savagery that was without bounds. The worst pictures of the
world's religions only touch the surface. And yet the torment cleanses
one's being.

Here the experience of an individual person is being replaced by the
experience of a group. Here dying wears a collective face. Though it
is not adequately conveyed in these two snapshots, the transition
from individual to collective perinatal experience was gradual and
systematic. It sounds strange to put it this way, but one literally has
to learn how to sustain suffering of this scope and intensity. If you
move into these regions too quickly, you simply "pass out" from experiential overload, as happened in session 13. The subsequent two
sessions, which I will not reproduce here, showed signs of a shift to
BPM III, with the pain intensifying to the point that it became ecstatic, frenzied energy rather than pain alone.

At this stage I was still trying to conceptualize these dynamics
in terms of a person-centered psychology of self, following the implicit lead of Grof's focus on the transformation of the individual and
reinforced by Eastern spirituality's focus on self-purification. I knew
that the *Bardo Thödol* described the Chönyid Bardo as a dimension
in which one experiences one's unconscious mind projected outward
and appearing in a multitude of external forms. The positive aspects
of one's psyche manifest as the "Peaceful Deities" and the negative
aspects as the "Wrathful Deities." In this interlife dimension one appears to be confronting many external forms, but all forms are said
to actually derive from one's mind alone. I speculated, therefore, that
the thousands of lives I was experiencing were possibly projective re-

flections of my own mind. Like entering a complex hall of mirrors, the images were many but the source was one—myself. Given the highly condensed nature of COEX systems, this seemed to be a reasonable hypothesis, and if I extended the formula to include former lives, this interpretation became even more viable. If I assumed that not just my present life but my entire karmic legacy was somehow stored in these highly compressed perinatal structures that were being unraveled in the sessions, this might account for the extraordinary scope of these ordeals. And yet, something didn't fit. The pain was growing to such proportions that I found it difficult to believe that it was all coming from inside me, even an expanded "me" of many incarnations.

I had a lot of time to ponder these questions because I interrupted my work at this point for reasons that are not part of this story.[10] During a hiatus of nearly seven years I continued a regimen of spiritual practice and personal growth work. This included *vipaśyanā* meditation, Gestalt-oriented therapy, body work, and several years of past-life therapy. While this helped me manage the powerful forces set in motion in my sessions, it never reached into the perinatal depths that were always there beneath the surface, waiting for my return. When I resumed psychedelic work, I began exactly where I had stopped, immersed in profound collective suffering. As soon as I opened to these depths again, it became immediately clear that the interpretation that I had crafted was completely inadequate.

Session 18

The most difficult aspect to describe from today's session is the pain / agony / frenzy. Terrible pain. Driving, explosive, convulsive horror. It was beyond anything before, beyond massacres, beyond wars. It blended feeling-tones of primordial civilizations and galactic cataclysm. It somehow comprised all human history but went beyond even human experience, encompassing experiential dimensions I am unfamiliar with. It was enormous in scope and complexity. It had little to do with my individual human history. Its intensity was not the intensity of compression. I could have lived on earth ten thousand years and not begun to touch the range of pain experienced today.

If this suffering could not be understood in terms of a model of compression, what could it possibly represent? If it was not an expression of my private history, by which I mean my extended karmic history, what was it doing in "my" therapy? These questions were the beginning of the unraveling of all my assumptions about what was mine and not mine, about what was me and not me. It marked the end of one way of thinking and the uncertain start of another.

In the following twenty sessions spread over three years, two developments took place. First, the pain continued to deepen and expand its boundaries, repeatedly jumping its banks like a river in flood. Secondly, the ecstatic portion of the sessions introduced a series of experiences that began to place the pain in a larger context, causing me to reframe my entire understanding of its source and possible function. They began to show me truths about how life is configured beneath physical appearances and beneath the shadows cast in the deep psyche by spacetime experience. It was as if a jigsaw puzzle were being dumped into my mind piece by piece, and it took many years before I could see how all the pieces fit together.

As long as there is self-conditioning in the system, one's ability to see clearly in these states is always compromised. As more structures are dissolved, the veil becomes thinner and one begins to be able to see more clearly, though always incompletely. Because one's ability to grasp what one is being shown is always compromised, emphasis should be placed not on individual experiences but on the trajectory being actualized across multiple sessions. The direction truth is taking shows itself sooner than its final destination. In the end, *all experiences in this inquiry are but forms through which still deeper realities express themselves*, and with persistence these forms will eventually dissolve, opening the way for still more subtle and profound forms to emerge until that which is beyond form is realized. While they stand, however, these forms focus our awareness and afford us insights into the particular level of the chain of being from which they are drawn. In the two accounts that follow, I include some of these experiential forms as they presented themselves in my work. After they are on the table, we can begin to try to solve the riddle of this collective anguish.

Session 19

After a long time, darker experiences began to emerge, but I was able to remain physically open and let them come, not resisting. Again there was the suffering that I cannot put into words. It is a frenzied, chaotic, physical, psychological anguish. At several places I found myself wondering what all this pain was about. I was open and letting it come through me, but where was it coming from? I could not tell, but it broadened and deepened for a long time.

My consciousness was expanding and opening to more and more suffering. Eventually I had the sense that my being stretched from horizon to horizon as I experienced a suffering that involved tens of thousands of people. Because I had gone into this state more slowly than in the previous session, however, it was not as confusing as before. Eventually through the field of suffering I caught a glimpse of something behind it, something enormous and familiar from the previous session. Then the field of suffering closed back in on me. I reached more deeply into it and eventually broke through again to this larger dimension.

Early on I had the experience of the dissolution of boundaries. I was experiencing the physical world, and everywhere boundaries were melting away. Discrete "objects" were shown to be but different nuances of a single energy. "No boundaries. No boundaries anywhere." There was not even a real boundary separating the physical and nonphysical dimensions of existence, and I experienced the worlds of matter and spirit as a seamless whole. It was all one massive Energy, one Being.

In most of my sessions I have simply been carried along from one transpersonal experience to another. Only once before have I had the experience of being able to consciously engage and direct my experience. Now it was happening again. A circle opened around me and created a space that became an arena of dialogue between myself and a larger Consciousness. I discovered, much to my surprise, that the experiential field within the circle was responsive to my thoughts. When I first discovered this, I had the ecstatic sensation of confronting an enormous Intelligence that included and surrounded my own. "That's right," it communicated to me. "That's exactly what is happening."

I began to ask it questions and it answered by orchestrating my experience in the circle. It was an extremely subtle process and the line between "my" consciousness and this larger Consciousness was invisible to me. At times my reactions to what was being shown me interacted with the content of the answer to distort or sidetrack the lesson being given. I learned that I could stop these unwanted deviations by taking control of my thoughts. I could "clear the board" by stopping my reactions and waiting for the space I was in to clear. Once my mind was still, the lesson would continue.

After some intervening experiences, I was brought to an encounter with a unified energy field underlying all physical existence. I was confronting an enormous field of blindingly bright, incredibly intense energy. Though the energy was not difficult to look at, experiencing it was extremely intense and carried with it a sense of ultimate encounter. This energy was the single energy that comprised all existence. All things that existed were but varied aspects of its comprehensive existence. I had encountered this energy in previous sessions, but never as completely and consummately as today.

The experience then changed into an extremely powerful and moving experience of the COSMIC TREE. The energy became a massive tree of radiant energy suspended in space. Larger than the largest galaxy, it was comprised entirely of light. The core of the tree was lost to the brilliant display but limbs and leaves were visible around its edges. I experienced myself as one of its leaves. The lives of my family and close friends were leaves clustered near me on a small branch. All of our distinguishing characteristics, what made us the individuals we were, appeared from this perspective to be quite minor, almost arbitrary variations of this fundamental energy.

I was taken around the tree and shown how easy it was to move from one person's experience to another and indeed it was ridiculously easy. Different lives around the globe were simply different experiences the tree was having. Choice governed all experience. Different beings who were all part of Being Itself had simply chosen these manifold experiences.

At this point I WAS THE TREE. Not that I was having the full range of its experience, but I knew myself to be this single, encompassing Consciousness. I knew that Its identity was my true identity. Though I had taken monism to heart years before, I was now actually experiencing the seamless flow of consciousness into crystallizations of embodiment. I was actually experiencing how consciousness manifests itself in separate forms while remaining unified. "So that's how it works," I said to myself. I knew then that there was fundamentally only One Consciousness in the universe. From this perspective my individual identity and everyone else's appeared temporary and almost trivial. To experience my true Identity filled me with a profound sense of numinous encounter. "So this is what I am." The freedom was sheer bliss.

As I left the experience of the Cosmic Tree, the sensation of intense energy subsided and I felt myself to be once again in conscious communication with this vast, surrounding Consciousness. My experiential field was extremely clear.

For the next several hours, this Consciousness took me on an extraordinary tour of the universe. It was as though It wanted to show me Its work. It appeared to be the Creator of our physical universe. It would "take me somewhere" or open me to some experience and I would come to understand some aspect of the working of the universe.

*Over and over again I was overwhelmed at the magnitude, the sub-
tlety, and the intelligence of what I was witnessing. "That's incredible." "I'm beginning to understand." The beauty of the design was
such that I was repeatedly left breathless by what I was seeing.
Sometimes I was so staggered that I would stop and It had to come
back for me. "Keep up. Keep up," It said, taking delight in my awe.
Sometimes I was not sure what I was seeing and It would do something and it was as if everything became larger and I would suddenly
understand. Then It would take me on to something else.*

*This tour was the most extraordinary journey of my life. The vis-
tas of intelligent design repeatedly swept me into cognitive ecstasy.
The irony, however, is that except for the small pieces I shall describe
below, I am unable to recreate the details of what I was seeing. I simply can't yet fit the understandings I had into my ordinary, smaller
mind. This does not lead me to question or doubt my experience. Even
though I have lost large sections of the experience, I retain an unshakable epistemological certainty that this knowing was of a higher order
than any knowing I am capable of in my ordinary consciousness.*

*At one point I was taken through a complex labyrinth of churning
forces until I emerged above the turbulence into a wonderfully spacious and calm experiential field. I was told that we had come
through the emotions of human experience. They had a restless,
gnawing quality to them and comprised such a mass of tangled energy that I was not surprised that they could blot out this subtler experience of peace and tranquility.*

*My elevation into the field I was now in had the subjective quality
of remembering, as did all my experiences on the tour. I was reawakening to levels of reality that I had previously known but forgotten.
Over and over again I was reawakening to a level of experience left behind long ago. Remembering, remembering. It was not about dying at
all but waking up and remembering. I was then lifted into another
"higher" or "larger" experiential field and then another. With each transition I entered a new level of quiet and bliss-filled peace. It was as
though an amnesia lasting billions of years was being lifted from me
layer by layer. The more I remembered, the larger I became. Wave after
wave of awakening was pushing back the edges of my being. To remember more was to become more.*

*Finally I was lifted into a particularly spacious and peaceful di-
mension. As I remembered this dimension I was overcome by an overwhelming sense of homecoming and felt fully the tragedy of having
forgotten this dimension for so long. I cannot describe how poignant
this was. Being fully restored to this dimension would be worth any*

cost. I asked what had happened and It explained that we had left time. Then It said, "We never intended so many to get caught in time." It felt like time was simply one of the many creative experiments of the multidimensional universe I was being shown.

Though these experiences were extraordinary in their own right, the most poignant aspect of today's session was not the discovered dimensions of the universe themselves but what my seeing and understanding them meant to the Consciousness I was with. It seemed to be so pleased to have someone to show Its work to. I felt that It had been waiting for billions of years for embodied consciousness to evolve to the point where we could at long last begin to see, understand, and appreciate what had been accomplished. I felt the loneliness of this Intelligence having created such a masterpiece and having no one to appreciate Its work, and I wept. I wept for its isolation and in awe of the profound love which had accepted this isolation as part of a larger plan. Behind creation lies a LOVE of extraordinary proportions, and all of existence is an expression of this love. The intelligence of the universe's design is equally matched by the depth of love that inspired it.

Somewhere in here I realized that I was not going to be able to take back with me the knowledge I had gathered on this journey. The Intelligence I was with also knew this, making our few hours of contact all the more precious to It. There was nothing I was going to be able to do with this knowledge except experience it now. My greatest service was simply to appreciate what I was seeing. It seemed extremely important to mirror existence back to its Creator in loving appreciation. To see, to understand, and to appreciate.

Such an experience draws to a head many months, even years of work. At the same time, it infuses extraordinary energy into one's system. This energy lifts one's entire psychophysical system into a new register which eventually triggers another round of purification. This *cycle of purification* is an important facet of psychedelic work, which, as best as I understand it, can be summarized as follows. When augmented awareness is focused within, it opens one to a "higher," more intense energy field. Connecting with this field activates powerful resonances between it and one's system that raise one's energy. This heightened energetic state triggers a detoxification process. When this detoxification, or off-loading of conditioning, has continued for a sufficient time, a breakthrough into a still higher energy and clearer experiential field eventually occurs, and the cycle repeats itself. Until all spacetime conditioning is exhausted, therefore, each breakthrough will be followed by a phase of even more acute suffering, because one is engaging progressively deeper structures of unconscious conditioning. The infusion of energy into one's system from positive transpersonal experiences draws to the surface more and more elemental patterns of conditioning contrary to Oneness, reminding me of Saint John of the Cross's observation that "Two contraries cannot coexist within one subject." This cyclic pattern of ecstasy and pain is well recognized in the mystical traditions of the world (see appendix A).

It is worth noting that the dynamic operating here is essentially the same as occurs in meditation. Ken Wilber, for example, writes:

> Meditation, in my opinion, is not a means of digging back into the lower and repressed structures of the submergent-unconscious, it is a way of facilitating the emergence, growth, and development of the higher structures of consciousness. . . . However, when a person begins intensive meditation, sub-mergent-unconscious material (e.g., the shadow) frequently begins to re-emerge, or occasionally even erupt into consciousness. It is this "derepression of the shadow" that has contributed to the notion that meditation is an uncovering technique and a regression in service of the ego. I believe this derepression does in fact frequently occur, but for a very different reason (possessing very different dynamics). Meditation, because it aims at developing or moving consciousness into higher levels or dimensions of structural organization, must break or disrupt the exclusive identification with the *present* level of development. . . . This happens very often in the initial stages of meditation, but it definitely seems to be a secondary by-product of the practice, not its goal . . .[11]

What is unusual in the context of psychedelic therapy is simply the scope of the detoxification being effected.

Session 21

I was surprised and caught off guard by how painful this session was. It was not personal and had little to do with my biological birth. If only it were a matter of undergoing a personal death, how easy that would be in comparison. The pain was clearly related to the birthing of the species first, and my birthing second. My experiential boundaries stretched to include the entire human race and all of human history, and this "I" was caught up in a horror that I am incapable of describing with any accuracy. It was a raging insanity, a surging kaleidoscopic field of chaos, pain, and destruction. It was as if the entire human race had gathered from all the corners of the globe and gone absolutely stark raving mad.

People were attacking each other with a rabid savagery augmented by science fiction technology. There were many currents crossing and crisscrossing in front of me, each composed of thousands of people, some currents killing in multiple ways, some being killed, some fleeing in panic, others being rounded up, others witnessing and screaming in terror, others witnessing and having their hearts broken by a species gone mad—and "I" was all their experiences. The magnitude of the deaths and the insanity is impossible to describe. The problem is finding a frame of reference. The only categories I have available to me are simplistic approximations that can give only a vague sense of it. It was a convulsing of the entire human species, a convulsing of the universe itself.

What happened next emerged in the context of this larger field of agony. It was in one sense foreground against the backdrop of the horror, but in another sense it was not central at all. It is difficult to describe how one's experience can be simultaneously so inclusive and so selectively focused. Like a small spotlight focusing our attention at one spot on a lighted stage upon which hundreds of actors are dancing and singing, we see it all and we see one part highlighted. My experience comprised the entire stage, and this more personal element was simply a focus of partial attention that was intimately coordinated with the larger background flow.

At the center came forward the theme of sex. At first sex emerged in its pleasant form as mutual delight and erotic satisfaction, but soon it changed into in its violent form, as attack, assault, injury, and hurt. The forces of sexual assault were building in the crisscrossing fields of humanity as well. I was facing these brutal forces, and behind my back was a child. I was trying to protect this child from them, to hold them back and prevent these destructive forces from reaching it. The horror intensified as the child became my three year old daughter. It was she and all the children of the world simultaneously.

I kept trying to protect her, to hold back the attack that was pushing through me, and yet I knew that eventually I would fail. The longer I held the forces in check, the more powerful they became. The "I" here was not just a personal "I" but thousands of people. The horror was beyond anything I can describe. Glancing over my shoulder I could feel the field of frightened innocence, but now there was an-

other element added to it—a strain of mystical embrace. Super-imposed upon the child was the Primal Female, the Mother Goddess herself. She beckoned to me to embrace her, and I knew instinctively that there could be no greater sweetness than that found in her arms. In holding myself back from violent sexual assault, I was also hold-ing myself back from the mystical embrace of the Goddess, yet I could not bring myself to rape and kill my child no matter how sweet the promise of redemption.

The frenzy continued to build until eventually I began to turn. Still holding back the terrible onslaught of killing, I was now facing my victim and being torn apart by the forces of passion on one side and protection on the other. My victim was at once my helpless daughter and the Primal Woman inviting me to a sexual embrace of cosmic proportions. No matter how hard I fought what was happen-ing, I was being drawn to unleash the fury. In horror and blind thirst I was turning to attack, to rape, to kill, and yet I continued to fight what was happening with every ounce of my strength. The struggle drove me to deeper and deeper levels of intensity until suddenly some-thing broke open, and I came to the shattering realization that I was turning to kill and rape MYSELF.

This breakthrough was very multi-dimensional and confusing. The intensity of the struggle drove me through a breaking point where I sud-denly confronted the reality that I was both the raping killer and victim. In looking into my victim's eyes, I discovered that I was looking into my own face. I sobbed and sobbed. "I'm doing it to myself." This was not a karmic inversion, a flip into a former life where victim and victimizer change places. Rather, it was a quantum jump to an experiential level that dissolved all dualities into a single, encompassing flow. My per-sonal sense of "I" exploded into an underlying oneness that subsumed all persons. It was collective in the sense of including all human experi-ence, but utterly simple and undivided. I was one, aggressor and victim. I was both killer and killed. I was doing it to myself. Through all of his-tory, I have been doing it to myself.

As this discovery was taking place at the center, it was also tak-ing place in the crisscrossing fields that encompassed all humanity and all creation. All the unspeakable horrors that I had been expe-riencing were mine in this larger sense. All the pain experienced in the violent creation of galaxies was caused by me and felt by me. The pain of human history was my pain. There were no victims. Nothing was outside of me doing this to me. I was responsible for everything that I was experiencing, for everything that had ever happened. I was looking into the face of my creation. I did this. I am doing this.

I chose for all this to happen. I chose to create all these horrible, horrible worlds. Why?

Then in the distance I began to see something that looked like a galaxy. It was our solar system, our galaxy, the entire universe. It was the physical cosmos and the underlying constitutive forces that built the universe and sustain it. It was something both physical and archetypal. It was not a symbolic representation of the universe but the real thing. It was continuous with the universe I had experienced on the cosmic tour, but many times larger and more complex. It was beautiful beyond words and absolutely captivating. I was becoming larger as I expanded into what I was seeing. I learned by becoming what I was knowing. I discovered the universe not by knowing it from the outside but by tuning to that level in my being where I was that thing. All I can do at this point is to sketch the highlights of the experiences that followed, which will not do justice either to their cognitive structure or to their experiential intensity.

What stood out for me in the early stages was the interconnectedness of everything to form a seamless whole. The entire universe was an undivided, totally unified, organic phenomenon. I saw various breakthroughs—quantum theory, Bell's Theorem, morphogenetic fields, holographic theory, systems theory, the grand unified theory, and so on—as but the early phases of the scientific discovery of this wholeness. I knew that these discoveries would continue to mount until it would become impossible for us not to recognize the universe for what it was—a unified organism of extraordinary design reflecting a massive Creative Intelligence. The intelligence and love that was responsible for what I was seeing kept overwhelming me and filling me with reverential awe.

The unified field underlying physical existence completely dissolved all boundaries. As I moved deeper into it, all borders fell away; all appearances of division were ultimately illusory. No boundaries between incarnations, between human beings, between species, even between matter and spirit. The world of individuated existence was not collapsing into an amorphous mass, as it might sound, but rather was revealing itself to be an exquisitely diversified manifestation of a single entity.

As my experience of this seamless universe progressed, I came to discover that I was not exploring a universe "out there," as I had in session 19, but a universe that "I" in some essential way already was. Somehow these experiences of cosmic order led me step by step into a deeper embrace of my own reality. I was exploring the universe as a dimension of my own existence, slowly remembering aspects of my be-

ing that I had lost contact with. This exploration seemed to answer a cosmic need not only to know but to be known.

Initially I was on a cosmic tour not unlike session 19 when I realized again that this larger field of consciousness that I was with (or in) had been waiting a long time to be seen and known. Again I began to cry as I felt its heartfelt longing to be known. Then I asked something I had not asked before. I asked, "Who am I talking to?" With that question my experiential field began to change, and I shifted to a new level. It was as though I made a quantum jump to a deeper operational level where I discovered that I was, in fact, with MYSELF. The creative impulse that had at the previous level been other than me was at this level Myself.

This mysterious progression repeated itself many times and in many variations. It continued for hours. I would be at one level far beyond physical diversity, and as I sought to know this reality more deeply I would experience a kind of falling away, a kind of death, and would slip into a new level where I would discover that this duality too was but another facet of Myself. Over and over again in detailed progressions I cannot now reconstruct, I was led to the same fundamental encounter. This experience of gently dying was quite poignant and was often followed by a period of mild disorientation as I got my bearings on the new level. No matter how many times I died or how many different forms I was when I died, I kept being caught by this massive SOMETHING, this IT. I could not leave IT, could not escape IT, could not not be IT. No matter how many adventures I had been on, I had never stepped outside IT, never stopped being IT. There simply was no outside to MY being. There was no other in existence.

As I moved into these levels of increasing ontological simplicity, I entered a profound stillness unlike anything I have ever known in my life and yet which seemed to reawaken a distant, vague memory. "Where have I known this before?" By following this stillness I was guided back to what seemed like a time before creation, back to the ontological fount of creation. In this stillness I was "with Myself" in ways that I had once been long ago, but not for billions of years. It was a time of reunion, a time of being whole after a terribly long separation.

In this condition I continued to ask my questions, "What is happening here?" "How does this work?" "What has it been like for You?" And with each question my experiential field changed, opening me to one cosmic process after another. I cannot describe these experiences adequately because the categories of thought derived from spacetime experience do not lend themselves to remembering clearly or translating into words experiences of realities that lie outside spacetime.

My ordinary waking consciousness, though it is being gradually changed by these experiences, is still too cognitively restricted to be able to hold onto them in sufficient detail. What I experienced, however, repeatedly swept me into ecstasy. "Amazing!" "So that's how that works!" "Oh, Goodness!" "How much do you want to see?," I was asked. "More!" I answered, and always more would unfold. It kept unfolding for hours.

It may seem that we have drifted far from our project of understanding the suffering that emerges in perinatal experience, but this is not so. To reframe our understanding of the perinatal domain, we have to understand more than the scope of the suffering involved. We must, in addition, begin to situate this suffering in the context of the larger trajectory of our evolutionary history. We must try to grasp, however incompletely, the cosmic process that brought our species into existence and that is continuing to reshape us even now. Unless we understand something about where we came from and where we are being taken as a species, we will never comprehend the deeper logic driving these experiences.

Before leaving this session behind, it should be pointed out that its perinatal themes were clearly BPM III in contrast to the hellish BPM II themes of earlier sessions. Sex, violence, and killing are prototypical BPM III themes, and the basic existential posture has shifted from that of victim to victimizer. In BPM II one experiences oneself as the passive recipient of violence, while in BPM III one becomes the perpetrator of this violence, or both, eventually transcending the entire polarity altogether. Pain has escalated into frenzied passion, a blind, animal hunger that destroys everything it touches. The conflict between this frenzied, sexual bloodlust and the attempt to protect my daughter seems to have been a device that allowed this energy to build to enormous proportions before shattering the fundamental dualism that created the conditions of conflict and hunger in the first place (BPM IV). The mystical embrace of the Primal Woman was an archetypal fragment, a symptom of the emerging "divine marriage," the *hieros gamos* that occurs when differentiated essence (the masculine principle) reunites with the primal essence (the feminine principle).

Another transition has been made between sessions 19 and 21. In the ecstatic portion of the earlier session, the universe was explored as a reality outside oneself. In this session, however, it is explored as the inner depths of one's own being. This transition is symptomatic of the gradual breakdown of dualistic consciousness being effected by repeated immersion in these states. What was previously viewed as lying outside one's boundaries is subsequently recognized as being but another dimension of one's deeper being.

While one may hear in the background of this account the echoes of an individual person struggling to be reborn, these are secondary to the larger drama that is being enacted. Remember that everything that took place at the center of the stage was also taking place in the surrounding, crisscrossing currents of humanity. The form in which these BPM III energies were expressing themselves was *first* the collective experience of humanity and only *secondly* an individual person. If we fail to keep this collective dimension clearly in sight, we will miss the true scale of the transition taking place and the import of this partial immersion in approximate nonduality.

Collective Perinatal Suffering and Morphic Fields

I do not think the kinds of experiences recorded here are adequately explained by Grof's paradigm in its current form. What is experienced as collective suffering of this scope and duration cannot be explained by any model of consciousness that focuses exclusively on the transformation of the individual. In order to make sense of these experiences, we need to look beyond the individual to that which the individual is part of.

As the above sessions illustrate, at the perinatal level of consciousness one often experiences personal anguish deeply intertwined with collective anguish. Sometimes this collective anguish focuses on various groups within human history while at other times it seems to embrace the human species as a whole. In some instances it seems to reach beyond the human species and to tap directly into the archetypal forces of creation itself. Whatever form it takes, however, it is always experienced as an expansion of one's present identity. Collective perinatal pain may initially be experienced as someone else's pain, but eventually this defense breaks down. When the last boundary has fallen, it is not a personal "I" experiencing the anguish of thousands of dying soldiers but something larger than personal consciousness. And yet paradoxically this something larger is still experienced as being "me."

It is important to grasp the significance not only of the extension of consciousness that has taken place, but of the coherence of this extension with one's ordinary sense of identity. In psychedelic states one's awareness can open to previously unbelievable limits, but this enlargement always begins with and is coherent with one's self-awareness as an individual human being. This experience of the coherent expansion of one's present identity to a larger identity is the phenomenological starting point of our attempt to understand the appearance of collective suffering in an individual's therapeutic process.

In psychotherapy, therapy heals the patient present. Following this simple logic, we must speculate that *if the patient in these intense states of awareness has expanded beyond the individual person, then the healing being realized through these exercises also reaches beyond the individual person.* If the awareness experiencing these ordeals is genuinely beyond-the-personal, as many have testified, then the healing that is taking place is also focused beyond the personal level. I think the fact that we are accustomed to thinking of psychotherapy primarily in terms of the individual, combined with the fact that these therapies do indeed benefit the individual, have conspired to blind us to the possibility that these experiences might also have a therapeutic impact on systems that transcend the individual. Furthermore, it is not immediately obvious who or what this enlarged "patient" might be. If the therapeutic impact of these experiences reaches beyond the individual, to what does it reach?

The concept of a centralized, integrating intelligence, an *anima mundi* or "World Soul," that underlies our individual life is ancient, but the attempt to provide empirical evidence for its existence is a relatively recent undertaking. Beginning with C. G. Jung's early attempt to demonstrate the existence of a collective unconscious, the movement to give empirical precision to this concept has rapidly gained momentum as the Newtonian-Cartesian scales have fallen from our eyes. Quantum theory either invites or at the very least tolerates such an "implicate" intelligence, depending on whose interpretation of the calculus one reads.[12] J. E. Lovelock's Gaia hypothesis directs us to a planetary intelligence in order to make sense of otherwise enigmatic shifts that have taken place in the Earth's ecosystem over billions of years.[13] In the anthropic cosmological principle, John Barrow and Frank Tipler have marshaled large amounts of scientific data to reintroduce the notion of design and teleological intent into scientific discourse, inviting us to look afresh at the extraordinary series of unlikely coincidences that have led to our existence.[14] One of the important attempts to give empirical precision to this concept of an integrating intelligence has been Rupert Sheldrake's theory of formative causation and morphic fields. Sheldrake uses the term "morphic field" as a general category that includes several different types of fields including morphogenetic fields, behavioral fields, social and cultural fields, and mental fields. Here I am primarily concerned with the field that Sheldrake calls the "group mind."[15]

Sheldrake has argued in a series of books—*A New Science of Life* (1981), *The Presence of the Past* (1988), and *The Rebirth of Nature* (1991)—that the individual members of every species are networked in a group-mind that constitutes the dynamic blueprint of that species. Sheldrake's innovation has been to suggest that this field not only contains the blueprint of the species' physical form and behavioral tendencies, but that it collects and incorporates into itself the new experiences of its individual members, constantly synthesizing at a central level the diverse experiences of its physically discrete parts. Thus, morphic fields can be thought of as mediating between the parts and the whole of a species, and also between the past and the future of a species. They are seen as extending the past into the present while simultaneously collecting and digesting the experiences of the present in order to facilitate the collective acquisition of useful innovations for the future. Sheldrake insists that his theory is empirically testable because we can in principle test the rate at which a new skill is acquired by a species. The early reports of attempts to carry out such tests are encouraging.[16]

Sheldrake suggests that between the individual and the morphic field of the species exist numerous intermediate fields that correspond to various subgroupings that the individual is part of—family, community, nation, race, and culture, to name a few. The species-field is in turn nested in a series of larger fields that encompass the planet, the solar system, the galaxy, and so on. As in general systems theory, Sheldrake's vision is of fields nested within fields nested within fields, with lines of communication running from the largest to the smallest and back again.

Sheldrake's theory suggests that the mental processes we see operating within an individual human being might be paralleled by similar processes operating in the species-mind, if we make allowances for the enormous differences involved. Thus, just as we remember in a coherent fashion the experiences of our individual body-mind, the species-mind would remember its vast experiences. Just as the integration and management of our individual experiences reflects intelligence and choice, the species-mind might possess a higher order of the same capacities. Similarly, the larger system of which the human species is a part might also possess these capacities, and so on. We soon lose track of the progression, but we do not need to map the entire terrain in order to unravel the logic of collective perinatal experiences, which is our task here.

It is striking how well Sheldrake's hypothesis of morphic fields meshes with Grof's experiential data. If we combine their perspectives, new possibilities emerge for understanding the collective suffering that surfaces in deep inner work. Very simply put, it would appear that the therapeutic target of such work is something larger than the individual yet something that the individual is part of. Following Sheldrake, I suggest that this "something larger" is the species-mind.

Before going further, let me insert an important qualification. It is the testimony of both the perennial tradition and practitioners of psychedelic therapy that the species-mind is but one layer of a vast Cosmic Intelligence that in this volume I am calling Sacred Mind. I focus on the species-mind here because it is the layer most immediately relevant to our problem, which is trying to explain the vast quantity of human suffering that sometimes surfaces in perinatal experience. Eventually, however, we will have to look beyond this layer to fully comprehend the dynamic involved. As Sheldrake himself has said, his model can explain the persistence of the habits of history into the present but it cannot explain creativity. To explain the creativity involved in these therapeutic exercises (and in life itself), we need to reach deeper into the fabric of being than the concept of morphic fields alone takes us. Let me therefore acknowledge that when I use the term "species-mind," I am using it in a sense that goes beyond Sheldrake's intention. I am suggesting that these dynamic fields of collective memory are embedded in other forms of intelligent agency that include knowing, planning, and innovating. Nonordinary experiences such as those recorded here allow us to extend Sheldrake's argument by recognizing that these fields of mind that show the imprint of history also reveal orders of creativity and initiative on a scale that is difficult to imagine but that can be directly experienced under the right conditions.[17]

If we assume for the moment that the dynamics of this species-mind parallel the dynamics of the personal psyche to some degree, we can speculate that just as problematic experiences can collect and block the healthy functioning of the individual, similar blockages might also occur at the collective level. This suggests that the unresolved anguish of human history might still be active in the memory of the species-mind, burdening its life just as our individual unresolved anguish burdens ours. Continuing the parallel, if conscious engagement of previously unresolved pain brings therapeutic release at the personal level, the same might also occur at the species-level. Normally we would expect such an engagement and release to take the form of mass social movements or cultural shifts in which large numbers of persons in some way or another confront and absorb some painful legacy from their collective past. Modern examples might be the movements to abolish slavery, to enfranchise women, and to end child molestation. Within the context of intense experiential psychotherapy, however, a new possibility seems to be emerging.

When we follow the roots of our pain in psychedelic states, we discover that our individual suffering is embedded in an historical web of suffering. The life of the individual appears to crystallize patterns that extend beyond the individual, both socially and historically. As our inner life unfolds in this intense arena, we spontaneously find ourselves being opened beyond our individual existence to encompass various aspects of a larger surround, and this surround is, at one important level, the historical experience of our species. Furthermore, the experience is not one of becoming something other than what we are, but rather of reaching into deeper levels of what we already are. We do not take on the species-mind, but rather we open to that part of our being where we already are the species-mind. And as this happens, we suffer, at least initially.

Some suffer more than others, but all suffer. The extreme nature of this suffering can be partially explained in terms of the principle of summation, reflecting the insight that the psyche stores experience in experiential aggregates (COEX systems). If we include in these complex amalgams trauma from previous incarnations, we significantly expand the theoretical explanation of the levels of anguish that can be involved. However, the principle of summation by itself is insufficient to explain the full scope of this anguish for two reasons. First, the sheer *quantity* of pain can exceed anything that could reasonably be explained in terms of even a long succession of incarnations. Even more telling, however, is the peculiar *quality* of the suffering. This pain is inherently collective. Its organizational patterns are the historical patterns of a species, not an individual. Its sweep is the sweep of whole groups of people arching against the backdrop of millennia. As Grof has demonstrated, there are somatic and emotional parallels between this pain and the personal pain one may be simultaneously experiencing. Going beyond Grof, however, we should speculate that there is (at least) *a two-tier structure of healing operating*—one at the level of the individual and a second at the level of the species.

By the same logic, we must conjecture that there are at least *two tiers of the death-rebirth process*. The transition that marks the culmination of a perinatal ordeal that has been strongly focused on the collective level is too large to be described merely as ego-death. When an individual's perinatal process has slanted strongly in this direction, when the pain being integrated has primarily been not the pain of an individual but of human history itself, the rebirth experience that follows similarly tends to be profoundly collective as well. The two tiers of healing lead to two tiers of death and rebirth, one operating at the individual level, the second at the collective level. If we call the first ego-death, we might call the second *species ego-death*.

These two tiers are often so deeply intertwined in perinatal experience that it is difficult to distinguish them. In *Realms of the Human Unconscious*, however, Grof presents an experience of ego-death in which the individual and collective aspects of the process are unusually well differentiated. This account allows us to mark both the parallels and the differences between the two tiers. The subject was a clergyman who had lost his faith in any transcendent reality.

> Suddenly my wild symphony took over. It was as if I were first at the top of a roller coaster gradually being drawn over the precipice, losing control, and being quite unable to arrest the downward plunge that I could see was ahead of me. One analogy I thought of was that this was like swallowing a keg of dynamite with the fuse already lit. The fuse was inaccessible, the dynamite was going to explode, and there was nothing I could do about it. The last thing I can remember hearing before my roller coaster began going down was music that sounded as though it came from a million earphones. My head was enormous at this time, and I had a thousand ears, each one with a different headset on, each earphone bringing in different music. This was the greatest confusion I have ever felt in my life. I was aware of being on the couch; I was dying right there and there was nothing I could do about it. Every time I would try to stop it, I became panicky and terror-ridden. The only thing was to go toward it. The words "trust and obey," "trust and obey" came through to me and in what seemed like a flash, I was no longer lying on the couch and did not have my present identity. Several scenes began to take place; it seemed as though they happened all at once, but let me string them out to try to make some sense of them.
>
> The first scene was plunging down into a swamp filled with hideous creatures. These creatures were moving to-

ward me, but they were unable to reach me. All of a sudden
the swamp was transformed into a canal in Venice just under the Bridge of Sighs. My family, my wife, and my children
were standing on the bridge looking down at me in this
swamp. There was no expression on their faces; they were
simply standing there looking at me.

The best way of describing this roller coaster and this
entrance into the loss of control would be to compare it to
walking on a slippery, very slippery surface. There would be
surfaces all over the place and finally all of them would become slippery and there would be nothing left to hold on to.
One was slipping, slipping and going further and further
down into oblivion. The scene that finally completed my
death was a very horrible scene in a square of a medieval
town. The square was surrounded by Gothic cathedral facades and from the statue niches in these facades and from
the gargoyle downspouts in the eaves, animals, persons,
animal-human combinations, devils, spirits—all the figures
that one observes in the paintings of Hieronymus Bosch—
came down from the cathedrals into the square and moved
in on me. While the animals, the humans, the demons
pressed in upon me in the square before these Gothic cathedrals, I began to experience intense agony and pain, panic,
terror, and horror. There was a line of pressure between the
temples of my head, and I was dying. I was absolutely certain of this—I was dying, and I died. My death was completed when the pressures overwhelmed me, and I was
expelled into another world.

At this point in the narrative, a reader familiar with Grof's
work might justifiably expect the next paragraph to describe a
scene of spiritual rebirth, for this man has undergone a profound
ego-death experience. Aspects of fetal experience echo through his
account: the enlarged head, confusion and loss of control, the downward plunge, a slippery, slimy environment, a Venetian "canal"
(known for its polluted waters), and pressure across the temples.
There is nothing left to break down at the personal level; his death
appears complete. Nevertheless, he does not make the transition to
rebirth yet. He continues:

It turned out that this outer world was to be a continuation
of deaths at a very different level, however. Now the panic,

the terror were all gone; all that was left was the anguish and the pain as I participated in the death of all men. I began to experience the passion of our Lord Jesus Christ. I was Christ, but I was also everyone as Christ and all men died as we made our way in the dirgelike procession toward Golgotha. At this time in my experience there was no longer any confusion; the visions were perfectly clear. The pain was intense, and the sorrow was just, just agonizing. It was at this point that a blood tear from the face of God began to flow. I did not see the face of God, but his tear began to flow, and it began to flow out over the world as God himself participated in the death of all men and in the suffering of all men. The sorrow of this moment is still so intense that it is difficult for me to speak of it. We moved toward Golgotha, and there in agony greater than any I have ever experienced, I was crucified with Christ and all men on the cross. I was Christ, and I was crucified, and I died.

This second death is markedly different from the first. The confusion and panic have vanished, his experiential field is clear, and the agony has intensified as he moves to a collective level where he becomes the entire human race. Religious imagery consummates this sense of expanded identity as he experiences a death that touches all humanity and seems to involve even God, the field of all fields. I think we should take this man at his word and honor the distinctions he has so carefully drawn. This second death is not a mere recasting of ego-death against a larger background, but a new movement in the death-rebirth symphony. Something larger is dying at this level, something that seems to involve and affect the entire species. The rebirth that follows continues in this collective vein.

When all men died on the cross, there began the most heavenly music I have ever heard in my entire life: it was incredibly beautiful. It was the voice of angels singing, and we began slowly to rise. This was again almost like birth; the death on the cross happened, and there was a swishing sound as the wind rushed from the cross into another world. The gradual rising of all men began to take place. These were great processions in enormous cathedrals—candles and light and gold and incense, all moving up. I had no sense of my personal existence at this time. I was in all the processions, and all the processions were in me; I was every man and every man began to rise. The awe and splendor of this rising was almost beyond description. We were rising toward light, higher and higher, through majestic white marble pillars. We left behind the blues, the greens, the reds, and the purples, the gold of the cathedrals, and the royal garbs of some of the people. We rose into whiteness; the columns we were rising between were white and pure. The music was soaring, everyone was singing, and then there occurred a vision.

This vision has an entirely different feeling about it from anything else I experienced in the whole LSD session. It still feels like a vision—as if a vision were actually given to me— it is so real. The resurrection garment of our Lord touched me. Yet you have to understand: it did not touch me; it touched all men and yet in touching all men it touched me. When it touched, several things happened at once, as they did many times during this experience. We all became very small—as small as a cell, as small as an atom. We all became very humble and bowed down. I was filled with peace and feelings of joy and love; I loved God completely. While this was happening, the touch of the garment was like a high voltage wire. Everything exploded, and it exploded us into the highest place there is—the place of absolute light. It was silent; there was no music; it was pure light. It was like being at the very center of the energy source. It was like being in God—not just in God's presence, but in God and participating in God.[18]

I believe that we deeply underestimate the true impact of such a powerful experience if we call it ego-death and monitor only how it changed this individual human being. Despite the problems inherent in verifying such a claim, we need to recognize that both the cleansing and ecstatic vision this man so eloquently describes were experienced not in a personal state of consciousness but in a transpersonal state that reached deep into the species-mind. *What died that day was not just this man's individual ego, but part of humanity's ego.* Correspondingly, the transformative vision he describes poured its blessings not simply into his private mind but directly into the depths of the collective unconscious, making it slightly more aware of its true relation to the divine consciousness. The resurrection garment touched all of us that day. Though we may be hard pressed to measure its distributed effect, I am deeply convinced that this man's death and rebirth carried a little piece of all of us into God-awareness and in so doing drew us all one step closer to awakening.

Having said this, I want to be careful not to overstate the therapeutic impact that these exercises may have on the species-mind. Even taking into account the fact that this cleansing is being mediated by a transpersonal state of consciousness, we must realistically ask how large a therapeutic effect can hours of such purgation have on the collective unconscious of the entire human race? How can we even begin to calculate such an thing? If I add up the total number of hours I have spent in these states and multiply them by the number of persons I subjectively sense to be involved, the total is but a pittance compared to the historical suffering humanity has endured. And yet, I would not want to underestimate its therapeutic impact either and consider the principle more important than any calculation of the ratios.

While I hope that readers will feel the weight of the evidence presented for this conclusion and see the logic of the argument, some may hesitate before drawing such a radical inference. I understand the enormity of the step I am proposing. It took me years to accept this conclusion myself, even after undergoing the experiences that compelled it. Because the interpretation that I'm proposing cannot be empirically verified, or at least I cannot see how it soon could be, some may choose to consider it simply a "speculative" thesis and let it go at that. While I understand this assessment, I think it would be a mistake. What may be a speculative opinion for one person may be a confirmed hypothesis for another, and what may not be verifiable to the eye of the flesh may be verifiable to the eye of the spirit. The scope of this hypothesis may not permit empirical verification at present, but it can be experientially verified by persons willing to undergo the regimen that generated the hypothesis in the first place. Persons can judge for themselves what they see through the telescope of psychedelic states.

Expanding the Concept of the Perinatal

In order to provide a comprehensive rationale for collective perinatal experiences such as those reported here, I think we need to make two basic moves. First, we need to surrender our habit of viewing what happens in psychedelic therapy solely in terms of the individual and expand our frame of reference to include the species-mind (and by extension those living systems which cradle and sustain the species-mind). Second, we need to extend Grof's concept of COEX system to the species-mind itself. As the first proposal has already been presented, let me briefly explain the second. After this has been done, I will outline a way of seeing the perinatal domain that integrates its personal and transpersonal dynamics in a balanced synthesis.

As defined earlier, a COEX system is a constellation of memories and fantasies from many periods of an individual's life that share a common emotional theme. As a general principle, it reflects the fact that the psyche tends to store experience in emotionally indexed clusters drawn from multiple layers of experience. In collective perinatal experiences, a person is absorbed into powerful collective currents of distress involving thousands of lives drawn from multiple periods of history and a variety of cultural settings. This fact suggests that the organizational tendency Grof has identified repeats itself at the level of the collective unconscious. Not only do individual minds have COEX systems, but the species-mind appears to have them as well. I propose that we call these massive COEX systems the *Meta-Matrices* of the species-mind. Furthermore, I suggest that just as there are many COEX systems in the individual psyche, we should assume that there are many Meta-Matrices in the collective psyche, at least four of which correspond thematically to the four Basic Perinatal Matrices Grof has identified.[19]

Once this concept is in place, we can go one step further and suggest that an individual's COEX systems can be thought of as clusters within the corresponding Meta-Matrices of the species mind. This gives us an elegant way of summarizing the interpretation of collective perinatal suffering that has been emerging in this chapter. What is happening in these ordeals, I believe, is that in the process of engaging his or her individual COEX systems, the psychedelic subject has been drawn into the corresponding Meta-Matrices of the species mind. From this perspective we can view Grof's concept of the Basic Perinatal Matrices as representing something of a bridge between the COEX systems of the personal psyche and the Meta-Matrices of the collective psyche. Seeing the perinatal matrices in this light helps us comprehend the complex multidimensionality of these systems, combining as they do elements from so many organizational levels of the psyche. It also underscores the inappropriateness of tilting this bridge toward the personal shore by suggesting that fetal experience constitutes the "core" of these systems.

Once we let go of our focus on the individual subject and begin to think in terms of the interpenetrating fields of consciousness that we discover ourselves to be in transpersonal states, our description of the perinatal dimension necessarily shifts. Instead of seeing it primarily in terms of the death-rebirth of the individual, we begin to see a much more complex ontology unfolding. The liberation of the individual is simultaneously part of the liberation of humanity, which in turn is part of the larger trajectory of involution/evolution. In order to systematically integrate these collective dynamics into Grof's account, we must clarify and extend his account of the perinatal.

While Grof's model distinguishes three levels of consciousness, it seems to be the case that the perinatal level does not have the same status as the personal and transpersonal levels for the simple reason that it does not endure. Perinatal symptoms eventually consume themselves in experientially oriented psychotherapy and disappear. Over the course of extended work, subjects eventually cease to experience perinatal complications as the transition to transpersonal states of consciousness becomes less problematic. While it is operationally active, however, the perinatal domain appears as an intersection of the personal and transpersonal levels of awareness, possessing characteristics of each.[20]

As a conceptual exercise, therefore, let us experiment with modeling consciousness in terms of only two basic levels, the personal and the transpersonal, with the region of overlap being designated the perinatal. This is consistent with Grof's model and represents only a shift in emphasis. In this model, the term "perinatal" identifies not so much a distinct "level" as a region of interface and interpenetration of two more fundamental modes of awareness. We might think of it as a standing wave that exists between the personal and transpersonal realms. It is a middle zone that functions partially as a bridge and partially as a buffer between these two worlds. Awareness functions differently on either side of this zone, which must mediate and integrate these differences.

The advantage of shifting to this simpler model is primarily a gain in conceptual clarity. It emphasizes the fact that the perinatal stands "midway" between the personal and the transpersonal levels and participates completely in both. That is to say, it is completely balanced in its makeup, fully partaking of both levels and performing discrete but integrated functions in each. The personal is not more fundamental to it than the transpersonal. The perinatal is not a domain that makes primary sense in personal categories and less sense in transpersonal categories. Rather, it is an operational mode of consciousness in which the personal and transpersonal blend, sharing organizational patterns and structures. At the perinatal level the distinction between "self" and "surround" is dissolved and replaced by a holographic dance in which self and surround move in rhythmic harmony, blending at deeper and deeper levels until they come to express a single design.

As Grof makes clear in many places, *the essence of the perinatal process is the death-rebirth dynamic.* The deepest force driving experience at this interface is the need to recover our true identity, to let die everything that is not essential and to awaken to what is essential. The hybrid nature of the perinatal domain, however, allows this death-rebirth process to express itself in a variety of forms. Perinatal experience typically combines both personal and transpersonal components, and on any given day it can manifest in a form that is slanted toward either side of the perinatal interface. Going one step further, a careful comparison of my own experiences with those Grof has published leads me to believe that the overall trajectory of one's journey through the perinatal domain may arch toward one side or the other of this polarity. The archetypal core of the death-rebirth experience is the same in both cases—the death of *samsaric* identity and the birth of transcendental awareness—but the form that this experience takes may vary significantly in scope and focus.

If one's perinatal process slants in the direction of the personal psyche, fetal elements may play a significant role in one's experience. The physical, cognitive, and affective vulnerability of the fetus may combine with the arduous nature of the birth process to make it the prototypical correlate of the death-rebirth dynamic.[21] Thus in the highly energized context of psychedelic therapy, one may experience the systematic destruction of one's personal identity and the recovery of one's spiritual identity intimately interwoven with reliving one's biological birth. Collective experiences may be present, but they would tend to be less prominent and therefore might be viewed as having been drawn in through resonance to that which appears to be primary. The psychospiritual trauma of being stripped of our body-based identity seems to parallel and mimic the ordeal of being physically born. In addition to the sheer trauma possibly involved in both processes, there is a logical symmetry that connects the taking on and the dissolving of one's physical identity. It is in the womb, so to speak, that we exchanged our comprehensive spiritual identity for our more narrowly focused human identity, and therefore it is not surprising that the reacquisition of this more comprehensive awareness should trigger womb memories. Furthermore, spiritual death-rebirth also stimulates memories of physical deaths and life-threatening experiences from across the full spectrum of our incarnational history. The womb and grave have been the revolving door through which we have entered and exited spacetime countless times, and thus they are naturally drawn into the saga of rediscovering that part of our being that extends beyond spacetime.

Even if fetal experience saturates the process of recall, however, I don't think that biological birth is the essential core here, nor is physical death, aging, or threats to one's life. These all give expression to and mark the stages of the archetypal dynamic that is driving these experiences, namely, *the death-rebirth dynamic*. All forms of biological birth and death are ultimately subservient to the spiritual process of shedding our egoic, spacetime identity and awakening to the transcendental dimensions of existence.

Because the collective unconscious is a deeper layer of one's psyche, one may also experience the death-rebirth dynamic in a more collective mode. If one's perinatal process slants in the transpersonal direction, one may undergo the entire death-rebirth sequence in deep and profound identification with the human species. Fetal themes may recede far into the background and the birth canal may become the birth canal of human history (and in extreme instances the birth canal of evolution itself). In this situation, the death-rebirth of the individual becomes part of a larger drama that wells up from deep within the collective unconscious. Through some alchemical shift that we can recognize but not as yet map, the patient expands to become the species itself. In these sessions, it is the species that is convulsing in agony and trying to be born, not just an individual human being. The therapeutic process of making conscious the trauma of the past, of holding that trauma in one's awareness until it dissolves, and of thus freeing the present from some measure of the burden of the past seems aimed at and in some sense even carried out by the species-mind itself.

The same death-rebirth archetype that we see operating at the personal level in the acute reliving of one's biological birth we see operating here in the acute reliving of the hatred and suffering that marks the history of an entire species still stuck at the egoic level of self-awareness. The same spiritual forces that well up from the ground of one's individual existence, driving one to shed all identities save one, here seem to be welling up from the depths of the collective unconscious, driving humanity in a similar manner to shed its restricted vision of itself before it is too late. If there is a rebirth that follows death in this context, it is the rebirth of a species, not just an individual person, even though it is mediated by the initiative of an individual. Here our vision naturally shifts from the story of the evolution of the individual to the story of the evolution of the human species as a whole. Our focus turns from the spiritual awakening of an individual cell to the awakening of the entire body of humanity.

It is important to understand that neither the personal nor the collective form of perinatal experience is the "real" perinatal experience but rather that these are simply two different modes in which the death-rebirth dynamic can express itself. Neither of these modes is primary to the other. Because life is unified at the outset of psychedelic work and not simply at its conclusion, the death-rebirth process can express itself in its more encompassing forms at any stage of perinatal engagement.[22]

The interpenetration of the individual and the species surfaces in deep psychedelic states as a dramatic manifestation of the dynamics of morphic fields. These heightened states of awareness amplify and make obvious a connection that is usually so subtle as to escape detection. While having jarring implications for the modern view of human identity that stresses individual autonomy and independence, this interpretation of perinatal experience is consistent with the postmodern themes of holism and interpenetration emerging in quantum theory, general systems theory, ecology, feminist theory, and process philosophy.

Let me introduce a simple picture that may help anchor the expansion of perinatal theory being proposed. In this picture the perinatal dimension is represented by a circle with the four roman numerals representing the four Basic Perinatal Matrices. The area inside the circle represents the psychodynamic field of consciousness and the area outside it the transpersonal field. When I am using this diagram in class with my students, I often draw a series of spirals around each perinatal matrix to suggest the powerful experiential vortexes that each represents. These circles also visually represent the fact that each matrix draws its content from both inside and outside the perinatal boundary, integrating personal and transpersonal elements in the death-rebirth cycle.

We can represent a perinatal experience that slants toward the personal side of the perinatal interface by means of a spiral drawn inside the perinatal circle. Transpersonal elements may be present, but there is a sense that the focus is the death-rebirth of the individual. If, on the other hand, one's perinatal experience slants toward the transpersonal side of the interface, we can represent this by drawing a larger spiral outside the perinatal circle. Though the

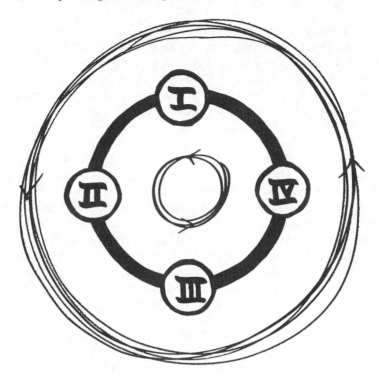

Figure 3.1

essence of the death-rebirth cycle is the same in both instances, the scope and focus have expanded dramatically in the second. When one's perinatal experience is primarily collective in nature, the focus shifts to the death-rebirth of the species and drives toward species ego-death rather than just individual ego-death. The archetype of death and rebirth is the same on both fronts, but the scale of the collective pattern is larger.[23]

This expansion of perinatal theory is in large part simply a clarification of Grof's original project, for he has always emphasized the multidimensionality of perinatal experience. And yet in his focus on the individual patient, in his tendency to see the birth trauma as forming the core of perinatal experience, and in seeing transpersonal elements as being drawn in through thematic resonance to this core, Grof's description of the perinatal dimension was inflected toward the personal psyche. It is not that these observations are false, but they seem to describe better a mode of perinatal experience that is slanted toward the personal side of the perinatal interface than one slanted toward the transpersonal side. What I have tried to do is to round out his account by presenting a more complete rationale for collective perinatal experience on its own terms.

One last point before we bring this chapter to a close. If the essence of the perinatal transformation is the death-rebirth process and if biological birth is less central to some forms of this process than to others, one might ask whether we should continue calling this level of consciousness the "perinatal" level at all. To do so seems to court unnecessary confusion, for the term always points us in the direction of biological birth. I am repeatedly correcting students who, despite hours of lectures and reading, cannot resist summarizing the perinatal domain in terms of the birth trauma, and even as sophisticated a student of the transpersonal as Ken Wilber has consistently fallen prey to this mistake (see appendix A). Persons who have not actually experienced this complex realm cannot help but tend to think of it disproportionately in terms of the birth trauma, as this is the more familiar ground. While this represents a misreading of Grof's theory, it is a reading that the term "perinatal" continuously invites. On the other side of the ledger, the advantage of keeping the term is that it has come to anchor a wide range of important insights into the role of fetal experience in our psychological development and in the recovery of our spiritual nature. Furthermore, birth is an extremely powerful archetype, and the perinatal vocabulary draws us into this multifaceted mystery. On balance, I believe that the term's disadvantages have come to outweigh its advantages and that the time has come for us to search for a different vocabulary for this domain. In the interest of continuity and clarity of presentation, however, I will continue to use the term in this volume. In the chapters that follow, I will often use the terms "perinatal dimension" and "death-rebirth dimension" interchangeably.

The expansion of perinatal theory presented here is but one part of the systematic rediscovery in many disciplines of the profoundly integrated nature of reality. For millennia the perennial philosophy has told us that all existence is a unified expression of a single intelligence, but only slowly are we grasping the true complexity hinted at in this assertion. Our individual lives are embedded in the larger life of our species. Here they are so tightly interwoven that, like ivy climbing a brick wall, one strand cannot be pulled without affecting others near it and some far away. As we push past the floor that doesn't exist at the bottom of the personal unconscious, we discover the undulating rhythms of a collective life that moves intelligently and precisely, as if following a timetable or script of which we had been previously unaware. Like the ebb and flow of tides that move in rhythm with a distant moon, the life of the individual moves in rhythm with the life of its species, which in turns moves in rhythm with something larger than itself. No longer atomistic selves bouncing around in a Newtonian universe, we discover that the details of our individual lives express currents that flow in quantum configurations through the whole of our kind. This discovery creates a new starting point for philosophical reflection, which we will take up in part III when we turn to explore the field dynamics of mind.

Before exploring this new starting point, however, I want to examine two additional sets of experiences that come from completely different arenas—near-death episodes and out-of-body experiences. The states of consciousness discussed in the present chapter have been entered into voluntarily. They have been deliberately cultivated and freely initiated. In the next chapter we will examine a set of experiences that I think are closely related to perinatal experience but which have entered people's lives without their consent or preparation. These are frightening near-death episodes.

Chapter Four

Solving the Riddle of Heaven's Fire

Of naked spirits many a flock I saw,
All weeping piteously, to different laws
Subjected; for on the earth some lay supine,
Some crouching close were seated, others paced
Incessantly around; the latter tribe
More numerous, those fewer who beneath
The torment lay, but louder in their grief.

—Dante, *Inferno*

P M. H. Atwater, author of several books on near-death experiences, tells the following story in an article published in 1992:

> Once, when I was autographing copies of my book in a shopping mall, a man in his middle thirties stopped at my table, looked at me straight in the eye, and with tight lips declared, "You've got to tell people about hell. There is one. I know. I've been there. All them experiencers on television telling their pretty stories about heaven—that's not the way it is. There's a hell, and people go there."[1]

For those who have taken comfort in the stories of the blissful white light waiting for us when we die being told by persons who have come close to dying, this man's urgent testimony of a darker side to postmortem existence strikes a chilling chord. Just as it was looking like the widespread near-death experience of an infinitely patient and forgiving God was beginning to erase the specter of a God who is willing to sentence some of his creations to an eternity of torture for their mistakes, along comes this man's disturbing insistence that hell is real after all. And he's not alone. Researchers are finding more and more persons whose near-death experiences have not followed the familiar pattern of blissful ascent into the white light but instead have turned aside into darker territory, in some cases territory so dark that these people insist that they entered hell itself.

The concept of hell is arguably the most terrifying notion that humanity has ever recorded. The idea that there is a place where one suffers excruciating pain for all eternity is the most frightening nightmare humanity has ever dreamed. To be forever isolated from everything that is beautiful and good seems a punishment that is both disproportionate to our finite status in the universe and incompatible with the concept of a truly loving Creator. And yet, many religious traditions have affirmed the existence of such a place, and now modern researchers have uncovered something that at least looks like hell.

The "hellish NDE" is part of a larger family of disturbing negative near-death experiences that British researcher Margot Grey summarizes in her book *Return from Death* in the following manner:

> A negative experience is usually characterized by a feeling of extreme fear or panic. Other elements can include emotional and mental anguish, extending to states of the utmost desperation. People report being lost and helpless and there is often an intense feeling of loneliness during this period coupled with a great sense of desolation. The environment is described as being dark and gloomy, or it can be barren and hostile. People sometimes report finding themselves on the brink of a pit or at the edge of an abyss, and state that they needed to marshal all their inner resources to save themselves from plunging over the edge. Alternatively, some people felt that they were being tricked into death and needed to keep their wits about them to prevent this from happening.
>
> The hell-like experience is defined as being one which includes all the elements comprehended in the negative phase, only more so in that feelings are encountered with a far greater intensity. There is often a definite sense of being dragged down by some evil force, which is sometimes identified with the powers of darkness. At this stage, visions of wrathful or demonic creatures that threaten or taunt the individual are occasionally described, while others recount be-

ing attacked by unseen beings or figures which are often face-
less or hooded. The atmosphere can either be intensely cold
or unbearably hot. It is not uncommon during this phase of
the experience to hear sounds that resemble the wailing of
"souls" in torment, or alternatively to hear a fearsome noise
like that of maddened wild beasts, snarling and crashing
about. Occasionally, respondents will report a situation that
resembles the archetypal hell in which the proverbial fire and
an encounter with the devil himself are experienced.

In the early years of near-death studies, researchers largely
overlooked these frightening NDEs (FNDEs), and though they have
begun to pay them more attention of late, progress in explaining
them has been slow. Descriptive typologies have been constructed
and piecemeal insights collected, but so far the attempt to integrate
FNDEs into the models of reality constructed from the study of ecstatic NDEs has produced mixed results. There is at present no consensus on whether the frightening NDE is a different type of NDE,
an aborted NDE, or even a real NDE at all. The field of near-death
studies does not at present appear to have a model of consciousness
that is large enough to incorporate these cases. While not wanting to
follow the fundamentalist voices that see them as proof of the existence of a literal hell, researchers have not been able to come up with
an alternative explanation that is convincing while being true to the
horrific nature of the ordeal.

One of the reasons they have been unable to do so, I will suggest
below, is that their approach to the problem suffers from the same
subtle theoretical bias toward the personal psyche that marked
Grof's description of perinatal experience. The psychological models
they have brought to bear thus far have been too centered on the
personal unconscious to do justice to the powerful collective and
transindividual aspects of these negative experiences. Only when
the collective features of FNDEs are appreciated, I believe, will we
comprehend the true scope of the trials that these persons have undergone, and only then will we be able to design therapeutic interventions that can help them deal with their experiences.

In this chapter I want to propose a solution to the riddle of
FNDEs by exploring their parallels to psychedelic perinatal experience. I believe that Grof's model of consciousness, as expanded in the
previous chapter, can provide us with a comprehensive framework
for understanding these experiences. A careful analysis of cases will
show, I believe, that FNDEs are rooted in the perinatal level of

consciousness. This excursion into near-death studies will deepen the line of inquiry we are developing and will lead to some startling conclusions about the nature of hell itself.[2]

The Ecstatic NDE

Frightening NDEs are the exception to the rule that deep NDEs are usually positive experiences. In order to set the scene for our investigation of these difficult experiences, let me first give one example of the more common "ecstatic NDE." Ecstatic NDEs vary in depth and intensity, and the following NDE is an example of what Ring calls a "core NDE," that is, a particularly deep NDE that seems to reach into the essence of what the NDE is all about. In core NDEs, one is carried beyond the peace, serenity, and level of existential insights that characterize milder NDEs into a particularly intense and extended encounter with the transcendent reality represented by the white light. In them we seem to see more clearly the destination toward which weaker or less complete NDEs are moving. This account comes from Beverly Brodsky and bears a certain resemblance to the psychedelic experiences cited in the previous chapters.

> I was raised in a nonobservant Conservative Jewish family in an overwhelmingly Jewish neighborhood in Philadelphia. The atmosphere was materialistic and, for me, claustrophobic. In high school girls were judged by their clothes and beauty. Bookish, shy and serious, I went through my teens as an atheist. Since learning, in very muted terms, of the Holocaust at age 8, I had turned angrily against any early belief in God. How could God exist and permit such a thing to occur? The secularism of my public school education and the lack of any religious training added fuel to my beliefs. I went through a period of depression growing up which was not treated due to my parents' unfortunate adherence to the belief that psychological treatment was disgraceful, and that personal problems or family secrets should never be aired outside the home. I had reached a desperate phase upon graduating from high school. Too upset to go to college despite my brilliant academic performance, I had trouble facing the future. To make things worse, shortly after graduation, at age 17, my father died suddenly from a heart attack. He had been my rock, my strength, in this world.

My mother went through an emotional crisis of her own after this loss, simultaneously entering menopause. No longer able to bear this unhappy environment, I left home at age 19, living first in Philadelphia's center city, and later moving out to California, where people then wore flowers in their hair and spoke of peace and love for all mankind. I had learned to meditate and for the first time had some hope that I could start over. To me the journey out West was like Hesse's "Journey to the East"—a quest for a new world.

In July, 1970, I suffered a fractured skull and numerous broken bones in my head due to a motorcycle accident that occurred in Los Angeles, California. I had just arrived in California the day before. The motorcycle ride, my first, was part of the celebration of arrival; we were returning from seeing the play, "Hair." I was a passenger on a small highway where helmets were not required, and was struck by a drunken driver. I was thrown head-first. When the police arrived, they initially took one look at me and started to book the driver of the car on manslaughter charges since my head was so badly mangled.

I spent two weeks in the hospital, where my fracture was sutured and I was given morphine for the pain. Then I was sent home and told to take aspirin. Since my pain threshold has always been very low, and my self-image was shattered by the contusions which had torn off half the skin from my face, I went home to my temporary apartment with the firm intent that the first night home would be my last. I lay down on the bed and, becoming an agnostic in this moment of trial, as many atheists do, prayed fervently for God to take me; I could not live another day. At 20 I had no goals but to enjoy life and find someone to share it with. The pain was unbearable; no man would ever love me; there was, for me, no reason to continue living.

Somehow an unexpected peace descended upon me. I found myself floating on the ceiling over the bed looking down at my unconscious body. I barely had time to realize the glorious strangeness of the situation—that I was me but not in my body—when I was joined by a radiant being bathed in a shimmering white glow. Like myself, this being flew but had no wings. I felt a reverent awe when I turned to him; this was no ordinary angel or spirit, but he had been sent to deliver me. Such love and gentleness emanated from his being that I felt that I was in the presence of the messiah.

Whoever he was, his presence deepened my serenity and awakened a feeling of joy as I recognized my companion. Gently he took my hand and we flew right through the window. I felt no surprise at my ability to do this. In this wondrous presence, everything was as it should be.

Beneath us lay the beautiful Pacific Ocean, over which I had excitedly watched the sun set when I had first arrived, but my attention was now directed upward, where there was a large opening leading to a circular path. Although it seemed to be deep and far to the end, a white light shone through and poured out into the gloom to the other side where the opening beckoned. It was the most brilliant light I had ever seen, although I didn't realize how much of its glory was veiled from the outside. The path was angled upward, obliquely, to the right. Now, still hand in hand with the angel, I was led into the opening of the small dark passageway.

I then remember traveling a long distance upward toward the light. I believe that I was moving very fast, but this entire realm seemed to be outside of time. Finally, I reached my destination. It was only when I emerged from the other end that I realized that I was no longer accompanied by the being who had brought me there. But I wasn't alone. There, before me, was the living presence of the Light. Within it I sensed an all-pervading intelligence, wisdom, compassion, love and truth. There was neither form nor sex to this perfect Being. It, which I shall in the future call He, in keeping with our commonly accepted syntax, contained everything, as white light contains all the colors of the rainbow when penetrating a prism. And deep within me came an instant and wondrous recognition. I, even I, was facing God.

I immediately lashed out at Him with all the questions I had ever wondered about; all the injustices I had seen in the physical world. I don't know if I did this deliberately, but I discovered that God knows all your thoughts immediately and responds telepathically. My mind was naked; in fact, I became pure mind. The ethereal body which I had traveled in through the tunnel seemed to be no more; it was just my personal intelligence confronting that Universal Mind which clothed itself in a glorious, living light that was more felt than seen since no eye could absorb its splendor.

I don't recall the exact content of our discussion; in the process of return the insights that came so clearly and fully in Heaven were not brought back with me to Earth. I'm sure that I asked the question that had been plaguing me since childhood about the sufferings of my people. I do remember this: there was a reason for everything that happened, no matter how awful it appeared in the physical realm. And within myself, as I was given the answer, my own awakening mind now responded in the same manner: "Of course," I would think, "I already know that. How could I ever have forgotten!" Indeed it appears that all that happens is for a purpose, and that purpose is already known to our eternal self.

In time the questions ceased, because I suddenly was filled with all the Being's wisdom. I was given more than just the answers to my questions; all knowledge unfolded to me, like the instant blossoming of an infinite number of flowers all at once. I was filled with God's knowledge, and in that precious aspect of his Beingness, I was one with him. But my journey of discovery was just beginning.

Now I was treated to an extraordinary voyage through the universe. Instantly we traveled to the center of stars being born, supernovas exploding, and many other glorious celestial events for which I have no name. The impression I have now of this trip is that it felt like the universe is all one grand object woven from the same fabric. Space and time are illusions that hold us to our plane; out there all is present simultaneously. I was a passenger on a Divine spaceship in which the Creator showed me the fullness and beauty of all his Creation.

The last thing that I saw before all external vision ended was a glorious fire—the core and center of a marvelous star. Perhaps this was a symbol for the blessing that was now to come to me. Everything faded except for a richly full void in which That and I encompassed All that is. Here I experienced, in ineffable magnificence, communion with the Light Being. Now I was filled with not just all knowledge, but also with all love. It was as if the Light were poured in and through me. I was God's object of adoration; and from His/our love I drew life and joy beyond imagining. My being was transformed; my delusions, sins, and guilt were forgiven and purged without asking; and now I was Love, primal Being, and bliss. And, in some sense, I remain there, for Eternity. Such a union cannot be broken. It always was, is, and shall be.

Suddenly, not knowing how or why, I returned to my broken body. But miraculously, I brought back the love and the joy. I was filled with an ecstasy beyond my wildest dreams. Here, in my body, the pain had all been removed. I was still enthralled by a boundless delight. For the next two months I remained in this state, oblivious to any pain. I wonder now if this were not the purpose behind the experience—to enable me to get through this period of recovery. . . .

I don't remember too much of this period, except that I did some things that were, for me, incredible. In the past I had been painfully shy and had felt myself unworthy of being loved. I went out, my head swathed in bandages like a creature from a horror film, landed a job in one week, made many friends, and got involved in my first serious romantic relationship. After the earthquake in 1971, I moved back East, went home to my mother, with whom I became reconciled, and started college at 23, another thing I never thought I could handle, and graduated Phi Beta Kappa. Since then I have married, become a mother, pursued a career, and have sipped deeply from the cup of life's blessings that I had never believed would come my way in those dark years before I had found the Light. In that encounter with death, I was given joy and purpose to continue on with life.

Although it's been twenty years since my heavenly voyage, I have never forgotten it. Nor have I, in the face of ridicule and disbelief, ever doubted its reality. Nothing that intense and life-changing could possibly have been a dream or hallucination. To the contrary, I consider the rest of my life to be a passing fantasy, a brief dream, that will end when I again awaken in the permanent presence of that giver of life and bliss.[3]

Against this uplifting portrait of the afterlife, frightening NDEs cast a dark shadow indeed, which we now turn to explore.

The History of FNDE Research

Premodern accounts of frightening near-death experiences go back to the Middle Ages, but these show such strong ecclesiastical and literary influences that it is difficult to estimate from this distance how much is true autobiography and how much has been added for our religious edification.[4] Modern accounts of FNDEs started showing up in the 1970s but in compromised contexts which delayed their being taken seriously by researchers. In *Glimpses of the Beyond* (1974), Jean-Baptiste Delacour described several allegedly real hellish NDEs, but his work showed signs of plagiarism and fictionalization which raised problems as to its credibility.[5] In *Beyond Death's Door* (1978) and *Before Death Comes* (1980), the cardiologist Maurice Rawlings reported a number of frightening and hellish NDEs, but his findings were rendered problematic by his flawed methodology and his strong commitment to fundamentalist religious views. Rawlings interpreted the frightening NDE as confirmation of the existence of a literal hell and recommended acceptance of Christ as the only way to avoid its fire. He has continued to promote this interpretation of FNDEs in books that have enjoyed wide sales, but his methodology has continued to be problematic.[6]

The scholarly study of FNDEs began in 1981 with the appearance of the Evergreen Study which was a survey of NDEs in the Pacific Northwest.[7] In 1985 Margot Grey devoted a chapter to negative NDEs in her book *Return from Death,* a comparative study of British and American NDEs. Grey documented that, though few in number, such cases definitely existed and offered the beginnings of an explanation of them inspired by the *Tibetan Book of the Dead,* which I will return to later. Other authors publishing in the 1980s provided further evidence of the existence of these types of cases but did little more than present case histories, summarize their features, and try to estimate their frequency of occurrence.[8]

In the 1990s the scholarly study of frightening NDEs shifted from description to analysis. In 1992 Bruce Greyson and Nancy Bush published a study of fifty distressing near-death experiences collected informally over ten years. They proposed a typology of FNDEs that quickly became the working vocabulary of the debate. Subsequently, the *Journal of Near-Death Studies* devoted two entire issues in 1994 and 1996 to frightening NDEs. In what follows I wish to lay out a more complete version of the interpretation of FNDEs I first presented in that forum.[9]

Surveying the Landscape of FNDEs

In their study Greyson and Bush distinguished three distinct types of frightening NDEs—(1) inverted NDEs, (2) meaningless void NDEs, and (3) hellish NDEs. Our first task is to summarize each type of experience and to illustrate the more important categories with case histories.

Inverted NDEs

Inverted NDEs are basically identical to ecstatic NDEs in structure but are experienced as being terrifying rather than joyful and comforting. People experience leaving their body, making the transition to another realm, and perhaps even beginning to confront the light, but instead of feeling increasing peace and serenity, they become frightened. The source of the disturbance seems to be their fear of ego-death, including the fear of losing contact with life as they have known it. Whereas most people experience the near-death invitation to expand into a larger reality as exhilarating, they experience it as terrifying. Instead of letting go, they clutch, and a battle with their fear begins. If they are able to surrender to the process, however, the experience converts to the classical NDE, sometimes with a life review and always with feelings of ecstatic transcendence. Compared to the other two categories of FNDEs, inverted NDEs are relatively mild traumas, and their dynamic seems to be reasonably well understood.[10]

Meaningless Void NDEs

Meaningless void NDEs represent a much more severe trial than inverted NDEs. In them people typically find themselves in a featureless dark void, completely cut off and alone. They are mocked by voices or demonic presences who insist that their life has been a complete illusion, a cruel joke completely devoid of meaning. There is sometimes a mechanical quality to the torment, and persons may see visions of discs or gears that move in a mechanical manner and make clicking sounds. Though they fight with all their might to prove that their life is real and does have meaning, they do not succeed. Time dissolves into an eternal emptiness, and they must face the worst kind of existential despair.

As an example of this kind of NDE, Greyson and Bush cite the case of a twenty-four-year-old office manager who had her experience when she was exhausted from three days of labor trying to deliver her second child. It may be premature to classify her experience as an NDE, because although it had certain NDE features, there is no indication that she was ever close to death during delivery. Whether or not it ends up retaining its classification as a genuine

NDE, the case is still instructive and contributes a piece to the interpretation of nonordinary states being presented here.

> I remember being in extreme pain and I remember thinking this is as far as pain can go, and then I lost consciousness. I then found myself floating in a narrow river toward a beautiful arched bridge. The bridge was made of large stones. I could see the shadow of the bridge getting closer and closer, and I was looking forward to getting in the shadow because I knew I would then be dead, and I wanted to die. I was floating with my body all down in the water, except my head was floating above it and bobbing up and down. I was very peaceful, but I wanted to get into the shadow.
>
> After I reached the shadow I was in the heavens, but it was no longer a peaceful feeling; it had become pure hell. I had become a light out in the heavens and I was screaming, but no sound was going forth. It was worse than my nightmare. I was spinning around and around and screaming. I realized that this was eternity for all mankind. I had become all mankind and this was what forever was going to be. You cannot put into words the emotions that I felt. I felt the quietness, except for the screaming within my own body, which was no longer a body but a small ball of light. I felt the aloneness, except the awareness that I was all mankind. I felt the emptiness of space, the vastness of the universe except for me, a mere ball of light screaming. . . .
>
> It was very realistic to me and an experience I will never forget for the rest of my life. I wrote this poem a few weeks later:
>
> > I have been to Hell.
> > It is not as you say:
> > There is no fire nor brimstone,
> > People screaming for another day.
> > There is only darkness—everywhere.[11]

As this woman's poem indicates, the line between meaningless void experiences and hellish experiences is sometimes blurred. While her experience did not contain any of the classic images one usually associates with hell, she clearly perceived it to be her personal version of ultimate torture, and what is hell if not this?

Hellish NDEs

Hellish NDEs are often saturated with archetypal images of devils, fire, dark pits, and collective suffering. The experiencer feels pulled on or dragged down by malevolent forces or grotesque beings, and a sense of evil pervades everything. Obviously such experiences are terrifying beyond words. Like all NDEs, hellish NDEs vary widely in scope and intensity. Some contain only a few hellish features while others contain many. Let me give two examples. Our first account comes from a man who had a cardiac arrest. He writes:

> I was going down, deep down into the earth. There was anger and I felt this horrible fear. Everything was grey. The noise was fearsome, with snarling and crashing like maddened wild animals, gnashing their teeth. I knew where I was without having to ask. I was in hell. There was this terrible feeling of being lost. It wasn't all fire and brimstone like we were taught. I remember this feeling of coldness. There were other things there whirling about. And there were two beings of some kind near me. I believe one was evil, maybe the Devil. He was the force that was tugging me deeper and deeper down into that awful place. I felt enveloped by dark, black evil. I remember frantically trying to put this two-piece puzzle together. I had to get it done or suffer some terrible, nameless punishment. You don't hear any words, you sense it all. Well, there was no way this puzzle would fit and I remember being in a panic. The other being I'm sure now was Jesus. I remember somehow knowing that He could save me. I tried to shout His name but I couldn't, there was this screaming in my head. Then I felt I was rushing through that black void again. I opened my eyes and my wife and the doctors were leaning over me, telling me everything was going to be alright.[12]

In the second example, the subject actually had three NDEs spread out over several weeks. The first and third NDEs were positive experiences, but sandwiched between them was the following ordeal, which is presented here in an abridged form:

> I went downstairs! Downstairs was dark, people were howling, (there was) fire, they wanted a drink of water. . . . we went down . . . it was pitchblack. . . . It was not a tunnel,

more than a tunnel, a great big one. I was floating down. . . . I seen a lot of people down there, screaming, howling. . . . No clothes at all . . . I'd say about, almost a million to me. . . . They were miserable and hateful. They were asking me for water. They didn't have any water. . . . he was there. He had his little horns on . . . I'd know him anywhere. . . . The devil himself![13]

Before turning to analyzing these cases, let me step back and identify a general problem that I see in NDE research and explain how my approach to NDEs differs from other commentators.

The Methodological Limitations of the NDE Database

Near-death episodes are short, intense, and usually unrepeated immersions into states of consciousness that lie far beyond sensory consciousness. They appear to give us snapshots of another world, glimpses into the inner workings of a dimension that surrounds or underpins physical reality. Researchers try to piece together many individual near-death experiences into a composite model of this other dimension. They want to understand its landscape, inhabitants, and dynamics. Toward this end they have to organize the many NDE snapshots they've been given. They have to identify their distinguishing features and decide whether these features indicate something significant about this dimension. Thus they create typologies of NDEs, but in doing so they are always limited by the fact that their database is a collection of, for the most part, unrepeated experiences. Studying a large number of NDEs gives us a more complete picture of this territory, but we are always limited by the fact that our snapshots were taken by people who experienced this realm only once. The one-time-only quality of this data tends to obscure the deeper, organic processes involved, and I believe that the key to understanding FNDEs lies precisely in these transformational processes.[14]

One way to highlight this methodological restriction is to imagine what we might learn if we could study a person who had not one but ten NDEs. The few cases of multiple NDEs that I am aware of suggest that subsequent NDEs tend to begin where the previous one stopped. Thus, experience in these nonordinary states is progressive. This is a point that is sometimes difficult for NDErs themselves to fully appreciate. A deep NDE is an exceptional state of awareness marked by an intense hyperclarity. NDErs take in much more information in a short period of time than is possible in their ordinary state of consciousness. When a person is suddenly propelled into a state that represents such a quantum jump in experiential intensity, they are usually overwhelmed by the reality that confronts them, whatever it is. The gulf between their usual state of consciousness and the state they now find themselves in is such that they immediately know that they are confronting something that is more real and more true than anything they have experienced prior to this. As a result, there is an understandable tendency for NDErs to take their NDE as a definitive read of this other reality. Their experience is so existentially powerful, so ontologically saturated that they cannot question its legitimacy, and therefore they seldom discover its limitations. This sometimes leads to problems down the road when they learn that other NDErs have had experiences that were equally legitimate to them but that are metaphysically incompatible with their own. One person learns that reincarnation is real while another learns that it's not. One discovers a God so loving that they "know" that hell is a metaphysical impossibility while for another hell becomes un undeniable reality. One person learns that all religions are fundamentally true and therefore equal in value while another returns saying that Jesus Christ is the *summum bonum*. All this can lead to interesting but confusing confrontations on the talk-show circuit.

It is very difficult for persons who have limited experience with extreme nonordinary states to understand that an experience that can be so overwhelmingly true in the moment can also be incomplete. *It is all too easy to mistake experiential intensity with metaphysical completeness; indeed, it is practically impossible not to make this mistake.* It is only by repeatedly entering these extreme states that one discovers that their revelations are always compromised or qualified by the residual patterning of one's consciousness. Of all the triggers that may propel one into a nonordinary state, nearly dying is surely one of the most powerful, temporarily disrupting one's egoic structures sufficiently to allow one to drink deeply from the transpersonal well. But if someone were to have this experience not once but five, ten, or fifteen times, she (or he) would discover that one can drink from different levels of this well. She would begin to recognize patterns or structures that had been invisible in the rush of insights that flooded her that first time. Because each NDE changes one's baseline consciousness to some degree, her capacity in subsequent NDEs to take in new experiences would expand, allowing her to move deeper into the experience, all other things being equal.

Because it is not possible, let alone ethical, to induce multiple NDEs in a single subject, the NDE database will always have this inherent restriction of being a collection of unrepeated "first dates" with transcendence. Obviously, you cannot learn everything you want to know about marriage from studying even a large collection of first dates. Fortunately, however, we are not restricted to this database to understand this reality but can supplement it with insights that come from other sources.

The similarity of psychedelic states to NDEs has been recognized for many years, and what these states may sometimes lack in comparative depth in individual episodes is more than made up for by the fact that they can be induced multiple times. In psychedelic states one gets extended and repeated access to states of awareness that overlap *and subsume* the NDE experience, both its ecstatic and frightening varieties. Here too, studying the experiences of many persons stabilizes and extends our vision, but the great methodological advantage of psychedelic therapy is repetition. Repeated immersion in psychedelic states draws out the organic processes involved, showing us more clearly how one state systematically unfolds into another. Processes that we see piecemeal in individual NDEs are seen more comprehensively across a long string of therapeutically focused psychedelic sessions.

Coming to the study of NDEs after many years of working with psychedelic states, I am convinced that the varieties of frightening NDEs that researchers have identified are in fact *permutations of a single transformational process,* the perinatal death-rebirth process. The categories that Greyson and Bush have created to catalogue these experiences mark variations on a theme, and the theme that unites them is more important than the variations that distinguish them. While accurate typologies are important, what is needed now, I think, is a comprehensive model of how these different pieces fit together and what they represent, and I think this can be had by viewing them in the context of Grof's paradigm.

Parallels with Perinatal Experience

The phenomenological parallels between perinatal experience and frightening NDEs are extensive and justify, I think, seeing frightening NDEs as being rooted in the perinatal level of consciousness. These parallels should already be sufficiently clear to require only a brief summary here.

While the entire perinatal sequence is relevant to understanding FNDEs, Basic Perinatal Matrix II seems to be particularly prominent in them. BPM II is the "no-exit" matrix in which a subject experiences an overwhelming assault against which he or she is utterly helpless. It is often the first matrix to appear in therapeutic work, and this may explain its high profile in near-death settings. (That is, if someone were to experience a series of FNDEs, we might expect their later NDEs to introduce themes of BPM III and IV.) The following summary of this matrix highlights the themes that are relevant to a perinatal interpretation of FNDEs. As we will see, BPM II combines all the features of both hellish and meaningless void NDEs. Grof writes:

> The characteristic elements of this pattern can be experienced on several different levels; these levels can occur separately, simultaneously, or in an alternating fashion. The deepest levels are related to various concepts of hell, to situations of unbearable physical, psychological, and metaphysical suffering that will never end, as they have been depicted by various religions. . . . Another typical category of visions related to this perinatal matrix involves the dehumanized, grotesque, and bizarre world of automata, robots, and mechanical gadgets, the atmosphere of human monstrosities and anomalies in circus sideshows, or of a meaningless "honky tonk" or "cardboard" world.
>
> For a person experientially tuned in to elements of BPM II, human life seems bereft of any meaning. Existence appears not only nonsensical but monstrous and absurd, and the search for any meaning in life completely futile and, *a priori*, doomed to failure. . . . This existentialist crisis is usually illustrated by a variety of visions depicting the meaninglessness of life and the absurdity of putting forth any effort to change this fact. . . .
>
> Agonizing feelings of separation, alienation, metaphysical loneliness, helplessness, hopelessness, inferiority, and guilt are standard components of BPM II. Whether the individual looks at his present situation and behavior or explores his past, the circumstances and events of his life seem to confirm that he is a worthless, useless, and bad human being. . . .
>
> An interesting variety of the second perinatal matrix . . . is experienced in LSD sessions as an increasing awareness of an imminent and vital danger or as *cosmic en-*

gulfment. There is an intense anxiety, but its source cannot be identified; the atmosphere of insidious threat may result in paranoid ideation. Not infrequently, the subject interprets these alarming feelings as evil influences coming from members of various secret organizations or inhabitants of other planets, as poisoning, noxious radiation, or toxic gases. Intensification of this experience typically results in the vision of a gigantic and irresistible whirlpool, a cosmic maelstrom sucking the subject and his world relentlessly to its center. . . . A less dramatic form of the same experience seems to be the theme of descent into the underworld and the encounter with various monstrous entities.[15]

If one compares the accounts of FNDEs that appear in this chapter with the psychedelic sessions recorded in the previous chapter, I think that the parallels will be clear. In addition to parallel content, the dynamic patterns that surface in both settings are consistent. In both contexts fighting the experience simply intensifies it while yielding to it causes it to resolve itself into a positive transpersonal experience. If allowed to run their full course, both experiences culminate in ego-death followed by spiritual rebirth. These parallels strongly suggest that severe FNDEs are rooted in the perinatal level of consciousness.[16] But what exactly does this mean and how does it help us understand what is happening in these traumatic episodes? To answer these questions, let me set out an interpretation of frightening NDEs in light of Grof s concept of the perinatal.

A Perinatal Interpretation of FNDEs

One of the important insights in Kenneth Ring's book *Heading Toward Omega* was that what occurs during an NDE "has nothing inherently to do with death or with the transition to death." His articulation of the parallels between transcendent NDEs and the mystical experiences that emerge in various meditative disciplines demonstrated that nearly dying is but a trigger that catapults persons with some consistency into higher states of consciousness that can also be cultivated through any number of consciousness expanding techniques. What happens, however, if for some reason the thrust toward this higher state of awareness does not carry someone all the way to the point of transcendence? What happens if the consciousness-expanding power of his (or her) NDE is sufficient to carry him beyond his personality consciousness but insufficient to open him to the transcendental level of his being?

The indications from psychedelic therapy are that this person would get caught somewhere in the labyrinth of the perinatal level of consciousness. When someone experiences a transcendent NDE, they have been catapulted through this labyrinth and end up beyond it. They have not dissolved it but have pierced it to reach the larger reality it screens. If he does not get this far, however, he will be susceptible to a perinatally tainted NDE. We might think of such a person as stuck in the tunnel that most NDErs pass through without complication. The tunnel here represents the transition from the personal level of consciousness to the transpersonal, that is, the transition through the perinatal domain.[17]

A perinatal interpretation of frightening NDEs allows us to incorporate and deepen observations made by other researchers. In *Return from Death*, for example, Margot Grey suggested that hell-like NDEs might be caused by the release of negative emotions that had been trapped in the psyche. Directing our attention to the negative postmortem *bardos* described in *The Tibetan Book of the Dead*, she suggested that FNDEs reflect the subject's "unfinished business" in life.[18] While this suggestion has much to recommend it, in its current form it fails to account for the rather narrow thematic content of these experiences. That is, if individuals were simply confronting unfinished business from their lives, we would expect these confrontations to show a much greater variety than they in fact do. A perinatal interpretation of these experiences, however, both affirms and deepens her suggestion.

Grof's paradigm identifies a level of consciousness deeper than the personal unconscious where the nature of one's "unfinished business" go beyond anything envisioned by conventional psychodynamic theory. At the perinatal level of consciousness, our idiosyncratic histories begin to yield to a narrow set of issues that are intrinsic and universal to human existence—birth, physical pain, disease, and death. The experiences that distinguish us as individuals begin to yield to experiences that unite us with all other members of our species. The unfinished business of the perinatal level, therefore, derives less from our individual histories and more from our collective history as a species. At this level of consciousness we confront the limitations of a species whose self-awareness is still largely trapped within its body. Here we face the fear that accompanies surrendering the limitations we have taken on by incarnating *as this humanity*.

Ken Ring made a similarly important but incomplete contribution to the discussion when he suggested that frightening NDEs were generated by our fear of losing our ego-identity. Taking his lead from *A Course in Miracles*, he wrote:

> If, upon having an NDE, a person is strongly identified with his ego and sufficiently attached to it that he clings to it like a drowning man might clutch to a raft, he will naturally bring a great deal of fear into his experience. . . . Such an individual's emotional state will then tend to generate images consonant with that fear which will only cause it to strengthen. The person will therefore continue to feel deeply menaced, as he is indeed threatened with extinction—as a separate ego.[19]

Ring put his finger on a critical issue, but in its current form his proposal runs into a fundamental problem of proportion. As we have seen, estimates of the frequency of frightening NDEs tend to hover around 1 percent. Even if we were to increase this estimate tenfold, Ring's proposed explanation would run into trouble for the simple reason that the condition of overly identifying with our egos is surely much higher than this. Among the millions of persons who have had NDEs, surely most were overidentified with their egos at the time of their NDE. Why, then, did only a small percentage of these people experience a frightening NDE? While personality rigidity, religious indoctrination, or situational trauma may intensify an individual's fear of death in specific cases, the fact is that our culture is pervasively frightened by death, and people in general are terrified at the prospect of surrendering their body/mind identities. When so many people are frightened of ego-dissolution, why are so few being propelled into frightening NDEs?

A perinatal reading of FNDEs supports Ring's assertion that frightening NDEs are driven by our resistance to ego-death, but it deepens it by emphasizing that this resistance is more than individual or situational. Our personal resistance to ego-death is rooted in our species' resistance to ego-death and is therefore embedded in the deepest levels of the collective unconscious. This resistance reaches into the very depths of our individual *and collective* existential confusion about what we are and our group failure to grasp the most fundamental spiritual truth about ourselves.

It would seem that a perinatal interpretation of FNDEs, however, has only worsened the problem of proportion. If our resistance to ego-death is rooted in the perinatal level of consciousness and if this level is a universal structure of consciousness, it would appear to be even harder to explain why so few persons who nearly die experience frightening NDEs. A perinatal reading of FNDEs does not so much solve this problem as redefine it and thereby shift where we should be looking for answers. It suggests that the reasons some people have frightening NDEs while others do not lie less in the psychodynamic particulars of the individuals involved and more in the variables inherent in their NDEs. While I think that Ring is correct that some individuals hold on to their ego-identities more fiercely than others, I suspect that the larger share of the explanation for perinatally tainted NDEs lies in the conditions that cause some NDEs to be weaker than others.

Why do frightening NDEs occur so infrequently? I don't know. Perhaps it happens more often than we have yet identified, as some researchers think. Perhaps more people have frightening NDEs and either do not remember them or do not report them. Alternatively, it may be the case that once a strong NDE is initiated by a biological trauma, deviations from the prototypical script are simply rare. Perhaps once certain thresholds are crossed, the psychospiritual impetus generated by nearly dying is simply strong enough to carry the large majority of persons through the perinatal and into the transpersonal dimension of consciousness without complications arising. In this context we should take note of the fact that many of the frightening experiences being reported as "NDEs" did not, in fact, involve any immediate threat to the subject's biological existence. If the threat of biological death is lacking or diminished, the resulting nonordinary state may be less empowered than a truly life-threatening experience and therefore more susceptible to perinatal entanglements. There is much we do not understand here and much work to be done. The important point to grasp at this time, however, is that the experiences of those few persons whose journey to the light is interrupted or sidetracked closely parallel experiences that occur in therapeutic contexts that are better understood and better mapped. By recognizing the perinatal features of frightening NDEs, we can incorporate them into a comprehensive model of consciousness that makes sense of them and in this way lessens their sting.

Bias in Psychological Models

Both Grey and Ring's interpretations of FNDEs contained important insights but ran into problems, I think, because of a subtle bias in the psychological models they brought to the issues, the same bias that hampered Grof's exposition of the perinatal domain. This bias is a general tendency to think in terms of models that are more oriented to the individual than to the species. Grey recognized that FNDEs involved confronting unfinished business but failed to appreciate that it was the "unfinished business" of the collective unconscious. Similarly, Ring recognized the role of fear of ego-death in FNDEs but failed to grasp the significance of the fact that this fear is endemic to the entire species. In both instances, *there is a habit of mind which causes a failure to recognize the play of the species-mind in the data and an insensitivity to its collective dynamics.*[20]

The transpersonal paradigm has radically expanded our estimate of the depth and breadth of human consciousness. Perhaps it is our long history of contemplative spirituality with its strong vertical focus, but we seem to be appropriating the significance of our mind's depth more quickly than its breadth. This point needs to be emphasized because I believe that one of the greatest challenges facing psychology and philosophy today is to grasp the full implications of our interconnectedness. We must surrender our atomistic models of mind and shift to a more holistic self-awareness. The fundamental polarity of our nature is the polarity of individuality and wholeness, and wholeness includes both depth and breadth. For several thousands of years we have strengthened and celebrated our individuality at sometimes terrible cost to our relational self. The challenge now facing us is to recognize the intimate ways we participate in each other's lives, to identify and appreciate the symptoms of our collective life, and to feel into the rhythms of our collective evolution into ever greater depth.[21]

A perinatal reading of frightening NDEs alerts us to the fact that in these arduous experiences, individuals sometimes open directly to the species-mind. This turn toward the collective typically expresses itself in a turn to the *universal themes* of death, birth, disease, and so on. It sometimes, however, expresses itself as a turn to a *collective mode of experience*. If we are drawn deeply enough within, we find that our personal experience of perinatal themes begins to expand into a collective experience of these same themes, just as we saw happening in psychedelic therapy. When this happens, we are drawn into collective experiences of previously unimaginable proportions and intensity. If a person has a perinatally tainted NDE, therefore, he or she may move into a state of consciousness that blends individual and collective dynamics. The life process of the individual may open to the life process of the species, and the two may begin to move in synchronized rhythm. Greyson and Bush have, in fact, already provided us with an excellent example of this phenomenon, though they let it pass without comment, I suspect because they did not recognize its significance. You may remember that in the example of meaningless void experiences given above, the woman said the following:

> [I]t had become pure hell. I had become a light out in the heavens and I was screaming, but no sound was going forth. . . . I was spinning around and around and screaming. I realized that this was eternity for all mankind. I had become all mankind and this was what forever was going to be. You cannot put into words the emotions that I felt.

I think that we should take this woman at her word and recognize that she had connected with the morphic field of the species-mind. Her claim to have become all mankind is not simply a figure of speech but a genuine experience. As in psychedelic therapy, we can recognize that a transition has taken place from the individual to the collective level of experience, but we still know very little about how this occurs or what end it might serve. What we are coming to see clearly, however, is that in the psycho-plastic world one enters during an NDE, personal and collective components can be synthesized into experiences of devastating intensity. The "hell" that this woman experienced is much more than just a personal hell. It might be better thought of as a pocket of suffering within the species-mind to which she gained access through her NDE. The archetypal quality of such an experience derives from the fact that she is confronting dimensions of suffering that "live" in the collective unconscious.[22]

FNDEs and the Dark Night of the Soul

Survivors of frightening NDEs are doubly alienated in our culture. First, they must manage the general failure of large segments of our society even today to accept the reality of their near-death experience. Secondly, and more importantly, while the majority of NDErs report basking in divine light, they were taken to the doorstep of "hell." How could they not take this as some sort of commentary on the moral tenor of their life? How could they not conclude that they were deliberately singled out for harsher treatment by some higher intelligence? This reaction is reinforced by simplistic theological interpretations of FNDEs that see them as foretastes of the eternal punishment that awaits the morally lax or unconverted.

In the context of Grof's paradigm, however, it becomes clear that a frightening NDE is not an alternative NDE but *an incomplete NDE*. It is not necessarily a reflection of the individual's moral character at all, but represents instead an encounter with some of the deepest structures of the individual *and collective* unconscious. Why one person is carried through these structures while another is not has less to do with the moral fiber of the person undergoing the experience than with the as yet unidentified variables that cause some NDEs to sputter out early while others drive through to their final destination.

One of the clearest ways to make this point is to remind ourselves that the "descent into hell" has been experienced by some rather saintly persons. It happened, for example, to St. Teresa of Avila, the famous sixteenth-century Catholic mystic. Teresa regularly entered into nonordinary states of consciousness while in deep prayer and not infrequently left her body during these episodes. While in the out-of-body state, she had many experiences that were exceptionally painful. In her autobiography, which was written not for publication but to allow her superiors to assess her spiritual experiences, she described in detail one particularly difficult ordeal, a descent into hell:

> The entrance, I thought, resembled a very long, narrow passage, like a furnace, very low, dark and closely confined; the ground seemed to be full of water which looked like filthy, evil-smelling mud, and in it were many wicked-looking reptiles. At the end there was a hollow place scooped out of a wall, like a cupboard, and it was here that I found myself in close confinement. But the sight of all this was pleasant by comparison with what I felt there. . . . My feelings, I think, could not possibly be exaggerated, nor can anyone understand them. I felt a fire within my soul the nature of which I am utterly incapable of describing. My bodily sufferings were so intolerable that, though in my life I have endured the severest sufferings of this kind . . . none of them is of the smallest account by comparison with what I felt then, to say nothing of the knowledge that they would be endless and never ceasing. And even these are nothing by comparison with the agony of my soul, an oppression, a suffocation and an affliction so deeply felt, and accompanied by such hopeless and distressing misery, that I cannot too forcibly describe it. To say that it is as if the soul were continually

being torn from the body is very little, for that would mean that one's life was being taken by another; whereas in this case it is the soul itself that is tearing itself to pieces. The fact is that I cannot find words to describe that interior fire and that despair which is greater than the most grievous tortures and pains. I could not see who was the cause of them, but I felt, I think, as if I were being both burned and dismembered; and I repeat that the interior fire and despair are the worst things of all. In that pestilential spot, where I was quite powerless to hope for comfort, it was impossible to sit or lie, for there was no room to do so. I had been put in this place which looked like a hole in the wall, and those very walls so terrible to the sight, bore down upon me and completely stifled me. There was no light and everything was in the blackest darkness.[23]

NDErs who have had similar experiences might be interested to know that Teresa considered this and her many other painful experiences in the out-of-body state to be especially beneficial to her spiritual development. She did so not because she harbored any masochistic tendencies but because she had come to recognize that these ordeals were a kind of purification process. Through them something negative was being lifted from her soul. By submitting to them and following them wherever they took her, she found that her experiences of mystical union deepened. Teresa is not alone in experiencing such ordeals, nor in recognizing their purifying function. In fact, the descent into hell is simply an extreme instance of a large set of arduous experiences that are a common feature of the mystic's journey. In the Christian tradition, these difficult experiences are called the dark night of the soul, and Teresa's close friend, St. John of the Cross, is perhaps their best-known chronicler. Collectively, these experiences represent a series of difficult purifications aspirants must undergo as they uncover the transcendent core of their being.[24]

In appendix A at the end of this book, I demonstrate that the purifications that occur in the dark night of the soul are essentially the same as the perinatal experiences that occur in psychedelic therapy. Recognizing the perinatal character of the dark night and frightening NDEs completes the triangle that has been emerging in this study. The fact that the experience of hell occurs on the psychedelic subject's journey to Wholeness, the NDEr's journey to the Light, and the mystic's journey to God is a striking confirmation of Ring's contention that we must place the NDE in the context of our spiritual traditions in order to understand it fully. Not only in its ecstatic forms but also in its most problematic forms, the NDE shows itself to be a coherent part of humanity's spiritual pilgrimage. We should, therefore, be able to illumine the hellish NDE by drawing upon insights garnered in these two other settings.[25]

When we do so, we find that in its deepest form the experience of hell is a painful process of confronting everything within us that is inconsistent with the deepest truth of our being. We might describe this confrontation as fundamentally a confrontation between our *nature* and our *history*. That is, it is a confrontation between what we essentially *are* and what we have as yet been able to *become* in spacetime. In all three contexts—the mystical, the psychedelic, and the near-death—our nature is discovered to be inherently divine. Our essential being is recognized as synonymous with Being Itself. From this perspective, everything we see, touch, and feel in spacetime is recognized as being part of our essential being. When we turn to our history, however, we often see how poorly and incompletely we have embodied this transcendental truth. Through countless incarnations, we have fallen into a fragmented condition, and thus our actions often fail to represent the inclusive truth of our primary nature.

As we indicated above, persons who have ecstatic NDEs have not dissolved their perinatal matrices but have been carried through them by the power of nearly dying to contact the transcendental dimension of their being. When their NDE ends and they return to their body, they find themselves back in their karmically conditioned life. As the clouds of spacetime close back around them, the Light recedes and they find themselves once again separated from the deepest level of their being. *Now their real work begins.* The spiritual baptism that opened their eyes must be followed by the long and laborious process of bringing the whole of their life into line with the spiritual truths that were shown them. If they had died during their NDE, the odds are that many would have continued this work of realignment in a subsequent incarnation. According to the *Bardo Thödol*, everyone encounters the Light upon dying, but few are able to sustain the full impact of this encounter or to recognize that the Light is in fact one's own true nature revealing itself. To do so requires that our history has become sufficiently transparent to our nature, and this is said to require many incarnations of conscious spiritual transformation.

In an ecstatic NDE, one has not purified one's entire history but temporarily slipped free of it to experience the transcendental nature that surrounds it. We might ask, therefore: What would happen if instead of slipping free of one's history, one somehow managed to bring it along with him or her into the Divine Presence, thus forcing the juxtaposition of one's conditioned history and one's unconditioned nature? The evidence from psychedelic therapy and mystical practice is that if this were to happen, the person would suffer terribly. She (or he) would suffer not because she was being rejected or punished, but simply because the unconditioned truth of her essential nature was inconsistent with the conditioned truth she had thus far lived.

Rethinking Hell

So far I have been largely speaking about the "hell-experience" and not about hell itself and thus have avoided making metaphysical commitments. While it would be safer to stay on the metaphysical fence and say that we are simply examining people's experiences and not drawing conclusions about the actual nature of postmortem existence, this cautious approach strikes me as lacking courage. Surely one of the things that interests us about the hell-experience in whatever context we study it is the thought that it might give us some insight into what actually happens to us after we die. Indeed, unless we are willing to go out on a limb and make some tentative metaphysical commitments here, we lose much of the real value of recognizing the purificatory role of the hell-experience, namely, that it strips postmortem hell of its cruelty and vindictiveness and restores to the universe its mercy and love.

A perinatal interpretation of hell tells us that if there is an astral hell like the one some FNDErs experience, and I for one can no longer doubt that this is the case, *its function is not damnation but spiritual transformation*. The metaphysical vision that emerges is one that balances accountability with compassion. It balances the necessity that we learn from our mistakes with the realization that our ability to make mistakes is one of the things that makes us precious to the Creative Intelligence. Instead of being the final resting place of those who have rejected God, hell is part of a developmental sequence of imperfect persons who are drawing closer to their inherent perfection. For spiritual practitioners, it is their passionate impatience to awaken to the transcendent dimension of being, and to awaken others, that causes them to plunge deeper and deeper into this purifying ordeal.

As we draw near to the source of our existence, to that from which we originally came and in essence always are, we approach it as a small flame drawing close to a large fire. Fire merges with fire effortlessly, but due to our history, our fire-nature has partially crystallized into the constricted patterns of fragmented consciousness. As we draw near to the larger fire, our inner flame flares as if in response to its presence. The closer we come, the more brightly it glows until it begins to burn away and set free everything in our history that constricts it. Because our history is a record of our life in spacetime, as it is burned away we suffer the excruciating "loss" of that life. The more brightly the flame burns, the more we suffer until we think that surely there is no surviving this, and there *is* no surviving it. That is the point.

Only when its work is finally done can we possibly begin to understand hell's mercy. Only when it has freed us from that which we mistakenly cherished most can we comprehend its love. *Hell is not heaven's opposite but the guardian at the door of that which heals everything.* Hell is God's closest companion, for in truth it is simply the transient flash of pain experienced by our urgent return to our source. There is no punishment here and certainly no banishment. Rather, there is simply the brief if terrible combustion that results when we feel we must shed our history as fast as possible, when safely staying out of the Divine Presence is a worse fate than suffering in It. Hell's intensity reflects our impatience as much as it does our mistakes. *Hell is heaven's purifying fire.*

A recently published NDE beautifully illustrates how closely heaven and hell, suffering and deliverance, are sometimes intertwined in nonordinary states of consciousness and gives support to the line of interpretation being developed here. This episode resulted from the trauma of involuntary electroconvulsive therapy. Though the patient was never in danger of biological death, she was terrified of the procedure and absolutely convinced that she was about to die. Her subsequent experience was virtually indistinguishable from NDEs caused by life-threatening biological trauma. The case has many interesting aspects, including a precognitive glimpse of an event two years in her future, but it is the intimate juxtaposition of hellish torment and spiritual rebirth that I want to focus on here. We pick up on the author's paraphrase of the woman's experience well into the episode:

> Then there were no more disruptions or intrusions of scenes to distract her gaze or brake her speed; and the threat of being swallowed up and consumed in the light loomed as the imminent, and ultimate horror.

Drawn, "as if by an inconceivably powerful electromagnet," into that blinding radiance, her terror mounted and matched the light in intensity as she shot down the tunnel with such acceleration, "it felt as if I were being sucked into a black hole in space." And though it was "a thousand times worse than even Dante's most horrifying images of hell," the desire to let go and go into the light was "infinitely compelling, absolutely irresistible."

The struggle had left her totally exhausted, with no energy left to fight against the light; and, having long since passed the point of no return, with courage born of desperation, she at last willed to let go and go into the light, knowing only that death would be release from "unendurable tension, unbearable anxiety."

It was then that she gave herself up to be burned away in the light, to die, to lose her mind, to be hurled into the belching mouth of hell, if that was what was to be. And finally having given up and let go to go freely into the light, in a moment, "in the twinkling of an eye," she knew herself to be one with the light itself, and was lost—and found—in a state of "absolute ecstasy."[26]

The high spiritual character of the suffering inherent in death and rebirth is also suggested in the iconography of Tibetan Buddhism. In this tradition, deities are often represented as manifesting in either of two forms, in a wrathful aspect or a peaceful aspect. As depicted in Tibetan art, the wrathful aspect is frightening to behold. These high spiritual beings often appear surrounded by exploding flames, standing on wild beasts, having multiple heads with fierce expressions, and waving multiple arms holding spears, knives, and other ritual objects. They ornament themselves with cadavers, wear human skins as robes, and sometimes drape a chain of skulls around their neck or waist. Their posture is confrontational and they appear poised to strike. When the *same beings* appear in their peaceful aspect, however, the effect is quite different. Now they appear serene and radiating supreme bliss. Often seated on lavishly decorated thrones in the center of glowing orbs of light, they hold flowers and are generously ornamented with precious gems. Their entire demeanor is ethereal tranquility poised in compassionate manifestation.

The important point for our purposes is that Vajrayana Buddhism sees these two images as portraits of a single life force. How we experience this high spiritual energy depends entirely on our condition. If we are in an egoic condition, the spiritual power of its presence will ignite into fiery experiences of threatening, death-bringing confrontation. If we are in a non-egoic condition, the same power will meet no resistance in us and instead lift us into the clarity and rapture that is its abiding condition.

The wrathful form of a deity, therefore, might be described as perinatal hell incarnate. Tibetan Buddhists see its fierce and grotesque form as expressing supreme compassion, for its considerable power is focused on liberating us from our overidentification with our body-mind egos. The skins and skulls it wears are symbols of its capacity to free us from our addiction to dualistic existence, as they are the corpses no longer needed by the beings it has already liberated into spiritual realization. The more powerful and compassionate the deity, the more plentiful its bizarre raiment. Thus, they represent the dynamic aspect of enlightenment, the part that answers our sincere and steadfast request for help by tearing away from us the obstacles that block our spiritual realization.

Drawing upon these religious parallels, we might suggest that NDEs also have a wrathful and a blissful aspect, a frightening and an ecstatic face. The fiery dungeons and taunting demons in hellish and meaningless void NDEs might be seen as their wrathful form. Though difficult and painful to confront, their intent is simply spiritual purification. Paradoxically, *the severity of our pain in this confrontation is a measure of how much more we are becoming than we have yet managed to be, both individually and collectively*.

Conclusion

We began this chapter with a story of one man's tormented message that hell was real. I hope that the line of thought presented here will reframe his message and soften both his anguish and the anguish of others who have been caught up in realms little understood by most physicians and psychotherapists today. Most modern thinkers would prefer to believe that hell is not real. They would prefer to think that it was the macabre creation of an overactive religious imagination or a medieval ploy to extort moral conduct from the masses. And yet the hell-experience keeps showing up, now in hospitals of all places.

The hell-experience *is* real. The question is, what is the nature of this reality? What does it tell us about the universe we live in and the life process we are part of? I have tried to show that the sting of hellish NDEs is lessened when we locate them in the larger context of spiritual disciplines that systematically uncover the deepest roots of our self-clinging. When we do so, they become more intelligible and the universe becomes more benign.

In spiritual traditions that affirm reincarnation, the experience of hell is seen as but the harsh confrontation in the interlife with the anger and hatred that one has generated in his or her just-completed life. Buddhism, for example, dispassionately catalogues the eight "hot hells" and the eight "cold hells" that together with the various "neighboring hells" and "ephemeral hells" constitute the interim fate of those whose minds are still plagued by a variety of violent emotions. And yet, something important is frequently left out of these discussions. Despite the emphasis placed on emptiness-of-self and nonduality in this tradition, Buddhist portraits of the bardo tend to focus exclusively on the fate of the individual mindstream and *fail to address the collective fields of consciousness that these evolving streams together comprise.* The story of the evolutionary ascent of the individual, even a Bodhisattvic individual, overshadows the story of the ascent of the species as a whole, with the result that the relationship between the two is not addressed in any detail. To explore this and the nature of postmortem existence further, let us turn to consider the out-of-body experiences of Robert Monroe.

Chapter Five

Beyond the Soul

There is no beginning, there is no end.
There is only change.
There is no teacher, there is no student,
There is only remembering.

—Robert Monroe, *The Ultimate Journey*

Robert Monroe was a vice-president for NBC living the executive life with a home in Connecticut, a plane in the hanger, and a boat at the dock, when his career in broadcasting was diverted by his spontaneous out-of-body experiences that began when he was forty-two years old. In time he became a pioneer in consciousness research and founded the Monroe Institute in Faber, Virginia, just south of Charlottesville. There he and his colleagues created a sophisticated technology that helps people enter specific states of consciousness through the psycho-acoustic entrainment of their brainwave patterns. Thousands of persons have come to the institute from around the world to learn how to enter these states in order to gain systematic access to realities which are invisible to sensory consciousness. Monroe also published three highly regarded autobiographical books—*Journeys Out of the Body* (1970), *Far Journeys* (1985), and *The Ultimate Journey* (1994)—which contain a description of the extraphysical universe as he experienced it in the out-of-body state. Monroe died in 1995, and his trilogy, therefore, can be viewed as a completed whole, reflecting almost forty years of out-of-body experience. In this chapter, I would like to bring Grof's paradigm into dialogue with Monroe's and to compare the cosmologies that emerge from their respective explorations.

It is not surprising that mainstream philosophers have ignored
Monroe's work, as it presents a profound challenge to the materialist vision that rules the modern mind. It *is* surprising, however, that
his work has received relatively little attention in the transpersonal
community. Apparently the Blue Ridge Mountains of Virginia are far
removed from California in cultural as well as physical miles.
Nevertheless, I think Monroe's work deserves the careful attention
of transpersonal thinkers for a number of reasons.

First, Monroe's work brings to the discussion a sophisticated understanding of the *bardo*, the "interlife" state one enters between incarnations. The *bardo* is a important concept in consciousness
research not only because it is essential to understanding the larger
rhythms of the reincarnation process but because it underscores the
depth of conditioning that spacetime experience exerts on human
consciousness. To underestimate the *bardo* is to underestimate the
true scope of human evolution and to miscalculate the many layers
of programming that must be shed before the essential nature of
mind can shine forth in its true splendor. In this context, it is noteworthy that Monroe's account of this realm closely accords with how
it has been described in established spiritual traditions. Indeed, his
description of the interlife in *Far Journeys* is deeply resonant with
its portrayal in the *Bardo Thödol*, or *The Tibetan Book of the Dead*.[1]

Second, introducing Monroe's experiences allows us to under-
score how difficult it is to transcend the soul in transpersonal experience. For over three thousand years, the Western religions have
taught the doctrine that we are, in essence, souls and that souls are
ontologically discrete spiritual entities. This atomistic conception of
our spiritual nature is deeply ingrained in the Western psyche, as reflected in the widespread belief in a day of final judgment when God
will separate the blessed from the damned and send them to their
respective rewards for eternity. It is our ontological discreteness that
allows God to divide us into these separate piles, as a child might divide a bag of marbles. Ken Wilber has argued that the concept of the
soul is, in fact, an essential component of the theistic worldview, for
they both emerge out of and reflect a specific stage of humanity's
psychospiritual development. To see the Divine as a single, differentiated intelligence, separate from the physical universe but in
charge of it, goes hand in hand, he says, with experiencing oneself as
an integrated, self-initiating being who is well differentiated from
the physical universe and other persons. Beyond the soul, an entirely different experience of the both the self and the Divine opens.
In this respect, Monroe's story is illuminating both for what he sees

and for what he doesn't see in the out-of-body state. In his candid reporting of his OOB experiences, he outlines a profound vision of human evolution, and yet, as I hope to show, his experiences stop short of transcending the soul. As a result, the universe that he describes continues to be a fragmented universe composed of discrete parts.

A third reason for considering Monroe's work has to do with sharpening our appreciation of the role that method plays in transpersonal disclosure. What one experiences in nonordinary states depends on how one's consciousness is structured at the moment of disclosure. By bringing Monroe's out-of-body experiences into dialogue with psychedelic experience, we are comparing not just two different sets of experiences but two different methods for accessing nonordinary states, both applied over many years. This comparison will allow us to articulate more precisely how transpersonal disclosure works, to distinguish those features that are method-dependent from those that are consistent across different methods. This is an important consideration if we want to persuade a skeptical mainstream audience that the universe as experienced in nonordinary states is self-consistent and coherent, and therefore deserving of critical attention.

A final reason is more autobiographical and for that reason may be more revealing. Monroe's writings were very helpful to me at a particular period in my life, even though exploring the out-of-body state has never been part of my personal path. Before I had come to it myself on experiential grounds, he gave me permission to believe that the majority of intelligent life in the universe is actually nonphysical. He lifted the ceiling of my metaphysical vision and encouraged me to extend my sight to a larger horizon. I also felt his courage and personal integrity as he relentlessly pressed beyond his personal limits, and this supported me in my own work. At the same time, the universe that was revealing itself in my psychedelic sessions was quite different from the universe Monroe was describing, and I had to figure out why. When everything is said and done, it is this combination of deep respect and my need to understand our differences that lies behind this chapter.

Monroe's vision of reality assumes the concept of reincarnation, and therefore it is a vision that sees human beings developing across enormous tracts of time. Taken together, however, all our lives on Earth represent only a small portion of our true existence. According to him, our life before we began incarnating on Earth and after we stop is largely screened from our awareness by the heavy conditioning that spacetime exerts on us while we are part of this system. Not

even death can be counted on to restore to us the memory of our
larger history. However, if we begin to understand and integrate the
hidden half of our life cycle, the half that takes place between death
and rebirth, we can begin to reappropriate the larger trajectory of the
soul-being that we are underneath our present human identity. To do
this requires that we understand what Monroe calls the "rings."

The Rings

Monroe describes postmortem existence, or the interlife, as taking
place in a vast landscape that he divides into a series of four rings
surrounding spacetime. To the extent that I visualize these rings
spatially, I imagine them to be somewhat like a series of concentric
spheres surrounding spacetime. Each ring in the series represents a
specific range of consciousness. When people die, Monroe says, they
eventually find their way to the ring that corresponds to their level
of development. This is the ideal scenario, for a number of variables
can sometimes cause a person to get stuck at a lower level, such as a
particularly sudden or traumatic death.

    According to Monroe, the innermost ring is populated by per-
sons who have died but do not realize it. Unable to let go of their
physical lives for a variety of reasons, including emotional and biological addictions, they are completely focused on physical reality
and are often frustrated and confused by their inability to influence
that reality. They appear to be surrounded and dominated by emotionally based fears and drives that they repeatedly act out without
satisfaction. A second, smaller population of beings in this ring also
do not realize they are dead but do know that they are somehow different from how they were before. This difference releases them
from their previous social restraints and obligations, and they give
themselves over to acting out all manner of desires in the only way
they know, through replicas of physical activity. Because they can
see physical life taking place around them, they relentlessly try to
interact with the physical world, leading to many bizarre activities
that are sometimes injurious to those they interact with.[2] The first
group Monroe calls the "Locked-Ins" and the second the "Wild
Ones." In his experience, these beings are so tightly focused by their
addiction to life as they had known it that it is practically impossible to get their attention or to communicate with them from the
OOB state. They literally cannot experience anything other their
own powerful emotions and are oblivious to other activities taking

place in their immediate vicinity. They can remain locked in this condition for years, even centuries.

The next ring out is much smaller and is populated by persons who know they have died but who have little awareness of any possibility other than the life they have just left. Though more aware than those in the first ring and less dominated by their lower emotions, they are still largely trapped within the awareness of the life they have just completed. Monroe describes them as often stunned by the loss of their body and unable to do more than passively exist in a self-contained, motionless state while they simply wait for something to happen. In contrast to those in the lowest ring, however, they are able to be contacted, and therefore are able to receive guidance from helpers from the outer rings. Because of this receptivity and the continuous assistance available to them, their numbers are small and the turnover in this ring is high.[3]

The third ring is a vast territory composed of many sub-rings covering a wide range of awareness. Monroe says that one could spend thousands of years exploring this domain and not come close to exhausting it. At this level of consciousness people know they have died, and they engage in activities that reflect their specific interests and abilities. In the psycho-plastic world they have entered, their thoughts, beliefs, and desires become their lived reality. Here one's experience is determined not by the conscious ego alone but by the entire psychic makeup of the individual. Repression and suppression are impossible, and all of what one is registers "up front," so to speak. Because people have widely varying beliefs about the nature of the afterlife and what is available to them there, their experiences vary enormously. At this level their awareness has expanded sufficiently to enable them to experience other persons, and the principle of "like attracts like" allows various groups to develop that reflect their aggregate world view. One gets the impression of an assortment of different astral villages organized around various themes and endeavors, some of which might surprise us. The varieties of experience available appears to be practically limitless.[4]

This vast territory is divided roughly in half, says Monroe, by a line that he describes as the midpoint of two interpenetrating fields of energy. This "null point" is the point of transition between two overlapping fields of influence. Below the null point, people's experiences are still highly colored by spacetime experience. Their mental habits and assumptions transfer the patterns of spacetime conditioning into this astral realm, causing it to resemble to varying degrees the physical world they have left behind. The influence of spacetime is strongest at the lower edge of this ring and diminishes as one moves outward. Beyond the null point, says Monroe, people's experiences come increasingly under the influence of nonphysical reality. The categories of spacetime fall away as the hypnotic spell of matter yields to the increasing clarity of an energy often described as pure consciousness. Awareness progressively expands and deepens into its "natural" condition, and the human shape begins to yield to the form of light, a light that becomes brighter and clearer the farther one goes in this direction. (Monroe describes the lower rings as grey, dense, and filled with psychic static while the upper rings are increasingly light-filled, spacious, and expansive.)

In his last book, Monroe calls the lower half of the third ring the "Belief Systems Territories." Here one finds persons who during their lifetime subscribed to some organized system of beliefs concerning the nature of postmortem existence. Here are the heavenly paradises and hells described in the world's major religions. Persons for whom these belief systems were important guides will find themselves in conditions that approximate their expectations. However, Monroe also says that one of the things people discover in the postmortem state is that reality is always richer than they had anticipated. Thus, people not only encounter their expectations by living them after they die, they are always being invited to outgrow their expectations by becoming more self-aware. This appears to be a general feature of the *bardo* at all levels. Reality is always richer than we are making use of. As a result, there are always cracks in our experience, fissures through which we can pass into an even richer mode of experience. (When you stop and think about it, isn't this true of our experience in spacetime as well?)[5]

Beyond the null point, Monroe says, people's experiences become less and less describable in terms that correspond to spacetime categories. The influence of Earth surrenders step by step to the influence of nonphysical reality. Time yields to timelessness, shape and color to pure light. Boundaries that created the conditions of learning in spacetime first soften and then dissolve to reveal increasingly inclusive patterns.

In the last ring live the "Last Timers" and the "First Timers," persons who have one last incarnation to take before they leave physical existence behind altogether and those who have just started their calculated descent into the spacetime experience. At this level, Monroe says, persons appear simply as light with occasional sparkling patterns around them. Their entrance into their final incarnation is practically indiscernible and their exit after their "death" looks like a sparkling, glowing light that moves swiftly through the rings, sometimes pausing for unknown reasons. When they pass the outermost ring, they suddenly disappear from perception altogether. Where they go can be known only by those who are able to follow them.

Though Monroe describes the rings in spatial terms, it is clear that they represent not actual places but states of consciousness. The geometry of concentric rings is in the final analysis a metaphor for the different experiential possibilities inherent in different states of consciousness. Like television signals that share the same physical space without conflict because they vibrate at different frequencies, persons occupy the same "space" after they die but experience this space differently depending on their state of awareness. The sequence of Monroe's own evolution confirms this point. In the early decades of his work, Monroe had the sensation of traveling from place to place while in the out-of-body state. By the end of his second book, however, he reports that this sensation had been replaced by the sensation of simply shifting his "phasing." To think of extraphysical reality in spatial terms, therefore, is still to be under the influence of spacetime conditioning. Technically, one does not "travel" in this reality so much as simply shift one's operational mode of awareness. All images of space are metaphors of state.

Monroe's description of postmortem existence is more complex and subtle than this brief overview can capture, and part of the beauty of his writing is that he enlivens these categories with many stories of contact with beings who live at each of the levels. Enough of an outline has been provided, however, that we can now turn to consider the changes that took place in Monroe as he explored the rings over many years.

The Developmental Trajectory of Monroe's Experiences

One of the most striking things about Monroe is how much his experiences evolved over four decades. The metaphysical vision contained in his first book, *Journeys Out of the Body,* is primitive compared to that found in his second, published fifteen years later, and his third is more complete still. This perpetual deepening is one of the characteristics that Monroe's work shares with Grof's therapy. What becomes available in nonordinary states is always governed by the consciousness one brings to the encounter. Repeated immersion in these states slowly changes one's baseline consciousness, and as one's baseline changes, new levels of reality open around one. Thus, Monroe is constantly outgrowing himself. In addition, he discovers over the years that many of his earlier experiences had contained subtle clues to possibilities that he had missed at the time. Always the candid reporter, he never tries to hide his foibles from his audience and allows the reader to follow him through all his mistakes and uncertainties.

This perpetual deepening of experience comes not just from repetition of experience, of course, but from confronting with awareness the limitations that are restricting one's experience at any given level. Here too, Monroe's willingness, even eagerness, to engage his personal limitations parallels the temper of serious psychedelic work. Whether through the intense learning exercises arranged for him by his Inspec friends[6] or through his own adventures, Monroe comes back from his OOB experiences deeply changed, and the trajectory of these changes has already been suggested in his description of the rings themselves.

In order to be able to experience a certain reality in the OOB state, one must to some degree be like what one is seeing, or at least be sufficiently like it for it to enter one's awareness. In his first book, Monroe was working for the most part below the null point, in the lower half of the *bardo*. In his second book, his range had extended to include all the rings, and this expansion reflects a long process of personal transformation. For him to become aware of and able to communicate with persons in the outer rings, he had to clarify his consciousness to the point that he could participate in their reality. In his third book, his transformation had deepened further, and his vision had become clearer and more comprehensive. Thus Monroe's description of the beings who occupy the successive rings can be read as reflecting the stages of his own development. Taking this approach, then, we might ask: What are the patterns of development that Monroe records as he progresses through the rings?

If we wanted to identify the most salient features of this developmental trajectory, I think three points stand out. First, as one moves from the lower to the upper rings, the working identity expands from the egoic personality to the soul, or from what Monroe calls the "I-Here" to the "I-There." The egoic-personality is the working identity of postmortem existence only in the lower rings. Because spacetime heavily structures our experience of reality at that level, the identity we assume there tends to be our most recent historical personality. As we follow Monroe into the outer rings, we find that the working unit of identity changes. The persons he meets at these levels are not only clearer but also larger in that they are the conscious integration of many incarnations. In one encounter, for example, Monroe meets an old friend, Lou, whom he had worked with at NBC and who had died several years before. By now, however, this being had already completed two subsequent incarnations, so the Lou-identity was a conscious part of a much larger being.

Second, as the above example suggests, time itself appears to become porous as one moves through the rings. From Monroe's temporal perspective, only a few years had passed since Lou's death, but from Lou's perspective, this apparently was enough "time" for him to experience two entire incarnations, presumably of more than a few years duration each. Monroe says that as he transcended the influence of material conditioning, he found that the restrictions of linear time also fell away. He learned, for example, that persons can reincarnate in any historical period they choose. The perception that one must follow the track of history in one's subsequent incarnations appears to be a lower bardo distortion, which yields at a higher level to a rich field of multi-temporal possibilities.

If one follows this insight to its logical conclusion, it would seem that time might dissolve so deeply that the concept of *re*-incarnation might deconstruct with it. That is, it may be the case that seeing our life process as a linear series of incarnations might be a partial truth within a larger temporal illusion. There may be a reference point from which reincarnation might appear more accurately as multiple incarnations being lived simultaneously. Monroe himself does not take the possibilities this far, but this may in the end be the more natural way of understanding the entire exercise. For our immediate purposes, it is sufficient to point out that according to Monroe, time is part of the fabric of spacetime, and as such it slowly dissolves as one moves away from that fabric and opens to new temporal modalities that wreak havoc with our temporally bound logic, which keeps shouting "That's impossible!" One is reminded of Alice's protest in Lewis Carroll's *Through the Looking Glass*:

"I can't believe *that!*" said Alice.

"Can't you?" the Queen said in pitying tone. "Try again: draw a long breath, and shut your eyes."

Alice laughed. "There's no use trying," she said. "One *can't* believe impossible things."

"I daresay you haven't had much practice," said the queen.[7]

Third, not only does time become porous as one moves through the rings but our minds do as well. The beings Monroe encounters in the outer rings often know what he's been doing and why he's come to them before he is able to say anything. One gets the impression that as we move into these realms, we become increasingly transparent to each other. Private thoughts seem practically impossible to keep, or perhaps they simply become unnecessary or even silly. We might initially interpret Monroe's experiences as indicating exceptional clairvoyance and assume that all the citizens of the outer rings are simply capable of "super-psi," and yet this interpretation may be missing the true significance of these exchanges. If our minds become exceptionally transparent to each other at this level, might this not suggest the existence of comprehensive patterns of integrated awareness rather than simply separate souls in telepathic dialogue? That is, just as the working unit of consciousness shifts from the egoic-personality to the integrating soul in the middle rings, might it not be the case that the soul yields to still more encompassing and inclusive forms of consciousness at still higher levels?

Monroe does not go this far, but there are subtle clues in the conversations he records that seem to suggest something like this. In one of his early conversations with his Inspec friend, for example, he asks how many Inspecs there are. The answer he receives back is that it is difficult to say because of the "melding." The Inspecs simply don't keep track of themselves that way. One gets the impression that our numerical measures of individuality, which were created to manage the conditions of spacetime plurality, do not apply well to the natural form reality takes at this level.[8]

But these are only possibilities that one must infer indirectly from bits and pieces of Monroe's narrative. On the whole, the description he gives of extraphysical existence is soul-centered. While there are hints of expansive textures and blended edges, what stands out in the end is the individual soul. It is, to be sure, a profound and expanded soul, but it is always an individual soul with well defined edges. In *The Ultimate Journey*, for example, he describes a large assembly of souls that appeared to him as a multidimensional carpet of lights. As suggestive as this image is, he does not take us the next step and explore what the inner experience of such an assembly might be if it were a single, self-conscious entity. Instead, he leaves us with an inspiring image of a vast assembly of separate luminous beings, companion voyagers gathered at a meeting point beyond the outermost ring, preparing to leave spacetime together in one massive exodus.

Monroe makes his readers work, often giving them pieces of information indirectly and almost seeming to delight in suggestion and innuendo. He sometimes uses terms or concepts before he has introduced the experiences that explain them, and you have to read his books several times to catch everything that is happening. Perhaps that was his intent. I suspect that most of these convolutions result from the fact that Monroe is distilling his narrative from decades of OOB experience, weaving thousands of journal entries together into a simplified account, and he's only willing to go so far to make this story look more organized than the original experiences actually were. Furthermore, he repeatedly warns us that what he is giving us is only an approximation of events, a story line that suggests but does not capture the full reality of his actual experiences. Given this fact and given Monroe's love of open-ended suggestion, it is difficult to pin down exactly how far his experiences actually took him. All we can do, I think, is take his account at face value and trust that he has done a good job of representing himself. In the end, we are not interpreting the man but a text, and the text is a selective representation of a richer field of experiences.

Having outlined the developmental trajectory of Monroe's evolving OOB experiences, let me begin to bring his portrait of extraphysical reality into dialogue with Grof's paradigm.

Comparing Monroe and Grof

Let me begin this comparison by sharing an observation that comes from years of introducing students to Monroe and Grof. When my students read Monroe, they usually come away feeling uplifted and less fearful of what is waiting for them after death. Monroe does not sweeten postmortem existence, but on the whole his portrait of it is reassuring and positive. If there is a measure of torment in the rings, there is far more space given to joy, peace, and perpetual self-transformation. When they read Grof, however, their reaction is often ambivalent. They value the expanded understanding of consciousness that he gives them, but they are often disturbed by the extreme suffering he describes in the perinatal dimension. The cosmology that they intuitively extrapolate from his description of the three levels of consciousness appears to them to be less forgiving, less friendly, and less kind than Monroe's cosmology. Grof's account of the perinatal ordeal and his apparent confirmation of the reality of hell often leaves them feeling fearful of what might await them at death. In essence, they are afraid of the tortures they think they will have to endure in order to become one with God when they die. I'm not saying that their interpretation of Grof is correct on these points, but their reaction is understandable. I might add that because my description of the perinatal domain is even darker than Grof's, there is a risk that my account will seed an even greater existential dread among readers, and this would be the last thing I want to do. In order to avoid this reaction, it is absolutely essential that we understand what the perinatal dimension is and isn't. We must grasp what these horrific experiences are telling us about the universe we inhabit.

I think that my students are right to point to the lower profile of suffering in Monroe's account of nonordinary experience and its prominence in Grof's. With the exception of the experience I will cite below, there is very little in Monroe that matches the concentrated psychospiritual anguish and shattering confrontation with death that characterizes psychedelic perinatal experience. The question is: What are we to make of this difference? The students want to know which is the truer picture of the universe. Is it Monroe's kinder universe with hosts of spiritual beings constantly trying to lift us out of our self-imprisoned worlds into larger, more satisfying realities, or is it Grof's harsher universe where entry into hell is the price one must pay for spiritual liberation? The answer, I think, is that they are both true portraits. The difficulty is getting the students to see that the head-to-head comparison they are drawing is too simplistic.

In order to understand the significance of this contrast between Monroe and Grof, we must carefully examine the different methods being used to shift consciousness and compare how these methods impact consciousness over time. As I have already said several times in this volume, what experiences emerge in nonordinary states depends to a large degree on how our consciousness is structured at the moment of disclosure. One's mind acts as a seed-catalyst that draws forth specific experiences from a field of infinite possibilities. Thus, we must consider how psychedelic therapy and out-of-body work affect consciousness over the long term if we are to understand the different facets of the universe that come into view using these two different psychotechnologies. When we do so, there are three points that I think need to be made.

The first is that the out-of-body state is a much gentler method of personal transformation than psychedelic therapy, especially when the latter involves the use of psychoactive agents. I believe that much of the traumatic nature of perinatal experience derives from the sheer efficiency of the methods being used to provoke this confrontation with the deep psyche. Where one's inner obstacles are melted more gradually, the result is a gentler erosion of illusion rather than a convulsive spasm of awakening. For an analogy, if you were to place an ice cube near a candle flame, the steady warmth of the flame would melt the ice cube slowly, causing small drops of water to run down its face and fall away. On the other hand, if you dropped the same ice cube into a cast iron skillet heated to a high temperature, it would jump around the pan, popping and crackling as its water molecules explode against the hot surface. In a similar manner, the OOB state purifies one's system more gradually than psychedelic therapy, spreading its transformations across thousands of small ego-deaths instead of concentrating them in a few large, dramatic ones, and *this gives the appearance of a gentler universe*.

In actual fact, there is a great deal of transformative suffering in Monroe's story, but it is hidden by being broken up into many smaller episodes rather than being grouped into a few large and dramatic ones. We might recall that Monroe's first book was based on almost six hundred OOB experiences, and his later books reflect thousands more. As Monroe describes the OOB state, when consciousness shifts its phasing from its spacetime coordinates, it becomes more susceptible to influences from the deeper layers of the psyche. Monroe attributes the deeper perspective of his second book to a decision he made after many years to turn his OOB experiences over to the guidance of the Inspecs, which we later learn meant turning them over to his soul or Total Self. By surrendering conscious control of his OOB experience, Monroe encouraged a series of confrontations with his deep psyche that gradually wore away his ego-structure over many years. This posture of engagement and confrontation is the same as that adopted by the psychedelic subject; the difference lies in the intensity of the confrontation with the unconscious.

The second point is that the catalytic power that causes psychedelic therapy to bring about its effects more quickly also allows it to reach more deeply into our unconscious conditioning. Perinatal suffering is the distinctive pain of surrendering the deepest roots of one's private existence. The fact that Monroe continued to experience extraphysical reality as a collection of separate selves suggests that when all is said and done, his basic operational mode of consciousness continued to be that of the private self, or at least the semiprivate self. Though his sense of self expanded enormously through the years, his experience remained centered in a dualistic medium of discrete selves. Given this fact, it seems that part of the reason for the lower profile of suffering in Monroe's account is simply that the deepest roots of the self had not yet been challenged.[9]

The third point is that, as we saw in chapter 3, psychedelic therapy sometimes triggers episodes of collective suffering that must be framed in terms of the species-mind, not the individual mind. These particularly intense ordeals represent not the harsh treatment of an individual person but the healing of some aspect of humanity's collective unconscious, in response to the initiative of the individual.

In summary, then, why is there so much more suffering in Grof's account of transpersonal experience than Monroe's? It is because psychedelic therapy challenges egoic conditioning *faster* than the OOB state, because it reaches *deeper* into that conditioning, and because it sometimes triggers a form of *collective cleansing* that redounds to the benefit of both the species and the individual.[10] *The appearance that Monroe's universe is kinder than Grof's, therefore, is mistaken.* The differences in method make it appear so, but it is the same universe revealing itself through two very different mediums of self-transformation. Monroe's universe appears to be gentler because the out-of-body state asks less of us in the short term, but in the end there is no greater kindness than freedom, and in psychedelic states we may have as much freedom as we can endure.

If I may inject a cautionary note at this point, it is possible, of course, to accelerate one's spiritual development more than is wise. The psychospiritual technologies that are becoming available to us today present us with the possibility of doing too much rather than too little. The fact that we can do something does not necessarily mean that we should do it. In my case at least, I recognize with hindsight that I at times pushed my system harder than was wise. Not living in a culture that understands and guides these undertakings, I had to find my own way about and in the process stumbled many times. Changes of consciousness are changes of one's entire being, and these changes must be absorbed at many levels, by our body, mind, emotions, subtle energy, social relationships, and so on. Asking one's system to absorb too much change too fast stresses these levels. As in all things, it is a matter of balance and paying careful attention to the feedback one's system is giving you.

Returning to my students, they want to know what is going to happen to them when they die. Will their experience be closer to Monroe's description or Grof's? If given just these two options, I tell them that I think Monroe's portrait more closely reflects the progression of most people's lives. Nature tends to move slowly, polishing away our impurities gradually. While it can be demanding at times, it generally allows us to proceed at our own pace. If, however, persons were to choose to accelerate the pace of their development, either here or in the *bardo*, their experiences might begin to resemble those seen in Grof's paradigm. The challenges of purification increase the more we accelerate the pace of our transformation, but so do the rewards. It is entirely up to us.

I don't want to overstate this contrast between Monroe and Grof, however, because they are clearly plowing the same field even if using different methods to do so. My concern has been to figure out how their different experiences fit together and what is responsible for the differences in the first place. Furthermore, it would be a mistake to say that the perinatal dimension is not represented in Monroe's experience at all. If the essence of the perinatal dynamic is ego-death and rebirth, surely Monroe is no stranger to this process. In addition, there is one particular experience that Monroe underwent near the end of his life that has striking perinatal features and resembles the death-rebirth experiences that occur in psychedelic therapy. It comes near the end of *The Ultimate Journey* and is the culminating experience of the book. Given the fact that this volume is the capstone of Monroe's trilogy, it is arguably the culminating experience of all three books and thus of all Monroe's OOB experiences. It therefore bears looking at closely.

Monroe had set himself the task of finding his ultimate point of origin. Having discovered many years before that he came to Earth from a nonphysical energy system that he calls KT-95, he was now seeking the source of his existence prior to even that existence. Going beyond all the rings, Monroe returned to KT-95 and then turned deeply inward, driving his awareness toward its source. We pick up his narrative at this point:

> . . . careful, careful . . . it feels much stronger now than it did then . . . the movement . . . the music is fading . . . clouds dissolving . . . the curls are gone[11] . . . nothing now, nothing but a spiraling mass of energy moving outward . . . moving inward bit by bit . . . like swimming upstream . . .
>
> . . . the spiral becomes tighter, tighter . . . narrowing, very narrow . . . the current is stronger . . . hard to move against . . . but still moving . . . hard, hard . . . takes too much strength . . . ahead of me the vortex point . . . a little more, little more . . . too small, can't get through it . . . concentrate energy . . . skip . . . skip . . .
>
> . . . a surge deep inside me . . . another, larger . . . taking me over . . . another wave . . . it hurts but it is beautiful . . .
>
> (and a part of me is left behind)

. . . skip . . . skip . . . a larger surge . . . hurts terribly all through me, but so beautiful, so exquisitely beautiful . . . nothing can be so magnificent as this . . .

(I lose another part of what I was)

. . . skip . . . another surge . . . nothing can hurt so deeply . . . nothing can be so all-encompassing in joy . . . but I can't stand much more . . .

(not much of the old me left)

. . . skip . . . the greatest surge . . . this is it, this is it . . . there is nothing greater than what I feel, nothing so total, total joy, total beauty, total . . .

****

What? Why did I wake up this way? I need to put my consciousness back together . . . There, that's more like it! Now, what happened? Yes, the dream. Dream? Or did I live it? Was it real—or someone else's dream?

. . . Now everything is in place and operating . . . the dream is fading quickly . . . something about clouds and curls . . . and moving along an Interstate . . . and life and death, whatever that means . . . something called time-space . . . and a blue planet . . . a sun . . . strange, strong energy . . . millions of suns . . . and love . . . never forget the feelings of that even if it was only a dream . . . a complicated dream . . . took so much energy to wake up . . . here in this bright coolness . . . .

. . . my consciousness is filling out more . . . remembering how it happened . . . yes . . . was part of the Whole . . . one by one, parts were placed here and there, taken from the Whole and placed . . . where? Can't see it clearly . . . the excitement . . . joy at a new adventure . . . one by one, those around me were placed . . . then it was my moment . . . the wrenching . . . the uncertainty . . . then the Whole was gone . . . what terrible loneliness . . . alone . . . need to get back to the Whole . . . consciousness falling apart . . . fall asleep . . . sleep . . . what is sleep? . . . losing consciousness, falling apart . . . that was it . . .

. . . Now I am moving back . . . back to the Whole, where I belong. I can feel the beginning of the radiation, becoming more intense as we move . . . what joy to return . . . .

Yes, now I know what I am, what I have been from the beginning, what I always will be . . . a part of the Whole, the restless part that desires to return, yet lives to seek expression in doing, creating, building, giving, growing, leaving more than it takes, and above all desires to bring back gifts of love to the Whole . . . the paradox of total unity and the continuity of the part. I know the Whole . . . I am the Whole . . . even as a part I am the totality.[12]

The correspondence with psychedelic perinatal experience is striking: a sense of tight constriction and narrow opening, building energy pushing him through a vortex, surging waves that repeatedly carry him beyond his breaking point, a pain so extreme that it becomes indistinguishable from pleasure, losing large pieces of his personal identity as he is stripped down to essentials, and rebirth into a more inclusive spiritual reality.

When Monroe then moved on to return to the Whole, he eventually found himself outside an aperture that he called the "Emitter," a massive device that was projecting the hologram that we know as spacetime. He could not pass through this aperture until he had regathered and integrated the energy of all his incarnations, a process that was not yet complete for him. Later, as part of the same exercise, he returned to spacetime and drove his awareness into the core of physical matter, deep into quantum reality, and discovered there a beam that led him again to the same Emitter. This experience convinced him that the entire reality he had been exploring all his life, both its physical and extraphysical dimensions, were in fact an integrated, holographic projection from another reality that was ontologically more basic. Physical existence and the bardo realms comprise a single world, one of but many. In making this discovery, Monroe reproduced the ancient insight of the perennial tradition, that heaven and earth sprang into existence together and are an integrated expression of something more fundamental still. Even our heavenly paradises are part of a dream from which we will eventually awaken into something even more extraordinary.

If we are correct in drawing attention to the perinatal features of this experience, it constitutes an important point of contact between Monroe's and Grof's paradigms. Grof, too, has for many years used holography as an analogy when describing how physical reality appears in transpersonal states. And yet, when all is said and done, we are left with the fact that Monroe did not appear to probe the inner workings of this hologram as deeply as Grof. I suspect that if Monroe had lived for another decade and given us a fourth book, the overlap in their paradigms would have increased. As their systems currently stand, however, we must come to terms with their differences. Before continuing, however, let me insert a brief comment as a footnote to the previous chapter's discussion of hell.

Hell and the Bardo

With the possible exception of the experience just quoted, one does not find in Monroe's description of the *bardo* anything that approximates the extreme metaphysical anguish or existential despair that characterizes the hell-experience that occurs somewhat regularly in psychedelic therapy and occasionally in frightening NDEs. Monroe locates "hell" in the Belief Systems territory of the lower third ring, but he does not describe what it is like other than to say that one's cultural beliefs script one's experience there. If there are indeed pockets of "hell" in the bardo, they appear to be an exceptionally small part of a much gentler postmortem environment. The impression that one gets from Monroe's description of the bardo is that while there may be isolated pockets of suffering here and there, in general the postmortem world is much kinder and gentler than most religious traditions have led us to believe. This brings us back again to the question of what role hell plays in postmortem existence and in the larger scheme of our evolution.

There may be persons whose actions on Earth are so heinous and whose hearts are so closed that drastic measures may be called upon in the *bardo* to pry them open. And yet, by Monroe's account at least, such severe measures seem comparatively rare. What appears to make them rare is the malleable, self-generated nature of one's experience in the postmortem state. The psycho-plastic quality of the *bardo* allows us to confront our inner contradictions there very powerfully, but it also seems to allow us *to avoid these contradictions to some extent if we choose to do so.* It is precisely the fact that our mind creates our reality there that allows some persons to refuse to face certain truths about themselves for long periods of time, such as the simple fact that they've actually died. One might also recall the examples Monroe gives of his many failed attempts to convince persons he meets in the rings that there is a larger reality beyond the one they are currently experiencing.

If one reads the literature on the *bardo* from classical as well as contemporary sources, one gets the impression that between incarnations people tend to wrap themselves in astral cocoons. Change and growth are stimulated by engaging contrasts, and the self-generated nature of one's experience in the bardo tends to reduce these contrasts and therefore actually slows one's growth. In the *bardo* one lives in a reality where one is surrounded by beings pretty much like oneself. Everyone shares a similar worldview and has approximately the same capacities. In such a world one cannot fully avoid the familiar problem of suburban neighborhoods whose residents resemble each other too much to be very stimulating. Indeed, commentators no less than Sri Aurobindo point out that what makes Earth such a rich environment for accelerated spiritual growth are the contrasts that exist here as opposed to the relative sameness of one's experience in the *bardo*, however pleasant it may otherwise be. On Earth, beings from all the different rings walk down the same street and rub shoulders, and the resulting friction of values, priorities, and capacities creates a fertile mix that encourages us to become more than we now are.

If we follow this line of thought to its logical conclusion, we can begin to appreciate why intense suffering represents something of an anomaly in the bardo. It is not that the *bardo* rules out the possibility of these self-generated exercises of self-confrontation and purification, but *the self-generated condition of postmortem existence actually seem to discourage them.* Why would someone enter a condition of extreme suffering in the *bardo* if they didn't have to? To do so voluntarily would reflect an unusually refined awareness of the treasures lying beyond one's immediate reach and a rare commitment to seizing them. Suffering is something the ordinary person instinctively avoids, and it requires a rather advanced understanding of the dynamics of spiritual transformation to freely embrace the ordeal of self-purification. We can understand if most persons would choose to pursue their evolutionary climb through the slower, more circuitous route of rebirth.

Understanding the Differences

If we place the work of Monroe and Grof side by side, we note, first, that Grof's paradigm includes the full range of contact with extraphysical beings that Monroe describes. Grof discusses contact with deceased individuals, for example, in *The Adventure of Self-Discovery* where he presents two cases that yielded specific information about recently deceased persons that was subsequently verified.

In one of these cases, a subject in a psychedelic session became aware of a discarnate presence who gave his name, the name of his parents, their address and telephone number, and asked that his parents be contacted and reassured that he was doing fine. A phone call later confirmed that a son by this name had died just three weeks before. Elsewhere Grof discusses contact with spirit guides and with life forms that appear to be from parallel universes.[13] His survey of transpersonal experiences, however, includes a wide range of phenomena that do not show up on Monroe's screen at all.

In Monroe, for example, there is no hint of the species-mind that we saw registering so strongly in chapter 3. In his account, the points of light that represent separate souls, though clairvoyantly porous to each other at higher levels, never congeal into a unified field of awareness. In psychedelic experience, on the other hand, the inhabitants of the rings, instead of existing as separate points of light, sometimes merge into luminous strands that appear to form the sinews of massive forms of intelligence, described here as the species-mind, or the Gaia-mind that cradles the species-mind. It is as if the rings can organize themselves into different configurations in response to different catalysts and, in fact, this is exactly what I think happens.[14] Furthermore, psychedelic subjects frequently experience realities that are superordinate to the rings, such as the archetypal architects of creation. By contrast, the power or forces responsible for creating spacetime remain outside Monroe's purview. The Inspecs describe their function as being to improve the learning curve of human experience, but they report that they did not create the garden they are tending. The creator of the garden and the means through which the garden was created are not discerned.

The key to understanding these differences in transpersonal disclosure once again lies in understanding how psychedelic therapy and out-of-body work affect consciousness over the long term. As one engages the perinatal matrices in psychedelic work, the roots of our private existence are brought into conscious awareness. As one purgatorial crisis after another is navigated, pieces of our conditioning fall away. When one moves into a transpersonal state of consciousness after such a therapeutic melt-down, the experiences that crystallize around one reflect this increase in freedom. A less constrained observing consciousness draws forth a more expansive experience from the fertile transpersonal ground. As ego is gradually weakened, the trans-egoic structures of existence come more easily and naturally into view. I use the metaphor of sight here, but in these sessions one learns not by seeing but by becoming. It is *education by participation.* The dynamic is the same as we saw operating in Monroe; the difference lies in the intensity of the purification orchestrated by psychedelic therapy and the corresponding depth of deconditioning realized.

As mind slowly empties itself, nature undresses herself. Genuine transpersonal disclosure at the subtle level of existence occurs in spite of the fact that not all egoic constrictions have been surrendered and precisely because they have not been surrendered. That is to say, if ego were completely expunged in the beginning, I suspect that one would skip the psychic and subtle dimensions altogether and "move" directly into the formless causal realm. Thus, it is only because these residual structures are still present in the psyche to some degree that we learn something about the mechanisms operating at these cosmological levels at all. These structures will organize our experience in pervasive ways that will be difficult to detect and that may become apparent only in later sessions when one's system has undergone even further purification. If one accepts the partial and perspectival nature of one's participation in these realities, one can learn a great deal about how reality is organized at these levels.[15]

Monroe's narrative reveals the softening of boundaries that occurs in transpersonal states, but the boundaries never disappear from his account. If the species-mind or other "broad bandwidth" phenomena did not register in his experience, I think it is ultimately because his mind, as expansive as it was, was too structured by egoic patterns for him to participate in these levels of reality. Here egoic consciousness has no functional role all. Monroe saw the vertical dimension of consciousness that gives the psyche its great depth, but he did not see the great expanse of Sacred Mind. The connections that link us together into larger operational units, and eventually into a single field, are missed. In order to experience these inclusive fields of being, one must first surrender one's private being. Thus, the greater suffering in Grof's paradigm is directly tied to its greater disclosure, for this suffering is simply the fleeting pain of surrendering our smallness as we open to the larger being that we are.

Grof has generously illustrated the many textures of transpersonal experience, but the way he organizes his material does not lend itself to illustrating all of the dynamics operating in these exercises. For example, by separating perinatal experience from transpersonal experience and discussing them in separate chapters, the organic connection between the cleansing phase of a session and its ecstatic phase is disrupted. Insights into how progressive clarification at the perinatal level is reflected in deepening transpersonal disclosure have been set aside in favor of other concerns. Furthermore, in presenting a comprehensive typology of transpersonal experience drawn from thousands of subjects, he does not delineate the progressive stages of unfolding beyond the fourfold perinatal movement. Similarly, the intimate way in which breadth and depth unfold together is sacrificed as part of the fine grain of psychedelic work that is not represented.

As a complement to Grof's inclusive approach to presenting these states, therefore, I would like to stay with my own experience to illustrate the collective fields of experience that are missing in Monroe but which are a frequent component of psychedelic work. I do so not because my experiences are in any way unique in this respect but simply because following one person through the multiple layers of the hologram brings out the continuity of progression. If there is any epistemological validity to these experiences, it lies precisely in the fact that they are *not* unique, and this demonstration rests upon their essential congruence with the broad database that Grof has established.

In the interest of efficiency, the following narrative is a composite drawn from sessions 24 through 28, which took place over nine months. These sessions deepened the theme of the second tier of healing introduced in chapter 3 and began to distinguish different levels of archetypal reality—one being the morphic field of species memory and the second being the creative archetypal level. Moving beyond this second level revealed a field largely devoid of form altogether but saturated with transcendental clarity. Immersion in this field then brought into clearer focus a web of "mind-fields" that underpin physical existence.

Sessions 24–28

Within a context of deep serenity and love, I began to experience pain, and I saw that the pain was not about dying or biological birth at all but about reliving one's entry into physical existence itself. More broadly, it had to do with the trauma of spirit being born into matter in some collective sense that was larger than my individual identity. Later in the session the direction of the birthing process was reversed. At this level what was happening was that "I," again in some collective sense, was being reborn back into spiritual existence. I was reversing the process of being born into matter by being reborn back into this preexisting, nonphysical world.

The pain deepened and broadened for a long time. It again breached the boundaries of history, and I saw more clearly than before that this suffering could only exist in some domain that gathered the experiences of humanity in some collective embrace. I had a clearer sense than in previous sessions that I was not experiencing multiple, discrete historical epochs so much as a domain that was once-removed from temporal experience. As always there were millions of persons involved and tens of thousands, even hundreds of thousands of years. The suffering was enormous. Any attempt to describe it would simply become a repetition of extremes.

Although the suffering was worse than in previous sessions, there was also something new present. The pain had begun in love and I was shown in the beginning that it did not represent a rupturing of love but was itself an expression of this love. Being born into spacetime, even the very birth of spacetime itself was an expression of unshakable divine love. This love was like a faint halo surrounding the pain that I would sometimes be aware of and sometimes lose. I began to sense that by consciously experiencing this pain as an expression of divine love, I could transform it. Humanity had endured all this suffering without realizing why it had done so. By re-experiencing the pain knowing that it was part of a creative impulse rooted in transcendental love, some small part of the species was being healed. I realized that the more pain I could take in, the more healing I could mediate. At that point I began to embrace the suffering, to actively seek it out and take in as much of it as I could. Pain became my ally.

It is hard to describe how one can reach out and absorb suffering of this magnitude. It was as though I could open and take in the pain of whole groups of people, of whole collective endeavors, of wars and rebellions, of droughts and social upheaval. As I did so, the sweep of the pain kept getting larger and larger, reaching deeper into human and prehuman history. The process kept accelerating until it reached an unbelievably frenzied pitch. It became a feeding frenzy. Enormous energies were involved. Eventually these energies reached such gigantic proportions that the sensation became one of frenzied power rather than pain. I had moved into a state of ecstatic power feeding on the pain of the planet.

Eventually I found myself slowly emerging from this mayhem. Still surrounded by the chaos, I began to see a larger world beyond it and to sense the atmosphere of transcendence. To enter this world again filled me with delight, exhausted relief, and reverential awe.

The feeling tone and texture of this level was completely different from what had preceded it. It was ancient, archetypal, and extremely powerful. It felt more inherently "alive" than spacetime. I saw powerful forces that I knew were the living forces driving physical existence, but their forms were felt more than seen. Visually they resembled massive galactic displays, something akin to the majestic sweep of distant galaxies spinning through deep space, but this is only an analogy. I saw deeply into the fact that events in spacetime echoed the intentions of these beings. Somehow it was THEY who were living and working through the collective patterns of human history. It was THEY who were loving through the embrace of thousands of Romeos and Juliets across the planet. Living forces too different from me and too foreign to grasp accurately, I could only catch glimpses of their mode of being. Ancient. Huge. Panoramic in scope. Celestial but facing earth. Creating through humanity. Living through humanity. Satisfying themselves through humanity. The world of Cosmic Archetypes.

The energy generated through my embrace of collective suffering had carried me into this pre-existing archetypal domain and here it continued to build to unbelievable extremes. The energy formed currents that looked like rivers of liquid fire—white-hot lava but more supple, exploding sun flares but more controlled. Usually these currents surrounded me in displays of extraordinary power and beauty, but several times I was drawn into them. The liquid fire poured through me, completely consuming and transporting me. There is no experiencing these things without being changed at the core.

After some time at this level, things changed again. What happened is hard to describe. Everything around me began to spin and become very confused. I grabbed onto some focus at the center of this cyclone and held on. I was not resisting the change, but was holding still so that the change could happen to me. It was like being in the center of a tornado, at the center of an exploding sun. The energy moving through me was enormous. This archetypal meltdown was tearing things away from me, burning things out of me. Eventually I began to realize that I was being transported to an entirely new reality still. The walls of the energy tornado were melting away, and sparkling through on the other side was a different experiential field.

Breaking through to this level carried with it a sense of supreme accomplishment. The most distinctive feature of this field was its extraordinary clarity. It was infinitely spacious, infinitely extended, saturated with intelligence, and clear. Clear beyond imagination. Suddenly I appreciated as never before how much the human mind-field constitutes a constant background static to our individual minds. Somehow I had moved beyond the species-mind, and here I experienced being conscious in a completely new manner. I was clear. I was as I was meant to be. I opened myself and embraced this realm and was embraced by it. I cannot describe the enormous sense of release.

Having reached this region of incredible clarity, I was not carried deeper into the transcendental side of things but instead was directed back into spacetime, but now experienced from a completely different perspective. I was experiencing it not as I had previously experienced it through the physical senses but as the interplay of what, for want of a better term, might be called quantum mind-fields. By restricting ourselves to physical sensation, we actually experience a very small fragment of the total reality of spacetime. In my current condition I was experiencing the interlaced mind-fields that saturate physical systems and weave them together into larger collective systems. This phase of the session opened with a moving experience of collective healing.

I was on an African plain where hundreds of natives were dancing a dance of celebration. (I have no idea why this particular culture was selected.) The lions were far away, there was no danger, there was food and no one was hungry. The tribe had survived the rigors of life for another year and they were dancing their thanks. They were dancing their celebration of life. This was an extraordinary sensation. I was able to take in the experience of these many people whole. I was the tribal mind reveling in celebration. Their infectious joy and dance-induced ecstasy blended them into a single field of celebration. They knew what was happening, and they kept giving themselves over to the process, letting it deepen and deepen until they were completely awash with the unifying joy of their tribe, the plain, the earth, etc. They were one with themselves, each other, and their environment. I had never experienced anything like this before in my life, this melting into a communal embrace, and it was profoundly moving. How impoverished we are that we have lost these rituals that activate the deeper weave of our interconnectedness.

My reference point for experiencing all this was an intelligence that saturated everything—the people, the animals, the fire, the Earth itself. If I had to name it, I would call it Earth Consciousness. I discovered that not only did this celebrating dance heal the tribe— cleansing them of the pains of the year's losses and setbacks and healing the frictions of interpersonal conflict—it also, much to my surprise, healed the Earth itself. I actually experienced a release of energy that healed not only the tribal mind-field but the energy field of this geographic region.

As I was experiencing the melting into the unified field of these people and their surround, I was also experiencing a truth about myself, a truth that would be repeated many times in many forms. In the physical world we experience membranes encapsulating our bodies and know life from within these membranes. Now, however, I was experiencing fields of consciousness that run through and unite physically discrete forms. There were many interlaced fields. The tissues of these fields were differentiated but seamlessly intertwined. Many layers of intelligence were active simultaneously. Just as a human being shares his or her biological existence with many different types of smaller life forms whose lives are intertwined around one's own, so at the mental level there are many larger life forms around whose lives we are intertwined.

In this context I witnessed many patterns in society as a rippling of the species-organism at the transindividual level. Like a scientist who can focus his or her microscope at different levels of a tissue, I could focus my vision at a deeper-than-individual level of society. At this deeper level, collective patterns suddenly jumped into focus. They had always been there but had been undetected because I had not been focused at that level. Now that I saw them, I was able to see how certain dynamics in society represented coordinated influences from deep within the collective psyche. I clearly saw patterns of change rippling through society as archetypal forces reaching up through the experience of the species as a whole. In this context I saw that individuals whose lives resonated with the archetypal elements active in any given historical period would be particularly sensitive to and responsive to the dynamics of these themes moving through society.

We are taught that the thoughts we experience arising within our individual awareness are our private creations, but this is not true. Many of them are not "ours" at all but are simply the registering in our localized awareness of a collective thought that is arising in some part of the species, a thought that has been initiated at a collective level of intelligence. These unfamiliar thoughts pass through us, tugging at our awareness, and we dismiss them as a passing mood or an idea that did not make much sense at the time and let it go at that. We think our mind is bound by our physical senses, but it is not. I experienced clearly that the individual and collective energies of everything that surrounds us creates a collective net of influences that flows through our conscious and unconscious awareness. We do not usually notice the subtle distinctions in the many fields that together create the flow of our awareness, yet in my current state I could clearly distinguish their distinct patterns of vibration.

This was the interpenetrating tissue of manifesting intelligence. These fields of energy that are porous to surrounding vibrations are brought into focus by our individual body-minds, but they are not

*confined there. The body / mind lives a few years, but its field endures
as a cell in a still larger field. My body / mind would end, but another
would materialize to take up where it left off. In this way my individual energy field would grow and evolve as the larger field I am part
of grows and evolves. No absolute boundaries in either space or time.
Only the blending tissues of fields of porous energy with many levels
of intelligence running through it all.*

Repeated immersion in fields such as these slowly melts our deeply
ingrained habit of thinking of mind in categories derived from physical experience. Specifically, it melts our habit of experiencing our inner, spiritual being as a private soul. Whatever organizational
pattern the soul represents, it is a porous reality. If sufficiently
pressed, the soul-pattern will explode to reveal these vast, inclusive
fields of consciousness that constitute the deeper patterns of existence, patterns that lie beyond the soul. The atomistic soul is simply
too small a concept to bring to these vast fields of mind.

To those who have experienced these dimensions of the deep psyche, our sensory-based culture looks as out of balance as a civilization that refuses to allow itself the joy and wonder of seeing the
night sky. It lives in a state of denial, rejecting half its natural existence and exhausting itself in relentless consumerism. Withdrawing
behind locked doors every sunset, our civilization comes out only after the sun has hidden the larger context within which life takes
place. But the sweet night will not be denied and each year draws
closer. The future is tumbling in upon us almost faster than we can
keep up with. The pace of discovery taxes us all, including the discovery of our capacity under repeatable conditions to enter transpersonal states such as those described here. We are only just beginning
to learn to think in terms of the holistic paradigm that these experiences imply. Richard Tarnas describes our challenge well when
he writes:

> The Western mind must be willing to open itself to a reality
> the nature of which could shatter its most established beliefs
> about itself and the world. *This* is where the real act of hero-
> ism is going to be. A threshold must now be crossed, a thresh-
> old demanding a courageous act of faith, of imagination, of
> trust in a larger and more complex reality; a threshold, more-
> over, demanding an act of unflinching self-discernment.[16]

This is the task we take up in part III.

Part III

The Field Dynamics of Mind

Chapter Six

Beyond Personal Karma

> When something happens here at point A which touches upon or affects the collective unconscious, then it has happened everywhere.
>
> —C. G. Jung, *Letters*

One of the fundamental insights to emerge in the twentieth has been the discovery that no single part of life can be comprehended independently of the systems in which it is embedded. Physics taught us this when it showed us that matter is pure process, that its most basic "parts" are not parts at all but sets of relationships, that underlying the stability of the visible world is an invisible dance of energy in which particle-patterns flicker in and out of existence, moving back and forth between spacetime and a more fundamental implicate order (Bohm) or quantum vacuum (Laszlo). For a time the sheer invisibility of the quantum realm buffered us from the full implications of these breakthroughs. Mainstream philosophy and psychology took refuge from the holism and indeterminacy of the quantum domain in the determinism of the molecular world where separate "things" are an obvious reality and local effects predominate. Though intellectually unsatisfying since the 1930s, this false sense of security has now been undermined by chaos theory, for this new branch of mathematics has shown us that the macro-realm we walk around in is no less interconnected than the micro-quantum realm.

Other disciplines are concurring. Process philosophy has articulated a metaphysical vision in which the notion of an enduring self has been dropped altogether. Feminist writers have persuasively argued that the concept of an atomistic self is an inherently masculine creation that contrasts sharply with what some have called the "connective self" that flows more naturally from women's experience. Meanwhile, the science of ecology has shown us that the postulate of existential separation is at odds with everything we are learning about how nature actually works. In the natural world, living systems interpenetrate so profoundly that to isolate one species within this matrix is heroically difficult and ultimately misguided if it were to suggest that any of us would be what we are if we lived in a different eco-matrix.

While not wishing to overstate this convergence by collapsing the distinctions between these disciplines, that there is a pattern here seems clear enough. The seminal insight being articulated is the discovery that parts cannot be meaningfully isolated from the systems in which they exist. In the subatomic world of quantum mechanics and the macro-world modeled by non-linear mathematics, *all individual, particulate existence shows itself to be inseparable from its corresponding fields.* Individual pieces of life cannot be realistically isolated from their surrounding matrix. Not only is it impossible to do so except as a rough approximation, but at a deeper level it is misguided to attempt it. Our challenge at this point is to internalize this fundamental insight and firmly grasp the fact that what is true of the living systems that surround us is also true of ourselves in the deepest possible sense.

The concept of karma is central to the vision of reality held by the wisdom traditions of the East and is a fundamental concept for most transpersonal thinkers. Conventionally, karma is described as the principle of cause and effect that orchestrates the evolution of the individual toward the eventual realization of his or her inherent oneness with the whole of existence. And yet, if the separate self is a relative truth operating within the larger truth of interpenetration and holistic embrace, then the traditional concept of karma is deeply incomplete. If existence is truly united in the One, then we move as One not only at the end when this fact breaks into our conscious awareness but at every stage leading up to this point. If we are truly empty of a self-existent self (*súnyatā*), then there must be a sense in which every struggle we have taken on in our individual lives is part of the larger evolutionary development of the whole. And if this is so, then the customary exposition of karma is lopsided at the very least. By overemphasizing the story of the spiritual development of the individual, it tends to neglect the deeper story of the development of the species and fails to address the intimate way in which these two stories are intertwined. If this meta-story is not fully appreciated, the concept of karma will tend to be squeezed into the myth of individual enlightenment.[1]

The purpose of this chapter, therefore, is to rethink the concept of karma in light of the deepening experience of mind that unfolds in psychedelic states. In some respects we might also describe this project as a feminist revision of the concept of karma, for it resonates deeply with the feminist critique of patriarchal culture. Our religious vision of the last several thousand years has emphasized the forging of the individual in the karmic fires of history and has attended less to the collective karmic sinews that weave individuals into larger wholes that are simultaneously evolving. How different the history of the concept of karma might have looked if women had had an equal share in writing it.

Having said this, I also think that the essence of what follows is consistent with the teachings of our deepest spiritual traditions, though it presses its edges in new directions. Wherever the shell of self has been broken and Sacred Mind exposed, the field dynamics of collective karma have been recognized. In Vajrayana Buddhism, for example, one is said to make progress toward spiritual realization by the practicing the "two accumulations," first the accumulation of karmic merit and then the accumulation of wisdom. Somewhat paradoxically, however, at the end of every spiritual practice in this tradition one gives away the karmic merit one has just generated in doing the practice, distributing it to all the beings who live in the various realms of the samsaric universe. One constantly empties one's karmic cup, so to speak, in order to drive home the lesson that there is no separate self here seeking enlightenment in the first place. One practices not to lift a private self out of ignorance, but to lift all existence. To grasp this fact is to grasp the true condition. Thus, the highest motivation for spiritual practice is said to be *bodhicitta*, universal compassion, which unites merit (the power generated by good activity) and wisdom (living free of the illusion of separate existence).

And yet, Buddhism, and Eastern thought in general, has viewed the bulk of humanity as so mired in karmic illusion that it has considered it to be incapable of spiritual liberation en masse. Accordingly, it has tended to focus its greatest efforts on the liberation of the comparatively few in each generation who are capable of undertaking serious spiritual training. These few will continue to work for the good of the whole even after their death, voluntarily returning to earth as *bodhisattvas*, but the final liberation of all sentient beings from the samsaric mind-set is seen as lying so far off in the future that it is seldom discussed. As a result, in these traditions the story of the heroic ascent of the individual tends to overshadow the story of the ascent of the species, and the relationship between the two is seldom addressed. The details of how collective karma actually works are not explored or presented in any detail.

Because the transpersonal movement has historically been deeply influenced by Eastern spiritual thought, it is not surprising that this habit of thinking in terms of individual spiritual development has been carried over and shows up in many transpersonal writers. In part II we saw that while Grof described the death-rebirth sequence as culminating in the discovery that one is much more than the individual self, his discussion of the impact of this discovery consistently focused on the individual and did not address the larger systems that the individual is part of. We also saw that NDE researchers missed the collective import of frightening NDEs because they were still thinking in person-centered categories and that Robert Monroe kept the story of spiritual discovery essentially at the soul-level of individual awakening. These authors are simply reflecting our conceptual habit of isolating the individual from his or her context and subtly asserting the spacetime dualities that dissolve at deeper experiential levels. We have a deep residual tendency to experience ourselves as separate from the larger fabric of life and therefore to think in terms of "units" that have only provisional existence. Even the work of Ken Wilber, who appreciates in theory the interplay between the individual and the collective, is lacking on this score. Wilber describes how the slowly evolving group consciousness is the platform from which individuals push off in their spiritual practice and which in turn is uplifted by their efforts, but the story is told with an insufficient feeling for either the true intimacy of the process or the true cost.[2]

The metanarrative of spiritual awakening must be broadened. Transpersonal thinkers must extend their analysis beyond individual persons and begin to address the larger systems that persons are part of. *We must learn to think in terms of the encompassing patterns that emerge in transpersonal experience itself.* We must find our way to a new vocabulary that allows us to describe the dynamic of spiritual awakening from the perspective of the unified reality that is awakening, while not losing sight of the individual. To address the issue of karma and the species-mind is, I hope, one step in this process.

Setting the Categories to Be Used

Karma is the generic name given to the conditioning of our mind-stream, and I propose that we distinguish between the *temporal* and *spatial* aspects of this conditioning. For the purpose of this exercise, let us think of ourselves as existing at the intersection of time and space, conditioned by forces that reach us through both these dimensions. Though completely integrated in reality, they can be isolated conceptually in order to articulate more precisely our inner experience. Thus I will speak of the temporal and spatial *vectors* of our mind, by which I mean the temporal and spatial conditioning of our mindstream. "Mindstream" is itself a metaphor that reflects a bias toward the temporal vector, for the term emphasizes movement in time. The term "mindfield" might be a more suitable metaphor for the spatial vector, as it suggests omnidirectional spatial extension.[3]

I believe that most transpersonally informed persons today are reasonably familiar with the workings of the temporal vector of mind. Because of the growing acceptance of reincarnation, either through contact with Eastern thought, Ian Stevenson's research, or clinical studies in past-life therapy, many of us have grown accustomed to thinking of ourselves as life forms that exist across enormous tracts of time. Indeed, what most people mean by "karma" is precisely the conditioning that reaches us through the vector of time. But there is a second mode of karmic conditioning that reaches us not through time but through space. To see it we need to look not "vertically" through time but "horizontally" through space, at life as it is spread out around us. As we turn in this direction, we begin to recognize that *our minds are part of an extended web or field of consciousness composed of all the beings who are simultaneously sharing this present moment.* Less recognized than temporal karma, the karmic conditioning that reaches us through this spatial vector is just as real and just as important to understanding the human condition.[4]

Another way to make the distinction between temporal and spatial karma is to say that the concept of the soul that often accompanies reincarnation theory, especially in popular thought, heals the fragmentation created by time but *perpetuates* the fragmentation created by space. With the concept of rebirth our sense of identity is enormously expanded in time, with our egoic identity yielding to an encompassing soul-identity that integrates all our incarnations. If we stop here, however, we will not have escaped the conditioning of spacetime. We will simply have taken the experience of spatial discreteness into transpersonal theory and created the myth of the individual soul, a temporally extended but spatially constricted reality. We will still be caught in the astral mirror that is simply reflecting back to us the spatial dualism of physical existence.

In what follows I want to take advantage of the fact that we are more familiar with the workings of the temporal vector and use this familiarity to begin to illumine the workings of the spatial vector. I want to suggest that we use what we have learned about how karmic conditioning works across time to begin to articulate how it works across space. We will not reach any closure in this exercise but will simply be making a start on learning to think in this new direction. Toward this end, I want to begin by reviewing a few points about the workings of karma in the temporal dimension and then import these insights into a description of its operation in the spatial dimension.

The Temporal Vector

As past-life therapists have demonstrated in multiple volumes, our former lives constitute a dynamic field of influence on our present awareness. The causal patterns that arch through time are increasingly easy to trace in clinical settings.[5] What is considerably more difficult is deciding how we should conceptualize this influence. Should we think of our past as a kind of impersonal momentum registering in our unconscious (as karma is often described), or should we think of it as a collection of still vital agents with whom we are in unconscious contact, as former lives still existing in the *bardo*? If we choose the latter, should we see ourselves in dialogue with many beings at once or with a single awareness (the soul) that integrates all these lives and speaks with one voice, albeit with different accents from time to time?

These questions are far from being resolved by reincarnationist thinkers and may yield different answers at different stages of a person's development. As difficult as they are to solve, however, they cannot be avoided once we accept the temporal depth of our minds. Once we open to the fact that our mind's experiential "age" exceeds the age of our current body, we have no alternative but to ponder these issues. Our present personality is drawn from this larger field of experience. Specific pieces of a larger past have been woven together into the composite that we now are. These pieces were once parts of other composites, and before that other composites still. The soul is constantly sending out new combinations of itself, reaching out to become more than it was, challenging itself in new ways, and sometimes suffering the fragmentation that accompanies experimentation.

If one undertakes a form of therapy that uncovers one's former lives in a systematic manner, different aspects of one's karmic lineage tend to stand out at different stages of one's work. In the beginning, what often stands out are the former lives themselves. As one confronts one's former lives and becomes familiar with the historical details of their existence, it is as if one suddenly inherits, for better or for worse, a bunch of eccentric relatives one never knew one had before. What makes them eccentric is simply the fact that they're all dead and they're all you. As these lives are worked with, however, and integrated into one's present consciousness, a shift often occurs. What begins to stand out at this point are the streams of karmic causality that weave these many lives into a single developmental river. These karmic streams are often experienced as being larger and more basic than the specific lives that have contributed to them. One's desire to create beauty, for example, is larger than the several incarnations that may have fanned this flame. Similarly, the hunger to understand the universe is more basic than the multiple lives that may have fueled this hunger. One can picture these overarching karmic patterns as streams of energy weaving themselves in and out history, crystallizing in different forms in different centuries.

While the first gestalt emphasizes one's former lives as points of integration of these streams, the second gestalt emphasizes the continuity of the causal river itself. As the second gestalt replaces the first, one's previous lives tend to lose their solidity, their stand-aloneness, and begin to dissolve into the more fundamental patterns of energy that gave birth to them. They do not dissolve in the sense of disappearing altogether, but they become porous to encompassing currents which arch through time. They can still be resurrected, but their forms tend to become *transparent* to these larger patterns of energy.[6]

Some reincarnationists believe that our future lives exert an influence on us that is just as real as the influence exerted by our past lives. They hold that it is only the resistance of our cultural indoctrination that prevent us from recognizing that our future "draws us" as tangibly as our past "pushes us."[7] Others believe that in order to preserve free will in the present, the future must be kept open-ended. We have a great deal of evidence of influence from the past, they observe, but evidence of influence from the future is far sketchier. Fortunately, it is not necessary for us to solve these problems, because what is important here is only that we sharpen our appreciation of *the dialectical relationship that exists between our present consciousness and a larger temporal stream*. While we are clearly more familiar with influences that reach us from the past, I suggest that we leave open the possibility of influence from the future and represent an individual's previous and future lives as a series of dots on a vertical line that represents time, with the center representing the present. The karmic streams running through these lives can be represented by a series of curved lines connecting all the dots and pointing toward the present.[8]

Whatever position we take toward future lives, as we open to the temporal depth of our being, we cannot help but become more sensitive to the paradoxical both/and quality of our present condition. We are both our present incarnation and, in a less obvious but just as real sense, we are also the former lives that have given this life its

Figure 6.1

shape and content. We are who our body and personal history tell us we are, and yet we are also more, because the significance of this body and its history only comes into view when we place it in the larger context of our extended existence. Our sense of identity thus stretches to include both these aspects of our being. Our present form emerges out of the karmic momentum of our mindstream, which defines the challenges our life was designed to embody and which will receive our efforts when we are finished with this life.

Because of the both/and nature of our being, dialogue is the fundamental rhythm of our inner life. The more conscious we become of our historical depth, we more we begin to recognize that *there is a subtle inner dialogue constantly taking place within us.* This dialogue is the breathing in and breathing out of soul, a continuous trafficking between our present awareness and the historical depth of our being. Like a computer program that accomplishes its task by inconspicuously shuttling back and forth between RAM and the hard drive for the information it needs, we function by maintaining a continuous dialogue between our present body-mind awareness and our deeper soul-awareness.

The more keenly we discern the depth of history behind our every thought, the more paradoxical becomes our immediate condition. Our distant past impinges continuously on our present. The less conscious we are of its influence, the more it tends to structure our awareness automatically. Conversely, the more conscious we are of it, the more a sense of dialogue replaces linear conditioning, opening the way to the exercise of greater freedom in the present. Dialogue encourages communication, differentiation, integration, and greater freedom of choice. Attending carefully to our stream of consciousness sets in motion a process that slowly frees us from blindly repeating the patterns of the past.

In general, then, learning to live consciously in a reincarnating universe involves opening to a multitiered sense of identity that develops into a temporally expanded sense of self. The words "I" and "my" begin to take on an expanded temporal reference as we stretch language to describe the multiple levels found to be operating within our moment to moment experience. Careful distinctions between the present personality and the temporally encompassing soul-identity allow us to articulate inner processes so subtle as to usually escape detection. All the while our sense of identity is becoming increasingly porous. It does not become mushy or lose its shape, but rather is experienced as a transparent reality in continuous exchange with a larger field of awareness created by our previous life experiences. As our sensitivity to this exchange increases, our basic sense of identity shifts, becoming progressively deeper. While the danger of ego-inflation is always present, the ego claiming more and more experiences as its own, this is transpersonal pathology pure and simple. When contact with one's deeper past is healthily integrated, the ego is deflated, not inflated, because things that we had initially thought of as being "me" are now recognized as being merely a karmic inheritance. As with inherited money, it would be foolish to mistake our inherited traits as personal accomplishments, however much we are entitled to enjoy them. Rather than grow larger, our sense of self becomes lighter.[9]

In this way, reincarnation deepens our sense of identity by shattering the temporal boundaries of the self, and yet there is a distinct narrowness to this self. In this model, one's karmic lineage is the trajectory of a single entity moving in and out of time. If there were a dozen people in a room, there would be twelve distinct lineages present, perhaps intersecting at different points in history but always representing the evolutionary development of twelve separate beings. The concept of rebirth opens us to our historical depth, but to the extent that the reincarnating soul remains a solitary individual, it remains inevitably a small thing. However hoary with age the soul may be, *it is a cell devoid of a larger organ.*

The Spatial Vector

Thus we make the transition to the spatial vector, but this transition has not been easy for me personally to make. The habits of atomistic thinking were so deeply ingrained in me that when I first tried to describe the spatial vector of karma, I found it difficult even to say the words. It kept feeling as though I were speaking either heresy or sheer confusion. As we let go and experientially open to the spatial breadth of our being, a breadth that includes everything that we see around us, it feels like we are shattering our last piece of privacy. It is one thing to open to time which we can't see, but another thing entirely to open to the full complexity of space which we can see. At least the concepts of reincarnation and personal karma allow us the privacy of individual progress. If we open to the whole of humanity, it initially seems that we will lose ourselves entirely in the developmental currents of our species.

And yet something like this surrender is demanded by the collective experiences that regularly emerge in psychedelic states. Long before it is extinguished in Causal Oneness, the ontologically separate self is challenged by being repeatedly immersed in many permutations of collective awareness, such as those recorded in Grof's books. What needs to be emphasized here is that these collective or transspatial experiences are not simply temporary states but rather are profound encounters with the being one always is. These glimpses awaken us to the larger being we are at this and every moment. After the shock wears off that contact with such collective fields of awareness is possible, the greater shock settles in as we realize that this contact is taking place *continuously* beneath our conscious awareness. The interlaced quality of our existence may move in and out of our attention, but it never ceases for a moment to be our functioning reality.

We can begin our exploration of the spatial dimension of karma by expanding the earlier picture of the temporal vector. Now the vertical line of time is intersected by the horizontal line of space. The dots of our past and future lives are now complemented by dots representing other members of our species sharing the present moment (and by extension other life forms as well). The lines of causal influence that enter our present awareness through time are now complemented by lines of influence that reach us through space, from the human species as a whole and from specific subgroups to which we are particularly connected. When one's present awareness is penetrated deeply in meditation or in psychedelic states, both these vectors of influence eventually come into view and are seen to contribute to our moment-to-moment awareness. Similarly, by reversing these arrows, we can represent the continuous flow of the karmic effects of our individual decision-making back into these fields.

The same both/and quality that we saw operating in the temporal vector of mind also characterizes the spatial vector. The same dialectic, the same intimate and subtle dialogue between our present consciousness and a deeper subjective ground emerges. Now, however, the dialogue is taking place not between the individual and his or her former lives but between the individual and the species. The expansion of one's sense of identity beyond egoic time into deep time repeats itself in the expansion of one's sense of identity beyond egoic space into the deep space of the species-mind. As we come to recognize the subtle patterns of interaction constantly taking place between ourselves and our kind, our sense of self again becomes more porous, but in a different direction. Our individuality does not become mushy, but rather transparent to the vast and subtle field of the species-mind, and what lies beyond the species-mind. (Though my discussion in this volume emphasizes the species-mind, our

Figure 6.2

spatial embeddedness does not stop with our species, of course, but extends to include the entire cosmological life process and all the life forms it has birthed.)[10]

It is not just experiencing the species-mind from many different angles that forces one to redraw the boundaries of one's identity, but experiencing *the detail of one's placement in that mind and the precise and subtle ways that one's individual life reflects this larger field.* The conventional exposition of karma emphasizes individual agency exercised over time. It stresses the fact that our present form emerges causally out of our deep past and that we alone are responsible for our condition. By emphasizing the temporal vector and individual agency, however, this account leaves out of the picture an equally important facet of karma, namely, that our individual choices take place within and reflect the general condition of the species-mind as well.

Our choices derive from and feed back into not only our individual soul's evolutionary trajectory but the evolutionary trajectory of our species via Sheldrake's principle of formative causation. The evolution of the individual is part and parcel of the evolution of the group and cannot be meaningfully isolated from it. Though we can appreciate the pastoral intent of spiritual traditions that emphasize individual responsibility and the refining of individual capacity over time, we must also recognize the imbalance created by any presentation of cause and effect that diminishes the lateral web of causal relationships that weave all of us into an integrated whole. A more rounded discussion of karma will seek to remove this imbalance by emphasizing the intimate participation of the species in the life of the individual and the individual in the life of the species.

The shortsightedness of overemphasizing individual karmic agency can be quickly appreciated if we try to imagine any individual problem in isolation from its larger cultural manifestation. Whatever problem we might be wrestling with, whether it be anger, greed, irresponsibility, addiction, fear, or even disease, our individual version of this problem is always part of a larger disturbance of the social fabric. It is difficult to imagine anyone who is hard pressed by a problem that is entirely personal, that lacks some larger societal dimension. The usual pattern, I think, is that our individual dilemmas crystallize and bring into focus larger patterns that exist within our species. When we are born into the world, we inevitably soak up, lifetime after lifetime, the social assumptions, cultural priorities, and community values of our historical setting. As children we draw them into ourselves, and they become part of our sense-of-self, part of who we experiences ourselves as being. As we grow up, we apply these values and priorities to our life circumstances and refine them by finding out what works and what doesn't work. We experiment with what should be dropped and what strengthened, and our experiment becomes part of our karmic legacy to our species. Even our physical diseases have collective dimensions to them. Many of our illnesses reflect the pathology of our collectively imbalanced lifestyles and the toxicity of our now omnipresent industrial environment. They also reflect the evolutionary limits of our species' collective inability to consciously control its biological processes, a limit that psycho-neuroimmunology has taught us can be shifted with training.

We can make this general point another way if we borrow vocabulary from chaos theory and say that *karma is a fractal phenomenon*. Fractal geometry has mesmerized us with its visual displays of self-similarity, that is, the repetition of detail at descending scales.

Commenting on the fractal geography of coastlines, canyons, and internal anatomy (with its repetitively branching veins and arteries), John Briggs and F. David Peat write in *Turbulent Mirror*, "The complex systems of nature seem to preserve the look of their detail at finer and finer scales. . . . Images from vastly different scales evoke a feeling of similarity and recognition."[11] What is true of the outer world also seems to be true of our inner life as well. Fractal images such as one finds in Briggs's wonderful book *Fractals: The Patterns of Chaos* are powerfully suggestive of the mysterious way that the individual's life reflects the constitutive karmic patterns of the species. In nonordinary states of consciousness, one sometimes experiences that what is large in the life of the species as a whole registers in the lives of its individual members, while what is karmically prominent in the lives of individuals reflects something prominent in the whole.

The karmic challenges we face and the blessings we inherit can be described from within *both* the temporal and spatial frames of reference, for these two perspectives are complementary. If described within the temporal frame of reference, the story of karma is one in which the individual inherits and advances the derivatives of choices made in his or her previous lifetimes. If described within the spatial frame of reference, however, the story becomes the story of the individual inheriting and advancing the derivatives of his or her species' previous choices. Viewed from this perspective, the individual appears to be a distillation of collective karmic currents. This is not an either/or choice, for *both these perspectives are true*. The collective norms of the group become the karmic context of our individual decision-making. The species-mind is the matrix within which our individualized agendas unfold. As karmic cause and effect crystallizes in our lives, therefore, it can be as seen as being both individual and collective, as simultaneously reflecting both the temporal and spatial dimensions of mind. Similarly, our responses to our karmic challenges generate an energy which flows into both vectors, echoing through time and space, affecting both our individual future and the future of our species.

Psychedelic Therapy and the Field Dynamics of Karma

These observations on the dynamics of karma follow immediately from combining Rupert Sheldrake's hypothesis of formative causation with the concept of karma and rebirth. As the mental field of the species, the species-mind both defines the edge of learning for each generation and integrates the learning of its individual members at a centralized level of awareness. This concept by itself seems to demand an immediate expansion of our usual way of thinking about karma. The line of thought developed in this chapter, however, is driven less by theory than by experience, though the convergence of experience and theory is welcome. Above all, it is the repeated *experience* in psychedelic states of the intimate symbiosis of the individual and the species that fuels these observations.

In chapter 3 I presented a series of psychedelic experiences in which we could discern two tiers of healing operating—one focused on the individual and a second focused on the species. These sessions suggested that the individual and the species are united in a symbiotic dance that is much more complex and intimate than we have generally appreciated. The boundary between the individual and the species gets progressively harder to identify as one moves deeper into the death-rebirth labyrinth. The healing of deep personal pain sometimes elicits a corresponding healing in the collective psyche. If this experience of symbiotic participation is repeated often enough, it eventually redefines one's frame of reference for the thinking about the problem of suffering. Instead of seeing "my" pain as existing separately from the suffering of "others," it becomes more natural to see it as a distinct nodal point within a collective field of suffering that runs throughout the species. Though this pool of suffering may register locally in our individual awareness, it lives as a much larger field within the species-mind. (The same applies to our positive qualities as well.)

An analogy from massage therapy may help illustrate this point. Massage therapists often work with "trigger points" in a muscle. These trigger points are points that collect and focus the toxins of a larger muscle group. It is as though the muscle is able to focus all its stress on one particular spot or series of spots. When a trigger point is pressed, a sharp pain is felt, followed eventually by a soothing heat that flows outward as the entire muscle begins to relax. The point of the analogy is that though the pain may register locally, it actually "belongs" to a larger field, and thus the release of that pain impacts the entire field.

Something like this is sometimes experienced very clearly in psychedelic therapy. At the death-rebirth level, personal pain can blend with collective pain so deeply that they cease to register as separate phenomena and are instead experienced as but different localized expressions of a single movement. Pressing into this pain and bringing it forward is both excruciating and profoundly liberating. One can feel actually that the pain involved comes from the collective and that the healing being generated is reaching into the collective through clearly defined channels. It is as though the species-mind has its own system of metameridians, similar to the personal meridians traced by acupuncturists on the human body. When one "presses down" on these collective trigger points in a session, the cleansing that occurs eventually transforms these karmic sinews into brilliant filaments of light. When restrictive conditioning is "taken into the light," these fibers are quite literally changed into pure light, and this light flows into the larger whole that the individual is part of. (This is the spatial counterpart to the experience of temporal healing that sometimes occurs in past-life therapy, when the karmic burden of multiple former lives is healed through the initiative of the present incarnation. Here, some small portion of the collective karmic burden of the species is being healed through the initiative of one of its members.)

We can take a different approach to spatial karma by returning to the experience of moving beyond the species-mind reported at the end of the previous chapter. At this high subtle level, one begins to confront luminous fields of clarity that become brighter and more intense as one's experience in this realm is gradually purified. Persons may experience this field differently. Some may respond most deeply to its love while others may feel most keenly its dynamic creativity. What has stood out for me is its extraordinary clarity—brilliant, luminous, diamond clarity. Even brief immersion in this reality completely reframes one's understanding of what incarnating as a human being actually involves. It is as though by moving temporarily beyond the field of the species-mind, one becomes sensitized to the species-mind's pervasive and distinctive "coloring" of one's consciousness.

From this luminous vantage point, what is collective in one's experience stands out clearly from what is idiosyncratic to the individual. One is instilled with a deep sense that in order to incarnate as an individual human being with a specific karmic script, one must first incarnate as a human being per se. *When one incarnates, one first takes on the group consciousness of the species at a particular point in its history, and only within that context does more individualized human experience articulate itself*. In ordinary states of consciousness these two levels of mind are so deeply intertwined that they are difficult to disentangle, but in nonordinary states of consciousness they can sometimes be clearly differentiated, with one standing out from the other as clearly as the solo instrument from the orchestra in a concerto.[12]

The threads of our individual life are part of the fabric of humanity, and this fabric has a life of its own with its own rhythm, needs, and aspirations. If the reader will indulge me, incarnating on Earth might be compared in this respect to enlisting in the army. If you enlist in military service, you are allowed to choose your area of specialized training. This choice is an expression of your individual preferences. However, you must make your choice from a list, and this list reflects the needs not of the individual but of the army, which has a life of its own with its own needs and goals. In order to fulfill its objectives, the army knows that in a given year it needs so many radio operators, heavy weapons specialists, nurses, and so on. The training you want may not be on the list at the time you enlist, or the available slots may have already been filled. Compromises may have to be made and individual plans adjusted to accommodate the larger interests involved.

The army's agenda is distinct from but obviously not completely separate from the agenda of its enlistees. The armed services require the voluntary participation of individuals to realize their ends, and the recruits require these larger organizations to realize their individual ambitions. Give and take is called for on both sides. The opportunities extended at one level and the choices made at another merge to form careers which hopefully serve the interests of both parties. The individual may leave the army at the end of his (or her) tour or re-enlist. If he re-enlists, the army he returns to will not be the same army he had previously enlisted in, and one of the differences will be the contributions he himself made to this institution during his prior enlistment. If most people's contributions are too small to register significantly on the status quo, the influence of individuals higher in the chain of command is more evident. Large or small, however, every soldier's contribution feeds into and affects the overall vitality and creativity of the organization.

If we bring these observations back to bear on reincarnation and karma, they can be used to illustrate how the conventional discussion of karma has generally neglected the pervasive feedback loops that sew us into the larger social fabric we are part of. The fact that we detach ourselves from and return to this fabric many times and that our points of entry are shaped by our points of exit ought not cause us to lose sight of the fact that while we are here, our form is given to us by humanity and our destinies are part of its collective evolutionary project. As long as we are "enlisted" in spacetime as a human being, our tour of duty serves the interests of both ourselves and the species as a whole.

As the collective unconscious becomes a consciously experienced reality, one begins to recognize that much in our life that we had taken to be "personal" actually derives from the collective field of the species-mind. To return to our analogy of the recruit, imagine that this soldier were to wake up one day having lost his memory of having enlisted. Unaware of how he came to be where he is, he simply accepts his circumstances without question and goes to his assigned job. Later, however, he begins to ask questions and eventually discovers how he came to be doing the job he is doing. As he becomes more conscious of his situation, he begins to reconstruct the complex series of events that have come together in his career. He goes to personnel and sees his signature on his enlistment papers, and so on. He remembers the string of choices he made as an individual and discovers the string of collective choices made by others, which have converged to create the conditions that his life now embodies. If he has a philosophical bent, he might even observe that there are, in fact, many "levels of reality" converging within his military career, and he would be right.[13]

We might push this analogy one step further. If our recruit comes to understand and accept the larger organization he (or she) is now part of and finds a meaningful life for himself there, he may even choose to place the army's needs above his personal needs. He may come to embrace a larger sense of identity by identifying with the collective good of this institution and the country it serves. Thus, he may be willing to sacrifice a great deal at the personal level in order to support and advance this larger good. Note, however, that in opening to this more "selfless" identity, the soldier advances the greater good through the medium of his individuality. He cannot serve the army by ceasing to be the individual that he is or by undermining his distinctive capacities. Rather, he serves the army best by (1) developing his individual abilities to their fullest capacity and (2) coordinating his activities with other individuals to collectively express a larger intentionality. From one frame of reference, one might say that his individuality has been extinguished, in the sense of ceasing to provide the sole motivational basis for his conduct. A more subtle reading, however, would be that his individuality has become transparent to a larger field of concerns. *The form of the self remains, but the life of the self has expanded exponentially.*

As we become increasingly sensitive to the multiple fields that combine in every human being's experience, the suspicion grows that the cumulative product of our life experience must be shared with all these fields. That is to say, we need to speculate that the learning that comes from the human experience is not like gold coins that must be in either your pocket or mine, but more like computer disks that can be duplicated and shared without loss or dilution. The purpose of this simple analogy is to suggest that we need to think more flexibly about who or what can retain and benefit from "our" life experience after our life is over. In chapter 9 I will argue for the existence of a true individuality that emerges from the death-rebirth process. If such an individuality inherits the learning generated in my present life experiences, why should this learning not also be inherited by other levels of the system I am now part of?

When we die, I think that our experience is retained both by the individual and the species-mind (and who knows how many other fields of nested intelligence). The sweat equity of our learning is not diluted by being shared. It is a wonderful if sobering thought that wherever we go after we leave here, whatever we become part of after we no longer choose to be part of this particular universe's exercise, the energy of our life experience will live within the collective experience of this species. Our personal victories in the short term will contribute directly to humanity's victories in the long term. William James expressed a similar sentiment when he said, "God himself, in short, may draw vital strength and increase of very being from our fidelity. For my own part, I do not know what the sweat and blood and tragedy of this life mean, if they mean anything short of this."[14]

It is strangely liberating to discover that some of the reasons that our lives are the way they are may not have as much to do with us personally as we thought, in the sense of simply being part of our individual karmic legacy, but are in some measure determined by the needs of others. It is invigorating to feel the larger landscape that we are part of. Though it opens the door to new forms of transpersonal pathology if handled poorly, it also gives us the opportunity to glimpse a larger, more genuine identity if handled well. Our lives *as they already are* fit into and express a larger pattern of evolutionary intent. Our foibles as well as our strengths are part of this larger design. There are causal sinews that run through us, that weave us into humanity and through humanity into Gaia and through Gaia into the pulse of evolution itself.

Collective Karma and the Problem of Suffering

Understanding the spatial or collective dynamics of karma opens new horizons for addressing the historically intractable problem of suffering. When one confronts a person who suffers deeply with only the conventional understanding of karma, one has little alternative but to end up speculating that somewhere in this being's past, mistakes must have been made that are registering only now. Even jettisoning the narrow interpretation of suffering as punishment and adopting a more benign reading that sees it as serving an educational function, conventional karmic theory inevitably leaves us wondering what possible mistakes this soul might have made in the past that are requiring such a harsh corrective in the present. When we confront the most heinous acts committed against the (apparently) innocent, however, this approach eventually falters. Sometimes there is simply too much pain in a person's life to see it as plausibly deriving from their former lives alone, even a long series of such lives. A new dimension to the problem of suffering opens when we begin to recognize that our lives reflect and embody collective as well as personal karma, and therefore that they may have the potential to beneficially impact whole groups of people.

At the center of this chapter is the conviction that psychedelic therapy merely intensifies and augments natural processes that are taking place more subtly in daily life in general. Thus, the symbiotic participation of the individual and the species that sometimes emerges so powerfully in psychedelic sessions merely dramatizes, I think, the ongoing interpenetration of the individual and collective mind operating in the population at large. If this is correct, then it is not just in extreme nonordinary states that our lives may connect with and bring forward pains that lie deep in the collective psyche, but also in the more subtle rhythms of daily living. As the Zen master Thich Nhat Hanh says in *Being Peace:*

> The kind of suffering that you carry in your heart, that is society itself. You bring that with you, you bring society with you. You bring all of us with you. When you meditate, it is not just for yourself, you do it for the whole society. You seek solutions to your problems not only for yourself but for all of us.

This gives us an entirely new perspective from which to view the problem of suffering. As long as human suffering is approached simply on an individual basis and not viewed collectively as part of the larger drama of the spiritual development of our species, we will fail to grasp the deeper story of humanity's struggle against its evolutionary limits taking place *inside* our very lives. We will tend to *overly personalize karma* and thus fail to recognize that much of the suffering we endure in life comes not just from personal failings but from *the unfinished state of the human condition itself*. We are living in a house only partially built; no wonder rain gets in. If we attend only to the case histories of individual karmic entanglement and disentanglement, then even when we can trace this sequence into the heroic breakthrough of enlightenment, we will miss the larger story of humanity's collective evolution and divinity's progressive involution into spacetime.[15]

Suffering is a very personal matter. I have several close women friends who were sexually and physically abused as children, and as I have pondered the problem of suffering through the years, their lives have been the measure of the adequacy of the answers I have contemplated. We all make mistakes, and though terrible mistakes may lie behind great suffering, I believe that this is too simple an explanation for the horrors that these individuals have endured in their lives. If we extrapolate insights derived from psychedelic therapy and apply them to everyday life, a different possibility begins to emerge. (The example of sexual abuse will be used to illustrate a general principle that can be applied to many forms of human suffering.)[16]

Fathers have been raping their daughters for countless centuries, and thus the pain of incest has karmically accumulated not just in individuals but in the collective tissue of the human psyche. This ancient pain now seems to be pouring into our collective awareness as part of the re-emergence of the feminine and the re-empowerment of women. It might help us understand the intensity of this modern epidemic if we consider the possibility that in it we are confronting the psychic injury of not just one generation of abused women but of *many generations summed*. The convulsions we are experiencing around this horror express, I think, the rising into our awareness of a pain that has been collecting for thousands of years. The cry we are hearing is the scream of children raped throughout history. If something like this is happening, then those who are carrying this injustice in their present life may be carrying the karmic burden of not simply their personal history but our collective history as well. The brutality they have personally endured may represent the surfacing of a much deeper wound. By forcing their abusers out into the open, they are bringing a long-denied justice to scores of invisible women. In healing their own lives, they are working to heal us all.

I have many times had the experience in psychedelic sessions that each one of us carries within us the collective diseases of our time. If our society is ill, each of us has a share in its illness, some more than others, perhaps, but we are all implicated to varying degrees. If our society is racist, sexist, violent, or consumed by greed, these diseases live in our collective soul. The cells of these cancers are distributed among all of us because our lives are the tissues that make up the psychic organs of the species-mind. And just as a disease that lives in a physical body may manifest itself by attacking one particular organ, a disease of our collective soul may manifest itself disproportionately in the lives of specific individuals. If it does so, the suffering that these individuals endure should be thought of as serving a collective project and not just an individual project. If we persist in pondering the riddle of suffering in terms of only personal karma, we will miss the larger pieces of the puzzle.[17]

If this seems to dilute our karmic accountability by asking "us" to shoulder responsibilities that rightly belong to "someone else" or, conversely, by letting "others" take over burdens that are rightly "ours," clearly that is not my intent. Remember that the same argument has been used in the past against the concept of personal karma. The habit of thinking in terms of incarnating only once made the justice of temporal karma hard for many Westerns to recognize at first. Why should "I" inherit problems left over from some "other" person's life, and why should "my" failings be foisted onto "another" who will follow me. The solution to this apparent injustice, of course, lies in deepening our sense of identity beyond our present incarnation until it expands sufficiently to include our entire karmic lineage. Only when we can *feel* the continuity across multiple lives that coexists with our incarnational uniqueness can we recognize the exquisite perfection of the system that we are part of. A similar expansion is required here, only this time the challenge is to expand our sense of identity beyond our individual karmic lineage to our collective karmic lineage. Here too, it is when we begin to be able to *feel* our fundamental oneness with the human condition in all its forms that a profound compassion begins to open in which a narrow, personal justice is exchanged for a higher order of justice that serves a larger good. When we can feel the continuity of our essential humanity coexisting with our irreducible uniqueness, we can then feel the higher octave of the same exquisite perfection.[18]

When we see great suffering, therefore, I think we are seeing one of three things: either a great sinner, a great saint, or a mixture of both. It is never possible to judge the blend, of course, but I think there are more saints among us than we have suspected. I wonder, for example, when a child is struck down by an incurable disease whether this might sometimes be the action of a great soul who has voluntarily shouldered this role in order to galvanize our collective determination to find a cure for this disease and thus free future generations from its threat. If persons are in fact working off "bad" karma in the narrow sense when they take on great suffering, I personally think they are seldom doing only this. We live in a century when the waters of the collective unconscious appear to be rising. As we will see in chapter 8, many ancient and modern voices have suggested that history is rapidly drawing humanity toward a decisive choice-point. Everywhere our individual efforts seem increasingly to carry the weight of our collective past. If this is the case, it is especially important at this time in history to understand how our individual lives reflect and advance larger evolutionary processes.

Chakras and the Species-Mind

Let me bring this chapter to a close by briefly suggesting a way of incorporating the concept of chakras into this discussion. The seven centers of consciousness known as the chakras are a well-established concept in spiritual circles, but as they are conventionally discussed, they tend to be viewed simply as the spiritual spine of the individual. From the base of material existence to the height of unitive consciousness, the chakras are represented as the psychic organs of the individual soul, the centers of awareness that integrate all our experiences from our present and past lives. The three lower chakras are said to anchor our individual physical existence (survival, reproduction, and power), the heart chakra our social existence (compassion), and the three upper chakras our connection to the universe as a whole (creativity, intuition, and oneness). While this description is correct as far as it goes, I don't think it goes far enough. Within deep psychedelic experience, the chakras sometimes appear to be the psychic organs not only of the individual but of the species itself. Furthermore, they appear to be the nodal points through which the experience of the individual and the species flow into each other in a precise and calibrated fashion.

This can be visualized by drawing upon the long history of imagining the chakras as spheres of colored light. Light is a vibratory phenomenon and the different colors of the chakras are often said to reflect their different rates of energetic vibration. As vibratory phenomena, the chakras tend to generate spontaneous resonances with other nearby chakra systems. That is to say, *it is natural for sympathetic resonances to occur between persons at chakra-specific frequencies.* This is obviously an oversimplified account of an extremely subtle and complex process, but the basic principle is straightforward. If you picture a room full of people and imagine the chakras as glowing orbs of light within each person, you might visualize these interpersonal resonances as lateral bands of colored light stretching horizontally across the room.

Research has demonstrated that persons meditating together tend to move into collective patterns of synchronized brainwave functioning. If we extrapolate these physiological observations to the subtle level, we can imagine an ideal situation in which all the heart chakras in a room, for example, could begin to move into deeper sympathetic resonance with each other until they eventually clicked into a stable pattern of integrated functioning. We might visualize this integrated condition as a plane of green light extending across the room at the heart level. (The heart chakra is traditionally pictured as green in color.) If this condition were sufficiently stable, it might begin to resemble a condition known in chaos theory as "phase lock." Phase locking occurs in nature when individual oscillating systems shift from a state of collective chaos to integrated resonance. For example, if individual cells from a chicken embryo heart are separated from each other, they beat erratically. If they are recombined one by one, when a certain number of cells are present, they spontaneously phase lock and begin to beat in unison. Another example would be the synchronization of women's menstrual cycles in student residences or other close living conditions.[19] Similarly, if the various chakras of a group of people were to enter into a sufficiently deep pattern of resonance with each other, they might phase lock to produce a highly integrated group consciousness. We might visualize this chakra-specific phase locking as horizontal planes of differently colored light passing through all the individuals present and integrating their individual awarenesses into a single metamind, if you will. The array of luminous chakras within each individual would move into resonance with the chakras of the other persons present to generate a rainbow field of energy representing the group mind.

I am not suggesting, of course, that this highly integrated state of energetic resonance always happens, but rather that *it is always trying to happen*. This is the important point. This capacity to enter into states of collective resonance is inherent in the life form that we are, though it is only slowly being recognized and its full potential can only be guessed at. The situation I have described of fully integrated chakra phase locking represents an ideal, the realization of a form of metaconsciousness that emerges when fields of energy become deeply integrated into a single encompassing field. The point is that this ideal is always trying to come into existence.

Clearly, we experience ourselves to be free individuals, capable of creating and recreating ourselves again and again according to our own choosing, and yet our creativity exercises itself within a living field that is composed of the pooled experience of our species. It draws from that pool and feeds back into it, and we can visualize this flow as a diastolic and systolic flow of light moving between human beings through our chakras. Being the vibratory phenomena that they are, our subtle systems are constantly reaching out and building energetic bridges with other persons, and they cannot help but do so. Our experience of the spatial expanse of our being may be weak and episodic, it may be sporadic and not well integrated, but the system we are part of is continuously reaching out to stabilize what is transitory, to make coherent what is incoherent. In psychedelic states, the fertile chaos that surrounds the shell of our private existence can sometimes reveal unanticipated orders of design. One discovers that our "private" intelligence is permeated by more inclusive fields of intelligence. Our "personal" feelings express vast pools of sentiment. Our "stream" of consciousness is fed by an ocean of awareness. We are only beginning to discover the layers of complexity that have been designed into us.

So far I have been speaking of the coalescing of individual energies to form a unified field of group consciousness, but what may come into acute expression for a small group is, I think, already operating in a more general way for the species as a whole. Any self-conscious attunement to each other takes place within the context of a more basic, unconscious attunement which is already established and which reflects our common evolutionary ancestry. This is the essence of Sheldrake's insight that we always exist within the historically conditioned soup of our species' collective experience. *Though we may become conscious of it only in exceptional states of consciousness, we are always processing at very deep levels the experience of the whole of humanity.* The concept of the collective unconscious suggests that we are already to some degree phase locked with each other, however unconscious we are of these connections. Indeed, our capacity to experience a consensual reality at all may involve a basic form of phase locking. The more we appreciate that our sensory experience of "the world" is imposed upon a shimmering dance of quantum energy at the subatomic level, the more we might legitimately suspect that our very perception of a common physical environment constitutes an extraordinary example of unconscious phase locking. If physical existence is in some essential respect a hologram, then something like phase locking might be allowing different persons to experience the same hologram from moment to moment.

There are many directions in which we might take these observations. They might help us understand why our inner experience shifts subtly in different group situations such as football games, karate tournaments, art exhibits, and spiritual retreats. They may help us understand why, as our spiritual practice deepens, we instinctively start to avoid certain kinds of assemblies while going to great effort to seek out others. We might discuss diffusion patterns, such as the consciously controlled resonance between a guru and disciple when giving *shaktipāt* or transmission for a spiritual practice, or the spontaneous contagion of a new idea rippling through a classroom as one student after another suddenly "gets it." Here, however, I want to bring this line of thought back to the therapeutic interplay of the individual and the species in psychedelic therapy.

If the reader will allow me the conjecture that the chakras function collectively as nodal points in the species-mind, we have another frame of reference within which to understand how an individual working on what first appears to be a personal problem might be drawn into the collective dimension of this same problem. Sheldrake has described the species-mind as a series of nested fields, each field reflecting specific groups that we are part of, such as family, local community, national community, ethnic group, and so on. Chakra theory might be a starting point for describing the organs that integrate these diverse fields into a unified whole. When a person is working at the perinatal interface in psychedelic therapy, the latent interpenetration of the group and the individual sometimes becomes manifest, and the usually hidden flow that unites them comes clearly into view. As already noted, when healing takes place at this level, the energy that is released can sometimes be clearly experienced as flowing out into the larger field of the species-mind. Chakra theory allows us to refine this perception by suggesting that these channels of flow are actually chakra-specific. The chakras are the nodes of the metameridians of the species-mind.

Eventually the dualism of self and species that this entire discussion has assumed becomes too clumsy a vessel for describing these transformative processes and yields to the simplicity of experiencing the entire process from the perspective of a completely unified, seamless field. When this happens, everything suddenly becomes much easier to grasp. From this deeper experiential perspective, it becomes clear that any understanding of this healing that focuses on any level subordinate to this unified field will be necessarily incomplete. In order to grasp the full ramifications of the dynamics operating here, we must expand our vision to see the larger organism being healed. Nature is concerned not only with individual incarnations but with souls, and not only with souls but with the human species as a whole, and not only with humanity but with the evolutionary project in its entirety. Each individual is cherished beyond measure, and yet our private efforts flow into a realization centered both within us and beyond us simultaneously. It is the awakening of humanity as a whole that is the current project of history; nothing less will satisfy the Creative Principle.

The field dynamics of mind show up not only at the macro-level of the species-mind but also in the smaller, transient groups that form within that mind. The collective intelligence in which we are immersed is continuously manifesting itself everywhere around us, once we give ourselves permission to see it. One of the areas of life where I have learned to recognize the signs of its presence is in the university classroom, to which we now turn.

Chapter Seven

Teaching in the Sacred Mind

If we are completely open, not watching ourselves at all, but being completely open and communicating with situations as they are, then action is pure, absolute, superior.

—Chögyam Trungpa

Sacred Mind is not a distant reality that surfaces only in nonordinary states of consciousness but the inner lining of everyday life. It is the unbounded awareness within which all individualized experience occurs, the living matrix within which minds meet and engage. The dynamics of Sacred Mind, therefore, are "hidden" in plain sight, but we fail to recognize them for two reasons. First, we habitually restrict our experience of mind to the nearby territory of ego and, second, our culture has not taught us to recognize the presence of this broader mental field, let alone how it functions. Because we are constantly taught that only individual beings have minds, we fail to recognize instances of transindividual mental functioning operating in our everyday life.

Once we have experienced the reality of Sacred Mind in nonordinary states, however, we cannot help but become more sensitive to its presence in everyday experience as well. Classically, this discovery is described as the awakening of the individual to the transcendental depths of experience. There is, however, a second dimension of this awakening, namely, the discovery of Sacred Mind alive within our everyday *collective experience*. Awakening inside Sacred Mind slowly sensitizes one to the fact that this Mind permeates every aspect of life. It is the medium within which we all exist, the mental field within which all minds meet. It is a living field with "sinews" and "fibers." It has "pockets" and "circles," "eddies" and "momentum." We must twist language to describe the undulations of the currents in which our lives are suspended.

I am a university professor, and outside of my spiritual practice, the most powerful context in which I have experienced the field dynamics of mind on a regular basis is in the classroom. It was in this setting that I slowly came to recognize that our culture's atomistic models of mind do educators a great disservice because they desensitize us to the subtler textures of the teaching experience. By failing to legitimate our experience, they obstruct our ability to understand what is actually taking place in our classrooms and thus stifle the full transformative potential of the student-teacher relationship. In this chapter I would like to describe how my students and I came to discover a deeper dimension of Mind alive within the everyday act of learning and to discuss some of the theoretical implications of this discovery. I hope this chapter will stimulate discussion of the transpersonal dynamics of teaching among educators. At the same time, I hope it will ground some of the theoretical discussion of previous chapters in a familiar piece of everyday experience.[1]

Transpersonal Pedagogy

There is a substantial literature on transpersonal psychotherapy, but as far as I know, little has been written on transpersonal pedagogy. This silence is striking. Educators are not yet discussing publicly the transpersonal dynamics of teaching or the potential of the classroom to trigger genuine spiritual transformation. Concerns for keeping church and state separate may be hampering this discussion in a society that still confuses spirituality with religion. And yet, as more teachers and professors take up deep forms of spiritual practice, it is increasingly important that these discussions begin because our individual evolution is intertwined with the evolution of those around us.

Research suggests that our individual mindfields interpenetrate the mindfields of those around us and, at a deeper level, that they emerge out of and remain connected to vast fields of collective intelligence. Our experience in meditative and psychedelic states is that as we move into deeper levels of awareness, we discover that our many lives are threads in a single, intentional fabric of complex design. There they are so tightly interwoven that they cannot be meaningfully separated from each other. These observations suggest that when one person begins to throw off the layers of illusion and recover his or her true and natural condition, surrounding persons will necessarily be affected. We can picture this if we imagine Sacred Mind as a large tablecloth spread out on a table. If we were to pinch the tablecloth at any one point and lift, the entire fabric is drawn up to some degree. Our spiritual ecology simply does not permit isolated realization.

As more teachers begin to actualize the deeper potentials of consciousness, therefore, we should expect to find resonances of clarity and cleansing spontaneously manifesting among our students. This will happen not because we have inappropriately assumed the role of spiritual mentor or guru but because of the *interpenetrating nature of mind itself* and the *contagious quality of clarified states of consciousness*. Furthermore, the deeper the natural connection between student and teacher, the more pronounced these resonances will tend to be.

Within the Newtonian-Cartesian worldview, teaching is conceptualized as the transfer of information between ontologically separate minds. Teachers pass along to their students the knowledge they have accumulated, or, if they are more gifted, they awaken their students' hunger for learning and then help them satisfy that hunger through a combination of readings, lectures, discussion, and directed research. Always, however, this exchange is conceptualized as taking place between separate minds. Information must be taken out of one mind, packaged in words or pictures, and projected to other minds where it is taken in, decoded, and assimilated into the store of information the students have collected in their previous courses. If all goes well and the transplant takes, they walk away with something growing inside them that wasn't there before. It is an unquestioned assumption of academic thinking that this exchange takes place between ontologically separate beings who are not connected in any way other than through physical channels. The perception that there are many separate minds housed within separate bodies is reinforced daily by the simple fact that the students don't know what the professor knows, that they have to work hard to learn what he or she has already mastered. And yet, from the perspective of nonordinary states, this undeniable fact of distance and separation is discovered to be not the final word.

Transpersonal experience shows us that beneath the levels of consciousness where our minds are separate and distinct are depths where they begin to interpenetrate until they eventually are enfolded within the undivided Sacred Mind itself. If we view teaching as an activity taking place within this Mind, our understanding of classroom dynamics begins to expand dramatically. In this context, teaching can be seen as an activity in which one part of Sacred Mind addresses another part of itself. There is no ontological gap, only a psychological gap which creates the appearance that we are separate beings. This different metaphysical starting point gives us a new context within which to view what takes place when minds "meet" in common cause in the classroom setting.

If mind is a field phenomenon, if it registers not only as our particle-like, sensory awareness but also as a wavelike, intuitive awareness that extends beyond our bodies, then teaching is more than just sending out information across an ontological chasm for students to catch. It is in addition *a direct energetic engagement of the mental fields of our students within the encompassing matrix of Sacred Mind*. It is mind directly encountering mind. Through this direct engagement, bridges of resonance spring into existence that support the exchange of information at the conscious level. Usually these resonances are so subtle that they pass undetected, like most of the operations of the collective unconscious. Under certain conditions, however, they can surface and make their presence consciously felt in the classroom.

For practically all the years that I have been a student of nonordinary states, using both meditative and psychedelic disciplines, I have also been a university professor. For most of my professional life, these two worlds have existed side by side in silence. As a matter of professional ethics, I did not talk to my students about my spiritual practice; and yet as my inner work deepened through the years, these worlds began to interact. My practice began to trigger noticeable and unexpected effects in my classes. It was as if, given the profoundly collective nature of my psychedelic work, my students were being drawn into my inner process, or I was being drawn into theirs. Completely ignorant of these dynamics in the beginning, I eventually realized that it was not possible to keep these two spheres of activity completely separate because mind is itself a field phenomenon that does not allow itself to be broken up into separate pieces. Because there is no such thing as an entirely private mind, there is no entirely private spiritual practice. Every practice emerges from and reaches into the extended fabric of Sacred Mind; it spreads out around us in circles, like ripples spreading across a pond's surface. Eventually the ripples became so pronounced in my classes that I had no other recourse than to begin to attend to them, both practically and theoretically. As I did so I began to realize that my students were actually verifying insights that had been emerging in my inner work about the participation of the collective in the life of the individual and the individual in the life of the collective. Furthermore, they were forcing me to learn how to manage the transpersonal dynamics of the classroom more effectively.

In this chapter I would like to share with you a brief outline of what my students have taught me about teaching. Everything that follows here comes from them and would not have occurred had they not been willing to invest their hearts as well as their minds in their learning. No teacher could ask for better students than I have had, and what they have given me is more than I can ever repay. We are only beginning to glimpse the collective dynamics of mind in educational settings, and every discovery leads to new questions. I hope that this exploratory overture will encourage increased discussion of these important issues among transpersonally-oriented educators.

I want to address primarily two themes here. Though presented separately, they are deeply intertwined. The first is the experience of spiritual resonance in the classroom—a particularly intense form of energetic resonance between teacher and student that emerges spontaneously and can generate powerful symptoms of kundalini arousal. The second is the hypothesis that individual classes have distinct morphic fields that can become a powerful influence in the classroom. I believe that one of the most important theoretical and practical challenges facing transpersonally informed educators today is learning how these fields operate, how to work with them directly, and how to manage the enormous energies that are sometimes generated when they are activated.

First, some background. I teach at an open-enrollment state university in northeast Ohio with about twelve thousand full- and part-time students, most of whom live at home and commute. Situated in America's heartland where the Rust Belt meets the Bible Belt, Youngstown State University (YSU) is a transpersonally naive campus. This naiveté, however, actually helps us from one perspective, because it underscores the fact that the resonances I'm going to describe operate for the most part unconsciously and independent of cultural encouragement. My students were not expecting what happened and neither was I. Other conditions also contribute to making YSU a most unlikely setting for the story I'm going to tell. With the collapse of the steel industry in 1978, Youngstown entered hard economic times. A dismal local economy, combined with the fact that these men and women are in many cases the first in their family to go to college, tends to make our students acutely career oriented.

Thus, courses in religious studies are usually seen as marginal to their "real" reason for being in college. These educationally inhospitable conditions are reinforced by local conservative religious traditions that in general have little use for meditation and transpersonal concepts in general.

On the positive side of the ledger, approximately one-third of our students are non-traditional age, which means that they are more seasoned than the typical college student. They have children and mortgages, and have often been through divorces, layoffs, and funerals. Non-traditional students have usually dropped the naive idealism of many traditional-age students and come to their courses better focused and with clearer objectives. As a result, they are often ready to vigorously engage the ideas of a course, and this intensity has an uplifting effect on the entire class. Furthermore, many of them have entered the middle phase of their life and are therefore naturally inclined toward deeper introspection. They tend to be willing to carefully re-examine their previous beliefs and make adjustments where warranted. With these students I study Eastern religions, psychology of religion, transpersonal studies, and comparative mysticism.

Transpersonal Resonance in the Classroom

In lecturing there is a moment that comes when a student has asked a question or when you are searching for just the right example to communicate a difficult concept to a particular group of students, with their distinctive capacities and limitations. There is a pause in the flow of your mind, a break in the continuity of thinking. These moments are choice points, opportunities for intuition to transform an otherwise predictable lecture into a lively improvisational exercise. A good teacher learns to enter these moments often, to reach deeply into the possibilities they present, and to use the inspiration that flows from them to do one's work more effectively. Through them the new and unprecedented enters the room.

When I first learned to enter these moments many years ago, I discovered a small door in the back of my mind. This door would sometimes open and through it slips of paper would be passed to me with suggestions written on them—an idea, an example, an image. I found that if I took the risk and used these gifts, something magical would happen. Something new and unexpected would come forth, the energy in the room would rise, and the students and I would move together in a creative direction instead of in a predictable loop. For five years I experimented with these moments, learning how to weave them into my lectures, how to integrate my prepared material with the novelty they unleashed.

Then about fifteen years ago, students started coming up to me after class when the room had emptied and they were sure no one could hear them and say something like, "You know, it's strange you used the example you did in class today, because that's exactly what happened to me this week." Once, for example, I was teaching a night class on Eastern religions and found myself taking a little unexpected detour in which I described someone who had had a precognitive intuition of his impending death. After class, an elderly woman came up to talk to me. She was not one of the usual students but a visitor brought by her friend who had felt she needed to get out of the house. Her husband had died three months before. He had owned a used car business, and shortly before his unexpected death, he had suddenly cleared out most of the cars from the lot and gotten all his financial affairs in order. Not long thereafter he and his wife were watching TV at night when he put down his newspaper and, in a way that was quite out of character for him, turned and said to her, "Darling, I just want you to know that if I died tomorrow, you've made my entire life worthwhile." A week later, he died in his sleep. This led to a long discussion of the challenges and opportunities his passing had created for her. After touching her grief, she got in touch with how overprotective he had been and how she was now being given an opportunity to develop herself in ways that his well-intentioned care had always prevented. She eventually came back to college, where she has thrived.

When these things first began to happen I was shocked, because I was completely unaware of making any paranormal contact with my students and certainly had not intended any. In fact, having always considered myself a psychic brick, I had thought I was incapable of it. Nevertheless, the trickle of such reports grew until these synchronistic "coincidences" became a not uncommon occurrence in my classes. My students were finding intimate pieces of their lives showing up in my lectures. Moreover, these pieces often hit sensitive points in their life or triggered substantive movement in a decision-making process they were already involved in, such as a career change or marital choice. The students also began to tell me that it was uncanny how often my lectures answered as if on cue questions they were feeling but were not asking. It was as if their souls were slipping messages to me, giving me hints on how I might reach them—telling me where they were hiding, where they were hurting, and, most importantly, what ideas they needed in order to take the next step in their development.

As you can imagine, these occurrences often affected the students deeply. When you take a class simply looking for four credits in the humanities and suddenly find the professor using your recent history to illustrate the point being made, it tends to catch your attention. Buried in the back of the room, safely anonymous in the crowd, suddenly your life is exposed, your heart pierced by words that seem aimed directly at you. Given such a personalized invitation, how could you not get more deeply involved in the course?

As my students continued to come to me with these reports and I saw how deeply their lives were being affected by this mysterious alchemy between us, which I had not intended nor had any conscious control of, I too was shaken. What were these powerful processes that were linking me to them in such an intimate fashion without either of us soliciting the connection? Did I need to protect them from what was happening? Obviously this was not what they had signed up for, or at least not what they had thought they had signed up for. How does one ensure informed consent when the dynamics are so involuntary? The only control I had over the situation was the choice of whether or not to lock this door in my mind and cut off all further communication with this deeper source of information. Though I considered this option, I eventually decided against it. In the end I chose to continue the exercise but to pay closer attention to my students as I worked, staying alert to signs of impact and possible distress. As I subsequently learned, these synchronicities were just the overture to a much deeper connection with them that was beginning to unfold and would continue to deepen in the years ahead.

At home with my wife, I started to call this mysterious interweaving of minds "the magic." When the magic happened, the walls of our separateness came down temporarily, secrets were exchanged, and healing flowed. When the magic happened, my students and I tapped into levels of creativity beyond our separate capacities. On a good day the room was so filled with new ideas that after class I too sometimes copied down the blackboard, having caught glimpses of a deeper trajectory of new concepts unfolding in our dialogue. The magic also signaled the emergence of a group of students who would guide my teaching into further uncharted waters.

I began to recognize that I was functioning at two levels on campus, with each level attracting a different group of students. For one group I was operating as a conventional professor. This group came looking for academic instruction and usually walked away reasonably satisfied. Our relationship seemed to be primarily about information exchange. As the years passed and the magic deepened, however, a second group emerged with whom I had a very different relationship. With these students the exchange of information seemed to become the vehicle for a deeper spiritual opening that happened spontaneously and involuntarily when we came together to learn. Sprinkled throughout my introductory courses, they began to collect in larger numbers in my more specialized upper-level courses, first in small groups and later becoming the majority there. With this second group, teaching became a true adventure—filled with many unknowns and great rewards.[2]

Truth spoken directly from the heart and skillfully illumined by the mind has an enormous power that cannot be eliminated even in the academic setting. As a teacher of world religions, the truths I work with are the perennial truths of our spiritual traditions. When students hear these truths simply spoken, when they are reminded of things long ago forgotten but always present at the edge of their awareness, there is sometimes a spark of recognition that can suddenly explode into a flame. This flame is contagious and sometimes stimulates energetic resonances with other students in the room. Students may collectively feel their energy begin to shift to higher centers of awareness, though they may not understand what is happening. Symptoms of chakra-opening and kundalini-type arousal may begin to manifest. Energy runs, hearts open, and insights arise.

A woman in her mid-thirties summarized her experience in one of my courses in the following manner:

> Sitting in class, I felt like I was inside one of those glassball snow scenes that folks use as paperweights. Shake the ball and mass confusion begins with flakes of fake snow swirling all around. . . . I couldn't *hear* the lecture. My mind struggled to focus and stay with your words, but I was missing it . . .
>
> Later . . . at home . . . alone. It would all return to me, the lecture. . . . Mostly feelings. Tears. Recognition. Understanding after I let it simmer for a while. Realization that if I didn't grab at it, it would be there waiting, this knowledge. These tiny bright spots of revelatory insight. I'd journal. I'd cry. Sometimes light and gentle, warm feel-good crying. Sometimes sobs, wracking and exhausting. I THOUGHT I WAS LOSING MY MIND A FEW TIMES.

Instead of hearing your lectures with my Brain-Mind-Intellect, I actually heard you from somewhere else. . . . Heart-Soul maybe? Ears of a type that I hadn't been exercising. They had atrophied. You gave them a workout. Or the class field was so intense that it penetrated my controlling dominant brain-mind and vibrated my heart-soul like cardiac shock paddles to bring it to life.

The result? I'm becoming who I was *long* ago. The field bypassed my intellect and went directly to my heart to pry it open. . . . I now know what I had deeply buried in me for years, and the gift of the pick and shovel for the ONGOING PROCESS comes from being in the energy of the folks in our classroom. It didn't come from me alone.

Teaching at this level in an academic setting, especially in a state university, quickly becomes a very delicate matter and opens the door to all manner of errors of judgment. It becomes necessary to protect your students from their own enthusiasm as well as from your personal shortcomings. Fortunately, all this developed slowly, and my wonderful students taught me what I needed to know about the process as we went along.

Again I want to emphasize that it was not my intention to trigger these reactions. In fact, fearing that they were out of place, I often tried to damp them down. This was impossible, however, without damaging the teaching process itself. Whenever we would gather and focus our energies on the common task of sharing understanding, these resonances would involuntarily occur—not always but often—drawing us for better or for worse into heightened states of awareness. I want to emphasize this point because it is important from a theoretical perspective to understand the unconscious depths at which these resonances operate. Beneath the level of material bodies, beneath conscious minds, these are resonances of the soul. At a deeper level still, I believe they are the *synaptic sparks of Sacred Mind*. My only choice was either to stop teaching or learn how to manage these states.

I should also mention, perhaps, that I do not teach meditation in any of my classes nor do I ever introduce my own experiences into the classroom except in the rarest of circumstances. This last point is important because it is critical to affirm the principle of protecting students from overzealous professors. When a professor introduces his or her own experiences into an undergraduate course, because of the professor's position of authority it tends to encroach upon the autonomy of the students, and this is never appropriate. As a matter of professional ethics, therefore, I did not reveal my inner life to my students, and yet our lives seemed at times to be moving in synchronous patterns. Though they were unaware of it, there were sometimes striking correspondences between my personal inner work and the issues that were surfacing in their lives. These correspondences were particularly pronounced as I was working through the various perinatal matrices, a process that lasted many years.

The perinatal dimension represents the interface between the individual and the collective psyche. In it are housed the most difficult and universal obstacles to spiritual awakening. As my inner work focused on this level, many of my students seemed to be having a particularly difficult time of it. It was as though we were all caught in a giant death-rebirth vortex that was breaking us down in different ways, uprooting fundamental pains, and crushing restrictive barriers. Conscientious students who took my courses during this time were often drawn into deep personal growth as their systems strained to break their bounds. Some chose to end bad marriages or heal wounded ones, while others left careers they had outgrown but had been holding onto. Some began to confront their addictions and others to recover dormant memories of incest. While these reactions may sometimes be an expected component of certain courses, such as those in counseling, for example, this was not the case for the courses I was teaching. Rather, these reactions seemed to be the *indirect effect* of our simply coming together to study various spiritual systems.

One woman in her mid-forties, for example, hints at the profound disruption of her inner and outer world that occurred in a course on Buddhism when she began spontaneously to recover terribly painful memories of child abuse:

> During and after having been in your classes, my internal world became increasingly chaotic as demons from painful psychological gestalts began to emerge, and eventually coloring my external world too, challenging everything I thought I was and dissolving familiar reference points. . . . As I struggled to break through powerful gestalts of pain, you spoke to and nourished my soul, making it possible for me to move more deeply into my spiritual journey.

Among the various possible explanations for these deeply synchronous patterns of spiritual trials and breakthroughs, two seem to stand out. The first is that my students and I were being simultaneously influenced by a common event, that some shift of the collective psyche was making itself felt in our separate lives. Archetypal transit astrology might help us identify such shifts in the collective field. The second possibility is that my students were unconsciously responding to the energy being generated by my individual work, or that this work was somehow coordinating our lives at a subtle level and fueling our synchronous development. Not mutually exclusive possibilities, both influences might be operating simultaneously, one reinforcing the other. Between the two, it is the second that I want to give attention to here. If transit astrology can identify shifts in the collective field that influence everyone, I nevertheless think that the immediate catalyst that was sparking the kind of synchronicities that were surfacing in my classes is deep spiritual practice. Any spiritual discipline that has the capacity to uncover and engage the perinatal level of consciousness, especially in its collective forms, and to tap into the high-energy transpersonal states that lie beyond it, will tend, I think, to trigger these sorts of connections between people, especially between people participating in intense group projects such as a college course.

The most sympathetic discussion of these phenomena that I have found in the spiritual literature comes from Satprem's biography of Sri Aurobindo, entitled *Sri Aurobindo or The Adventure of Consciousness*. In discussing Aurobindo's attempt to transform the single body of humanity, Satprem writes:

> But then, if the body is *one* with all other bodies, it means that all the other bodies are right there inside it, along with all the falsehoods of the world! There is no longer only one person's battle; it becomes the whole world's battle. . . . There is only one body.

He later continues this line of thought:

> Sri Aurobindo verified, not individually this time but collectively, that pulling down too strong a light causes all the darkness below to groan and to feel violated. It should be noted that each time Sri Aurobindo and the Mother had some experience indicating a new progress in the transformation, the disciples, without their even knowing anything about it, experienced in their consciousness a period of increased difficulties or even revolts and illnesses, as if everything were grating. Now we begin to understand how things work.[3]

If there is a single message that comes from this period that my students and I wish to share with the reader, it is this. If you are an educator who has chosen a form of spiritual practice that activates these very deep levels of the unconscious, you must expect to stimulate involuntary, sympathetic resonances in at least some of your students. Separate minds are an illusion of the senses. If you begin to drive your consciousness to the bedrock of existence and stimulate the purification processes that inevitably occur when self seeks True Self, you will not make this journey alone. As an educator, you must anticipate that at least some of your students will move in rhythm with your descent. You must expect it and you must prepare for it. Like ripples on water, these resonances are inevitable, and the better teacher you are, the more powerful you can expect them to be.[4]

Morphic Fields in Higher Education

When these synchronistic resonances first began manifesting in my classes, I thought of them as paranormal exchanges taking place between separate minds. As deeper patterns of interconnectedness emerged, however, I began to recognize that at least some of these experiences were better thought of as the manifestation of a group mind. I had read Rupert Sheldrake's books and had embraced his concept of morphic fields operating at the species level, but only slowly was I able to recognize the existence of these fields operating in my classes. Eventually, it simply became more elegant to conceptualize these phenomena as symptoms of a unified learning field that underlay and integrated the class as a whole.

Students were becoming more porous not only to me but to each other. They sometimes showed up in each other's dreams in significant ways. Synchronicities between them were increasing, and life-expanding coincidences were becoming almost routine. As one student who returned to college after a twenty-year absence reported to me:

Each quarter seemed to bring new and unexpected changes and synchronicities. I entered into a web of personal relationships and meetings with people that profoundly influenced my life. I was "finding" individuals whose circumstances were eerily similar to my own; people who knew friends of mine from obscure places in the world; people who seemed to be reading the same books at the same times and having experiences that were transforming them in the same shattering yet exhilarating ways.

The most important observation that pushed me toward a morphic field view of these events, however, was the sheer magnitude and intensity of the forces that were involved. Too many people's lives were being too deeply touched for me to conceptualize what was happening solely in terms of resonances with my individual energy. If my person was in some way a catalyst for these experiences to surface among my students, what was actually surfacing was something much larger than I could by generating. As I made the shift to thinking of this "something" in terms of the morphic field of the class, a variety of conceptual and experiential pieces began to fall into place. (At this point I need to inject an important qualifier. I don't think that the morphic field of the class is the final source of these energies but rather that it mediates our access to them. The important insight is that the class mind is a living entity that mediates the individual's experience of higher states of consciousness in group contexts.)

Sometimes when I am simply doing my job covering the day's assignment, it's as if the floor suddenly falls away. The atmosphere in the room becomes supercharged, and everyone seems to congeal into a superunified state. My mind becomes unusually spacious and clear, and my students' eyes tell me that they have moved into a particularly receptive state. Our hearts seem to merge, and from this open field of compassion comes a slow stream of thoughts that I, as spokesperson for the group, unfold and work with.

In these transient moments of heightened awareness, I sometimes have the acute sensation that there is only one mind present in the room. It is as if the walls that usually separate us have become gossamer curtains. Individual persons melt into a softly glowing field of energy, and this unified energy *thinks* and *feels* and *hungers to speak*. Because this field incorporates the life experiences of everyone present, of course we sometimes find the details of our separate histories surfacing spontaneously in it. Because it embodies our private hopes and fears, of course we are sometimes deeply touched by what comes out of it.

Many such experiences through the years have led me to draw the following provisional conclusions. I believe that regularly taught courses have distinct morphic fields associated with them. These "learning fields" reflect the cumulative discoveries of all the students who have taken this course through the years with this particular professor.[5] They record and carry the effort that previous students have invested in understanding the ideas involved, their break-throughs, and their resulting insights. They reflect both the depth of learning that has occurred and the quantity, becoming stronger year after year as more and more students take the course. Furthermore, these fields have at least two layers. The core of the field derives from the experiences of all the students who have taken the course through the years. The more immediate, second layer of the field derives from the current group of students taking the course this semester. I call the inner layer the *course mind* and the thinner second layer the *class mind*. Using this vocabulary, I believe that the class mind begins to congeal during registration as students choose their courses. As a field of focused intention, it grows stronger as they prepare for class—paying their tuition and buying their books—becoming an almost tangible presence on the first day. When the semester starts and the work begins, the class mind begins to integrate with the larger course mind, which unleashes its powerful currents into the collective sinews of this particular group of students.

I believe that these fields are always present wherever collective intention is focused in group projects of sustained duration and repeated form. Usually, however, they operate below the threshold of consciousness, and most of my colleagues, even the conscientious ones, are seldom aware of their existence. They appear to vary enormously in strength, reflecting a variety of factors including, for example, the commitment and focus of the students, their level of enthusiasm for the subject matter, and their individual temperaments and level of spiritual development. Under certain conditions, these fields can become strong enough to trigger a variety of phenomena in the classroom that are "paranormal" only from the perspective of an outworn atomistic paradigm. Within a transpersonal paradigm, these phenomena are entirely normal. They are simply the natural effects of the gradual surfacing of the deeper levels of mind in group contexts.

Exactly what conditions beyond those already mentioned are required for these fields to manifest in the classroom is still unclear to me. It may in part be a function of the subject matter of the course itself. I suspect that courses that try to penetrate the existential mysteries of life activate deeper levels of our being than are stirred by semiconductors, logarithms, and differential equations, but this may simply be a personal bias. If a professor lived and breathed these technical subjects and could inject his or her passion for them into their students, how could learning fields not form and make themselves felt around these courses as well? In general, I think that pedagogical techniques which stimulate strong student interest and participation and which invite high levels of critical reflection and the free expression of individual thinking will encourage the development of stronger course fields than techniques which emphasize regurgitative learning and passive engagement of the material. As intentional fields, they always reflect the intellectual and emotional vitality of the activities that generate them.

The key ingredients that must be present for these fields to form seem to be: (1) collective intention focused in group projects, (2) a project of sustained duration, and (3) repetition of the project in approximately the same form many times. If any one of these elements is missing, the field will be so weak as to be ineffective or at least undetectable. University instruction is only one of many activities that meet these conditions, and I'm sure readers will find many other settings in which these same dynamics arise.

The mental field of a university is defined by its project, which is learning. Learning is broken down into specific areas from which students select their courses, hopefully based on their interest in the subject matter. If they are not deeply interested in the subject when they walk into class on the first day, the professor's first job is to create that interest. My personal strategy is to hit them hard and fast on day one, give them a big jolt, show them the possibilities by taking them to some provocative place in their mind. Let them know with every gesture that this is not your ordinary course and that we are limited here only by our willingness to work hard and to think critically and creatively. The second task on the first day is to encourage those students whose interest cannot be fired up to move on to a course that does interest them. This can usually be done by designing a course with a heavy workload, an amount that is reasonable for the motivated but too demanding for the faint of heart. This, combined with an aggressive opening lecture, often weeds out the unmotivated. (This severity is actually a disguised kindness to all the students, both those that leave and those that stay.)

Interest is energy. Once interest is awakened, the next task is to focus that energy on a series of challenges that draw the students step by step into the project of understanding. The old saw that "You do not teach a course, you teach students" guides every aspect of the work. The barometer of the course is always the quality of engagement between the students and the course material. If the quality of engagement falters, then however much material may be covered, the course is failing. When the quality of engagement is high, one has the opportunity to accomplish something the students will remember for years. A high level of engagement does not guarantee a good course, for you can waste this energy or fritter it away on undeserving diversions. But active engagement is the raw material that makes great learning possible. When a high level of engagement can be focused in a sustained way on intellectually challenging and worthwhile projects, *great learning* can occur.

Great learning is learning that will stay with the students long after they've forgotten all the lesser details of their college career. It is learning that reaches into their hearts as well as their minds, that lifts their vision to a new horizon and gives them an understanding they will carry with them for years. Great learning has taken place when they keep their papers and journals and use them as a reference point in their lives, when they have heard their soul speaking to them as they struggle with their essays late at night, when a shattering "Aha!" lifts them out of their well-forged confusion, and especially when they fall in love with the open-ended journey of perpetual learning.

Engagement generates energy and university courses focus enormous quantities of energy in coordinated group projects lasting many months. Where several courses are tied together into larger learning sequences, these projects may last years, with students taking four or more courses with the same instructor. This sustained and repeated focusing of many minds on a single purpose creates strong currents within the larger field of mind.

In some ways we can imagine the mental field of a university community as something like a large lake, exquisitely sensitive to the movements of all its inhabitants and integrating their individual activities into its larger expanse. The waves created by single, unrepeated movements in a lake quickly die out, but sustained and repeated movements create a pattern of standing waves in the water. Thus the learning fields created by individual professors and their courses might be seen as stable whirlpools of energy spinning within the university mind, drawing people together for specific projects and releasing them back into the larger mind when their work together is completed. Because universities are not closed systems but open systems with a constant stream of students matriculating and graduating each year, we might deepen our analogy by imagining that our lake is fed by a river that enters at one end of the lake and flows off at the other. Thus our lake is being continuously stirred by a constant, gentle current moving through it.

This combination of a stable mental field with a slow but steady turnover of individuals is a fascinating setting in which to explore Sheldrake's theory of formative causation. The patterns that form in the university mind are more enduring than the constantly changing flow of students who temporarily become part of these systems. The learning fields we are discussing could not have come into existence without the efforts of many individuals, and yet once they exist, they have a life of their own which is larger than any of the individuals who contributed to them. *They are true structures within the group mind,* and they mobilize and shape our individual contact with the deeper dimensions of learning that are unfolding in the group field.

Applied to the university setting, Sheldrake's theory of formative causation suggests that the understanding which previous students have achieved actually makes it easier for subsequent generations of students to acquire these same concepts. This expectation is consistent with my experience, and other educators have told me that they have observed the same phenomenon in their classes. I find that every so many years I have to adjust my lesson plan because students are more easily grasping concepts that previously had required detailed explanation and argument. After years of using a tried and proven route to a specific intellectual outcome, it's as if the students have suddenly found a shortcut and are bored if I insist on taking them the long way around. This can be a very disconcerting experience for an instructor. You show up for a course with a prepared agenda that has been a winner for years, and the students signal you in the first week that they are several weeks ahead of you in the syllabus. Obviously many factors could be contributing to this effect, including general shifts in cultural insight, self-selecting student populations, and improved pedagogical delivery. Personally, however, I doubt that these by themselves are sufficient to explain the sudden changes in receptivity that periodically occur in student populations, as if following an unseen rhythm.

Another observation that correlates well with Sheldrake's theory is the way that these learning fields developed gradually over time. Sporadic paranormal phenomena began showing up in my classes after about five years of teaching, but it took another five to ten years before the fields gathered sufficient strength to become a significant, collective force in the classroom. This pattern of progressive strengthening matches Sheldrake's hypothesis. These fields begin small and become stronger with every group of students who take a particular course. Similarly, as one's teaching gradually matures, the quality of learning experience you can give your students improves, and this qualitative increase also strengthens a course's field.

I believe that these learning fields are present whenever the essential conditions are met—*collective intention focused in group projects of sustained duration and repeated form.* Their strength, however, will vary widely according to the variables already mentioned, together with other variables that we have yet to identify. Usually these fields function unconsciously in a course, their effects being so subtle as to easily escape detection. When the right mix of circumstances converge, however, they can become powerful forces in the classroom.

Whatever other factors are involved in drawing these fields into conscious expression, I believe that the instructor is the essential catalyst for their emergence. He or she is the spark plug and governor of the class engine. For morphic fields to manifest consciously rather than unconsciously, I suspect that it is a prerequisite that the instructor be intimately familiar with deep nonordinary states, that he or she be comfortable in these states and able to sustain them when they emerge without losing one's operational focus. Furthermore, I believe that systematic work at the perinatal and transpersonal levels plays a critical role in bringing these fields out into the open. Deep work at the perinatal level seems to act as a lightning rod, drawing forth powerful reactions from the group field. I could be wrong on this point, however, and may be overestimating the instructor's role. I could envision a situation in which the students were highly motivated and well focused and thus might stimulate these fields into action even though the professor may be less experienced in this area. How they might manifest without the additional catalyst of someone working consciously at the transpersonal level I don't know.

When these fields make themselves felt in a classroom, they unleash a power that can easily overwhelm both the student and the instructor and therefore require careful management. When they emerge it is as if the walls of one's mind suddenly fall away. New vistas of understanding can suddenly arise spontaneously and without effort. The depth of the human condition can suddenly be laid bare, and the intensity of the collective feelings that sweep through you can throw you off balance if you are not prepared for it. If students are overwhelmed by this intensity, they can retreat into the solitude of their private reaction, but the professor has no such retreat available and must maintain his or her public stance. He or she must maintain their operational focus and smoothly integrate into the work at hand the gifts that these fields can confer. Restraint is often called for. Ideas can come pouring in more quickly than students can effectively use. The self-referential reflex of ego can tempt one to use this energy to deepen personal understanding rather than serve the collective good of the students. All these distortions should be avoided.

Attention is energy, and in the field of the class mind enormous amounts of energy become available to the instructor. If the instructor is capable of focusing this energy and using it for the collective good, an escalating cycle of energetic exchange is set in motion. Animated by the collective field, the instructor opens and begins to function on a slightly higher level of awareness. As the insights that arise from this level find their targets in the room, the response of the students releases more energy into the class field, which then further empowers the instructor. When working with motivated and well-focused students, the energy can swell to enormous proportions. When all goes well, there is a crystalline quality to what emerges that every person in the room can feel. Like a great symphony that lifts the soul, what arises comes from depths that cannot be measured, and is aimed and guided by an invisible hand that finds its mark. What could not be accomplished separately becomes available to those who work together, and the wholeness that surfaces in these moments is characterized by a luminescent transparency. This transparency is contagious and its gifts precious. Each person draws from it gems unique to his or her situation. For me, the most precious gift of all is the transparency itself, as it is a token of the true nature of mind. (The surest indicator that the magic has happened is when students don't want to leave the room after the bell rings.)

These learning fields are the unregistered students in our courses. Though they do not show up on any roster, they are nonetheless tangibly present in the room. Once you recognize the existence of these fields, it is a natural step to begin working with them directly—not indirectly by working with the students but directly by engaging the fields themselves. This can be done both inside and outside the classroom. In a few of my upper division courses, I use visualization exercises to strengthen these fields. As intentional fields, they can be augmented by visualizations that image the constructive blending of those present into a common higher cause. Outside of class, there are a variety of meditative and shamanic techniques that one can use to cleanse and refine these fields, and I would encourage readers to experiment with the tools their specific traditions make available to them to work with these energies directly.

My own first attempt in this area involved the Polynesian ritual called *H'oponopono,* taught by the now deceased Morrnah Simeona. *H'oponopono* means "cutting." Boiled down to its essentials, this practice involves ritually forgiving all karmic debts which connect you to a specific circle of persons and asking that they similarly forgive you any karmic grudges they might be unconsciously carrying. More recently I have been using a Tibetan practice called *Chod.* *Chod* (also meaning "to cut") is a powerful cleansing practice taught in Vajrayana Buddhism that derives from Machig Lapdron, a deeply realized woman who lived in twelfth-century Tibet. My subjective perception is that when I began to include my students and our fields in my daily spiritual practice at home, especially the *Chod,* it had an immediate and beneficial impact on my classes at the university. Teaching went more smoothly and productively. I encountered fewer obstacles in the classroom and the students seemed to have an easier time learning at many levels. These are entirely subjective impressions, of course, without empirical assessment to back them up. In my more advanced courses where the most deeply involved students gathered, the disruptive effects of these fields seemed to be ameliorated, allowing them to arise with fewer disturbances and greater effectiveness.

These results were so striking that my current custom is to include my classes in my daily practice as soon as registration occurs, weeks before the course actually begins. I shudder sometimes at what my colleagues would think if they could see me performing the *Chod* ritual over a student roster for a course that has not yet begun, but to my mind this is simply an extension of my responsibilities as a teacher. *It is the logical consequence of recognizing the fields generated by our activities in the past and present, and discovering that we can influence these fields directly.* It is simply being efficient as an educator.

Just as important as opening and purifying the field before a course begins is the closing of the field when the course is over. All cycles have beginnings and endings, and if you do not consciously and decisively dissolve the class field at the end of the quarter, you will have students dribbling into your office for months, feeling strangely unable to let go of the course. It took me a while to recognize what was going on when this first happened. Initially, I took the appearance of these students at my door as a compliment, thinking that they had just really enjoyed the course. Only gradually did I realize that they were having difficulty letting go of the experience. Because the field had not been consciously closed, they were stuck, with no physical setting any longer to express the psychic link they still felt to the class mind.

The more powerfully the group mind has entered the classroom, the more important it is to dissolve that mind at the end of the course and to empower the individual students as self-sufficient fields of infinite awareness, whole and complete in themselves. For this purpose I sometimes use a visualization exercise in which we re-assimilate our collective work into our individual lives. Another effective integration technique is to invite the students to consciously distribute the merit of our work to all sentient beings, thus reaffirming the larger webs we are moving back into. In introductory level courses which do not allow me to address these processes that explicitly, many of the same ends can be accomplished by a well-choreographed "last day" lecture or group discussion. A final exam can also be an effective means of closing a course well, as the act of demonstrating what one has learned helps bring that cycle of learning to a decisive end. Lastly, what cannot be handled openly in class can be managed privately by using the practices available in one's spiritual tradition.

Before turning to consider the broader implications of these mental fields, I would like to ask a final question. What will happen to the learning field surrounding a course when the professor retires? Do we take these fields with us or do they simply atrophy from disuse like last year's muscles? Morphic theory suggests, of course, that their influence continues at more inclusive levels of the species-mind, and that they will help students wherever and whenever they set out to learn what students before them have learned. While this may be true, I also like to think that these specific fields might continue to manifest more locally as well. I would like to think that a lifetime of teaching, and more importantly a lifetime of thousands of students learning, would create currents in the local group mind that would help future students in this particular locale learn what we have learned before them, or better still to know intuitively things that we had to painstakingly piece together. Furthermore, I would hope that it might be possible for my successor, if he or she is of compatible ilk, to inherit not only my courses but also my learning fields, as I suspect I have inherited the fields of my predecessors. When all is said and done, these fields may be our most enduring contribution to our species.

The Broader Implications

We are so deeply habituated to thinking of mind as a private phenomenon that recognizing its collective component is extremely difficult and triggers a chorus of objections. We can immediately think of a hundred reasons why this suggestion must be wrong. It runs contrary to most of our daily experience. If we open our inner life to the possible influence of currents within the collective mind, we may feel the threat of being overrun by mass sentiment. If our private thoughts are this porous to the collective unconscious, have we not compromised our individual integrity? Aren't we eventually going to undermine individual effort and initiative? Surely our private mind is the norm and any bleed-through that occasionally comes from the collective level must be the exception that only demonstrates the strength of this rule. If we allow our individual autonomy to be compromised in the ways I have suggested here, what remains of our individuality?

I understand these objections and appreciate the shock and possible sense of violation that may arise when one begins to be conscious of the presence of collective fields of influence in our personal experience. What is required at this point, however, is not that we abandon our concept of individuality, but that we relocate this individuality within a transpersonal paradigm that allows us to recognize dynamics that are invisible within the Newtonian-Cartesian paradigm. We must let go of what we think we know about how mind works and open to new and startling observations drawn from carefully scrutinized experience. We cannot at this early stage tell where this shift in thinking will eventually lead us; all we know with certainty is that our previous paradigm of a stand-alone consciousness is hopelessly unable to deal with the facts of experience. While not abandoning our skeptical edge, we must push our critical faculties to explore uncharted territory.

The shift to thinking about mind as a collective as well as individual phenomenon leads to all sorts of unanticipated insights. For example, in the early years I observed a repeated synchronicity operating between my discovery of a given idea and the arrival of a student in one of my classes who needed this specific insight. I would read a particular book or have a certain experience that would allow me to understand something I had not previously understood. Not long thereafter, a student would show up in one of my classes and ask a question that was personally significant for him or her, which

I was able to be of some help with only because of my own recent breakthrough. Had the student come on the scene the previous semester, I could not have been of much use to him or her, but arriving when he or she did, the information was available and the connection was made.

When this had happened more than a few times, it became obvious to me that there was an invisible causal connection between the timing of my personal discoveries and the appearance of specific students asking for this knowledge. To begin to observe the subtle way the universe brings people together at the right moment to encourage the growth of a system larger than any of its parts awakens a sense of the sacred within the rhythms of our daily life. At this stage, however, I was still thinking about these things self-referentially and underestimating the scope of the processes involved. I thought that the universe was somehow capable of responding to my initiatives in such a way as to use the knowledge becoming available within me to nourish insights fermenting inside my students. It was only gradually that I realized how profoundly incomplete my understanding of these processes actually was.

As my experience of the class mind deepened, I began to realize that I had it backwards; I had put the cart before the horse. If from one perspective students were drawn to me because of my recent discoveries, from a deeper perspective my discoveries were sometimes better thought of as being driven not by my personal need to know but by my students' need to know. *The causal flow between student and teacher is a circle with no clearly defined beginning.* I slowly began to realize that the hunger fermenting within my students to understand some aspect of reality created a field around them that was actually influencing "my" desire to learn certain things. What I had previously thought of as my private desire to understand was in fact simply the registering in my personal awareness of a larger desire that was rooted in a collective field composed of me and my students together. We were much more deeply implicated in each other's lives than I had first suspected. Their need to know and my need to know were a single piece in the larger scheme of things. Their desire to understand and my capacity to articulate were but different sides of a synaptic bridge within the species-mind, and only when we came together and combined our resources did we fulfill our designed function.[6]

Here one either jumps entirely into a new way of thinking or one holds back thinking the jump too large—there is no middle ground. Within the conventional academic paradigm, what I am suggesting is unthinkable. It opens one to all manner of charges of ego-inflation and megalomania, of endorsing magic and abandoning critical thinking. And yet it is none of these things, but simply the tentative attempt to begin unfolding the implications of a transpersonal model of mind as it applies to education. In this model, mind is not the private chamber we had thought it was but an open field where different energetic streams converge. Some of these streams are personal and come from our immediate and distant past. Others, however, come from the lives of those around us, both those we can see and those we have yet to meet face to face. Persons discover the insubstantiality of the self in many contexts. I discovered it with my students, to whom I am eternally grateful.

I do not know what ultimately governs the processes I have been describing or what their limits are. If instructors were equally open to all approaching students, surely our students' needs would shatter our ability to function coherently. Why one student's message gets through the natural filters that "screen our calls" while another doesn't I don't understand, but that some calls regularly get through I can no longer deny. As Ram Dass once put it, one senses that one has "business" with one and not another. When the process works and the magic happens, when you manage to step far enough aside to let the alchemy work of its own accord, there is an exquisite sensation of delicate expansiveness. It is a state of heightened creativity similar to what artists and scientists sometimes report, but in this case taking place between partners meeting in the classroom. Not always but sometimes, one can feel the significance of the exchange. A sense of hallowed ground arises, a feeling of an arrow striking its target dead center, though hidden in the dark. It is a strange sensation of being a conscious part of an even more conscious whole. Sometimes this sweet sensation is so strong that it is hard to maintain my composure until I get back to my office, where private tears can fall.

A transpersonal paradigm allows us to entertain what is unthinkable from within the Newtonian-Cartesian model of education. Our conventional model of the classroom is a monarchial, trickle-down model. The professor, by virtue of his or her longer and presumably greater efforts, has gathered a certain store of information that confers a certain privileged status as a member of the academic aristocracy. To these educational barons, students come and knowledge is distributed, sometimes graciously and sometimes not, but always in a downward flow from a centralized source. In a transpersonal model of education, the possibility of a much deeper and more intimate meeting of minds emerges. While not flattening the differences between the roles or erasing the respective responsibilities of the people gathered, a transpersonal model recognizes the existence of fields of awareness and intelligence that are superordinate to the individuals present. While strongly resonant with feminist proposals for revisioning pedagogy, the transpersonal perspective goes farther to propose the existence of a collective wisdom running beneath the surface of dualistic appearances.

Beneath the traditional setting is a subtle field in which the precise boundary between professor and student becomes difficult to define. If my students' need to understand certain things has somehow entered me and either seeded or merged with my need to understand these things, then the course is a group project from the very start. What the students bring to our encounter and what I bring begin to take on the appearance of being two sides of a larger whole. We each have our respective roles in this drama, but one sometimes senses the presence of a playwright inside the scene even as we are acting it out. In the play's most transparent moments, one gets the acute sense that our individual roles contribute to the self-actualization of a single mind. At these moments our separate desires to understand seem clearly to come from a single source and to reflect a single aspiration seeking expression in the world. The forms of teacher and student become transparent to this larger dynamic. In our collaboration something larger is expressing itself. We can provisionally locate this larger intent in the species-mind if we remember that the species-mind is part of the even larger Sacred Mind unfolding itself in time and space.

Knowledge is the reason for our coming together, but the act of coming together itself activates dimensions of our collective existence that empower this knowledge in a profound way. The living power of the class mind not only injects vitality and a certain unpredictability into the distribution of information, but it can create a field of enriched creativity within which new discoveries can occur. When this happens, knowledge is not flowing down from a solitary source but arising from within the living presence of the class mind. Or it might be more accurate to say that this knowledge arises from Sacred Mind as it crystallizes in the transient field of the class mind. The circle of the class mind is not the ultimate source of this creativity but rather a powerful mechanism which allows us to tap more deeply into the creativity of Sacred Mind itself. When this circular field is sufficiently strong, the professor's store of knowledge can become an instrument played by a larger intelligence. Poised between things already grasped and things not yet understood, a living intelligence not housed in any one mind but evoked by the group mind begins to unfold its secrets, taking us the next step on our individual and collective journeys. In my experience, this particular magic tends to happen toward the end of one's more advanced courses, after the foundation has been carefully prepared through months and years of working together.

Having only begun to explore these field dynamics, my observations on their workings are exploratory and tentative. Even so, I believe that the observation of energetic resonance and morphic fields operating in educational contexts has the potential to transform not only education but a wide range of creative group processes taking place in board rooms, laboratories, think tanks, and so on. As we become more aware of the collective sinews of intelligence waiting to be tapped by those who learn to enter into states of *synchronized group awareness*, the possibilities expand exponentially. Studies have demonstrated that creativity is augmented when the two hemispheres of our brain begin to function in an electromagnetically integrated, whole-brain manner. The Monroe Institute has for many years marketed a line of creativity-enhancing tapes which use sound to stimulate states of hemispheric synchronization while shifting the brain's electrical activity into the theta frequency range associated with higher creativity. Similarly, a wealth of biofeedback and entrainment technologies today use every strategy imaginable to elicit whole brain functioning focused at specific frequencies for specific purposes. When the brain's hemispheres are phase-locked and working as one, a number of known benefits result, including heightened awareness, improved recall, more self-programming flexibility, and heightened creativity—in short, "superlearning."

From here it is a simple if substantial step to recognizing that our individual brains are neuron-clusters within the larger species-brain of humanity. Our individual mindfields are "cells" within Sacred Mind. When a number of minds come together and integrate their individual capacities, it is as though they become phase-locked in ways analogous to how individual neurons become phase-locked in hemispherically synchronized brain states. *When persons open themselves to each other and focus on a common goal, their individual energies meld in a way that mediates contact with levels of intelligence and creativity that are beyond the reach of these individuals acting alone.* It is as though by coordinating our emotional and intellectual energies, we can fashion ourselves into a more powerful receiver and begin to collectively pick up a signal that was always there but which we could not pull in as long as we were operating in a stand-alone mode. We literally must come together in an integrated manner for this novel mode of knowing to flow effectively.

No doubt there are persons who by virtue of the experiences gathered through many lifetimes are capable of reaching more deeply into Sacred Mind than a group of less talented individuals. One Einstein is worth more than many committees, no matter how well integrated they are. And yet, if one Einstein is capable of perceiving ideas that are beyond the reach of most of us, a group of Einsteins who have learned to capitalize on the mind's inherent capacity to form larger wholes with other minds will perceive still more. *It is not the specific level reached that is significant here but the discovery of the capacity of the integrated group mind itself.* The potential for refining this principle and applying it to new fields of experience seems open-ended. Whatever our individual abilities, our collective abilities are greater.

Our strong Western conviction has been that mind is generated by brain and therefore comes "after" brain, both historically and ontologically. Psychedelic experience, however, endorses the perennial perspective that mind precedes brain, and that the miracle of evolution is the miracle of a self-organizing universe that is creating the physical structures that allow a preexisting awareness to penetrate realms previously insensitive to its presence. From a transpersonal perspective, superconscient awareness already exists, and everywhere surrounds us. It has painstakingly created the organic form that finally has the capacity to support an increased measure of this awareness in the physical sphere, but we have not yet fully actualized this potential because of the mental habits formed during our earlier stages of evolutionary and cultural development. Everywhere this superordinate awareness presses in upon us, looking for points of entry, trying to reach us in our dreams, our meditations, and our moments of undistracted selflessness. Now, it seems, it is reaching out to us even in our classrooms.

Sacred Mind in Everyday Life

As we begin to awaken to the true dimensions of our mind in the classroom or in other settings, we begin to recognize that the symptoms of our expansive nature have in fact been with us for a long time, though we had been unable to recognize them for what they are. For example, when a person works on an engineering project that will not be completed during his or her lifetime, when someone foregoes the larger salary and chooses the job with greater heart, when the greater good of the greater number truly guides one's hardest choices, when the pain of others finally draws one into action, when the needs of future generations become as tangible to us as our own needs—in all these instances our choices reflect the breadth of our true being. We have tried to fit these "ordinary" experiences into the narrow model of the Newtonian self without realizing how poor the fit really is, leading some biologists to search in vain for the elusive "altruism gene." The mystery of an individual who is open to broader horizons, who hears and responds to a distant call, who lives and breathes a larger life is no less a miracle when he or she does it in the name of "common decency" or "just doing the right thing." The shell of the particle-like self gets thinner and thinner the more we respond to the summons of our higher ideals. To give one's life for one's country, to give more than one's share to one's community, to demand inclusive solutions to our social problems—these are evidence of the same mystery of self-transcendence that we have seen operating in the classroom setting. The mystery is the same; only the context and mode of expression is different.

Lifetime by lifetime, the scope of our care broadens as the full range of our nature expresses itself more completely. Eventually, the developments that have been fermenting within and around us for millennia begin to break into our conscious awareness. The true dimensions of our life simply cannot hide themselves any longer. When this happens we begin to awaken. Sometimes suddenly, sometimes slowly, a veil lifts and we glimpse the true scope of the being that *we already are.* Nature reveals her handiwork—a being unbound by time or space and yet focused in a specific time and place. The work has already been done; there is nothing to add or take away. There is only the harvest.

The insights that I have been articulating in this chapter are not new. The concepts of energetic resonance and group fields have long been recognized in the world's esoteric spiritual traditions, where it is common knowledge that the progressive anchoring of superordinate awareness is facilitated by community. This is why *saṅgha,* the community of like-minded spiritual seekers, is one of Buddhism's three refuges, and *ecclesia,* the Church, is frequently described as a boat that carries us safely to the distant shore. If there is any novelty here, it is only the report that these collective dynamics are being detected in the unlikely setting of a secular university classroom. Those who don't know me are free to suspect that this has happened because I have inappropriately blurred the line between spirituality and education and injected spiritual concerns where they don't belong. I understand this assessment and am saddened by the thought that some of my colleagues will opt for it rather than honestly confront the experiences that would otherwise rupture the epistemological and philosophical assumptions of their worldview. To these I can only say again that I know the boundaries of responsible university instruction at a state university serving a pluralistic student body, and have diligently kept within these boundaries. It is not misdirected missionary zeal that has produced these results, but something far more subtle and difficult to comprehend.

Even in the cathedrals of the rational enlightenment, in the citadels of secular humanism, the deeper fabric of our collective life shows itself if we allow it. The presence of such powerful collective dynamics in such an unlikely setting forces us to reassess our assumptions about the nature of mind. Moreover, and this is the direction we will turn next, it raises profound questions about the period of history we are living in. That we should be encountering these dynamics in such an "unspiritual" setting as the college classroom says something, I think, about the times we have entered. It draws our attention away from the specific individuals involved and toward the powerful currents churning within the collective unconscious that are driving these experiences from underneath. The suggestion that we are living in exceptional times has been a leitmotif of this entire book, and it is time to examine this thesis in greater detail.

Chapter Eight

The Great Awakening

There is, then, both a moral and a practical obligation for each of us to look beyond the surface of events . . . to feel the ground swell underneath the events and perceive the direction they are taking: to perceive the evolutionary trend as it drives social change in our world.

—Ervin Laszlo, *The Choice*

This is a chapter I have not wanted to write. I've resisted it strenuously, postponing its beginning many times. There are two reasons for my reluctance. The first is that I fear asking my reader to follow me beyond what even a liberally inclined audience can tolerate in good conscience. There is so much irresponsible apocalyptic hype in print as we approach the next millennium, or what many consider the even more fateful year 2012, that this is a area from which I would have preferred to keep some distance. The second reason is the painful nature of the subject matter itself. The topic of this chapter is the spiritual awakening of humanity. I believe that for there to be a genuine spiritual rebirth of our species, there must first take place a death of the species-ego, a complete collapse of our customary way of experiencing ourselves in the world, and the pain of such a massive collapse is extremely difficult to hold in one's heart. If the dark night of the soul is the painful price the mystic must pay to awaken to the Divine within, the dark night of the species-soul will be a particularly dark and potentially dangerous time in human history.

No matter how much I have tried to avoid it, however, this subject must be addressed for at least three reasons. The first is the simple fact that it is a theme that arises with some consistency in psychedelic work once a certain level is reached. This has been true not only in my personal experience but in the experience of many working with these states. Second, focusing on the patterns of spiritual awakening in the species follows logically from the experience of ego-death. When individual ego dissolves as the working unit of one's reality, attention is naturally drawn to the larger fields of consciousness in which one's existence is embedded. If we were to restrict our description of the death-rebirth process to the individual alone, we would still be operating under the subtle influence of the egoic myth. And third, one of the themes of this book has been the attempt to understand the sheer magnitude of the suffering that sometimes surfaces in psychedelic therapy. I do not think that this suffering can be fully comprehended without taking into account the historical context within which this therapy is taking place. For all these reasons, we need to broaden our focus and address our moment in history.

Voices of Change

For the last two decades, the number of voices predicting an imminent global crisis followed by the spiritual rejuvenation of the planet has increased exponentially, each voice citing different authorities— Nostrodamus, the Mayan calendar, the Book of Revelation, the *I Ching*, spirit guides, ancient prophecies, future life progressions, and alien abductors. I do not mean to dismiss outright any of these possible sources of information or to belittle the often heroic courage individuals have shown in bringing forward their personal stories. And yet, one cannot but sometimes wish that these modern prophets had more critical distance from themselves. One cannot help but suspect that if they recognized the convulsions of spirit taking place across the broad spectrum of humanity, they might take their experiences a little less literally and look to the larger picture.

One philosopher who takes just such a sympathetic and yet critical approach to these "endtime anomalies" is Michael Grosso. In an important series of books, Grosso has critically examined a wide range of paranormal experiences surfacing in modern times, including prophetic NDEs, Marian visions, angelic apparitions, and UFO abductions, and has explored the underlying forces driving these experiences. His analysis directs us time and again to a revolution taking place in the depths of the collective unconscious as humanity enters the greatest crisis it has ever faced—the crisis of global survival. In

The Final Choice, Grosso argues that the threat of nuclear annihilation is activating a powerful archetype in the collective unconscious that is ultimately behind these anomalous experiences, the archetype of Death and Enlightenment (the perinatal death-rebirth cycle by another name). More recently, in *The Millennium Myth* he demonstrates that this archetype has been active throughout the modern era, and he skillfully traces its themes through the Renaissance, the Enlightenment, the founding of America, the proletarian revolution, and even the Third Reich. By placing New Age thought and many contemporary paranormal anomalies in this larger historical context, Grosso paints a portrait of a species subliminally aware that it has entered a box canyon from which there is no escape except through global self-transformation. If death is a psi liberator, he argues, then the specter of global death that hangs over the postmodern era may be fueling a profound psychic transformation of our species.

Two other thinkers widely cited for their careful and provocative discussions of humanity's future are Duane Elgin and Peter Russell. Duane Elgin's *Awakening Earth* is a profound rethinking of how we came to this moment in history and where we are trying to go. Elgin retells the story of human evolution by dividing it into eight stages, each characterized by a distinct mode of consciousness, leading from our archaic past to full planetary citizenship. Our civilization, he argues, is coming to the end of the fourth stage as it struggles to transcend the limits of the fragmented consciousness that birthed the scientific-industrial era. Given the accelerated pace of cultural evolution, he speculates that if we succeed in making this transition, we may navigate the remaining stages in as few as five hundred years.

Peter Russell shares Elgin's conviction that the pace of change has been consistently underestimated by students of human evolution such as Teilhard de Chardin, Ken Wilber, and Arnold Toynbee. In his books, *The White Hole in Time* and *The Global Brain Awakens,* Russell makes the argument that our entire civilization is a creation of the ego and as such cannot be saved in its current form. He describes the technological, social, and psychological pressures that are driving the human species beyond its egoic self-understanding and toward a more integrated, trans-egoic consciousness. As technology relentlessly shortens our learning feedback loops, time is becoming compressed, pushing us, he believes, toward a psychosocial breakthrough of global proportions.

The observations of these careful thinkers are supported by other researchers who have demonstrated that the theme of global transformation sometimes shows up in the most unlikely places.

Ken Ring, it will be remembered, demonstrated in *Heading toward Omega* that many persons who have had unusually deep NDEs have had visions of the imminent death and rebirth of industrial civilization. These visions are generally consistent with one another, even though the persons involved had no knowledge of each other. In them, various geological catastrophes and global disruptions signal the complete collapse of life as we know it, to be followed by the spiritual rebirth of our species and an era of unprecedented global integration. As Ring summarizes it:

> Whether the earth is shaken by natural catastrophes, or nuclear warfare, or both, earth and the life upon it does survive. More than that, however: A New Age emerges and the devastating changes that have preceded it are understood to have been necessary purgations effecting the transformation of humanity into a new mode of being. By analogy, just as the individual near-death experiencer may have to endure the pain and suffering associated with the trauma of almost dying before positive personal transformation can take place, so the world may need to undergo a "planetary near-death experience" before it can awaken to a higher, more spiritual, collective consciousness with universal love at its core.[1]

After considering a number of interpretations of these visions, Ring steers away from a literal reading and recommends that we take them as a measure of the dramatic spiritual turning point humanity has come to. Quoting another but speaking for himself, Ring writes:

> For me, the cataclysmic prophecies that are rife in current literature foreshadow a revolution of the most astonishing proportions. . . . I sense the approach of a psychological earthquake the magnitude of which has not been experienced in the human awareness for millennia and may not have been experienced in the human awareness ever before.[2]

Psychedelic Experience and Humanity's Future

I have come to share the belief of these authors that evolution is driving humanity to a global psychosocial breakthrough of historic proportions not only because of the convincing way they have marshaled their evidence but also because it has been a regular theme of my own inner work for a number of years. In psychedelic states, one sometimes gains deep experiential insight into the larger trajectory of human evolution and the historical threshold humanity has come to. I think this may be particularly the case for persons whose death-rebirth experience has slanted in the direction of the collective unconscious and will return to this point later.

The natural expansion beyond individual rebirth into the larger trajectory of the spiritual rebirth of humanity follows the inner logic of ego-death quite naturally. Ego-death destroys the deep feeling of ontological separation that organizes our most basic sense of egoic identity. As the partitions that imprison experience are first softened and then surrendered, one discovers that one's life cannot be isolated from the rhythms of the species we are part of. At a deeper level still, the life of our species appears to be a fold in the Divine Garment. All individuated experiences at all levels of reality appear to be simply folds within the seamless garment of existence. In this condition, the beginning and end of one's individual life become completely unretrievable, and one realizes that one's life never existed as a separate "thing" even for a moment. If one never was a separate entity to begin with, then there never was such a thing as a private spiritual agenda. What we may have thought of as our soul's private spiritual hunger was the registering in our localized awareness of a broader spiritual hunger that is stirring in humanity as a whole, pushing it to shake off its sleepy past and to awaken as one. Every step each of us has taken toward our individual awakening has been, at a deeper level, part of humanity's journey toward collective realization.

When the boundaries between self and surround have dissolved this completely, it is only natural that insights into humanity's evolutionary trajectory should occasionally come into focus. We would be surprised if this did not happen. Even before final ego-death occurs, the restrictions of egoic vision can become sufficiently softened to enable the larger current that we are part of to come into view. Repetition sharpens the focus as bits and pieces of understanding congeal into stable patterns.

To set the stage for the discussion that follows, I want to put on the table some of the experiences that have shaped my perception of the transformation humanity is undergoing. These experiences surfaced over a number of sessions covering a two and a half year period. In the interest of efficiency, I have lifted them out of their original contexts and woven them together into an integrated narrative, editing them only as necessary to fit them together into a coherent story line. In addition to illustrating deep resonances with the thinkers cited above, these experiences will establish a baseline of reference for the real focus of this chapter, which is the exploration of the possible implications for human evolution of the coming ecological crisis.

Sessions 23–41

When I moved beyond the cleansing portion of the session, I was met by a large assembly of beings who appeared to have been called to participate in today's events. They had the feeling-tone of being master shamans. Under their watchful eye I was escorted to an arena where a day of disclosure had been planned. What "I" was at this point is difficult to describe. The hours of painful cleansing had already shattered my egoic reality and left me in an extremely porous transpersonal state. As we approached the arena, the procession was stopped at regular intervals and interrogated. In order to continue, one had to demonstrate one's knowledge of the inner workings of the universe. I was surprised to find that I appeared to possess the required knowledge, as I was always passed along. With each checkpoint, my experiential reality changed dramatically as deeper and deeper modes of archetypal experience of incalculable age and expanse opened. Eventually spacetime reality was left behind entirely, and I found myself "alone" in a condition that was seemingly without boundaries of either time or space, soaking in the bliss and clarity of transcendence.

I then learned that I was going to be shown a portion of the larger plan for the human species. As preposterous as this suggestion may sound to ordinary consciousness, in my current state it seemed entirely feasible. I had no time to debate these matters, for suddenly something opened and I was drawn into an even more refined and concentrated reality that felt to be the power and intelligence driving evolution itself. I entered into what for want of a better image could be described as a vast, concentrated "stream" underlying physical existence, and this stream seemed to be the formative intent of the Creator Itself. I dissolved completely into this stream and became one with it. The following experiences emerged while I was in this state.

I was first taken back to the primordial beginning before creation and there experienced human evolution in the context of a larger cosmic agenda. Suddenly I was overwhelmed by the most extraordinary Love, a love unlike anything I had ever encountered before. It was a romantic love, cosmic in scope and intensity. As I stabilized under this amorous assault, I began to remember a romance from deep

within my history. An ancient love, a divine love of unbelievable pro-
portions. I was a Cosmic Being being loved by another Cosmic Being.
Though at one level I had never been separated from my Lover, at an-
other level we had been separated for billions of years, and my return
was rekindling our ancient love.

    The pieces were hard to catch. Creation seemed to be a reality
that had come forth from the dynamic relation between two Cosmic
Beings, which had themselves emerged from a more fundamental
Primal Unity. One being, who felt more like a He, had remained fully
conscious outside of matter while the other had plunged Herself into
the task of creating the material dimension, knowing in advance that
She would lose Her self-awareness in this work and become uncon-
scious of Her true reality for billions of years. She had voluntarily
submitted to this long and painful exile in order to create the raw
substance of physical life that would in time become transparent to
divine intention as matter evolved into full self-awareness. This work
now largely complete, the self-imposed exile was coming to an end,
and the Lovers were being reunited at long last.

    The magnitude of the Love that lay at the font of creation was be-
yond description. To awaken to this Love was to remember a primor-
dial decision that I had somehow participated in. It was part of my
spiritual genetic makeup, something I had inherited along with
everything else that I had not understood about my life. Remember-
ing choices made before matter and time even existed, I reconnected
with the Divine Love that had inspired these choices. This experience
completely shattered my heart, and I wept deeply.

    From this perspective, I experienced all the suffering that hu-
manity had endured as taking place not outside this Love but inside
it. I realized that all the suffering inherent in evolution was noble be-
yond words. It was all part of a cosmic plan that had been entered
into freely by all participants, however unconscious of this fact we
had become along the way. The nobility of great suffering voluntar-
ily shouldered in the name of Divine Love, suffering that would
stretch across millions of years, suffering that would become so ut-
terly inscrutable that it would be used as evidence that the universe
itself was devoid of compassion, this was the nobility of humanity's
gift to the Creator. All of the suffering that humanity had endured
and would continue to endure, especially the suffering of forgetful-
ness itself, was part of a consciously chosen creative process, a process
that had not yet come to full fruition.

    I saw that out of the seething desires of history, out of the violent
conflicts and the scheming of individuals and nations, there was now

driving forward a new awareness in human consciousness. Its birth in us is no less difficult or violent than the birth of a new continent through volcanic upheaval. It drives upward from the floor of our being, requiring a transposition of everything that has gone before to make room for its new organizational patterns.

The great difficulty I have is describing the enormity of what is being birthed. The true focus of this creative process is not individuals but all humanity. It is actually trying to reawaken the entire species. What is emerging is a consciousness of unprecedented proportions, the entire human species integrated into a unified field of awareness. The species reconnected with its Fundamental Nature. Our thoughts tuned to Source Consciousness. Having moved beyond linear time into "deep time," I experienced this both as a projected destiny and also as a realized actuality. It was simultaneously something to be accomplished and something already accomplished. This quantum jump in our evolutionary status precipitated a wholesale reorganization of global culture. It signaled a turning point that would forever divide the human story into the before and after of THE GREAT AWAKENING.

I saw humanity climbing out of a valley and just ahead, on the other side of the mountain peak and beyond our present sight, was a brilliant, sun-drenched world that was about to break over us. The time frame was enormous. After millions of years of struggle and ascent, we were poised on the brink of a sunrise that would forever change the conditions of life on this planet. All current structures would quickly become irrelevant. All truths would quickly be rendered passé. Truly a new epoch was dawning. The lives of everyone living on the edge of this pivotal time in history had been helping to bring about this global shift.

As I witnessed this scene, I saw that though we did not know the deep future at a personal level, there was a more encompassing level of awareness that could see it very clearly. This was a deeply moving and clarifying experience. Just as we ask our children to do all sorts of difficult tasks that they do not understand yet that we know will be important to their future, there was likewise a "parental intelligence" that had set a task for humanity knowing what was just around the corner for it. We individual humans could not see what was coming and so did not understand why things were the way they were. Yet isolated from the future, the present makes absolutely no sense. To be ignorant of the future would be to be functionally blind, and our species is not blind. There is an intelligence within it, guiding it, that knows the future and is preparing us for it as systematically as we prepare our homes for the changes of the seasons.

I could not see the specifics of what the future held. What I experienced was overwhelming light and bliss, and though these may sound disappointingly vague, they in fact revealed more to me than any details possibly could. I knew the brilliant light to be the radiance of enlightenment and the bliss was the joy of liberation. The human species was poised on the brink of a profound and inclusive spiritual awakening.

From this perspective I saw that our culture's scientific "knowledge" about the origin of life was profoundly incomplete in two respects. First, our materialistic understanding of the actual mechanism of evolution is pitifully incomplete, and second, we have been basing our interpretations on what has emerged just up to this point in time, ignoring the obvious fact that we have seen only the early scenes of a much larger play. Imagine someone from antiquity who was completely ignorant of cars observing the early stations of an automobile assembly line and trying to comprehend what was being built. We simply see too little to guess what is coming and therefore do not properly understand what has gone before. The depth of our ignorance is measured by our conviction that our universe has been assembled by accident. In being given glimpses of the future, in touching the edges of the Creator's intent, I saw that evolution was indeed no accident but a creative act of supreme brilliance and that humanity was being taken across a threshold that would change it forever.

I then moved deeper into the unified field of existence and experienced the dynamics of humanity's awakening as movements initiated and orchestrated by a single, integrating Intelligence. Previously my frame of reference for understanding these processes had been individual human beings, and the themes of individual evolution are the skillful exercise of free will over vast epochs of time. Now I was drawn into a superordinate level of reality that revealed a deeper organizational pattern, a pattern that paradoxically did not contradict the reality of individual agency. From this perspective, I experienced the evolution of our species as the systematic growth of a Single Organism, a unified and unifying Being that all of us were part of. The subtlety of the cooperation of the parts with the whole was extraordinary. Nothing in our theological or philosophical systems does justice to the facts. To experience the incredible diversity of our species as a single unified field made many events clearer. New patterns sprang into view and the patterns made transparent sense.

What I "saw" was that the unified field was moving decisively and precipitously to become more aware of itself in spacetime.

Whereas previously it had existed as an extended fabric of being, largely unconscious of itself at the physical level, it was now waking itself up. Visually this took the form of energy coming together in swift, contractive spasms that created bright flashes of awareness. I repeatedly saw extended webs of energy suddenly contract and explode in brilliant flashes. In the past these flashes had not endured long and had been swallowed by the inertia of the collective unconscious of our species. Now, however, the flashes were beginning to hold their own. Not only were they not dissolving, but they were beginning to connect with other flashes occurring around the planet.

The next theme was that of purification. When an organism is called upon from within to become more conscious, it must first cleanse itself of the psychological by-products of living at its lower level of awareness. It must bring forward the residue of its past and purge that residue from the system in order to lay the foundation for a more refined level of operation. Our species was doing this in a wholesale manner and with great determination by crystallizing within itself generations that embodied this legacy. What I had previously seen simply as individuals reincarnating in order to clear individual karma, I now experienced as a highly centralized decision to cleanse the human mindfield of its collective karmic legacy in order to prepare humanity for what is coming. It was the coordinated exercise of the self-evolution of the species as a whole. At a deeper level it was the deliberate movement of the Divine Being that was evolving Itself through the experiences of our species. All our individual histories were expressions of this Being's larger history, our individual struggles were aspects of Its larger struggle. The process was so beautiful and so elegant that it swept me into a deep ecstasy that almost took me beyond my capacity to maintain coherence. It was not a vision but an experience of the reality itself.

From the center of this experience, it seemed to be the case that our current generation had been deliberately karmically configured to precipitate an intense cycle of collective purification. The poisons of humanity's collective past were being brought to the surface in us, and in transforming these poisons in our individual lives, we were making it possible for divine awareness to enter more deeply into future generations. We had volunteered for this role for both our personal benefit and the collective good. We were cells in a superorganism intent on rapid change. As such we were heavy with both the burdens of our collective past and the promise of our collective future. I saw that this century formed something of a watershed into which the karmic streams of history were flowing, and I knew that as this process came to fruition, our future condition as a species would be beyond anything we might project from our current state of fragmentation.

It is difficult to describe the jarring combination of emotions these insights stirred in me. On the one hand, I was deeply disturbed by the decisive and almost impersonal manner in which this transition was being effected. To experience entire generations of human beings as expressions of a larger evolutionary pivot was absolutely devastating. The entire process had the ruthlessness of Kali the destroyer, mercilessly cutting away the old to make way for the new. On the other hand, I also felt an exquisite tenderness coming from the Creator, who experienced with us every pain we had taken upon ourselves. Humans were so precious to the Creator that not a single ounce of pain, not a single tear was wasted. The depth of that divine care so moved me that no sacrifice seemed too large or unreasonable. Moreover, I could see that the future we were creating was a future that we ourselves would participate in through future incarnations. We were doing this for God, for others, and also for ourselves.

Eventually the multiplicity of perspectives from which this transition could be experienced became so overwhelming that it completely shattered me, and I exploded into a frame of reference that included all these levels. The remainder of the session was spent in this state of expanded, integrated plurality. The theme became the experience of "no-self." I experienced my work in the sessions as being not breaking through the shell of anything real (the death of a "self") but as the simple restoration of an open, inclusive wholeness that was and always had been the true reality. All else is mistaken illusion. For a short time the illusion was suspended and I experienced my life as pure process, a rippling of an expansive field of consciousness that supported endless ripples. What freedom of movement! What contentment in this spacious emptiness! How wonderful must be the experience of those who have stabilized this freedom.

These experiences reached beyond the ripple that was "me" into the morphic field of the species. It is difficult to describe this process because it was largely devoid of cognitive content, and I only began to grasp what was happening retrospectively. My frame of reference was not the usual self/surround polarity but the seamless fabric of unified existence, and yet there was a subtle agency operating that presupposed my individual historical existence as well. As best as I can put into words what was happening, it is this.

Just as my previous work had mediated the experience of collective anguish out of the collective field, my current task now seemed to be to mediate the experience of no-self into the collective surround. I experienced this primarily in terms of a flow of energy moving through me into the species-mind. To the extent that this flow took cognitive form at all, it took the form of becoming comfortable with the loss of boundaries. This had many aspects to it—being comfortable surrendering the boundaries of race, the boundaries of socioeconomic distinctions, the boundaries of nationality, the boundaries of religion. Wherever we had drawn boundaries around ourselves in history, there was fear. I seemed to be mediating a calming energy that encouraged the dissolving of these boundaries and the softening of these fears. This went on for a very long time as boundary after boundary fell to a social melding. Soothing energies moved through me and reached into the human field, making it a bit easier for persons to relax and yield to the flow of historical events that were challenging and dissolving the unreal divisions humanity had drawn upon itself. Together we were paving the way for a future that was radically unlike the present.

There is a social awakening coming, a time when we will have dropped our attempt to live in the atomized cells of our historical past and will have appropriated the truth of our inclusive nature. Everything we are currently undergoing both privately and collectively is paving the way for this future. The net result of these many experiences was to focus me on the question, "How can the entire species be awakened? What would it take for the whole of humanity to make this quantum jump in awareness?" Though I had seen that this awakening was our immediate historical task, I had not seen how it would be accomplished.

This is not a reading of history that one would necessarily form if one attended only to external events, for here the evidence is much more ambiguous. There are many encouraging signs, but for every positive indicator there are matching negative indicators. In some corners of the world, various liberation movements are healing the historical prejudices of race, gender, and sexual preference, but in other quarters long suppressed ethnic and religious hatreds are tearing nations apart. We have slowed the raping of our daughters but are accelerating the raping of Mother Earth. Genuine interest in spirituality is increasing, but so are private militias. The ecumenical movement is flanked by growing fundamentalist denominations that are hardening the caste distinction between the saved and the reprobate. Similarly, the spread of political democracy is being compromised by a growing social conservatism that is deepening the divide between "haves" and "have-nots," fueling new class struggles in the future. Meanwhile television continues to drive nails in our ecological coffin through its relentless barrage of advertisements for an environmentally hostile lifestyle and its mind-numbing banality.[3] Yet hidden within this pattern of increasing polarization are deep structural patterns of explosive evolutionary growth. One of these patterns is the accelerating pace of change itself.

The Pace of Change

Few have articulated the geometric acceleration of the pace of change more effectively than Peter Russell. One of the ways he makes this point in *The White Hole in Time* is by projecting the entire history of Earth's evolution onto New York's tallest building, the 108-story World Trade Center. Getting on an imaginary elevator on the ground floor when Earth was forming 4,600 million years ago, we travel through time to the present, covering approximately 42 million years with each floor. On this cosmological elevator ride, the simplest living cells don't emerge until the 25th floor, and photosynthesis occurs on the 50th. Oxygen breathing bacteria enter on the 60th floor, complex cells capable of sexual reproduction on the 70th, and multicellular organisms on the 80th. Fish appear on the 97th floor and crawl out of the sea on the 99th. Dinosaurs rule the Earth from the 104th to the 107th floor. Mammals do not appear until the penthouse, and *Homo erectus* shows up only a few inches from the ceiling.

It has taken 99.99 percent of life's journey to reach this point just inches away from the ceiling of the 108th floor, and our Neanderthal cousins have not yet even appeared on the scene. They do so a quarter of an inch from the ceiling, followed shortly by Cro-Magnon humans with language, clothes, and perhaps religion. Christ is born at about the thickness of a layer of paint on the ceiling and all modern history occupies approximately the space of a microscopic bacterium trapped under the paint.

It took the universe 10 billion years to create just over a hundred different elements, but with each shift in evolution from atoms to molecules to biological organisms, the pace of change has jumped exponentially. Molecules are more malleable than atoms, and biological organisms more malleable than molecules. When *Homo sapiens sapiens* appeared 50,000 years ago, the pace of evolution jumped again because now the universe's creativity could express itself in conceptual rather than just biological innovations. Now mind itself is the cutting edge of evolution, and underneath the paint, the pace of the mind's evolution has continued to accelerate.

One of the ways Russell illustrates this point is by looking at the rate at which scientific knowledge has been growing. If we let the entire sum of known scientific facts discovered between the emergence of *Homo sapiens sapiens* to the birth of Christ represent a single "unit" of collective knowledge, Russell estimates that it took approximately 1,500 years for this knowledge to be doubled to two units. It took much less time to double again, just 250 years, and only 150 years to double yet again. It next doubled in just 50 years, then 10 years, and then 7, and 6 years. Estimates are that the sum total of human knowledge is currently doubling every 18 months. No wonder we academics feel exhausted just trying to keep up in our fields of specialization.[4]

The same pattern of exponential growth is found if we look at the rate at which history-changing inventions have appeared. Drawing upon the work of Buckminster Fuller, Russell estimates that in 3000 B.C., an historically significant invention occurred about every two hundred years. By the time of Christ, that interval had

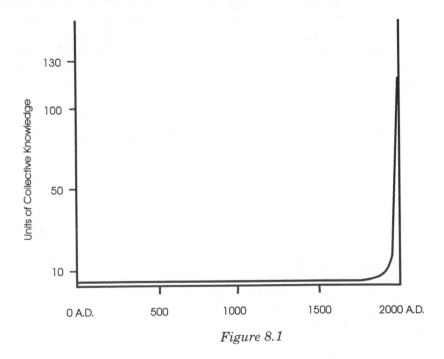

Figure 8.1

dropped to one every fifty years. By 1000 A.D., it had shortened again to thirty years, and by the Renaissance to one every three years. During the Industrial Revolution the rate dropped to one every three months and by 1950 it is estimated to have reached the staggering rate of one per month. Like an inward spiral, each turn of the evolutionary wheel takes less and less time to execute, thus in effect compressing time. Indeed, the world we are creating from our minds is today changing so fast that Russell believes the entire process is reaching melt-down proportions.

Getting across the Threshold

Russell's provocative analysis helps us appreciate the exponential rate at which change is taking place on the planet, but this by itself does not answer the specific question of how these changes might trigger the much awaited revolution in consciousness. In this area Russell seems to place the greatest weight on two factors—the telecommunications revolution and our reaching the population threshold of approximately 10 billion people, a threshold we will cross by the year 2030 given our current rate of growth.

The telecommunications revolution, combined with the increased ease of international travel, is profoundly changing our basic understanding of ourselves, taking us in directions few anticipated even as recently as a hundred years ago. Exposure to new experiences stimulates increased awareness, and increased awareness stimulates greater understanding and eventually more informed action. Through the eyes and ears of telecommunications, we are experiencing more of the world's cultural diversity than any previous generation on Earth, and thus we are being pushed to understand more and more as we try to come to terms with the entire human experience. This struggle to come to terms with the entirety of the human experience is shattering our religious, national, and cultural provincialisms and calling us to become what humans have never before been, world citizens. Our technology is summoning us to expand our sense of community until we *feel* identified with human beings everywhere, whatever their color, creed, or culture. This powerful force of expansion is also triggering the regressive reflex to retreat to an earlier time when we knew the world from inside smaller theological and national boxes. But the combination of the technology that connects and the technology that makes armed conflict no longer a viable option is forcing us to move beyond these boxes and enter a new and uncharted world that is at once both frightening and exhilarating.

Russell also draws an analogy between the growth of telecommunications, including the Internet, and the myelinizing of the human brain that is more subtle than this. His suggestion is that just as a minimum number of physical connections must be established in the brain to support a certain level of self-awareness, a minimum number of physical connections must similarly be established between human beings around the globe to support a higher level of species self-awareness. (As of 1995, the world had over 900 million telephones, about 17 for every 100 persons, and growing rapidly.) When the critical number of connections are in place, he argues, this fact itself will trigger the arising of a new understanding of our interdependence and thus a new understanding of ourselves. Telecommunications is literally shattering our physical isolation to the point that eventually it will no longer be possible for us to perceive ourselves as isolated individuals. If I understand Russell correctly, the idea seems to be that the medium of telecommunications will eventually reproduce at the physical level the psychospiritual reality of our interpenetration, thus stimulating us to awaken to our fundamental condition. He writes:

> As the communication links within humanity increase, we will eventually reach a time when the billions of information exchanges shuttling through the networks at any one time would create patterns of coherence in the global brain similar to those found in the human brain. Gaia would then awaken and become her equivalent of conscious.[5]

In addition, there is the provocative fact that at current rates of expansion, by the year 2000 the data-processing capacity of the global telecommunications network will equal the brain's. There is no guarantee, of course, that the capacity required to support individual self-awareness is the same as required to support species self-awareness, but the point holds an understandable fascination given the analogy Russell has developed.

The argument for the significance of the population figure of 10 billion hinges less on that exact figure than on the general fact that nature seems to require that certain concentrations of a phenomenon be reached before drawing forth from itself the emergent properties that bring a higher level of self-organization into existence. Patterns in the ascent of nature's self-organization from elementary particles to atoms to molecules to cells to organisms and to self-conscious organisms suggest that a critical number of a basic component is required at each level for the next higher level of self-organization to emerge. Russell cites a variety of physical data to suggest that 10 billion, or 10^{10}, is the approximate magic number required for a new order of existence to emerge. Very few cells, for example, contain less than 10^{10} atoms, and the average human brain cortex contains 10^{10} nerve cells. While I do not find his arguments for this particular figure convincing, the general pattern he has identified seems clear enough.

Russell's contribution to our understanding of the forces driving the spiritual renaissance of humanity extends far beyond the few ideas I have excerpted here. His book *The Global Brain Awakens*, a revised edition of his earlier book *The Global Brain*, is a rich source of information and insight into the factors contributing to global awakening including: the marriage of Western science and Eastern psychology to produce a new generation of pharmacological and electronic psychotechnologies, the rapid increase in the number of persons actively involved in consciousness work (doubling every four to five years), the fact that states of consciousness are contagious, and synchronicity as a symptom of increasing psychosocial coherence. There is only one important area where my perception of the future differs significantly from his, and it centers on the question of how much suffering a global spiritual rebirth might involve.

We have already seen that NDErs tend to see a time of extreme turmoil before the spiritual renaissance takes hold. Russell, on the other hand, seems to envision a transition that is less traumatic than this. Indeed, his portrait of the future is self-consciously optimistic, and he says he has deliberately chosen this emphasis because he believes that the images we hold of the future shape the future we actually create. A pessimistic vision of our future can easily become a self-fulfilling prophecy, and Russell wants to aim his reader toward a positive meeting with destiny.

Certainly Russell is correct about the danger of self-fulfilling prophecies and the cost of adopting negative scripts about a future we are still creating. And yet, if we do not address the suffering that such a transition might involve, I think we will undermine our ability to understand and manage this suffering should it overtake us. The risk of undermining our initiative must be balanced with a willingness to look deeply into the pain that this transition might involve in order to better understand and work with it. We do not want to augment the hardship in any way, but neither do we want to pretend that it will not be there, or that if it is there it means that something has gone wrong. Birth involves hard work, and if we do not prepare ourselves for the labor pains of this global birth, we will undermine our ability to experience these trials as a meaningful part of the transition we are making—a transition which in so many other respects Russell describes beautifully. For a genuine spiritual rebirth of our species to take place, there must first occur a death of our species-ego, and I believe that Russell underestimates the convulsions that this death will involve.

In turning to look more deeply into the darker side of this transition, I want to emphasize that I do not wish to subtract anything from Russell's account, but rather to add what I see as a missing piece to it. Far from fueling the forces of pessimism, I believe that the rebirth that is taking place is such an extraordinary opportunity for humanity that, like a new mother after the birth of her child, we will soon count our labor pains as a small thing. Though possibly overwhelming in the short term, they will quickly fall away as the future unfolds. Furthermore, far from undermining initiative and creativity, I want to empower them because I believe that as the impending historical events drive us to a point of critical instability, the choices we make will exert a disproportionately powerful influence on humanity's future. Only from a linear reading of history are we too close to the events in question to significantly affect their outcome. In a nonlinear reading of history, such as presented below, the influence of our choices increases dramatically as the critical transition draws near.

The Dark Night of the Species-Soul

The concept of the dark night of the soul is often used today as little more than a euphemism for a particularly difficult period in a person's life, but it is in fact a very advanced stage of psychospiritual growth reached by only the most committed spiritual aspirants. This arduous phase of development has well defined characteristics and shows up in all the mystical traditions under different names. The dark night is the final stage of a long spiritual process in which our identity as a discrete self is challenged at its core and ultimately surrendered. It culminates in a spiritual death and rebirth that is more profound than mere physical death. According to most mystical traditions, physical death alone does not unravel our deepest instinct for living as a separate self, and thus is usually followed by another birth. What dies in the dark night is precisely our deep attachment to separateness itself, and therefore the dark night represents the culmination of many lifetimes of spiritual effort.

If we extrapolate the experiences of our greatest mystics to the species as a whole, it would appear reasonable to speculate that the spiritual rebirth of our species cannot take place unless there first occurs a spiritual death. If ego-death is the term used to describe the spiritual death of the individual, we might describe the spiritual death of humanity as *species ego-death*. The question is: What form would such a collective transition take? What would it feel like?

At one level, this cultural death will involve the loss of certain deeply held ways of viewing the world, the collapse of deeply embedded intellectual paradigms, comparable to the earlier collapse of the medieval geocentric worldview. At a deeper level, I think this death will involve a deep shift in how we collectively *feel* about each other and the world at large. At this level, species ego-death may take the form of *the collective collapse of the experience of living in isolation*. It may be a falling away of feeling separate from everything, separate from each other and separate from the universe itself. In place of this sense of separation might arise a new feeling for the inherent wholeness of life, with circles of compassion rippling through life's web.

Our present sense of reality is one in which the edges of one person stop before the edges of another person begin. Our entire society is built upon this premise of ontological separation. It is the starting point of all our social contracts, all our moral debates. How we manage this separateness is what gives our life its distinctive flavor; it is the ontological prerequisite for everything we have understood life to be about. *Beyond the threshold of spiritual rebirth, however, separation is experienced as a smaller truth operating within the larger truth of interpenetration and common ground.* Parts are seen to cohere within and express the larger logic of the whole. Other persons are spontaneously *experienced* as partners in a complex dance, and because of this dance we are not just separate beings but vital parts of living patterns. We are the dancing itself. One's edges become softer and more porous, not in a pathological way that erodes individual agency but in a way which opens one to a *felt* connection with others and with the life-process itself. Self-interest is not diminished but extended exponentially. One literally begins to live a larger life.

The intellectual and social revolutions that have poured out of the modern mind are indicators that our species-ego has been falling apart for a long time now—the eclipse of biblical supremacy and the birth of global ecumenism; the ending of constitutionally sanctioned patriarchy and the growth of the women's movement; the collapse of the Newtonian-Cartesian worldview and the birth of quantum theory, followed by the new cosmology; the creation of weapons so destructive that they dare not be used; the emergence of the global economy; the discovery that our industrial civilization is ecologically unsustainable. Clearly whatever lies ahead is only the culmination of a process that has been underway for some time. And yet, I believe that the final death of the species-ego will have occurred only when the existential separation we presently feel has yielded to a collective experience of deep existential interpenetration, when narrowly defined self-interest has been replaced by a deeply felt, globally extended compassion. If this is so, the question then becomes: What would it take to push the forces of change already in motion to a point where we might open to this deeper experience of ourselves? What would it take for us to surrender our posture of existential separation en masse?

Religious fundamentalists look for external divine intervention to bring about this apocalyptic transformation, while some New Age authors expect massive geological disruptions to literally shake some sense into us. As different as these perspectives are, they have in common looking to something *outside* human experience to trigger the expected inner revolution. This approach to the problem, however, goes against the grain of all the lessons we have learned in the last several hundred years, which have taught us to look inside the system of which we are part rather than outside it to see to the true wonder. Ken Ring, it will be remembered, suggested that the earthquake scenario should be taken as an indicator of the magnitude of the approaching change rather than a literal description of how it would actually come about.

In *The Final Choice,* Michael Grosso emphasized the threat of nuclear destruction as the force that would drive us across the threshold. Because these weapons have come out of the human mind and heart, I think Grosso is looking in the right direction. In the nuclear scenario, it is our own intelligence and cold brutality that is driving our self-transformation. And yet, with the ending of the cold war and the break-up of the U.S.S.R., the threat of nuclear annihilation has receded for the time being. Nuclear terrorism by itself cannot generate the anxiety of full-scale species-extinction, for it takes two superpowers with large nuclear arsenals to enact this insanity.

Even as the global nuclear threat recedes, however, a new and more virulent danger has quickly emerged to take its place—the threat of ecological self-extinction. The crisis of ecological sustainability is even more lethal than the nuclear crisis because it is not being generated by an overzealous military minority but by the very fabric of modern civilization. The crisis is being driven by a lifestyle that all industrialized nations have come to expect and all pre-industrialized nations are clamoring to achieve. Thus it is a crisis that involves the entire human family and one that each of us contributes to each and every day that we participate in our consumer society. It is my belief that the crisis of sustainability will drive the forces of change outlined by Russell and others into the red zone and precipitate a melt-down of civilization as we know it. Because it will push humanity so completely beyond its historical limits, I believe that it has the potential to ignite the spiritual transformation we have been discussing. *If there is a species ego-death in our immediate future, I think it will be triggered by the impending ecological crisis of sustainability.*

The Crisis of Sustainability

Our best environmental estimates are that current industrial and social trends are driving humanity toward a devastating ecological and economic collapse that will take place probably within the next several decades. As we show no signs of pulling back from our suicidal policy of perpetual economic expansion, the only uncertainty seems to be how severe the ecological overshoot will be and how catastrophic the period or periods of recovery after the collapse takes place. Few have attempted to predict this approaching crisis more precisely than Donella Meadows, Dennis Meadows, and Jørgen Randers. In the early 1970s, they led an international team of researchers working in conjunction with the System Dynamics Group of the Sloan School of Management at M.I.T. to create a computer model of the world economy. They published their analysis of our global industrial, social, and environmental trends in a book entitled *The Limits to Growth,* which became an international bestseller. Their computer model, called World3, stirred great controversy by predicting that at current rates of growth, human society would exceed planetary limits within a hundred years. Twenty years later they returned with improved data and revised projections in their book *Beyond the Limits.* In addition to updating their forecasts, they explored various policy options by adjusting the variables in their model.

The sobering graph in figure 8.2 is their projection of the fate of the planet if we continue our current rates of population growth, industrial production, and material consumption. This scenario assumes that the world society continues on its current path as long as possible, that is, that the policies that influence economic and population growth remain essentially the same, that technology in agriculture, industry, and social services continues to evolve in roughly the same manner as now, and that there is no extraordinary effort to reduce pollution or conserve resources. In this projection, population and industrial growth continue until in about 2020 a combination of environmental and natural resource constraints constrict the capacity of the capital sector to sustain investment. As industrial capital falls, food production and social services (such as health care) fall with it, causing a decrease in life expectancy and a rise in the death rate.

Meadows's team found that even if they changed the variables and incorporated a number of more optimistic assumptions, a traumatic collapse was postponed but not avoided. The graph in figure 8.3 is their model's projection if the following assumptions are made: (1) twice the global natural resource endowment assumed in the first scenario, (2) an aggressive use of pollution control technologies starting in 1995 to bring pollution down 3 percent per year until 1975 levels are reached, (3) an aggressive use of technologies to increase

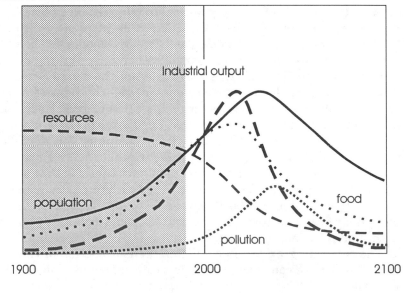

Figure 8.2

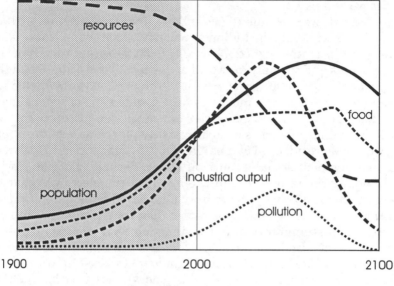

Figure 8.3

agricultural yield per acre 2 percent per year, and (4) a program to reduce global land erosion by a factor of 3. Even with these optimistic assumptions, a global crisis erupts by 2040. It takes a little longer to show up than in the first scenario and the rate of collapse is softer, but the collapse is nevertheless devastating.[6]

Not all of the test runs that Meadows's team ran on World3 resulted in economic collapse, but most did. This fact is a measure, they believe, not of any design flaw in their model but of just how far beyond sustainable limits our global economy is currently operating. The scenarios that avoided collapse required making fundamental shifts in our political and social priorities in addition to all the technological investments already mentioned. Specifically, they required a comprehensive global decision to (1) limit family size to two surviving children and (2) voluntarily lower our material demands to the goal of a simple but adequate standard of living. Furthermore, they required that these shifts be made immediately, starting in 1995. A delay of as little as twenty years in implementing these policies produced a major collapse in the world economic order by 2070. According to World3's calculations, the transition to an ecologically sustainable economy is achievable even now but requires an heroic commitment to a different future. Each year we delay deepens the price we will pay.

And yet, we continue to act as if we had time to spare. In 1992, over 1,600 scientists, including a majority of the living Nobel laureates in the sciences, signed a *Warning to Humanity* stating that "human beings and the natural world are on a collision course" and that "a great change in our stewardship of the earth and the life on it is required, if vast human misery is to be avoided and our global home on this planet is not to be irretrievably mutilated." Despite this and other warnings, the crisis of sustainability played no significant part in the 1996 presidential campaign. What little mention there was of the environment actually contributed to a deepening of the crisis by reinforcing the impression in the minds of the electorate that the "environmental issue" was simply a question of cleaning up toxic dumps and reducing emissions rather than confronting the deep ecological unsustainability of our civilization as it is currently structured. We may find the social wisdom and political will to avoid the collapse that Meadows and her team have forecast, and I hope we do, but the shortsightedness of politicians who can't see beyond their re-elections and the continued addiction of our religious and educational institutions to the myth of scientific progress suggest that we will stumble into hell before we cross into heaven.[7]

The ecotheologian Thomas Berry has offered the following sober assessment of our situation:

> The oppression of the natural world by the plundering of the industrial powers has so endangered the basic functioning of natural forces that we are already on the verge of total dysfunctioning of the planet. We cannot mediate the situation as though there were presently some minimal balance already existing that could be slightly modified so that a general balance could come into being. The violence already done to the earth is on a scale beyond all understanding. . . . Never before has the human community been confronted with a situation that required such a sudden and total change in life style under the threat of a comprehensive degradation of the planet.

In *Awakening Earth*, Dwayne Elgin describes humanity's near future in the following terms. (The reader might notice the striking use of perinatal imagery, which I believe is largely unconscious on Elgin's part.)

We are moving into a time of steel-gripped necessity—a time of intense, planetary compression. Within a generation, the world will become a superheated pressure cooker in which the human family is crushed by the combined and unrelenting forces of an expanding world population, a dramatically destabilized global climate, dwindling supplies of nonrenewable energy, and mounting environmental pollution. The circle has closed, and there is nowhere to escape [BPM II]. These forces are so unyielding, and the stresses they will place on our world are so extreme [BPM III], that human civilization will either descend into chaos or ascend in a spiraling process of profound transformation [BPM IV].[8]

Elgin describes the early twenty-first century as "superheated decades," and already the pressure is building. People are beginning to realize that the Earth cannot sustain perpetual economic growth, but most cannot yet see an alternative. The anxiety is building with each news broadcast of another environmental insult, another species lost, another calculated industrial "accident."

If Meadows, Berry, Elgin and many other environmentally informed writers are correct, this collective anxiety will intensify in the decades ahead as centuries of ecological IOUs come due. Without a fundamental realignment of our social priorities, we will be simultaneously overtaken on many fronts by events that get out of hand and can't be stopped. People will become increasingly alarmed as conditions relentlessly deteriorate, forcing them to let go of their assumptions at deeper and deeper levels. There will be less and less that they will be able to hold on to, fewer givens they can assume—how they will live, where they will live, what they will do for a living, what society can provide, what can be possessed. Panic will grow as what they had considered the normal and necessary structures of their world are torn away from them. Step by step, systems will collapse. Millions, possibly billions will die or find their lives pressed to desperate limits. "The world will seem to be going insane," predicts Elgin, and because the world is wired in a global telecommunications network, all of this suffering will take place right in front of us. The "electronic intimacy" of television will intensify the pain by showing us the global dimensions of our local suffering.

These scenarios are familiar to anyone who has read the ecological literature and do not need to be rehearsed further. The point I want to emphasize here is that if these events do come to pass, *they will stimulate the morphic field of the species-mind as never before in human history.* All individual human experience takes place within the field of the species-mind. Its presence is so subtle as to usually be undetectable, and we customarily feel our individual thoughts and feelings as taking place in a psychological vacuum. We feel our minds to be unconnected to the minds of persons standing to our left and right. This sense of ontological privacy is actually a tribute to the subtlety of the species-mind. If it were less subtle, we could not help but experience our interconnectedness and thus feel less separated from each other.

If the world becomes a "superheated pressure cooker," it will put the species-mind under enormous pressure. As the suffering and deaths mount, as the anxiety and despair deepens, all of this trauma will register not only in our individual minds but also in the species-mind. The scope and intensity of this crisis will be unlike anything we have ever faced before. It will not be like severe natural catastrophes that affect only a small percentage of the earth's population and are over relatively quickly; rather it will affect the entire planet and will last for decades, becoming only deeper with time.

Because the dimensions of this crisis will be historically unprecedented, we do not know how the species-mind will react. There are two possible scenarios we should consider. In the first, the species-mind would continue to function the way it functions now, as the quiet backdrop to the human drama. In this "business as usual" scenario, the collective unconscious would continue to be the silent partner, and only visionaries and meditators would know of its existence. The second possibility is that these events would impact the species-mind so severely that it would actually change the basic equilibrium of the collective unconscious. In this scenario, the ground of the human psyche would actually shift. Functions that had previously operated silently in the background might move forward and make themselves felt. Capacities which had been latent might be activated.

Both these responses are possible. Duane Elgin seems to envision something like the second scenario when he says:

> Despite all our good intentions, without this coming era of collective distress and adversity, the human family is unlikely to awaken to its global identity and evolutionary responsibility. It is the immense suffering of millions—even billions—of precious human beings coupled with the widespread destruction of many other life-forms that will burn through our complacency and isolation. Needless suffering is

the psychological and psychic fire that can awaken our compassion and fuse individuals, communities, and nations into a cohesive and consciously organized global civilization.[9]

I, too, think the second is more likely, but I have come to this conclusion primarily on experiential grounds and not on the basis of theoretical observations.

In chapter 3 I observed that when one's perinatal experience has been strongly slanted in the collective direction, the resulting death-rebirth experience also tends to contain strong collective elements. The final transition is simply too large to be described as mere ego-death. To help clarify this complex process, I suggested that we distinguish two tiers of the death-rebirth process—individual ego-death and species ego-death. In such a death-rebirth sequence, the death-rebirth of the individual tends to be subsumed into the larger drama of the death-rebirth of the species that is driving up from the depths of the collective unconscious. In these sessions time dilates, and one appears to gain selective access to the birth pangs of the species as it draws forth a new form of life from itself. One witnesses and actually *participates* in the death of our civilization and the birth of a new historical era.

Transtemporal experiences are notoriously difficult to interpret, of course, and the possibility of error must be acknowledged from the start. One's individual death-rebirth may be distorting one's perception of the larger collective process. It may be the case that these visions of cultural catharsis are simply the echoes of one's individual death-rebirth rebounding off the walls of some transpersonal canyon, that the existential collapse of "reality as we know it" is here simply taking the visionary form of the meltdown of global civilization. Furthermore, the history of those who, with noble intentions, have tried to take the measure of the future has on the whole been so dismal that this alone is reason to pause long before crossing this particular threshold. And yet, there is also the possibility of accurate perception arising in these special states of consciousness. Acknowledging fully the pitfalls involved and the highly speculative nature of the enterprise, I want to explore the second scenario given above and to offer a line of thought on the possible impact of the eco-crisis on human evolution. This line of thought will draw from multiple sources, but it is at core an attempt to interpret my own experience within a broader theoretical framework. After presenting the theoretical concepts, I will include the psychedelic experience that lies behind these observations.

Far-from-Equilibrium Systems and the Species-Mind

If humanity enters a sustained global ecological crisis, the field of the species-mind may be pressed so hard that it might be driven far from its previously "normal" operating equilibrium. It might, in effect, come to resemble what system theorists call a far-from-equilibrium system, or a nonequilibrium system. Its behavior might thus begin to resemble in certain basic respects the behavior of physical far-from-equilibrium systems. These are the three central assumptions that lie behind everything that follows—(1) that the species-mind is a unified psychic field, (2) that this field might be driven into a far-from-equilibrium condition by the eco-crisis, and (3) that its behavior in this condition might in certain respects resemble the behavior of physical far-from-equilibrium systems. I recognize that these are enormous assumptions that need to be carefully argued. Without setting out the full argument here, I propose to take certain insights from systems theory and chaos theory into the behavior of physical systems in the far-from-equilibrium state and use these insights to formulate a speculative hypothesis for how the eco-crisis may impact the mental field of the species-mind.

In the previous chapter, I described how my experience as a teacher first sensitized me to the experiential dynamics of group minds. I explained the long process through which I discovered that attention is psychic energy and that when group interest in a subject is strong and well focused, the energy in the room rises appreciably. When this happens, the minds present in the room sometimes stop functioning exclusively in their "stand-alone mode," and they become more transparent to their common ground. In this heightened state of awareness, both individual and group creativity is augmented, and deep personal transformations sometimes take place. The step from the class mind to the species-mind is very large but not theoretically complicated. One has only to imagine an exponential increase in the key variables to begin to appreciate what might happen if the entire species were forced by desperate circumstances to pay attention to itself in a similarly concentrated and sustained manner.

In physics when certain media are supercooled or superheated, or when they are subjected to high-energy bursts, they sometimes shift into a far-from-equilibrium state. While in this state they appear to do the impossible. Nonlinear behavior replaces linear behavior; systems phase-lock in unpredictable ways to allow previously separate systems to act as one. Nonlinear interactions at critical values sometimes produce spontaneous self-organizing forms called solitons.

Solitons reflect the fact that nature is profoundly interconnected and that sometimes these hidden connections can be triggered to produce a higher form of integrated order. Light, for example, may suddenly pass through an otherwise opaque substance, because the light and the substance have momentarily aligned themselves in such a way as to become a single system. This example of soliton penetration is called "self-induced transparency."[10]

If the species-mind were driven into something analogous to a far-from equilibrium state, it too might show increasingly nonlinear characteristics. Nonlocal psychological effects might become more prominent; something like psychological phase-locking might take place. Under these extreme conditions, systems that were previously isolated might spontaneously begin to interact with each other to form new connecting patterns.[11] *The capacity for synergistic experience that is inherent within the collective unconscious could emerge into our collective conscious experience.* If this were to happen, it would feel as though the human psyche were becoming alive at new levels, causing the human family to experience itself in new and previously impossible ways. Interconnections between people that had previously been too subtle to detect could start to become obvious. As our sense of psychological isolation began to break down, compassion for the now less-distant "other" would increase. And because these developments were being generated within a far-from-equilibrium system, they would occur much faster than anyone might have predicted on the basis of linear behavior alone.

Chaos theory tells us that when a system is driven beyond equilibrium, the subtle interconnectedness that lies latent beneath its surface can sometimes emerge to reshape the system itself. In his well-known study of dissipative structures, Ilya Prigogine has shown that one of the properties of far-from-equilibrium systems is their capacity for higher self-organization. When driven into far-from equilibrium conditions, some systems do not just break down; they generate new structures that pull higher forms of order out of the surrounding chaos. It is as if nature reaches into herself and draws forth higher orders of self-organization that are latent within the system, hidden and quiescent until their potential is actualized. The soliton is an example of a dissipative structure. Another example comes from the life cycle of the slime mold. For most of their lives, slime molds exist as single cell amoeba. When deprived of food, they send out a chemical pulse that signals other nearby cells. Thousands of cells begin to collect until they reach a critical mass, at which point they self-organize into an entity that can crawl across the forest floor. When they reach a location where the food is better, they develop stalks and release spores into the air from which new individual amoeba are formed. Prigogine sees examples of such self-organizing structures emerging everywhere—in biology, in the growth of cities and political movements, and in the evolution of stars. "Today," says Prigogine, "this seems to be a very, very simple thing, a nearly trivial thing. It's a law now that in the nonlinear range, far-from-equilibrium gives rise to structure, brings order out of chaos. In far-from-equilibrium, matter has radical new properties."[12]

If matter has new properties when pushed far beyond its equilibrium state, might not the same be true of mind? I want to suggest that the global eco-crisis may push the field of the species-mind so hard that it too may draw forth new structures from itself, structures that reflect its inherent capacity for higher degrees of self-organization. Under the stress of so much suffering, the balance of the collective unconscious might shift. If this were to happen, synergistic tendencies that are latent within the species-mind may become manifest, exerting a coordinating influence within seemingly disparate human activities. Synchronicities may increase. Realities that are unconscious to all but a few may become available to many. The ground of "common sense" may shift as the floor of the collective unconscious rises into awareness.[13]

It is widely recognized today that when individuals are thrown into life-threatening circumstances such as a near-death experience, their thought processes may accelerate to hundreds of times their normal rate. Ordinary consciousness often falls away suddenly to reveal underlying transpersonal capacities. Within seconds they may have access to mental capacities that are inherent within the human system but dormant in normal circumstances. Using the present vocabulary, we might say that the near-death episode throws their minds into a far-from-equilibrium condition that gives rise to the dissipative structures of transpersonal states of consciousness. Moreover, these transient episodes often have permanent aftereffects. Psychologists have shown that after the near-death crisis has passed, subjects are often left with permanent changes to their mental and psychic functioning, together with changes in their personal values and basic philosophical orientation.

From a Gaian perspective, the eco-crisis is overtaking humanity with similar lightning speed. Hundreds of years may seem like seconds to the species-mind. The question is, will our collective brush with possible extinction pull from the collective unconscious something analogous to what NDEs regularly draw forth from individuals? Can the mechanisms which we observe in cases of individual transformation give us clues to the mechanisms of collective transformation that might become operational for the species as a whole?[14]

Moving on to another point, if a system goes sufficiently far into the nonequilibrium state, it comes to a fork in its destiny called a bifurcation point. Bifurcation is an essential concept in Prigogine's thought. A bifurcation point is a moment of truth in which a system must "choose" which one of several evolutionary paths it will follow. At each such point, a flux occurs in which many possible futures exist. Decisions made at these points will cumulatively direct the system either toward higher forms of order or toward fragmenting chaos.

Chaos theory tells us that when a system approaches a bifurcation point, it becomes extremely sensitive to influence. Very small inputs are amplified by the constant feedback of iteration, or repetition, that is characteristic of far-from-equilibrium systems. As Briggs and Peat explain in *Turbulent Mirror*:

> A bifurcation in a system is a vital instant when something as small as a single photon of energy, a slight fluctuation in external temperature, a change in density, or the flapping of a butterfly's wings in Hong Kong is swelled by iteration to a size so great that a fork is created and the system takes off in a new direction.[15]

This ability of a system to amplify a small change into a major consequence constitutes an important part of the system's creativity and is characteristic of all far-from-equilibrium systems.

If the eco-crisis is indeed driving humanity to a bifurcation point in its history, we are entering a time when small changes may be disproportionately amplified by the hypersensitivity of the species field. In such a pressurized environment, the clarifying effect of the spiritual practices and "right action" of a comparatively small number of persons may become greatly disproportionate to their actual numbers. By any reasonable estimate, the critical mass needed to change the course of human history still lies a long way off if conditions were normal, but the point is precisely that conditions will *not* be normal in the future. *The severity of our crisis may actually be lowering the threshold of influence.*

Within a linear view of historical cause and effect, the forces that are generating the eco-crisis are so deeply entrenched in our behavior and social institutions that it may seem that there is little that individuals can do to change the outcome, especially with comparatively so little time remaining. But when chaos theory is combined with morphic field theory, a nonlinear view of causality emerges that exponentially increases the potential influence of individuals as the crisis deepens. According to this nonlinear view of history, as we spiral into the extreme crisis created by the eco-crisis, the collective unconscious will be put under increasing pressure from the global collapse of our industrialized civilization. This pressure will translate into highly unstable psychic conditions that will be both dangerous and filled with opportunity for humanity.

It goes without saying that the extreme nature of this crisis will severely tempt us to respond in a regressive manner. There will no doubt be many voices calling for the "necessary sacrifice" of a certain percentage of the population for the survival of the rest and others beating the national drums for a series of resource wars—the first of which we have already fought in the Persian Gulf—that may allow us to maintain our ecologically destructive lifestyle a few decades longer. All the measures of self-worth that have divided us in the past including race, gender, religion, nationality, and so on will be exploited to legitimize creating narrow definitions of our self-interest. We will have to make the difficult political choice of whether to be guided by our fragmented past or by a future vision of global inclusiveness. My point here is that *in this supersaturated psychic matrix, our individual choices may have enormous ramifications if they reflect our highest potential and seek the greatest good of humanity as a whole.* As we approach this fork in our destiny, the scale to the next step in human evolution—indeed the scale to survival itself—may be tipped by a much smaller number of individuals than we had previously suspected. Jung grasped this fact clearly when he wrote:

> We are living in what the Greeks called the *kairos*—the right moment—for a "metamorphosis of the gods," of the fundamental principles and symbols. This peculiarity of our time, which is certainly not of our conscious choosing, is the expression of the unconscious man within us who is changing. Coming generations will have to take account of this momentous transformation if humanity is not to destroy itself through the might of its own technology and science. . . . So much is at stake and so much depends on the psychological constitution of modern man. . . . Does the individual know that *he* [and she] is the makeweight that tips the scales?[16]

Ever since the publication in 1934 of Lovejoy's *The Great Chain of Being*, it has been widely held by transpersonal thinkers that the great saints and sages have given us glimpses into our evolutionary future. Their spiritual accomplishments are thought to have created the psychic blueprints that are functioning as *strange attractors* to focus the collective wave erupting within human awareness. And yet, if the events described here come to pass, I think it will fall to those who are actually living during these critical years to function as psychic bridges between these strange attractors and humanity's actual future. In the highly unstable, supercharged morphic field of tomorrow, those persons who have already made the transition individually that humanity is trying to make collectively, who have begun to think and act as ecologically responsible global citizens, who have truly lifted from their hearts the divisions of race, religion, class, gender, nation, and so on, may function as seed crystals working in conjunction with these strange attractors to catalyze new patterns in human awareness. In this setting, each of our individual efforts to bring spiritual, social, political, and ecological sanity into our lives may have far reaching consequences.[17]

A Transpersonal Perspective

I wish that I could give the reader an absolutely convincing proof for this vision of humanity's future, but I cannot. I know that the steps I am taking are large and that arguments from analogy are only as strong as our reasons for thinking that the analogy applies in the first place. Only time will tell if the parallels I am drawing between far-from-equilibrium physical systems and the collective unconscious will gather empirical evidence around them. Until that time, all I can offer is a line of speculation that is intellectually coherent and possesses a certain intuitive appeal. Beyond that, there is only experience, and while experiences can be rationally compelling for the person who has them, they obviously have less power for those who inherit them secondhand. Nevertheless, for those who understand psychedelic states and trust the insights that can arise in them, I would like to share the following experience. The material in this session may deepen the reader's appreciation of some of the experiential aspects of the collective transformation I have been outlining.

Session 55

The first two hours of the session were spent in very difficult cleansing. It seemed like it was endless, that I would never get to the bottom of the disturbance. . . . Then suddenly something happened. The pain I was dealing with suddenly broke apart. Something that had been experientially real suddenly became as brittle as painted glass and shattered. As it shattered the pieces fell away to reveal an entirely different reality underneath. It was as if the inner gestalt of the particular difficulty I was dealing with finally reached its perfect pitch and then shattered into a hundred shards. A voice said, "Enough of that," and it was finished. There was no gradual transition, but rather a sudden, abrupt transition from something artificial to something profoundly real, as if the backdrop of a theater production had been suddenly pulled up to reveal the stage crew working with props and wardrobe. One was vivid imagination, the other was real.

I entered this reality exhausted from my work, but my fatigue quickly disappeared. Now I was awake within a different reality, suddenly operational within a different sphere altogether. As I try to describe what happened in this sphere, however, I flounder for words, as there was no precedent for it in previous sessions. Whole new modalities of experience opened. This is my best approximation of what followed.

There was nothing personal about the state I was in, not even the residual personal of individual ecstatic experience. Instead, there was a wholeness that was species-wide; its movement was the movement of my kind. This movement of the species was itself part of the movement of God-in-time, so from another perspective the experience was one of being drawn into the inner workings of God's-experience-as-this-species in the larger sweep of history. It was vast and beyond measure. Linear fixed-time opened to holistic deep-time. As often happens, experience preceded understanding. I simply began to experience new things and only slowly did I get my bearings on what it was I was experiencing.

I began to experience states of arousal, anxiety, crisis, breakthrough, and a new beginning, but as a species experiences these things, not an individual person. It was how the entire human species would experience this if it were a single, integrated organism. I began to realize that "in me" were the experiences of countless human beings. The levels of arousal I was experiencing were ascending waves within the collective unconscious, and these waves were building up and breaking within me! It was like being able to experience a thunderstorm all at once, with every drop registering individually but subsumed into the patterns of the storm as a whole.

In time I began to realize that I was being allowed to experience some of the inner workings of the species that would be unfolding in response to events taking place over the next several decades, perhaps the next hundred years. As these developments take place, people will think that they are being overtaken by events outside themselves, but in fact it is the Divinity drawing forth from within Itself the actualization of new capacities that will be species-wide. In earlier sessions I had glimpsed the historical transition humanity was making. Today I was taken inside this transition and given the feeling of it from deep within the collective consciousness of the species, framed within the surrounding consciousness of the Creative Intelligence. I came away from the session exhausted from the knowledge of what lies ahead, exhausted from having felt the fear that humanity will feel as our world crumbles around us, and exhilarated by the new forms that are emerging.

The core scenario. Amidst a field of relative calm, a small anxiety began to grow. Slowly more and more persons were looking up and becoming alarmed. Like persons living on an island (before modern weather forecasting) who gradually become aware that a hurricane is overtaking them, humanity was gradually waking up with alarm to events that had overtaken it. Conditions got worse and worse. People became more and more alarmed as the danger increased, forcing them to let go of their assumptions at deeper and deeper levels. The world as they knew it was falling apart. Decades were compressed into minutes, and I felt their alarm deepen as they lost more and more of what they had considered the normal and necessary structures of their world. Step by step, events were forcing a rapid reassessment of everything in their lives. The events that had overtaken Earth were of such scope that no one could insulate themselves from them. The level of alarm grew in the species field until eventually everyone was forced into the melting pot of mere survival. We were all in this together. Families were torn apart, parents were torn from children and children from each other. Life as we had known it was shattered at the core. We were reduced to simply trying to survive.

For a time it looked as though like we would all be killed, but just then, when the storm was at its peak, the worst of the storm passed over and the danger slowly subsided. Though many had died, many were still alive. As the survivors began to find each other, new social units began to form. Parents and children from different families joined to form new types of families. Everywhere new social institutions sprang into being that reflected our new reality—new ways of thinking, new values that we had discovered within ourselves during the crisis. Every aspect of our lives was marked by new priorities, new perceptions of the good, new truths. These new social forms reflected new states of awareness that seemed to spread through the survivors like a positive contagion. These social forms then fed back into the system to elicit still newer states of awareness in individuals, and the cycle of creativity between individual and group spiraled.

The whole system was becoming alive at new levels, and this aliveness was expressing itself in previously impossible ways. It was as if the eco-crisis had myelinized connections in the species-mind, allowing new and deeper levels of self-awareness to spring into being. Repeatedly there was the message: "These things will happen much faster than anyone can anticipate because of the hyper-arousal of the species-mind." Thousands of fractal images drove this lesson home again and again. "Faster than anyone can anticipate." The pace of the past was irrelevant to the pace of the future. The new forms that were emerging were not temporary fluctuations but permanent psychological and social structures that marked the next evolutionary step in our long journey toward self-activated awareness. The entire process seemed to be being driven by strange attractors that were rapidly drawing the system into new patterns of self-configuration.

The time of rebuilding was suffused with an inner luminosity that signaled a profound awakening within the human heart. It was not the overwhelming brilliance of diamond luminosity that shines forth from individual awakening, but a softer luminosity that reflected the same reality but more gently present and more evenly distributed throughout the entire species. The whole of humanity was going to go through the death-rebirth experience, and the substance of awakening for the group was the same as for the individual, though realized more slowly and in smaller increments.

One scenario put the matter in theological terms. We were entering a period of "grace" in which the "sins" of the past could be set aside en masse. We did not have to expiate them linearly but could surrender them whole if we would but open ourselves to the forces that were moving powerfully in the present to recreate our lives. In a blending of Western and Eastern mythologies, I saw the present generations as carrying the full karmic burden of our prior evolutionary limits. I saw that the entire system was poised for a profound revision of those limits and that we who were part of this transition could actually free humanity from its past simply by enduring and responding deeply to the challenges of this radical transition. Collective

karma was being cleared exponentially. This time of great purifica-
tion was a time of great grace.

History is becoming psychedelic. Time is becoming increasingly
concentrated; developments are unfolding exponentially. The past is
rapidly catching up with us; debts put off for generations are coming
due; a new beginning approaches. The ecological crisis will precipi-
tate a death-rebirth confrontation that will shatter our psychospiri-
tual isolation and bring forward an awakening of common ground
within us. I saw that once we made this painful transition, we would
discover that all was gain. Nothing essential had been lost. We would
look with amazement at the depth of ignorance that had set us on a
course of self-decimation, and we would long not at all for that past.
All was gain, all was gain.

It took me more than a year to recover from this visionary experience. Perhaps it would be more accurate to say "adjust to" than "recover from." For six months I walked around the city where I live
feeling like someone visiting Hiroshima a week before the bomb was
to be dropped, with unbidden knowledge of the devastation that lay
just ahead. The juxtaposition of past and future, of life undisturbed
and life doomed, of plans consciously and unconsciously made was
difficult to manage. How blind a species we are. How noble. How
deep and profound the evolutionary currents that carry us.
Sometimes the darkness stands out for me, sometimes the dawn.
Increasingly it is the dawn.

Grounding These Observations in Intellectual History

In chapter 1 I outlined Richard Tarnas's description of the intellectual and cultural crises building in the twentieth century that have
rendered *all* human knowledge deeply suspect. It is under these
darkening clouds of epistemological doubt that Tarnas traces the
philosophical inquiry into mind from Descartes to depth psychology
where he quickly moves past Freud and Jung to focus on Grof's research. He zeroes in on Grof's discovery in the individual psyche of
the archetypal sequence of death and rebirth and then sets forth the
bold thesis that the human species as a whole appears to be undergoing precisely the same death-rebirth process as Grof's subjects on
a much larger historical scale. His argument is subtle and challenging as it combines a deep knowledge of perinatal dynamics and a
comprehensive grasp of Western intellectual history.

Tarnas believes that Western culture has for centuries been experiencing reality through the lense of a specific archetypal constellation, an experiential template that has selectively filtered and shaped human awareness—in my vocabulary, a Meta-Matrix of the collective unconscious. He uses Grof's theory to suggest that this constellation is a coherent part of an archetypal-perinatal trajectory that is expressing itself in the broad sweep of Western history. The basic arc of this trajectory is one in which consciousness emerges within and then detaches itself from a primal, undifferentiated unity, undergoes a process of painful but potentiating individuation, and finally experiences a death of identity that leads to a re-awakening to the original cosmic matrix, but now experienced on a new level that preserves the achievement of the entire trajectory. When the history of Western culture is viewed in its entirety, Tarnas contends, one begins to see that the West has been on this journey of transformation for thousands of years, and, furthermore, that it is presently undergoing the critical death-rebirth phase of the process on all levels—intellectually, psychologically, socially, politically, economically, spiritually, and ecologically.

Tarnas makes his case by delineating specific places where the archetypal-perinatal process can be recognized in the patterns of Western thought. It is not feasible to summarize his entire presentation, but I would point to the close correspondence that he demonstrates between the vision of reality that has come to dominate the modern mind and the condition of extreme alienation and isolation that Grof's subjects regularly experience when they are in the middle of the death-rebirth ordeal. As Tarnas summarizes them, the parallels are striking:

Here, on both the individual and the collective levels, can be seen the source of the profound dualism of the modern mind: between man and nature, between mind and matter, between self and other, between experience and reality— that pervading sense of a separate ego irrevocably divided from the encompassing world. Here is the painful separation from the timeless all-encompassing womb of nature, the development of human self-consciousness, the loss of connection with the matrix of being, the expulsion from the Garden, the entrance into time and history and materiality, the disenchantment of the cosmos, the sense of total immersion in an antithetical world of impersonal forces. Here is the experience of the universe as ultimately indifferent,

hostile, inscrutable. Here is the compulsive striving to liberate oneself from nature's power, to control and dominate
the forces of nature, even to revenge oneself against nature.
Here is the primal fear of losing control and dominance,
rooted in the all-consuming awareness and fear of death—
the inevitable accompaniment of the individual ego's emergence out of the collective matrix. But above all, here is the
profound sense of ontological and epistemological separation between self and world.[18]

When viewed in the combined context of Grof's paradigm,
Jung's archetypal theory, and postmodern philosophy of science, the
fundamental subject-object dichotomy that has defined modern consciousness can be seen as being rooted in an archetypal condition in
which all consciousness and value has been withdrawn from the
cosmos and relocated in the private self. In this powerful contraction of vision, the self is greatly empowered, but at the cost of being
profoundly cut off from the universe which gave birth to it. "The
Cartesian-Kantian paradigm," writes Tarnas, "both expresses and
ratifies a state of consciousness in which experience of the unitive
numinous depths of reality has been systematically extinguished,
leaving the world disenchanted and the human ego isolated."[19]
When the universe is experienced through this filter, it appears as
lifeless, other-than-self, objective, and machine-like. This condition,
which the modern mind experiences as "normal" and takes for
granted as the basis for any "realistic" experience of the world, is in
fact a temporary though long-lasting state, which Tarnas believes
we are now in the process of moving beyond, just as the psychedelic
subject eventually moves beyond the isolation and alienation associated with BPM II and III. When the basic predispositions and capacities of the modern mind are placed in this larger context, they
can be seen as reflecting a stage of psychospiritual development
that comes *before* a redemptive transformation in which the autonomous self enters into a new communion, not previously possible, with the ground of existence. From this perspective the entire
Promethean drive toward human freedom and autonomy can be
seen as an important and authentic stage in an archetypal process,
but just a stage.

This reading of history places the "deconstructive frenzy" of
much of postmodern thought in a new light. Under the relentless
skepticism of the hermeneutics of suspicion, our confidence in our
collective ability to tell truth from falsehood, right from wrong has

been crumbling. This "vast unmaking of the modern mind" (Hassan) has put everything in flux. Ideologies long dormant are reawakening, and the marketplace is overflowing with a confusing mix of new and ancient ideas and lifestyles. "The extreme fluidity and multiplicity of the contemporary intellectual scene can scarcely be exaggerated," says Tarnas, and yet this chaos of opinion and standards may be signaling the beginning of something extraordinary. Before something new can be born, the certainties of the past must be annihilated and a profound unknowing entered into. Tarnas writes:

> [T]he twentieth century's massive and radical breakdown of so many structures—cultural, philosophical, scientific, religious, moral, artistic, social, economic political, atomic, ecological—all this suggests the necessary deconstruction prior to a new birth. And why is there evident now such a widespread and constantly growing collective impetus in the Western mind to articulate a holistic and participatory world view, visible in virtually every field? The collective psyche seems to be in the grip of a powerful archetypal dynamic in which the long-alienated modern mind is breaking through, out of the contractions of its birth process, out of what Blake called its "mind-forg'd manacles," to rediscover its intimate relationship with nature and the larger cosmos.[20]

There is much in Tarnas's account that I am skipping over, but I want to mention in closing his description of the sacred marriage that he believes humanity is approaching. The Western project of the last four thousand years has from start to finish been an overwhelming masculine enterprise. Rather than see this tilt toward the masculine as a pernicious mistake, Tarnas argues that it has been an essential part of the entire endeavor. The Western drive has been to forge an autonomous, rational human self, separate from nature and capable of repeatedly transcending the achievements of previous generations. This project has largely succeeded, leading to historically unprecedented levels of individual achievement in every field of endeavor and an emancipation of human beings from many profound existential constraints. The cost of this achievement, however, has been the widespread and sometimes ruthless repression of the feminine on all fronts. The crisis of modernity, therefore, is essentially a masculine crisis, and Tarnas believes that its resolution is beginning to take place in the emergence of the feminine in its many and diverse forms.

Though long, the passage in which he lists the signs of this emergence is so rich that it deserves to be quoted in full. The rise of the feminine today, he writes, is seen not only in the rise of feminism and in the growing empowerment of women, but

> in the increasing sense of unity with the planet and all forms of nature on it, in the increasing awareness of the ecological and the growing reaction against political and corporate policies supporting the domination and exploitation of the environment, in the growing embrace of the human community, in the accelerating collapse of long-standing political and ideological barriers separating the world's peoples, in the deepening recognition of the value and necessity of partnership, pluralism, and the interplay of many perspectives. It is visible also in the widespread urge to reconnect with the body, the emotions, the unconscious, the imagination and intuition, in the new concern with the mystery of childbirth and the dignity of the maternal, in the growing recognition of an immanent intelligence in nature, in the broad popularity of the Gaia hypothesis. It can be seen in the increasing appreciation of indigenous and archaic cultural perspectives such as the Native American, African, and ancient European, in the new awareness of feminine perspectives of the divine, in the archaeological recovery of the Goddess tradition and the contemporary reemergence of Goddess spirituality, in the rise of Sophianic Judaeo-Christian theology and the papal declaration of the *Assumptio Mariae*, in the widely noted spontaneous upsurge of feminine archetypal phenomena in individual dreams and psychotherapy. And it is evident as well in the great wave of interest in the mythological perspective, in esoteric disciplines, in Eastern mysticism, in shamanism, in archetypal and transpersonal psychology, in hermeneutics and other non-objectivist epistemologies, in scientific theories of the holonomic universe, morphogenetic fields, dissipative structures, chaos theory, systems theory, the ecology of mind, the participatory universe—the list could go on and on. As Jung prophesied, an epochal shift is taking place in the contemporary psyche, a reconciliation between the two great polarities, a union of opposites: a *hieros gamos* (sacred marriage) between the long-dominant but now alienated masculine and the long-suppressed by now ascending feminine.[21]

Thus in Tarnas's view, the masculine principle informing the Western project has essentially helped drive the archetypal process of humanity's differentiation and emergence from the feminine matrix of nature and the *anima mundi*; and the current signs of the collective psyche's integration of all that which had been suppressed and lost with all that which has been accomplished during the trajectory indicate that a profound spiritual rebirth of humanity is taking place.

Tarnas's description of this historical sequence and its archetypal roots is deeply compatible with my discussion of the field dynamics of the species mind. He creates a strong case for his interpretation of history by arguing archetypally, illustrating and interpreting the parallels that exist between psychedelic therapy and cultural history. What I have tried to do is to explain some of the causal mechanisms that can be seen as underlying this progression. By incorporating Sheldrake's morphic field theory, chaos theory and nonlinear dynamics, Peter Russell's global brain theory, Kenneth Ring's observations from near-death studies, and ecology, I have tried to create a conceptual framework that, together with Tarnas's analysis, can help forge a stronger connection between Grof's paradigm and the death-rebirth that *Homo sapiens* is undergoing in our time.

Final Observations

In order to assess how a crisis as profound as the global crisis of sustainability might affect human evolution, I have suggested that we must look beyond individual human beings to the species-mind itself. We must deepen our feeling for the fundamental psychic matrix within which we exist and appreciate that this matrix is a mental field that behaves in certain basic respects like other known fields. History is turning up the fire under the soup in which we float. If the eco-crisis brings this soup to a boil, it could set in motion a series of evolutionary changes that would spread through us like wildfire. Driven by powerful nonlinear processes, an archetypal earthquake in the collective unconscious may shift the psychological ground out from under our feet, throwing us into our evolutionary future much faster than we would ever have predicted on linear considerations alone. And because nature tends to hold on to her successful dissipative structures, these new forms may become not just temporary fluctuations but permanent psychological fixtures within a restructured human psyche.[22]

The floor of the collective unconscious appears to be rising. As it does, it is bringing with it the psychic sludge of history. The first step toward greater realization is always purification. The karmic residue of the choices made by countless generations of half-conscious human beings is rising into our individual and collective awareness as we confront en masse the legacy of our past. If this process were linear, it might take us as long to clear our karmic mistakes as it did to make them, but fortunately for us, the process is not linear. The historical crisis we have entered is accelerating our collective transformation. There is a cost to this acceleration, however. To do the same amount of work in less time always requires a greater expenditure of energy, and all mothers know that a shorter labor is not necessarily an easier labor. The cost of accelerating our inner development is the intensification of the death-rebirth process.

These observations finally allow us to place chapter 3's discussion of collective perinatal experience in a larger historical context. If the floor of the collective unconscious is rising in response to or as part of the evolutionary crisis of a species that can no longer afford the luxury of its existential ignorance, it makes the presence of such strong collective elements in the therapy of individuals more understandable. Our individual lives are suspended within a larger living being; we draw the form of our individual existence from the raw material of its larger life. Usually, the subtle rhythms of the species-mind are too large or too distant to be experienced directly, but they are always present beneath us, like the rising tide that lifts a fleet of ships. Because we are cells in the mind of our species, our individual psychological processes cannot help but reflect its metaprocesses. If, therefore, the species-mind is responding to, or actually fermenting, this evolutionary crisis, we might even have predicted that this fact would show up in deep psychedelic work. If the forces of death and rebirth are building at the collective level, it makes sense that this larger dynamic would make itself felt in our individual death-rebirth experiences. Thus, I would be willing to predict that as the dark night of the species-soul intensifies in the decades ahead, the perinatal experiences of persons working in nonordinary states will increasingly reflect these collective dynamics. As the species plunges into the vortex of collective transformation, individuals will naturally be drawn more deeply into this whirlpool as well. Should this occur, they will have a rare opportunity to make a direct and potent contribution to the positive resolution of the global crisis.

The convulsions that will accompany the collapse of our industrial culture are the death throes of the state of consciousness that produced this culture. The fully empowered individual was the crowning achievement of the Enlightenment—strong, self-confident, critical of tradition, hungry to know the universe, disciplined and creative in exploring her. But also . . . deeply cut off from his fellow human beings and the common ground of our essential nature. Increasingly well informed on the workings of the physical world, he (and I use the masculine form intentionally) was incredibly uninformed on the workings of the inner life. When the dark night of the species-soul has done its work, however, we will find that none of the hard-won gains of the Enlightenment or the talents forged therein have actually been lost.

If the crisis of sustainability does bring about the ego-death of our species, what will have died, I think, is primarily our sense of being disconnected from each other and from everything around us. As the psychological debris of our difficult past is cleared away, we will begin to experience more clearly the web that weaves all life into a single fabric. This is the rise of the feminine in perhaps her most fundamental form, the Cosmic Goddess approaching her groom, fully differentiated consciousness, in eager anticipation. Purification is followed by awakening, and this great awakening marks a new beginning for humanity. The adventure is now inherently collective. The age of the hero is yielding to the age of the heroic community. If the community does not become heroically realized, no individual heroes will survive to chase dragons.

As the inherent wholeness of existence becomes a living experience for more and more persons, individuals will find themselves empowered by new orders of creativity that could not have been anticipated as long as we were trapped within the narrow confines of an atomistic, self-referential mode of consciousness. As the encompassing fields of mind become stronger, synergy and synchronicity will increase. The Sacred Mind will spring alive inside the human family in ways that seem impossible from our current fragmented condition. However difficult the journey, who could not feel uplifted by the privilege of being part of such an undertaking? The pain of this labor should not be feared but used creatively. We are building a new world for our grandchildren, indeed, a new species— *Homo spiritualis.*[23]

Chapter Nine

The Fate of Individuality

The Meta-universe does not subject beings to great suffering to become self-aware only to have them dissolve into the great All. Instead we are learning the skills needed to function as ethical, self-referencing beings in the infinite ecologies beyond our material cosmos.

—Duane Elgin, *Awakening Earth*

Let me summarize what I believe has been the core vision unfolding itself in this volume. As the illusion of the private mind slowly dissolves in spiritual practice, one discovers within the details of one's individual life the sinews of collective intent. Within the rhythms of our personal story, we find the pulse of a larger story, within our step the dance of creation itself; and with this discovery everything pivots. Our lives are no longer "ours" alone but belong in an unsuspected way to the universe from the very start. They reflect not just our personal karmic history but the history and aspirations of humanity itself. The threads that form the unique patterns of our never-to-be-repeated existence have been spun in the cosmic womb, in the collective evolution of a star-cluster, a planet, a people. The sins and victories of all flow into each of us. Is it surprising, therefore, that as we come together in common cause, higher orders of creativity should spring forth unannounced and unanticipated?

We must not pull back from this truth for fear of being overwhelmed, for we are only seeing clearly what has always been the case. Nothing changes here but our understanding and the opportunity to participate consciously in what had previously been a hidden arrangement. From the first, the sages have told us that our lives are not our own but God's. Only slowly do we grasp the import of their words. Life pours *Itself* into us, pours *Its* problems and capacities into our temporary forms, and we take these gifts and work with them, trying to purify the distortions and strengthen the virtues. The life well lived is our greatest gift to the Creator. It becomes part of the larger story that is unfolding everywhere around us.

This book has explored the extended fabric of our being, and the resulting vision has been a vision of wholeness. Now it is time to reverse our perspective and consider the implications of this vision for our understanding of individuality. The more one penetrates the transpersonal tapestry that registers covertly in our moment to moment experience, the more paradoxical our individual existence becomes. On the one hand, the self is being emptied of its private existence. Everywhere it is touched, our supposed separateness dissolves into fractal patterns of mutual participation. And yet in being emptied, the self is also being refined and transposed. As it dissolves, it is simultaneously elevated into altogether new modalities of experience. Dying at one level of existence is followed by rebirth into a new order of reality, followed by another and another. The questions I want to ask in this final chapter, therefore, are these. When the fires of death and rebirth have done their work and the self finally opens to Sacred Mind, is our individual identity simply expunged? What lives where the illusion of the private mind once resided? In essence, what is the fate of individuality in psychedelic therapy? I do not hope to give a final answer to these questions but simply to share some provisional reflections—a final exercise in talking myself in from spirit.

Psychedelic Therapy and Individual Identity

The sense of individual identity with which most people begin psychedelic work is rooted in common sense, and common sense tells us that our identity is ultimately defined by the range (and texture) of our individual experience. We feel that whatever I am must be a function of the experiences that this "I" has had. We can make the same point another way by saying that the experiences that others are having and which I am *not having* define the limits of my sense of self. Outside the circle of my personal experience is everything that is "not-me," and this not-me defines the limits of what I recognize as being "me." While the philosophers may argue about what this "me" is exactly and the psychologists how it works, it appears obvious that it must lie within this circle of experience.

In ordinary states of consciousness, one's circle of experience stays relatively constant, but in psychedelic states it can expand dramatically. In the beginning, these new experiences simply "stretch" one's sense of self-identity, but when the envelop of experience has been stretched many times in many directions, sooner or later it must give way. It simply becomes impossible to continue defining oneself by the experiences one is *not* having at this present moment when one discovers within oneself the capacity to enter into any of these experiences under the right circumstances. As Grof has documented, in nonordinary states one can be drawn into experiences that come from anywhere in the cosmos. There is nothing in the physical and extraphysical universe that cannot in principle become part of one's immediate and intimate experience. One does not have to experience everything that life has to offer before one realizes that the potential to experience the whole is present.

The rhythm of psychedelic work, then, is the repeated expansion of one's experiential field far beyond its conventional boundaries followed by the contraction of this field after each session. What one contracts back into changes slowly over time, but the rhythm of expansion and contraction is a dialectic that drives the question of our identity beyond these gradual adaptations. What are we that we are capable of such extreme fluctuations of experiential scope? What is the nature of the being endowed with such elasticity and range?

Faced with the vast scope of the experiences that arise in various states of consciousness, some philosophical systems, such as Vedanta, have simply swallowed the individual as a transitory illusion created by the Divine within the Divine. What is ultimately real, they have said, is not the individual but the One-without-a-second. To think otherwise is to be caught in the dualistic maze created by Brahman to know Itself from within diversity. We can experience everything that exists because in essence we *are* everything. In the final analysis, there *is* no small "I," there is *only* the One, the Divine Reality. So many have endorsed this interpretation that I hold it open as a constant possibility, and it may well be the case that this is the ultimate realization to which all these experiences finally lead. And yet, it seems to me that there is something left out of this account, something that is not represented in its pure monism.

When the circle of experience has been stretched and shrunk so many times that it is no longer a viable metaphor for one's identity, it explodes. For me, the language of the self is tied to this circle, so that when the circle explodes, the language of self explodes with it. If one were to attend only to the temporal vector of mind, the self could be stretched to the meta-self of the reincarnating soul, but as we have seen, this resting place is eventually ruptured by the vast expanse of humanity that repeatedly flows into one via the spatial vector. When one lets go of the attempt to hold onto a separate soul at *this* level, it feels as though there is no other point at which one can meaningfully recover any sense of individual identity at all. Beyond this point, it is a free-fall into the Divine. And yet, it's not that simple.

If one falls into the Divine in a methodical way, one finds that when the self explodes into the vast expanse of infinite possibilities, there is a subtle, residual sense of individuality that carries over. This sense of individuality is subjected to purification after purification, but no matter how much it is refined, it never disappears entirely, or at least it hasn't yet in my experience. (Again, I want to emphasize the tentative nature of these observations.) The sense of identity that I am describing is an identity that is not at all separate from the infinite field of experience, as this boundary has long since been erased. It is a sense of being conscious not as a person nor as a soul, but nevertheless as an individual, though not an individual within any frame of reference one is previously familiar with. Within the contextual presence of an Intelligence and Energy that is so vast that it can only be understood in terms of Divinity, this refined sense of individuality persists. It is not in any way other than the Divine Matrix but rather seems to be a delightful expression of it. If I were to try to say what this individuality consists of, I would say that, distilled to its essence, it seems to be *the capacity for consciously integrated experience.*

In extreme nonordinary states it is possible to so overdrive one's capacity to maintain coherent experience that this individuality is temporarily shattered. If this happens, one ceases for a time to be capable of integrated experience. One becomes lost within the flow of Sacred Mind, caught in the temporary rapture of transpersonal experience, but in the end unable to say what it was that one experienced. In falling too quickly into a given depth of the Divine Expanse, one has fallen, from our human perspective at least, into a state of "ecstatic unconsciousness." Individuality has temporarily exploded, and therefore these experiences cannot be integrated into one's coherent awareness. This problem is not unique to psychedelic therapy and occurs on other spiritual paths as well. Gurdjieff, for example, describes the difficulty of stabilizing conscious cognition at higher levels of awareness in the following passage:

If we could connect the centers of our ordinary consciousness with the higher thinking center deliberately and at will, it would be of no use to us whatever in our present general state. In most cases where accidental contact with the higher thinking center takes place a man becomes unconscious. The mind refuses to take in the flood of thoughts, emotions, images, and ideas which suddenly burst into it. And instead of a vivid thought, or a vivid emotion, there results, on the contrary, a complete blank, a state of unconsciousness. The memory retains only the first moment when the flood rushed in on the mind and the last moment when the flood was receding and consciousness returned. But even these moments are so full of unusual shades and colors that there is nothing with which to compare them among the ordinary sensations of life. This is usually all that remains from so-called "mystical" and "ecstatic" experiences, which represent a temporary connection with a higher center.[1]

While some spiritual systems see this explosion into the Divine as the ultimate aim of spiritual practice, Gurdjieff, and Sri Aurobindo, see it more as a sign of failure of practice than success. However ecstatic the experience, you have ceased to be useful to God because you are not able to integrate the experience into your individuated awareness. You are not able to bring it back and anchor it in the denser fabric of spacetime consciousness.

In sustained psychedelic work, such occasional lapses of excess occur against the backdrop of systematically learning how to coherently manage larger and larger vistas of experience without passing out or losing the capacity for conscious integration. Forgetfulness, even ecstatic forgetfulness, is not a virtue but simply a sign of hitting one's experiential limits. Though one regularly loses pieces of new transpersonal experiences around the edges, in carefully structured systematic work, one recovers those pieces in subsequent sessions and discovers how they fit together. The goal is always conscious integration of experience, not forays into fascinating transpersonal landscapes that later you can't recall. (For the same reason, I think ineffability is often overrated as a sign of genuine mystical experience. The fact is, if you can't represent even to yourself where you've been, you probably just got lost.)

One has to learn how to maintain one's cognitive coherence within the dramatically expanded experiential possibilities that psychedelic states make available. Because this is an important point, let me illustrate it with an example from a session. The following experience was an exercise in "learning how to learn" in transpersonal states, which resulted in a significant heightening of clarity in subsequent sessions.

Session 20

The intelligence that brought our universe into existence is enormously sophisticated, and the workings of this intelligence are far beyond our human capacities of comprehension. If you want access to its knowledge, this intelligence has to teach you how to receive it. Since this intelligence is nothing other than our own being, it's a matter of learning how to become conscious at deeper and deeper levels of our being, or Being Itself. The "council of elders" seemed to be a training exercise in developing the necessary awareness for this task.

The elders were the guardians of knowledge, the knowledge of what has been going on in the universe for billions of years. Because I sought this knowledge, I was brought before the council to get it. This knowledge is not just given to you, you have to work for it. First, you have to work to reach this level of awareness, and then you have to work to sustain the concentration necessary to receive the knowledge that they can make available to you.

I was sitting with the council of elders at what felt to me to be the primal core of the universe, in the bowels of the cosmos where the guardians of physical existence conjure and make things happen. A charged field of synchronicity that blended music and experience into a single field surrounded me. I wanted to know things. An idea of something I wanted to understand would come into my mind and immediately the council knew it and accepted it as a formal request. The head of the council would bellow a thundering chant—"He wants to know. . . ."— then the others would join in and they would start an invocation. They chanted to gather power because if you want to know certain things, you've got to gather the power necessary to access that reality. You've got to say the mantra so many times, etc. Even the council of elders had to gather power. And so they started chanting.

I learned the hard way that I had to be ready for what would happen next. I had to stay extremely focused, because when they released that power, a vast, all-consuming knowing would engulf me. If I was focused and centered when this knowledge hit me, it would carry me into the most exquisite, orgiastic ecstasy of knowing imaginable. If, however, I had not controlled my thoughts carefully while waiting and was not centered when it arrived, the knowing would shatter me. It would drive me beyond my ability to experience coherently and explode me into cognitive chaos. Both of these happened numerous times today.

Sometimes I would make a mistake; I would get distracted while the elders were chanting. When this happened someone or something would grab me right down to my bones and say: "Listen! Listen! Will you grow up! That's not what this is about! Now pay attention! All of these things have their place. But if you want to understand the structure of the universe, you've got to be able to take it on at deep levels. You've got to be able to experience it."

The council of elders gave me access to experiential knowing that allowed me to see many pieces of how the universe works. I could know anything I wanted if I could endure it, but to endure it, I had to be able to "go flat out with existence," that is, to expand to the size of the reality I wished to have knowledge of. Somehow my being able to know the universe in this way answered a longing so deep that I knew it had been driving me for thousands of years.

As this session indicates, in these states one learns how to learn not on one's own but under constant guidance. This guidance takes different forms at different times—sometimes plural, sometimes singular—but one always senses that one is surrounded by or immersed in a Presence that is instructing you, teaching you, drawing you out, breaking you down. Step by step you are bent backwards and forwards, turned inside out, fired and cooled by something that is absolutely trustworthy. And as the veil between "you" and this Presence gets thinner and thinner, even as it momentarily dissolves to give you a foretaste of what lies ahead, one gets the sense that it is diligently working to *protect your individuality* even while stretching that individuality to its absolute limits. As one learns how to cooperate with this process, one senses sometimes that one is being fed the experience of transcendence drop by drop, thus being allowed to assimilate the experiential possibilities gradually. Too great an exposure to the transcendental depths, as desirable as it may be from one perspective, seems counterproductive to what is taking place.

When either by luck or design one touches a state of consciousness that lies beyond one's present capacity to integrate, it can have a devastating effect. I sometimes think these jolts are given to help orient us to the larger project at hand. Let me give an example. This experience took place during the ecstatic portion of a session after a long and productive period of intense purgatorial cleansing.

Session 33

In my inner visionary state, life was spread out in front of me in a captivating display of exquisite diversity, subtlety, and finesse. I was enjoying the splendor of its harmonious complexity when suddenly I experienced the same reality from the perspective of the unified field that this diversity also was. This unified mode of experience was so concentrated, so intense that it shattered me. It literally hit me like a flash of light, blasting me instantly beyond any frame of reference I could imagine. It withdrew as suddenly as it had come, leaving me stumbling about, picking up the pieces of my mind, trying to comprehend what had happened. Making associations in the rapture left by its withdrawal, I knew that this had been a brief encounter with a reality that in previous centuries would have been labeled "God." How naive I have been. How completely unprepared for what lies ahead. I spent the remaining hours of the session digesting this experience, which could not have lasted more than one second.

In contrast to this jarring flirtation with future possibilities, when a lasting breakthrough occurs, one's experience is always coherent and well ordered. What opens is well integrated with everything that has gone before and often recapitulates vast experiential landscapes covering years of work, as the session I will introduce later will illustrate.

If the goal is not simply transcendence but *integrated transcendence*, then there must be a cognitive structure that anchors this integration. The universe itself seems to bend over backwards to support and nourish this cognitive structure every step along the way. The danger of overwhelming one's capacity for integrated experience is pronounced in spiritual methods that use powerful technologies to trigger radical shifts of consciousness, yet within these practices one learns how to let go and lose coherence at one level and then recover it in a completely new arena. It is the repeated recovery of coherence within ever deepening experiential fields that drives my sense that *even as the self dies, a deeper form of individuality is being liberated.* From my present perspective, I believe that it is not individuality itself that is the illusion but our sense of being isolated from the whole.

As the isolation of the private mind is consumed in spiritual practice, the self or ego dies, for this self is nothing more than the working identity of our isolation. From its ashes, however, springs forth not just the freedom of transindividual experience but a truer form of individuality as well. In this individuality is preserved the distinctness of our long and unique history, but now open to life on all sides. Furthermore, this individuality, this capacity for integrated experience, seems capable of infinite refinement, infinite extension and development. In this open-ended evolution, the body loses its significance entirely as providing the center of one's identity, and yet the experience of being a coherent center of conscious awareness is continuous with one's experience of being an embodied "I." What changes is the depth and range of experiences being integrated.

This description of post-egoic individuality is strikingly similar to John Briggs and David Peat's description in *Turbulent Mirror* of autopoietic structures. Autopoietic structures are forms of open systems that are self-renewing, highly autonomous, and have separate identities, and yet are also inextricably embedded in and merged with their environments. They write:

> Each autopoietic structure has a unique history, but its history is tied to the history of the larger environment and other autopoietic structures. . . . Autopoietic structures have definite boundaries, such as a semipermeable membrane, but the boundaries are open and connect the system with almost unimaginable complexity to the world around it.

Furthermore, contrary to what we might initially expect, autopoietic structures achieve greater autonomy not by severing their ties to their environment but *by actually increasing them*. "It appears that the greater an organism's autonomy, the more feedback loops [are] required both within the system and in its relationship to the environment. This is the autopoietic paradox."[2] Post-egoic individuality combines openness and uniqueness in a similar paradoxical fashion. Its increased communion with its environment, far from suffocating it, is actually necessary to sustain it.

When the circle of the egoic-self explodes, new images for this emerging individuality present themselves. One that has been useful to me is the image of a cross with equally balanced arms extending in the four directions (figure 9.1). This archetypal image conveys the sense of being open to the full field of experiential possibilities while

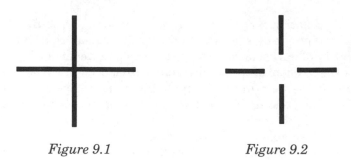

Figure 9.1   *Figure 9.2*

drawing all experience into a coherent center of integration. Experience is open on all sides but is localized; it extends (potentially) to infinite horizons, but is focused in this integrating center. Later, a modification of this image presented itself. As the boundary between the center and the surround became more porous, it seemed appropriate to draw the cross with an open center (figure 9.2). This image better conveyed the sense that that which integrates and that which animates are but different expressions of a single reality. The center and the field are not ultimately two but one. Localizing awareness within individual points of experience does not disturb the infinite field of Sacred Mind in the least. On the contrary, *it gives it great delight*.

A third image has been useful to me as a visual representation of the autopoietic paradox described above. The image in figure 9.3 visually represents the idea that as the "breadth" of our commerce with Being expands, so too does the "height" of our individuality. In this image, the horizontal beam represents our openness to and identification with our environment. It represents the breadth of our social commitments, that part of life for which we have accepted responsibility in some tangible sense—our family, some aspect of our community's well-being, some aspect of the planet's well-being, and so on. As one's zone of care expands and one becomes operationally active within a larger sphere of life, one's sense of identity must expand proportionately. The wider the horizontal beam, the higher the vertical beam. Like a snake shedding its skin, we outgrow ourselves many times. The transition known as ego-death is only one of many transitions we undergo as the flame of our individuality—our capacity for integrated experience—burns higher and brighter.

Unfortunately, it is not yet the case that these symbols of an open-ended field of awareness focused in localized experience de-

scribes an abiding condition for me. They are images of seed experiences still gestating within me, symbols that help anchor an awareness that still comes and goes. Pictures and theories tumble out
of experience, and experience is a deep well. I don't know whether
the images presented here will endure or whether they will in time
yield to still other images representing even deeper modalities of
experience.

After completing the first draft of this chapter, I came across a
passage in which Sri Aurobindo's consort, the Mother, described her
experience using an image similar to the four-armed cross but with
a different twist. She said:

> The ordinary individual consciousness is like an axis, and
> everything revolves about that axis. If it moves we feel lost.
> There is this tall axis (more or less tall; it may also be very
> small) fixed in time, and everything revolves around it. The
> consciousness may extend more or less far, be more or less
> high, more or less strong, but it still revolves about that axis.
> Yet for me, there is no longer any axis—it's gone, disap-
> peared! So it can move to the north, to the south, the east, or
> the west—forward, backward, or anywhere at all. There is
> no more axis.[3]

Figure 9.3

I ponder her words, "There is no more axis," and wonder what ex-periential horizon they reflect. Is she simply describing a profound inner freedom, or does she really mean to say that there is no longer a sense of center? I consult Ramakrishna, whom I frequently come to in these matters, and he is relentless in his assertion of the utter emptiness of individual agency:

> O friends of Truth, none of your meditative disciplines will be of any ultimate value unless you realize directly—here and now, before continuing even one step further along the path—that *akhanda satchidananda* alone exists, that you simply are indivisible Being, Consciousness, and Bliss, that Mother performs all action, including your own acts of devotion and meditation. Your aspiration to realize Truth is simply God longing for God.[4]

Yet still I wonder. Is it simply some unbaked remnant of self that makes me ask, "Would the part of God that has folded itself into God-as-matter only to rediscover God-in-all ever *be allowed* to drop its beautiful individuality altogether?" The God-intoxicated voice that sings the universal Presence is the sweetest voice of all. If such a voice is the supreme accomplishment of 15 billion years of evolution, will it now completely disappear back into bliss without remainder? If so, what has been accomplished? It is the illogic of the exercise that bothers me in this interpretation. Something is missing. A cadre of Bodhisattvas pictured in Buddhist art, whose ethereal forms depict a beatific existence beyond any I can imagine, suggests to me that there is an exquisite form of living that *only begins* once the self dies. Their idiosyncratic features suggests that this form *preserves our uniqueness* even while opening the floodgates of the universal. The paradox is due only to our limited capacity to comprehend what lies ahead. But then Ramakrishna returns:

> The genuinely human body and mind of the *avatara* is an opaque covering. Beneath this veil, there is no individual soul, no eternal facet of the Divine, but instead there resides the complete Divine Reality, with infinite facets.[5]

Does the phrase "with infinite facets" allow the kind of transparent individuality I am envisioning? Here I must let the matter stand and move on.

Early Dawn

Those who have had occasion to keep a vigil through the night know that dawn is a game of subtle shifts. First, the sky begins to glow ever so faintly, revealing the world in silhouette, and slowly color creeps into things. Finally the long awaited moment comes when the sun breaks the horizon, its light flooding the land. At this moment we mark the birth of a new day. It is but early dawn. It will be hours before all the shadows have been rounded up and vanquished, hours before the bright orb has reached its full power. Yet this is the decisive moment. We know that from this point on, it will be light in ever greater abundance. The long night is over.

In earlier chapters of this book, I asked the reader to follow me into great pain because I believed it was in fundamental respects not a private pain but a pain shared by all humanity, and therefore in need of being understood by all. It is part of the collective karmic legacy that lives within each of us, fueling the historical forces that are driving us to the brink of self-extinction. Now I invite the reader to walk with me a bit farther into a shared joy, which I hope will bring a sense of closure to this difficult phase of the journey. Like the pain, this joy is also a shared joy, because it reflects something that lives within all of us and is emerging within each of us. The following session was the first in a long series of death-rebirth transitions that took place over several years as the collective ordeal described in earlier chapters began to subside. It drew together experiences from several years of work, creating a small rise that afforded something of an overview of the larger process. After this rise came another valley and renewed cleansing, as the cycle of purification continued.

Session 38

Tibetan chanting carried me into a deeply chaotic state that was very disorienting. I was not experiencing pain, only confusion and chaos, and later fear. The confusion seemed to be reaching deeper and deeper into me, leaving less and less of "me" to orient to. The power of the thundering chants was dissolving me, breaking me into incoherent pieces. I kept feeling fear but could not find anything to be afraid of. I tried to focus on the content of these experiences to see more clearly what they consisted of, but they remained completely enigmatic. Indeed, their impenetrability seemed to be an essential aspect of them. Everything was sheer chaos. I register that for me chaos is a deeper layer of the unraveling than pain. The core of my experience was that where there had previously been an ordered singularity, there was now only a hopelessly disordered plurality.

After what felt like hours of this, I began to feel exhausted and completely spent. Now there was a panic growing in the chaos as my feelings shifted from stoic endurance to exhausted desperation. "I can't take much more of this. Please stop. Please let me go." I was completely and utterly overwhelmed by these voices that were dissolving me into their thundering cadence. . . . I could not remember anything that had happened in any previous sessions. . . . I was completely incoherent. . . . Once desperate to escape the chanting, now I was simply thundering vibration itself. . . . And the chanting continued on and on.

From somewhere the sense eventually came that it was time to move on, and I signaled this to my sitter. I was so disoriented, however, that I had absolutely no idea what should happen next. Then the spacious music of Paul Winter came on. In response to its soothing rhythms, my shattered mind began to move again. It slowly curved back in around the edges, coaxing me into motion with comforting strokes of intimacy. It felt to me as if I were a standing dead man, as if I had died and not even had the decency to fall down. The meaninglessness of the category of death cascaded through me and I laughed. From the middle of a profound emptiness I began to stir. Against complete darkness, I felt myself to be the silhouette of a human being, completely empty within. The figure began to move, and as it did, a world of color sprang into existence around me. It was a world of nature, of trees, birds, grasses, and flowers. As I moved within this familiar-looking world, suddenly I began to experience it in an entirely new manner that was completely and utterly intoxicating.

It was as though I were experiencing its many pieces all at once. Birds flying between trees and the trees themselves were not separate things but flowing strands in a single field. These strands were sparkling white and glistening with a diamond bright luminosity. My previous experience of nature had been so diluted and diminished. I had been able to experience only one piece of it at a time. Now I was experiencing the ecstatic wholeness of it; not an amorphous wholeness that blurred the distinctions between things but a brilliantly clear wholeness that preserved and delighted in the distinctions and suffered them without the slightest effort or compromise. I was not swept into this world quickly but entered it step by step, maintaining a clear perception of events and reveling in the ever widening circles of experience that were opening to me. And as the circles opened, what exquisite ecstasy!

As I began to [mentally] move about, I suddenly found that I had abilities completely beyond anything I had ever imagined. Capacities that I had never dreamed possible were now part of my spontaneous nature. I was like a kid in heaven's candystore. It took me a while to realize what was happening. These new abilities were actually new ways of being conscious. I was suddenly able to experience textures of reality, modalities of existence that had been completely unavailable to me seconds before, and that I had never touched in any previous session. Any lingering unfulfilled dreams or aspirations that belonged to my previous life suddenly fell away from me as irrelevant. The deepest left-over longings of my heart simply dropped away in the face of the simplest, most elementary mode of just being conscious at this new level. It was as if God had increased my allowance a thousandfold.

As I moved through this reality, new constellations of experience kept opening to me, and each constellation carried with it a different form of ecstasy. I cannot describe the experiences because they correspond to nothing in spacetime. Possibilities were opening faster than I could keep track of. I knew that I was just scratching the surface of this realm and that it would take me aeons to understand and tap its full potential. I felt like a child, deliriously happy to have been given more blessings than I could ever have imagined.

The quantum jump in experience between the chaos and this new level of consciousness was in time followed by still another quantum jump that was even larger than the first. The insights and experiences that follow derive from a different order of reality altogether, and words will be even less satisfactory to give a sense of their proportion or impact. I cannot reconstruct the exact sequence of events as they unfolded, so I will organize the telling in part according to themes and insights that emerged over time from multiple layerings of experience.

The falling away of the concerns of my present historical personality carried with it a sense of regathering the energies of my life. It was as though I was regathering energies within myself that I had strewn over centuries of historical time, presumably in multiple incarnations. As I did so, I became step by step more what I had been before I had entered spacetime, but at the same time I also focused and clarified what had been accomplished by entering spacetime. So there was both the sense of return, with profound feelings of homecoming, and also the sense of realization of accomplishment, of seeing clearly what had been the purpose of the entire exercise.

Once the first transition beyond my present historical personality was made, it seemed easier to regather other layers of energy. I felt that these other layers pertained to other lives, but I could not see specific details. As I regathered wave upon wave of energy, I "rose" to quieter and quieter levels of existence and into deeper intimacy with an intelligence that spoke with the authority of "God." Whatever its ultimate status in the cosmic matrix, it profoundly engulfed my minuscule awareness. As I ascended through these levels, many teachings from years of sessions returned and organized themselves into profound experiential exercises of instruction. The pieces of the puzzle were literally coming together and carrying me into an extremely concentrated distillation of experiential instruction. Many of the components of this teaching were familiar from previous sessions, but today they were demonstrated to me with devastating power. I will first describe the conceptual content of the teaching and then the experiential aspects.

Reduced to its essence, the teaching was as follows. Matter is nothing more than the canvas that mind paints upon. It has no capacity to act apart from the animating presence of consciousness and is completely passive to the direction of consciousness. Therefore, whatever our experience is in spacetime reality, we must have the courage to sit still and face the fact that we are experiencing nothing but the manifestation of our own consciousness. No matter how terrible the pain, no matter how horrendous the injustice or inscrutable the logic, our experience in spacetime is the direct expression of our consciousness in a higher order of reality. (The "our" was more than just personal consciousness, however. It was both personal and collective, both individual and species.)

If we do not face this terrible fact, we fail to understand the most basic fact of life. Matter is the canvas on which we practice and refine the art of creating. It is the notebook in which we draw sketches and explore possibilities. If our experience in this life is convoluted and torn by conflicting forces, it was transparently obvious that this is caused by the carryover of exercises from other spacetime encounters. The experience of matter is extremely intense and leaves a powerful impression on the mind. If we go to see a frightening movie, we may have nightmares later when we are home safe in our beds. Likewise, the impressions physical existence makes on our consciousness carry themselves over into other lives. It is as if we have tried to sketch too many drawings on the same page, and the pictures interfere with each other. "What we are is the result of everything we have ever thought." Yet there was a method to this madness, a direction to our experimentation.

We move into spacetime to experiment with our creative abilities. But the intensity of spacetime experience is such that we tend to get caught in the dreamy echoes of our experience. Home safe in our cosmic beds, we nevertheless still get caught by our dreams and return again and again to Earth, weaving new layers into the dream. Eventually, however, the time comes when we begin to collect the tangled threads of our experience. Lifetime by lifetime we rewind the threads of our dreaming and regather the energies of our exercises. As I rewound the threads of my existence, I began to experience more clearly what the entire exercise had been about. It had not been about what happened in any individual life. It had been about learning how to control the powers of creativity that were my innate nature. We were, in effect, learning how to be gods, learning how to create.

The fact that matter follows mind implies in principle the ability to control one's physical experience through the power of "coherent consciousness." (Coherent consciousness is to ordinary consciousness what a laser, or coherent light, is to ordinary light.) This cannot be done at the level of egoic-consciousness, of course, but requires a profound integration of the deeper levels of consciousness. Beginning to access these deeper levels first brings forward the unresolved fragments of other spacetime experiences (karmic impressions from former lives) and causes them to manifest in our inner life and in our physical world. Eventually, however, these threads are all rewound. When this happens, our physical existence begins to be transparent to choices originating in our deep consciousness, our soul, and in the larger field our soul is part of. To begin to be able to consciously direct our experience in spacetime instead of being unconsciously dragged around by our past represented a major accomplishment.

This step, however, was quickly superseded by yet another realization. To be able to control one's historical existence was a good thing, but to learn that historical existence itself served the function of developing and refining this creative ability, this was a development whose significance radically transcended physical existence. This was what the exercise of spacetime was all about. The goal seemed to be about becoming a fully conscious creative being.

These discoveries were not an intellectual exercise, as I have described them here, but rather a series of profound experiential realizations. Regathering energy led to conscious control of my physical existence. My historical existence became transparent to my soul's conscious intent with fewer complications arising from the shadows cast by pockets of unresolved karma. When I moved into the next level and discovered that the deeper purpose of the exercise was controlled creativity, the most brilliant, diamond-like light broke forth from my chest. I now understand why it is called Diamond Consciousness. Truly our experience of physical light is but a metaphor for the intensity and brilliance of this energy. It had the characteristics of brilliant light, of sparkling luminosity, but also perfectly aligned density. It was not hollow as light is, but extremely dense, yet at the same time perfectly transparent. It was perfectly focused power, capable of anything. I suddenly knew that all my experiences in spacetime served the cultivation of this Diamond Energy. This is what I was here for, what we were all here for, to learn how to consciously control this. This was the power that could create universes. In one second, my entire existence was redefined.

Let me backtrack to another layer of the experience. As I was reassimilating my life and ascending through various levels, I was also entering into intimate dialogue with a Presence that addressed me. It communed with me and "spoke" to me in messages that were only sometimes put into words. It was explaining to me what I was experiencing not so much with words as with direct illumination. When I reached the point of Diamond Luminosity, I was lifted beyond the dream of physical existence, beyond the bardo echoes of physical existence altogether. It felt like I had reassimilated all my experiences in spacetime, that I had brought back into one all my experiences of duality including the experiences of being both male and female. From this point, which carried the flavor of both "before" and "after" physical existence, the Presence illumined for me the human project.

With the deepest, most tender words of a divine parent, It said, "Go and create, My Children." It was setting us loose in a cosmos that contained many realms. The one I had just reemerged from was only one among many universes, some of which were physical while others were not. We were small aspects of this being, truly Its children, of the same type only smaller in size and capacity. Having just returned from a sojourn of countless years in spacetime, I knew that our creative capacity was enormous. I knew, too, that our capacity for creating destruction and pain was also enormous. And yet this being was setting us free, placing absolutely no limits on our creative abilities. Our absolute freedom seemed as precious to It as our creative ability. No limit was placed on our learning. "Go and create, My children." How generous and terrible the conditions. How immeasurable the wisdom behind the exercise.

I was different from my surrounding environment, and the difference was the Light that was shining forth from me. It was what I now was—a defined speck of infinitely dense, infinitely transparent Diamond Luminosity. This is what I had entered spacetime to actualize. This is why we are all here. I could feel many universes around me to explore and grow in. I felt the truth of the ancient mandalas that depict multiple universes all overseen by a cadre of divinities, each focused in a different project. These too were about expanding and refining one's potential, about becoming more through the disciplined exercise of awareness. The opportunities were infinite. Go and create, My children. I felt myself returning to a condition of undivided wholeness within myself. Regathering aspects that seemed to derive from some of these other realms, I rose through level after level until I felt myself to be alone with the source of my existence, suspended between worlds. The warmth of this reunion soaked me to the bone. The peace cannot be described.

There is nothing more that I can say at this point except to note that the experience was both personal and collective. It felt like some enormous ball of intertwined threads that did not begin or end in my private life was dissolving into this Light. The threads that were originally twisted into this form that I am derived in large measure from the collective, and therefore as this tangled knot dissolved into the Light, the luminosity flowed into the field of the species-mind, spreading itself deep into the fiber of the collective unconscious.

Meister Eckhart once gave the following piece of spiritual advice. "You should love God mindlessly," he said, "so that your soul is without mind and free from all mental activities, for as long as your soul is operating like a mind, so long does it have images and representations. But as long as it has images, it has intermediaries, and as long as it has intermediaries, it has neither oneness nor simplicity."[6] This session is cluttered with intermediaries, indicating how much work still remains. It comes from the subtle level of consciousness, beyond the psychic level and before the causal level.

Taken by itself, this session might give the impression that the purpose of working in nonordinary states is to reunite with these "higher" dimensions in order to ensure the abiding enjoyment of these realms upon death. Surely this is part of the game and an undeniable good that presents itself in the work. Is not the ancient Hindu name for realization *mokṣa* ("escape" from samsara) and does not the heaven of Christianity and Pure Land Buddhism promise a reprieve from the burdens of spacetime existence? And yet, as all who continue past this point in their work discover, the breakthrough to these ultra-clear, God-soaked dimensions represents only a midpoint on the spiritual journey. The bliss of reconnecting with the source of one's existence, of remembering who and what one is underneath the many layers of conditioning is not the final goal but only a turning point. This was not clear to me at the time of this session, any more than it usually is to NDErs who beg to be allowed to stay in paradise when they are told they have to return to Earth because they "have work to do." Lest this session, therefore, be mistakenly subsumed into an "up-and-out" cosmology such as one finds in Monroe, *The Celestine Prophecy*, or any religion that seeks salvation by spurning the world, let me quickly dispel that misinterpretation.

One of the pivotal discoveries that many people make in this work is the realization that these bliss-soaked, light-filled, God-intoxicated dimensions of being that initially appear to surround spacetime waiting for us to find them are relentlessly trying to penetrate spacetime. They are the matrix, the Cosmic Womb that has given birth to this realm, that holds it in existence moment by moment, and that is constantly working to saturate it in ever greater measure. When we first become conscious of these more refined realms, we may feel that we have been marooned in a harsh and barren world—cast out of the garden—but in time we discover that we are in fact emissaries and pioneers here. After the joy of reunion subsides, one sees more clearly that the task is not escape but just the opposite, greater Presence. Our individual and collective goal is to draw the Divine Impulse ever more completely into physical incarnation.

This is the meeting point between the wisdom traditions of East and West, between Buddha and Christ, between *nirvāṇa* and the kingdom of heaven on earth. Here we see the deep significance of the Christian belief in physical resurrection, for the archetypal message of this doctrine is that the physical universe participates fully in salvation. Aurobindo's integral yoga which seeks to draw the Divine Consciousness into ever greater embodiment, Mahayana Buddhism's declaration that *saṃsāra is nirvāṇa*, and the Dzogchen teaching that existence is perfect at every moment just as it is, all describe a form of spirituality that begins to ripen only *after* one has weathered the infatuation of reunion. Here we also feel the embrace of the Goddess and the deeper import of the emergence of the feminine in our time. By drawing Her most conscious species on Earth into the death-rebirth mystery, the Goddess is affirming, not abandoning, Her creation. By guiding us individually and collectively into the transformative fires of divine awakening, she is bringing creation into the springtime of its flowering, one of many springtimes in our long evolutionary ascent.

To discover that the passion of God is to awaken ever more completely *inside* creation shatters all dualities and completely reframes the spiritual impulse. Where shall we "escape" to? Where can we be that God is not? The challenge is not to exchange earth for heaven, but to awaken more completely to the heaven that everywhere presses in upon us. It may refresh us to feel the bliss of our deeper nature in the subtler planes of being, either in temporary ecstatic experiences or in the *bardo* recess between incarnations, but our true challenge is to transform our *embodied* existence in such a way that this bliss may become our continuous conscious experience. In this exercise, the conditions of spacetime are simply the weight upon the bar. Weight-lifters do not complain about the weight on the bar but use it to their advantage. Similarly, our task is to use the resistance of spacetime to accelerate the development of capacities that would emerge more slowly in the subtler planes of existence. Our challenge is to use this thick density that hides the truth of wholeness and interpenetration to become more conscious than we were before we incarnated (when we still inhabited those blissful planes), and in so doing serve both God's passion and our own evolution.

The connection between these observations and this chapter's theme of individuality is this: If the goal is not escape but greater Presence, then we see more clearly how important it is that there be a strong and well-developed individuality to anchor that Presence. Not an isolated individuality, as isolation is the very antithesis of the Divine Embrace, but a strong center of integrated awareness, a point where Creator and Creation can meet.

The paradox of transpersonal development is also the paradox of human evolution. It takes a strong individuality to surrender the ego and to endure the impact of transcendence without fragmenting. The forging of this strong center has been the patriarchal project for four thousand years. The trajectory of this phase of our cultural evolution has been to form us into highly differentiated, self-critical, self-empowered individuals—individuals who can evaluate and set aside centuries of tradition if we see fit, who can outgrow and remake ourselves at an unbelievable pace, jumping from the sand dunes of Kitty Hawk to the moon in less than seventy years. Only now as this phase is concluding do we begin to glimpse the larger arch that this patriarchal segment is part of. In our long isolation from the Goddess, under the tutelage of our many Father-Gods, *there has been gestating within us a strength of form that will allow humanity to withstand the assault of such unitive splendor as few can imagine.* Ahead lies a degree of incarnation of the Divine

Impulse that would have shattered us at an earlier stage in our evolutionary development.

I believe that this divine marriage of Individuality and Essential Ground, of the Masculine and Feminine, of *saṃsāra* and *nirvāṇa* is the dawn that humanity's dark night is driving toward. This is the dawn that, if successfully navigated, will unite humankind and elevate us into a form that has never before walked this Earth: a humanity healed of the scars of history, its ancient partitions reabsorbed; a people with new capacities born in the chaos of near-extinction. Only when we have made this pivot, when our long labor has birthed this future Child, only then will we fully understand what we have accomplished. And when this moment finally comes, I deeply believe that, like all mothers before us, we will count our pain a small price. This birth is our gift to the Creator.

Appendix A:
Ken Wilber and the Perinatal
Features of the Dark Night

In *Sex, Ecology, Spirituality*, Wilber distinguishes four stages of mystical development—the psychic, the subtle, the causal, and the nondual. He uses Teresa of Avila as his example of the subtle stage of development (Fulcrum 8), an advanced stage of transpersonal development that includes the ordeal of the dark night of the soul, which I have linked to perinatal experience. In his criticism of Grof later in the book, however, Wilber proposes that the perinatal level of consciousness be located at the lowest level of his developmental scheme, at Fulcrum 0 or the pre-birth fulcrum.[1] Wilber's reduction of the perinatal to the fetal represents a fundamental misinterpretation of Grof's concept, but it also constitutes a striking failure to recognize the close parallels that exist between perinatal experience and the dark night of the soul. This is such a glaring oversight with such important theoretical ramifications for the possible integration of Grof's and Wilber's paradigms that the matter deserves careful attention. In this appendix, therefore, I will profile Teresa of Avila's experience of the dark night and demonstrate the intimate correspondence between her experience and perinatal experience as it surfaces in psychedelic states. After this discussion, I will offer a general critique of Wilber's handling of the perinatal domain.

Though it is not uncommon for people today to describe any difficult phase of growth they may be experiencing as a "dark night," this usage trivializes the reference and distorts the true nature of the dark night experience. The dark night of the soul is at core the final stage of a long spiritual process of surrendering one's identity as a discrete self. To die here is not simply to pass through difficult times, but to die at the deepest level of personal identity. Because the dark night represents the final unraveling of self-identity, it represents, from the perspective of many esoteric traditions, the culmination of many lifetimes of spiritual development.

Not all mystics undergo dramatic psychophysical ordeals as part of their dark night transition, but some do, and among these there is great variability. For some the trials are short-lived and moderate, while for others they persist for many years and constitute great physical and psychological suffering. One for whom the latter was the case is the great Spanish mystic St. Teresa of Avila (1515–1582). Teresa's debilitating seizures were such an integral part of her path for so many years that they came to be regarded as one of the hallmarks of her spirituality. Because of them she was diagnosed at the end of the nineteenth century as suffering from "hysteria," eventually being heralded as the "patron saint of hysterics."

Teresa of Avila's Dark Night Experience

Teresa of Avila was born in 1515, on the eve of the Protestant Reformation. At the age of twenty-three, when she was a novice at the Carmelite convent of the Incarnation in Avila, she began to suffer serious fainting spells, fevers, and heart troubles. On a trip to Becedas for treatment, she was given a copy of Osuna's *Third Spiritual Alphabet,* from which she learned the prayer of recollection, experiencing quickly the "prayer of quiet" and even brief "union." In Becedas she was diagnosed as having "shrunken nerves," and her condition deteriorated steadily for three months. "The pain in my heart," she later wrote in her autobiography, "which I had gone there to get treated, was much worse; sometimes I felt as if sharp teeth had hold of me, and so severe was the pain they caused that it was feared I was going mad."[2]

Unceasing pains racked her from head to foot. One particular fit left her comatose for four days and so deathlike that a grave was prepared. Though she survived, her condition was pitiful: "My tongue was bitten to pieces. . . . All my bones seemed to be out of joint and there was a terrible confusion in my head. As a result of the torments I had suffered during these days, I was all doubled up like a ball, and no more able to move arm, foot, hand or head than if I had been dead, unless others moved them for me."[3] After a year and a half of treatment, Teresa returned to Avila uncured. Eight months later her condition slowly began to improve, but she did not fully recover from her paralysis for three years. The paralysis recurred intermittently for twelve years, between the ages of twenty-seven and thirty-nine.

In the years following Teresa's illness, her experience in prayer deepened and she began to receive four "divine favors." First, she began to enter the third and fourth degrees of prayer—the prayer of union and the prayer of divine union. Second, she began to experience visions and voices that instructed her, among other things, in the processes of her deepening spirituality. A third favor Teresa called by several names: rapture, elevation, flight, or transport of the spirit. In these experiences she left her body in some type of spirit-form and was taken usually to "heaven," where various theological and spiritual truths were revealed to her. However problematic Teresa's narratives of out-of-body experiences may be to Western intellectuals, she insisted that they happened just as she described them. She also insisted, to our surprise perhaps, that these out-of-body experiences were "much more beneficial" to her spiritual development than even mystical union! Admirers of Teresa have tended to sidestep her testimony on this point.

Coming after the three preceding favors was a fourth that Teresa was told to value more than the others because it would purify her soul of its imperfections. She began to experience various pains that came upon her without warning. While sometimes subtle, at other times these pains were times so severe that she was "unable to do either this or anything else. The entire body contracts and neither arm nor foot can be moved."[4] These convulsive spasms caused her bones to become so disjointed that she honestly thought she was near death, and prayed for the release death would bring. They were accompanied by chills, fluctuations in pulse, and occasionally a ringing in the ears. She writes:

> [T]the pain is so excessive that one can hardly bear it, and occasionally, according to those of my sisters who sometimes see me like this, and so now understand it better, my pulses almost cease to beat, my bones are all disjointed, and my hands are so stiff that sometimes I cannot clasp them together. Until the next day I have pains in the wrist, and in the entire body, as though my bones have been wrenched asunder.[5]

Elsewhere she speaks of being wounded in the heart with an arrow dipped in a drug that causes self-hate, and on other occasions with a spear tipped with burning iron. She also describes the experience of being thrown on a fire as fuel.

Though Teresa's agony was overwhelming, it was also paradoxically sweet: "No words will suffice to describe the way in which God wounds the soul," she writes, "and the sore distress which He causes it so that it hardly knows what it is doing. Yet so delectable is this distress that life holds no delight which can give greater satisfaction."[6] Teresa was never able to understand how such distress and bliss could coexist in the soul.

Though these "outer" bodily experiences caused her great pain, Teresa seemed to be able to maintain a positive psychological balance through most of them. She felt supported by God during these trials, which she experienced as playing an important part in her spiritual growth. There were times, however, when the physical traumas were accompanied by a particularly severe psychological anguish in which this fundamental spiritual security was shattered. In these instances Teresa was unable to maintain any sense of being connected to or protected by God. Not surprisingly, she attributed these torments to the devil. The devil caused her to forget all the divine favors given her and to become distrustful and doubtful of everything. She experienced herself as so completely evil as to be personally responsible for all the heresies of the Reformation, an assessment not even the scrupulous Teresa could accept. She felt herself alienated from God's mercy and confronted by a God "who is always wielding fire and sword." Burdened by her sins before this righteous God, Teresa came to know true despair.

On other occasions devils "played ball with her soul" by causing her to be unable to think of anything but absurd trivialities. Her faith numbed and asleep, her love of God lukewarm, Teresa felt trapped in hell:

> To go and say its prayers, or to be alone, only causes [the soul] greater anguish, for the inward torture which it feels, without knowing the source of it, is intolerable; and in my opinion, bears some slight resemblance to hell. Indeed this is a fact, for the Lord revealed it to me in a vision: the soul is inwardly burning without knowing who has kindled the fire, nor whence it comes, nor how to flee from it, nor with what to put it out.[7]

Deprived for days of the ability to think a single good thought, Teresa entered a pervasive depression and dissatisfaction that she could neither isolate nor dispel.

These bouts with the devil were often purely psychological in nature, lasting anywhere from one day to three weeks. The worst condition, however, was when both the psychological and physical distresses occurred together. She describes one particularly difficult episode in her autobiography:

> On another occasion the devil was with me for five hours tor-
> turing me with such terrible pains and both inward and out-
> ward disquiet that I do no believe I could have endured them
> any longer. The sisters who were with me were frightened to
> death...for the devil had made me pound the air with my
> body, head and arms and I had been powerless to resist him.
> But the worst thing had been the interior disquiet. I could
> find no way of regaining my tranquility.[8]

The closer Teresa moved to her peak mystical experiences, the more frequent and intense her physical and psychological suffering became. The latest experiences recorded in the autobiography involved an acute sense of being abandoned by God even as she drew closer to him. Sometimes beset by seizures and sometimes not, Teresa experienced herself to be suspended between heaven and earth. Having abandoned an earth that no longer offered any consolation whatsoever, she could not yet advance to heaven. As her hunger to be with God grew, so did her sense of abandonment. The only "help" she was given was a knowledge of God that actually augmented her torment, for she was still denied his presence. She described herself wandering alone in a "desert" without relief.

In this context Teresa introduces the interesting image of being strangled. The abandoned soul seeking companionship, she says, is "like a person who has a rope around his neck, is being strangled and trying to breathe."[9] She goes on to say that the desire that body and soul not be separated during these traumas (that is, that she not die) is "like a voice crying out for help to breathe." Not only was the same simile used in one paragraph for two distinct psychological experiences, but the comparison in both instances is unclear and somewhat confusing. One wonders whether strangulation and difficulty breathing were inherent aspects of Teresa's experience, which she is here trying to integrate into the flow of her narrative. I believe this is likely, given that she explicitly mentions in several other places having difficulty breathing.[10]

When Teresa was writing the *Life* in her mid to late forties, these physical and psychological trials were her almost continuous experience. Though she had many times experienced the thrills of rapture and had known mystical union of an advanced degree, *she counted these torments, even her bouts with the devil, as the most valuable gifts given her by God.* They were the means through which her soul was being purified, "refined like gold in the crucible," and cleansed of its impurities. They were her final purgatory before her deepest mystical unfolding, which did not occur, I believe, until some time *after* her autobiography was completed.[11]

Teresa's description of this "final cleansing" in *Interior Castle* is consistent with her earlier account. Writing twelve years after the fuller version of her *Life* was completed, when she was sixty-two years old, she placed these purifying torments in the sixth mansion just before entrance to the highest seventh mansion. Purifying fire is the most frequent metaphor, and she describes the same paradoxical abandonment—the closer she draws to God, the more she feels absent from him.

I would now like to summarize the parallels between Teresa's dark night experiences and contemporary perinatal experience.

Summary of Correspondences

The similarities connecting the two sets of experiences are extremely close and can be divided into five categories—physical symptoms, psychological symptoms, ego-death, the blending of pain and ecstasy, and the overall progression of experience.

1. Teresa's *physical symptoms* closely mirror the physical features of perinatal experience, namely: contractive spasms throughout the body that may last for hours and be so severe as to cause a temporary disjointing of bones, violent jerking and shaking of the extremities, chills, fluctuations in pulse, ringing in the ears, and excruciating pains throughout her body, especially around her heart. If the reference to strangulation has experiential import, we can add suffocation to this list. Finally, the fetal posture Teresa assumed for a period of time in her early illness is a frequent perinatal posture.

2. The *psychological distress* that often accompanied Teresa's seizures, peaking in her devil-experiences, closely resembles the psychological debasement, metaphysical alienation, and existential despair endured by someone in psychedelic states. Teresa's usual interior security is shattered by an extreme inner turmoil marked by a loss of love and trust. All of her once-quieted vanities and weaknesses return to plague her, and she feels herself to be profoundly worthless. She feels utterly estranged from God and condemned to perpetual exile from him. So deep is her sense of worthlessness and alienation that she succumbs to despair, experiencing God only as a

vengeful tyrant. This psychological torment is said to be worse than the physical seizures themselves. Being denied God's embrace, she says, is like being scorched by the heat of a fire over which she is helplessly suspended. She draws comparisons to purgatory and hell, images common in perinatal narratives. In a conceptual context that is meaningful to her, therefore, Teresa repeats the basic elements of perinatal experience: estrangement from all that is seen as good and meaningful, extreme alienation, personal worthlessness, futility, and hopeless despair. She despairs because she experiences this suffering and alienation as never ending, as does the person in an extreme nonordinary state.

3. Teresa's experience reproduces the perinatal experience of *ego-death*. Death of the self is a recurrent theme in Teresa's writing. Repeatedly sounding the refrain of radical self-surrender and self-renunciation, she describes the prayer of union as a "complete death to everything in the world and a fruition in God."[12] Using the silkworm as a metaphor for the soul, she writes: "The silkworm has of necessity to die; and this will cost you the most; for death comes more easily when one can see oneself living a new life, whereas our duty here is to continue living this present life, and yet to die of our own free will."[13] It is only after the silkworm dies, she says, that fullest union with God can be experienced.

In keeping with these ideas, Teresa experiences her torments as actually destroying her "old self." Like Meister Eckhardt before her, she understands this old self to be not merely her unregenerate habits but her very existence as a self-willing individual. The transformation she describes is nothing less than a complete realignment of this self-willing core. "When we empty ourselves of all that is creature," she writes, "and rid ourselves of it for the love of God, that same Lord will fill our souls with Himself."[14] This passage refers not to a temporary peak experience but to a permanent restructuring of consciousness.

So complete and permanent is this death of the ego that when describing the mystic's state of mind in the seventh mansion, Teresa speaks of a pervading forgetfulness of self: "[The mystic] lives in so strange a state of forgetfulness that, as I say, she seems no longer to exist, and has no desire to exist—no, absolutely none."[15] In the seventh mansion the ego is replaced by a mode of consciousness centered in God, not in self. Similarly in the context of experiential psychotherapy, ego-death is experienced as a total annihilation of the individual on all levels—physical, emotional, intellectual, ethical, and transcendental. All meaningful reference points collapse as one is emptied to the point of extinction. Having died as an ego, the individual suddenly finds him or herself experiencing mystical experiences of a unitive sort.

4. The peculiar *blending of pain and ecstasy* that so puzzled Teresa also occurs in psychedelic contexts. The pain experienced by subjects under the influence of the third perinatal matrix often reaches such high levels that it changes into ecstatic rapture of cosmic proportions that Grof calls *volcanic ecstasy*. "In the state of 'volcanic ecstasy,' various sensations and emotions melt into one undifferentiated complex that seems to contain the extremes of all possible dimensions of human experience. Pain and intense suffering cannot be distinguished from utmost pleasure, caustic heat from freezing cold, murderous aggression from passionate love, vital anxiety from religious rapture, and the agony of dying from the ecstasy of being born."[16] Thus, when Teresa reports extreme pain characterized by excessive sweetness, she is giving us an accurate description of a rare but not pathological experience.

5. *The overall progression* of Teresa's experiences parallels that which occurs in modern therapeutic contexts. Beginning only after she had begun to practice the prayer of recollection, Teresa's seizures become more frequent and more severe as her experience in prayer deepens, peaking immediately before her breakthrough to her highest mystical realization.[17] Similarly, perinatal symptoms intensify as the subject moves closer to the ultimate death-rebirth experience and peak in that experience. Equally important is the fact that Teresa's convulsions cease after she has entered the seventh mansion. Teresa's torments are the growing pains of a mode of consciousness that Teresa would have called God-consciousness. As such, they are transitional and end when this new mode of consciousness is fully established. This transition had not occurred by the writing of her autobiography in 1565, but it has by the time she writes *Interior Castle* twelve years later. It is a strange hysteria indeed that is cured by mystical union.

Telling though they are, these points of comparison do not adequately convey the extraordinary degree to which Teresa's descriptions of her experiences parallel in intimate detail the contemporary accounts of psychedelic states. This can only be appreciated by placing the respective narratives side by side and attending carefully to the language and imagery used. Enough has been said already, however, to justify a perinatal interpretation of Teresa's ordeal. Teresa's many hardships during her dark night can be seen as a profound encounter with the perinatal level of consciousness. The perinatal dimension is the sedimented core of the personal unconscious, the basement wherein are stored undigested fragments of a primitive sort concerning survival, bodily integrity, and by extension one's basic value and one's ultimate helplessness against life's destructive forces. It was only after she had exhausted these forces that she was able to enter the seventh mansion, the abiding presence of the Divine. Let us now turn to consider Ken Wilber's handling of the perinatal in light of this correspondence.

Ken Wilber on the Perinatal

Wilber separates Grof's perinatal dimension from the higher spiritual transformations associated with Fulcrums 7, 8, and 9, reducing the perinatal to the fetal and plugging it into an improvised Fulcrum 0, far from Teresa's dark night experience in Fulcrum 8. This marginalizing of the perinatal goes hand in hand with his disparagement of psychedelic therapy as the "back door" entry into spiritual realms. Psychedelic therapy's "regressive" states of consciousness, he says, produce temporary contact with transpersonal domains but are incapable of producing the stable and enduring developmental structures that characterize the prized "front door" methods, such as meditation. But this is just propaganda for Wilber's preferred form of spiritual practice. The extensive and intimate degree to which Teresa of Avila's dark night experiences parallel perinatal experiences that emerge in psychedelic therapy argues against his dichotomy. The question of the comparative efficacy of psychedelic therapy vis-à-vis meditation as methods of spiritual transformation is an important one, but it is much more complex than Wilber is recognizing.

But let's step further back and look at Wilber's ladder of fulcrums as a whole. Wilber's model of psychospiritual development is an attempt to represent in a comprehensive manner the cognitive stages an individual moves through over the course of his or her entire evolution as a human being. His model seems to assume some concept of reincarnation, as it is hard to imagine anyone who could cover this entire developmental span in just one lifetime. (This is also implicit in Wilber's endorsement of Vajrayana Buddhism, which affirms reincarnation.) This means that as persons move through Wilber's various stages, they are periodically dying and being reborn, presumably starting in some meaningful way where they left off in their previous life. Ironically, however, reincarnation is little discussed in his work. The nit-and-gritty complications that are part of constantly stopping and restarting our physical existence are set aside in the interest of identifying the larger trajectory of our psychospiritual evolution. That this is Wilber's focus is fine, but unless this focus is carefully managed, it can lead to oversimplifications that create precisely the kinds of misunderstandings that I think mar his discussion of the perinatal. I want to suggest that *Wilber's neglect of the reincarnational facts of life goes hand in hand with his failure to fully grasp Grof's concept of the perinatal dimension of consciousness*.

Wilber reduces the perinatal to the fetal and proposes placing it at the lowest rung of his developmental ladder. Setting aside for the moment the error of reducing this multidimensional domain to the fetal, let's see how well this approach works for fetal experience itself. Fulcrum 0 may be an acceptable place for Wilber to put fetal experience if we remember what he is actually saying when he does so. All he is saying is that in his map of the stages of our evolution as a human being, we begin our first incarnation as a fetus. In a developmental scheme in which the details of reincarnation have been set aside, Fulcrum 0 *must refer to our first incarnation and not our most recent incarnation*. Thus, Wilber says that the moment when we are farthest from cosmic unity is the moment when we are conceived. When he says this, I must assume that he is referring to our first incarnation, otherwise I cannot make sense of it. Hopefully we are closer to cosmic unity even as a fetus on our one-hundredth incarnation as a human being than on our first. In Wilber's model, therefore, Fulcrum 0 is not actually one's most recent fetal experience but an event that lies in the person's distant past.

Now Wilber could make Fulcrum 0 our most recent fetal experience if he chose to do so, but in order to do this he would have to adjust his presentation to describe the cycles within cycles that reincarnation actually involves. He would have to explain the subtle and complex ways in which we are always catching up with ourselves in every incarnation. He would have to explain how the fulcrums that we have successfully negotiated in our previous lives exist within us as latent capacities waiting to be actualized in this life. He would have to explain how when we navigate our way through the developmental ladder each lifetime, we do not do so from scratch but rather with a sophisticated internal radar that tells us where we are going, as though our former life experiences were acting as strange attractors guiding us to our growing edge in this lifetime. But the point is that Wilber does not do this, and therefore

the most honest reading of his scheme is that Fulcrum 0 is a reference to everyone's first fetal experience.[18]

All of this looks rather artificial, of course, when we consider
the actual facts of human experience. If it takes many lifetimes to
cover the evolutionary sequence Wilber has outlined, then *real* fetal
experience takes place at *many* places along the soul's climb up his
ladder, not just one. The point is that Wilber is not describing the
human experience as it actually takes place but is mapping its developmental milestones. The fact that there is a cyclic rhythm of
death and rebirth woven into the fabric of this evolutionary progression is largely left out of his account. And yet, if we want to understand the psychospiritual significance of fetal experience as it is
actually lived by human beings, we must begin with the following
facts of experience. We must begin with the fact that our evolutionary history is punctuated by many deaths followed by many births.
We must begin by understanding *how birth functions to bring into
focus one's karmic agenda for the life one is entering, serving as a
critical bridge-point between incarnations.* We must begin by understanding that *every birth re-enacts our primal separation from
spirit, and every death foreshadows our ultimate reunion with it.* We
must begin with the fact that at a deeper level *our psyche intimately
fuses birth and death,* as though the difference between them were
nominal.

But the perinatal is, of course, more than the fetal. The death-
rebirth experience is the surrender of our physical identity for an
identity defined by spiritual reality. Thus understood, it is not difficult to see where this transition falls in Wilber's model. His first six
fulcrums represent the progressive refinement of spacetime consciousness, culminating in the complete integration of body and
mind, the capacity for vision-logic, and so on. The next three stages
represent the stabilization of states of transpersonal awareness in
which physical existence is increasingly eclipsed and spiritual reality encountered at deeper and deeper levels until finally the duality
between spirit and matter itself is overcome. Material conditioning
is left behind primarily in the psychic and lower subtle stages of
transpersonal development (Fulcrums 7 and 8). Thus the perinatal
death-rebirth dynamic that Grof has identified correlates best, I
think, with Fulcrums 7 and 8. (It would be conceptually neater if we
could simply locate the perinatal matrices in one fulcrum, Fulcrum
7, and certainly much of their phenomenology suggests that they belong there. The problem with this placement, however, is that the
sheer intensity of Grof's therapeutic methods tends to blur these

well drawn categories, drawing elements from multiple fulcrums into powerful psychospiritual melt-downs of vast proportions. The death one undergoes at each fulcrum is qualitatively different, as Wilber points out, but these methods are so powerful that they often mix and combine these deaths, giving "perinatal" experience its distinctive multi-dimensional quality.)[19]

Wilber himself seems to be moving towards this placement, though with qualification and with some inconsistency. In his book *The Eye of Spirit* he writes:

> When frontal consciousness development itself passes the existential level (fulcrum-6) and reaches the actual psychic level (fulcrum-7), the psychic/soul dimension begins to enter frontal awareness. . . . For just that reason, this is precisely where a reliving of the birth trauma *might* occur, since that perinatal awareness/memory is carried, not by the ego, which did not exist at the time, but by the psychic/soul, which now emerges in frontal consciousness."[20]

The qualification is that Wilber insists that reliving the birth trauma is not a *necessary* component of this transition, but a *possible* component. (But this is what Grof has said all along.)[21] The inconsistency is that he also continues to argue that the perinatal matrices belong in Fulcrum 0.[22]

I have argued in this volume that the true "core" of the perinatal drama, if we choose to use that language, is the death-rebirth transition itself, not death, not birth, but the liberation of mind from matter, or as Wilber puts it, the self deconstructing "its exclusive identification with the bodymind and all its relations."[23] I believe that all of the other elements which Grof has identified as part of the perinatal process can be understood as meaningful components of this fundamental transition. If this is the case, therefore, we must ask whether the term "perinatal" is the best term to use to describe these complex experiences. I am increasingly convinced that it is not because at this point in time the term introduces unnecessary confusion. The task before us is to find a vocabulary that will preserve Grof's many insights into the subtle interplay of physical birth, death, and spiritual rebirth while reconfiguring these insights around the core of existential death and rebirth.

I have used Grof's language for so long that it is probably impossible for me to be entirely comfortable with another. For me, "perinatal" *means* the hyper-intense, multidimensional mixture of fetal, personal, collective, archetypal, and mythical elements that orchestrate and saturate one's spiritual death and rebirth when these particular transformative methods are used. But for those who follow, I think we should search for a new terminology. If we speak of levels, "perinatal" phenomena belong at the interface of Wilber's existential level and the transpersonal levels (the psychic, subtle, causal, and nondual levels). If we speak of process, might we not speak simply of the death-rebirth process, and perhaps rename the Basic Perinatal Matrices as the Death-Rebirth Matrices, or DRM I–IV?

In making this proposal, it is important that we distinguish Grof's arguments for the role that fetal experience and biological birth play in our psychospiritual development from his suggestion that birth constitutes the core of perinatal experience. We can affirm everything he says about the former while rejecting the latter. I completely accept Grof's insight that the womb is the immediate foundation of our present existence, the transduction point through which the karmic themes of our larger life process are woven into our present incarnation ("larger" in all senses—soul, collective, Gaian, archetypal, and so on). But the essence of the death-rebirth experience, as Grof himself says in numerous places, is the experience of dying to our physical identity and awakening to a completely different reality (and sense of self) that transcends and includes physical existence. It is the painful surrender of everything that matter has taught us that we are and the joyous discovery that we are infinitely more. The heart of this transition is overcoming the illusion of the duality of self and other that physical existence creates, the death of *saṃsāra* itself.

When consciousness first breaks free of the prison of material conditioning, it discovers the world of spirit, a seemingly endless, multidimensional world of intelligence, power, and love. In time, however, it also discovers the story of creation, the story of the voluntary movement of spirit into matter (the involution that precedes evolution). The pain one experiences in this process of self-awakening, as Grof demonstrates, is much more than the pain of a few hours of physical compression in the womb. Underneath this physical pain, saturating it but more fundamental still, is the pain of spirit being compressed into matter with the consequent loss of its felt connection to the Cosmic Womb. It is the excruciating existential isolation of infinite consciousness being imprisoned in a private mind for countless generations as our voluntary part in creation. And because this is a choice that we made collectively as well as individually, beneath our individual existential angst looms the larger pain of an entire species that has severed its conscious communion with its Source in order to create and grow itself into the species that we are becoming. All of this is compressed into the act of being born, which is what makes birth such a rich and multidimensional experience and potent symbol of spiritual transformation. We can affirm all of this, indeed, we should affirm all of it, without conceptualizing this transition in such a way that places biological birth at its center.[24]

If Grof overstated the role of birth when he suggested that it was the core of the death-rebirth transition, Wilber gives it less significance than it deserves. When he argues that Grof's model is "profoundly out of touch with the great preponderance of evidence from the meditative and contemplative traditions," he greatly overstates his case.[25] The issue is not whether one must relive the details of one's biological birth in order to be spiritually reborn, as no one is asserting this. Rather, the issue is whether components of one's biological birth sometimes work their way into and become part of the transition of moving beyond the egoic self. When the question is framed in this way, I think that the spiritual record will clearly show that they do. Let me close by giving two brief examples, the first from Teresa of Avila again and the second from Vajrayana Buddhism.

In one of Teresa's most agonizing and yet profitable dark night experiences, she experienced herself descending into hell. Descent into hell is a common theme of BPM II, and Teresa's journey is a compelling portrait of this matrix. In the following passage I have emphasized those features of the experience that bear a striking resemblance to physical birth.

> The entrance, I thought, resembled a very *long, narrow passage*, like a furnace, *very low, dark and closely confined*; the ground seemed to be *full of water which looked like filthy, evil-smelling mud,* and in it were many wicked-looking reptiles. At the end there was a *hollow place scooped out of a wall,* like a cupboard, and it was here that I found myself in *close confinement.* But the sight of all this was pleasant by comparison with what I felt there. . . . My feelings, I think, could not possibly be exaggerated, nor can anyone understand them. I felt a fire within my soul the nature of which I am utterly incapable of describing. My *bodily sufferings were so intolerable* that, though in my life I have endured the severest sufferings of this kind . . . none of them is of the smallest account by comparison with what I felt then, to say

nothing of the knowledge that they would be endless and never ceasing. And even these are nothing by comparison with the agony of my soul, *an oppression, a suffocation and an affliction so deeply felt*, and accompanied by such hopeless and distressing misery, that I cannot too forcibly describe it. To say that it is as if the soul were continually being torn from the body is very little, for that would mean that one's life was being taken by another; whereas in this case it is the soul itself that is tearing itself to pieces. The fact is that I cannot find words to describe that interior fire and that despair which is greater than the most grievous tortures and pains. I could not see who was the cause of them, but I felt, I think, as if I were being *both burned and dismembered*; and I repeat that the interior fire and despair are the worst things of all. In that pestilential spot, where I was quite powerless to hope for comfort, it was *impossible to sit or lie, for there was no room to do so*. I had been put in this place which looked like a hole in the wall, and *those very walls so terrible to the sight, bore down upon me and completely stifled me*. There was no light and everything was in *the blackest darkness*.[26]

Did Teresa relive her physical birth in this experience? Not in any obvious sense. However, the real question is: Was her experience of descending into hell shaped to some degree by the psychic imprint of her birth? Here I think we should answer yes. Why else should hell have so many features that mimic birth? To surrender one's exclusive identification with the physical self is to walk a trail that reaches back into the womb where the physical self took its present shape, and therefore it is only natural that memories of the womb should sometimes play a role in how we experience this surrender. The very custom of calling it re-*birth* makes the point.[27]

Secondly, Vajrayana Buddhism provides us with a striking example of a spiritual tradition choosing metaphors of the womb to describe the inner textures of spiritual awakening. In her study of Yeshey Tsogyel, *Meeting the Great Bliss Queen*, Anne Klein of Rice University explains that the essential mind in Buddhism is sometimes described as a "Buddha-womb." She writes:

Here . . . the womb expresses the ultimate spiritual discovery. . . . In Buddhist traditions, for example, the womb that is an "expanse of reality" is a ubiquitous matrix, participating in

and pervading all that is born from it. It is never left behind
as is the maternal womb of contemporary Western description. In contrast, most Jewish and Christian traditions understand God to have created the world *ex nihilo*, that is,
from a nothing that, like the maternal womb, is left behind.
In Buddhist understanding, there is no dead space left behind when existence manifests. The womb of the expanse is
an ever-replenished resource, and the wish to renew association with it is not regarded as regressive but potentiating.[28]

This womb is never withdrawn but is the ever-present matrix within
which sentient life exists moment by moment. To reunite with this
womb is to reunite with the ground of existence itself. As
Padmasambhava, the great eighth-century Tibetan sage, said:

> This is the basis of all coming and going
> The place of arising of all existents,
> The womb of the mother consort.[29]

Is calling enlightenment the "Buddha-womb" or the "womb of the
mother consort" devoid of psychological significance? Doesn't the
choice of these powerful images reflect the perception that a deep,
natural (and nonreductionistic) connection exists between birth and
spiritual awakening?

Appendix B:
Ego-Death and the Species-Mind

In Grof's paradigm, the perinatal process is said to culminate in ego-death. Ego-death is presented as a definitive transition from a personal to a transpersonal identity, just as birth represents a definitive transition from the womb to the world. In various places in this volume, however, I have suggested that by itself ego-death is too small a concept to describe the multidimensional opening that takes place as the perinatal death-rebirth process comes to fruition. Because it stands alone at this critical juncture in Grof's paradigm, the concept is overworked by default and forced to carry too much of the conceptual burden of explaining this complex transition. Ego-death is but one of many deaths that occur as transpersonal experience distills itself in increasingly refined forms. The hermeneutic of biological birth does not serve us well here, because physically one is either born or not born, but spiritual birth has many shades and degrees of realization.[1]

The main point I wish to make in this appendix, however, is more basic than this. If the individual and the species are as deeply interwoven as I have suggested throughout this volume, then individual ego-death presents us with something of paradox. How is it possible for any person to ever undergo *final* ego-death as long as there is ego left in the species-mind and we *are* the species-mind at a collective level? A final ego-death makes sense within a personal model of the psyche because there we assume that one's individual karmic history is finite and therefore exhaustible. Within the model of consciousness proposed in this volume, however, it's not that simple. If at the perinatal level of consciousness one can open to the suffering of the species-mind and begin to impact that suffering to some degree, how does it happen that the individual ever finishes his or her work at this level while there is still suffering in the species-mind waiting to be released? We must attempt to give some explanation of the fact that the karmic ordeal can in fact end for the individual even though it obviously continues for the species as a whole.

295

One key to solving this riddle, I think, lies in recognizing that the therapeutic value of the individual to the species-mind actually takes two forms, not just one. The first is the cathartic release of negative experiences *from* the collective unconscious; the second, as suggested in chapter 3 is the direct infusion of positive transpersonal experiences *into* the collective unconscious. If it is the case that tapping into the collective suffering of the species may beneficially impact the species-mind in some small way, by the same logic one's positive transpersonal experiences may also directly benefit the species as a whole. When an individual's death-rebirth ordeal is concluded, therefore, he or she does not detach from the species-mind, as if that were possible, but rather his or her therapeutic role vis-à-vis the species-mind shifts from that of providing cathartic release to that of infusing transcendental energies into the collective psyche.

Though in chapter 6 I stressed the karmic threads that weave humanity into a single design, each of us is, of course, more than our present species form. Just as our egoic identity falls away on the spiritual path, so too eventually does our species-identity. When this happens, we are shedding the conditioning of not primarily personal karma but collective karma, the biocultural conditioning that structures the fundamental cognitive and affective patterns of humanity at its current level of development. Ramakrishna frequently alluded to both these levels of conditioning in his teaching. He said, for example: "For the *avatara,* there is no *karma*, no limiting or binding impressions from the history of personal *and collective* embodiment." Elsewhere he said, "The person who has not courageously confronted the basic unreality of conventional structures—including both individual *and collective* egocentricity, including as well the very notion of a substantial universe—can never sincerely love the Real or long intensely for the Real, much less become Reality."[2] From this perspective, if we can penetrate beyond the species-ego and transcend the restrictions inherent in the collective unconscious, we are not abandoning humanity at all, but rather are mediating a great gift directly into the species-mind—*the gift of experiencing what we are beyond this species form.* Because it is a human being who has "reached beyond," the gift is being appropriated by the entire species via Sheldrake's principle of formative causation.

Even this, however, does not completely solve the question posed. The fact that the individual never detaches from the species-mind does not by itself solve the problem of timing. When one's inner process has opened profoundly to the collective rhythms of the species-mind, by what mechanism is the individual ever drawn beyond these powerful currents? Who or what decides when "enough is enough" and allows the individual to move on, even though much suffering still remains in the species-mind?

I do not have a complete answer to this question and have taken two different approaches to the problem at different times. The first approach was to see collective perinatal suffering as resulting from a series of resonances between the individual mind and the species-mind that were springing up spontaneously in one's work. The idea was that when a person uses particularly powerful techniques to hyperstimulate the psyche and brings forward a given perinatal matrix, energetic resonances can be *accidentally* or *unintentionally* created with the corresponding Meta-Matrices of the collective unconscious, forming something like standing waves within the species-mind. Through these *bridges of resonance*, the energies of the collective unconscious are drawn into the individual's awareness, bringing the undigested historical experience of the species into our conscious awareness.

In this "passive resonance model," the answer to the question "Why does collective suffering end for the individual when there is still suffering in the species-mind?" is relatively straightforward. What controls the entire process is the condition of the individual. When the individual has finally removed the last egoic distortions from his or her private system, these problematic resonances with the collective psyche can no longer occur because there is no longer the required hook in the individual to anchor them. The collective suffering ends for the individual but not for the species because there is no longer any COEX system or perinatal matrix in the individual that corresponds to the Meta-Matrices that still exist in the collective unconscious.

While this approach to the problem seems to capture some of the dynamics involved, I no longer think that it is a complete explanation of the process. In this model, the collective field is viewed as being essentially passive. It moves in response to the initiative of the individual but initiates nothing on its own. In my experience, however, the species-mind is not a passive field but a living intelligence that is *more alive* and *more conscious* than we are. From this perspective, these resonances appear to be not the accidental byproducts of a particularly intense therapeutic method but the manifestation of a higher order of intention and design. In a felt collaboration that I have not tried to describe in this book, the collective and the individual *cooperate* in this endeavor. An invitation is extended from the collective level and is freely accepted by the individual.

When we see another person in pain, the immediate instinct of most persons is to come to their assistance. It is the same here. When one begins to experience humanity's pain firsthand in psychedelic sessions, one's immediate instinct is to try to help relieve that suffering if it is within one's means to do so. If one is shown a way to help, it is only natural to do what one can. In this deep collaboration of soul and surround, choices are made whose full ramifications may not be visible at the time, but which clearly reflect the fact that a higher order of intentionality and design is expressing itself. At critical junctures, one *feels* a larger plan unfolding, as though all the parties involved had shown up as prearranged to accomplish a specific task. Furthermore, in my case, at least, it was not true that the collective ordeal ended after ego was expunged, as would have been predicted by the first model. In fact, it was only *after* the collective ordeal had subsided in my work that the sessions turned to the less difficult task of going after the personal roots of my egoic distortions. Until that point, my session experiences were not focused on trying to remove my private foibles (and somehow missing), but rather were *using* those foibles to reach into the collective mind and establish the resonances described in part I.[3]

We must conceptualize everything that happens in psychedelic therapy from the perspective of both the individual subject *and the larger life form we are.* We need to re-think the death-rebirth dynamic from the perspective of the Chain of Being. To use Ken Wilber's vocabulary, if we are a holon functioning as a part within a series of ever-enlarging wholes, then the death-rebirth dynamic may have different functions for different levels of reality, all of which are being realized *simultaneously.* From the perspective of the smaller holon, for example, the effect of death-rebirth may be liberation into that which is larger, while the effect of the *same* transition from the perspective of the larger holon may be to allow it greater access to and integration with the smaller field. An event that functions as spiritual "ascent" from below may simultaneously function as "descent" from above.

Thinking from this more unified perspective, it is still not clear to me why the suffering is allowed to end for an individual while it continues for the species. Is it that there is some hidden cosmic oversight that simply decides, "That's enough!"? Is it, as I suggested above, that the individual simply becomes more useful to the system as a conduit for drawing higher energies into the field than for drawing the toxic sludge of history out of it? Or is it simply that the confused and tormented species-mind is simply one of many points of interface that the individual negotiates on the journey to the core of existence? There is still much that we do not understand about these processes. All I can say with certainty is that the collective ordeal does eventually end, and a new phase of the work begins. In this new phase, the enormous field of energy that has been set free during the long phase of perinatal cleansing begins to be focused in such a way that one starts to break through a *series* of new experiential barriers. This work is not less challenging, but it is less painful and it is focused beyond the collective dimension of mind. In a later book, I hope to explore some of these experiences and the issues they raise for transpersonal psychology.

Notes

Chapter 1. The Pivot to Nonordinary States

1. The work of scientists such as Paul Davies, David Bohm, John Barrow, and Frank Tipler has revitalized our teleological awareness and is placing the argument from design on new empirical footing. The exploration of nonordinary states complements these developments by offering us the opportunity to deepen our *experience* of the intelligence that their research points us toward.

2. For example, Daniel Dennett's *Consciousness Explained* and Paul Edward's *Reincarnation.*

3. Huston Smith and Ken Wilber have demonstrated the existential and philosophical impoverishment that accompanies denying the transpersonal depth of human experience. See Smith, *Beyond the Post-Modern Mind* and Wilber, Sex, *Ecology, Spirituality* and *The Marriage of Sense and Soul.*

4. 1995: 276.

5. This is the approach recommended by John Heron in his book *Sacred Science.*

6. While emphasizing the universal nature of these experiences, it is an open question whether men and women will experience the deep psyche in exactly the same way. My early assumption that they would has eroded as I have assimilated the feminist critique of psychological models that too often fail to reflect women's experience. Most of the model-makers in transpersonal psychology thus far have been men, and most of the spiritual systems being interpreted are patriarchal. We must be careful, therefore, not to assume that the patterns of the male psyche are universal patterns. There may be some safety in the large number of male and female subjects contained in Grof's samples, but careful comparative studies have yet to be done.

The ego that we are attempting to transcend in transpersonally oriented therapy is a collective as well as individual construct, a construct that has been forged for the past four thousand years in the fires of patriarchal culture. Even putting our most enlightened foot forward, how could it fail to be the case that the psyches of men will embody this construct differently than the psyches of women and therefore that men and women will experience its dissolution somewhat differently? I fully expect, therefore, that some of the ideas presented in this volume will eventually need to be revised as our understanding of the role of gender in transpersonal disclosure matures. Until that time, women will have to determine for themselves the degree to which the observations made here apply to their own experience of the deep psyche.

7. After a hiatus of over twenty-five years, legal psychedelic research is slowly resuming. The Multidisciplinary Association for Psychedelic Studies (MAPS) is an international educational and research organization that publishes research initiatives on psychedelics in its quarterly newsletter. Its recent reports on LSD, MDMA, ibogaine, ketamine, DMT, ayahuasca, and marijuana research indicate that research on psychedelics is making a quiet, cautious comeback in medical and scientific circles. The FDA, for example, has given approval to Richard Yensen and Donna Dryer's study on the use of LSD in the treatment of substance abuse, pending approval from an Institutional Review Board (MAPS, vol. 4, no. 4). Juan Sanchez-Ramos at the University of Miami has had Phase I studies of ibogaine approved to assess its safety, metabolism, and pharmacokinetics in volunteers with an eye to its eventual use in treating drug addiction. Rick Strassman recently completed a tolerance study of DMT at the University of New Mexico and is continuing these and similar studies on LSD and psilocybin under funding from the National Institute on Drug Abuse. As this new generation of research continues, it is only a matter of time before the capacity of these substances to activate the very foundations of consciousness itself will once again become a matter of clinical record. MAPS has two internet addresses: rickmaps@aol.com and st.maps@cybernetics.net.

8. Put more carefully, neither method aims directly at the lower register of the unconscious but rather shifts consciousness toward its higher register. Consciousness thus aroused spontaneously and organically begins to throw off its impurities and distortions.

9. Ken Wilber has criticized Grof for failing to examine the "intersubjective worldspace" of the psychedelic subject. His contention is that Grof's phenomenological description of transpersonal experience simply assumes the subject who is having the experience and does not examine the intersubjective space that supports and allows the particular subject and the particular experiences to arise in the first place. The subjective space in which these experiences occur is not pregiven and unproblematic: it develops (1995: 745). Wilber has a valid point, I think. While not providing everything that Wilber is calling for, I hope that the observations on methodology and transpersonal disclosure that are scattered throughout this volume will contribute useful pieces to an eventual account of the intersubjective space that unfolds in psychedelic therapy.

10. My description makes the process sound more linear than it actually is. In fact, the process has many twists and turns, many cycles within cycles. Furthermore, when working in the deep psyche, not all months and years are the same (see Rick Tarnas, *Cosmos and Psyche,* forthcoming). Nevertheless, amidst all the variables and changing landscapes, a progressive unfolding can usually be discerned.

11. Ken Wilber's contention that Grof's therapeutic methods are not capable of generating long-term changes in a subject's baseline consciousness is simply not correct. While raising important questions about the difficulty of integrating powerful transpersonal experiences and therefore the relevance of these experiences for fostering genuine spiritual development, Wilber greatly oversimplifies the issues involved (1995: 585–588). He is quite correct to point out that for true transformation to take place, it is not sufficient for persons simply to have deep experiences. The essential question is, how much leverage can these experiences exert on the conditioning of our psyche? In this book I am going to assume, not argue, that psychedelic therapy is a legitimate form of spiritual practice, or in Wilber's terms that repeatedly entering into certain "states" can eventually effect the "structures" of consciousness. In a subsequent book I hope to discuss this issue in greater detail and to explore how psychedelic work might be integrated into other forms of spiritual practice, especially those found in Vajrayana Buddhism. In the interim, I highly recommend Jack Kornfield's interview "Psychedelic Experience and Spiritual Practice: A Buddhist Perspective" in *Entheogens and the Future of Religion*, edited by Robert Forte, and his interview "Domains of Conscious" that appeared in *Tricycle*, Fall, 1996. I would also mention Trungpa Rinpoche's observation, quoted in the same issue of *Tricycle*, that LSD functions as a kind of "super-samsara" and as such could be a useful method for confronting one's karmic conditioning (Rick Fields, "A High History of Buddhism").

12. Michel Zimmerman, "Deep Ecology and Ecofeminism: The Emerging Dialogue," in *Reweaving the World,* Irene Diamon and Gloria Orenstein, eds. See also *Deep Ecology for the 21st Century,* George Sessions, ed.

13. In their excellent book, *The Coming Age of Scarcity,* Michael Dobkowski and Isidor Wallimann write: "'Hell' is the fundamental instability that will arise as members of an overpopulated planet compete for increasingly scarce resources" (286–287, citing Heilbroner, 1980).

14. There is a more subtle esoteric vocabulary which distinguishes various aspects of Sacred Mind, but it is not necessary for our project. See Ken Wilber, *The Spectrum of Consciousness* and *The Atman Project.*

15. See Wilber, 1986: chapter 3; 1995: chapter 8. The resulting model of reality is the hierarchical model found in the perennial philosophy. Donald Rothberg has argued effectively that one can credit many of the

points made by the critics of the perennial philosophy without accepting their reductionistic alternatives or abandoning the core insight of a hierarchically structured universe. Specifically, endorsing a hierarchical ontology does not require devaluing matter, emotions, sexuality, women, or nature. I agree with him when he says:

> Development of non-hierarchical models may be seen not so much as contradicting the *philosophia perennis,* but rather as indicating that affirming the hierarchical ontology alone may be a one-sided and potentially dangerous mode of expression, stressing, as it were, the more "masculine" qualities of differentiation, ascension to the heights, activity and movement, and transcendence. What may be most needed . . . is an exploration of the corresponding, more "feminine" qualities: integration and openness, and immanence, the "always already" quality of enlightenment and liberation. (1986: 26)

As I understand it, this is precisely the tantric perspective. In tantra nothing is devalued, everything is sacralized. To affirm the depths of the Sacred Mind does not disparage the splendor of the Sacred Body. On the perennial philosophy, see: Huxley (1945), Schuon (1984), Smith (1976, 1982), and Wilber (1980, 1995). On the defense of the concept of a hierarchical ontology against its critics, see: Rothberg (1986), Wilber (1995, 1997), and Foreman (1990).

16. 1991: 420.

17. 1991: 353.

18. 1991: 400.

19. 1991: 364.

20. This epistemological lineage diverged into two streams in the twentieth century: depth psychology and cognitive science. Both traditions share the same drive to uncover the underlying psychological structures of the human mind but differ sharply after that. Cognitive science focuses on the study of ordinary states of consciousness and activities such as remembering, calculating, identifying, intending, and so on, which it explores under the strong influence of research on artificial intelligence, using computers to model mental processes. Although most philosophers of mind and epistemologists have placed their eggs in cognitive science's basket, I believe that depth psychology will have the larger impact over time.

21. 1991: 422.

22. Tarnas goes on to use Grof's paradigm to interpret the broad sweep of Western history in terms of a perinatal dialectic, suggesting that humanity as a whole has been undergoing a long death-rebirth process

which is now reaching a critical stage. I deeply agree with his read of history and will return to his proposal in chapter 8.

23. See especially: *The Spectrum of Consciousness* (1977), *The Atman Project* (1980), *Eye to Eye* (1983), *Sex, Ecology, Spirituality* (1995), *The Eye of Spirit* (1997), and *The Marriage of Sense and Soul* (1998).

24. "In psychedelic or advanced psycholytic sessions, events from an individual's intrauterine development are rather common. . . . Whenever it was possible, I have made attempts at objectively verifying such episodes. . . . On several occasions, I was able to get surprising confirmations by independently questioning the mother or other persons involved; it should be emphasized that this was done with all the precautions necessary to avoid any contamination of the data." Grof continues, "Another interesting aspect of these experiences that I found quite unusual was the fact that subjects, when discussing them, seemed to avail themselves of specific knowledge of embryology and the physiology of pregnancy that was far superior to their previous education in these areas. They have often accurately described certain characteristics of the heart sounds of the mother and child; the nature of various acoustic phenomena in the peritoneal cavity; specific details of positions, physical features, and behavior of the fetus; relevant facts about placentary circulation; and even details about exchanges between the maternal and fetal blood in the placentary villi. . . . Scientists from various disciplines . . . who volunteered for the LSD training program expressed astonishment at how convincing and authentic these experiences could be. These same sophisticated subjects usually emphasized that experiences of this kind occurred in their sessions in spite of the fact that, before the sessions, they did not accept the possibility of prenatal memories" (1976: 158–60).

25. See the case of Karl, who during a session relived what he felt was his death in a former life as a priest in the company of Spanish troops, but in a setting that looked incongruously like Scotland or Ireland. In his experience he saw a seal ring on his hand with clearly recognized initials. Being an artist, he produced a series of drawings of the fortress he had seen, its tunnels and underground storage spaces, the ring, and his death. Through a combination of fortuitous circumstances and careful research, he was subsequently able to verify what he had experienced in his session. The place was the old fortress in Ireland called Dunanoir or *Forte de Oro* (Golden Fortress), which was occupied during the time of Walter Raleigh by the Spanish and then besieged by the British. After negotiating a surrender of the fortress, the British broke their promise and slaughtered all the Spaniards. Karl discovered a document that revealed that a priest had accompanied the Spanish and had been killed with them. It also revealed that the initials of the name of the priest were identical to those that Karl had seen in his vision of the seal ring, which he had represented in one of his drawings (1988: 92–97).

26. See the case of Nadja, a fifty-year-old psychologist, who in a realistic identification with her mother relived a distinct and poignant scene that appeared to come from her mother's childhood, when her mother was three or four years old. Her mother subsequently verified the details of both the visual and the subjective content of the experience, which included the experience of being raised in an unusually strict home where the mother had made excessive demands concerning cleanliness and proper behavior (1976: 164–65).

See also the case of a young woman from Finland who during a session experienced a strong identification with her father and relived what appeared to be a battle that he had participated in fourteen years before in World War II. In this experience she relived being her father and hiding behind a tree when a bullet scraped his/her cheek and ear. She had no memory of her father ever having spoken to her about this incident, but the experience was extremely vivid and convincing. Later her father confirmed, to his astonishment, that her description of the scene and the environment was absolutely accurate. He also confirmed that he had never spoken to her of this event or to other members of the family because it was not sufficiently serious (1988: 80–81; see also the case of Renata, 1976: 165–67).

27. In one case a patient made telepathic contact during a session with a spirit presence who requested that the patient contact a couple in the Moravian city of Kroměřž and let them know that their son, Ladislav, was doing alright. The message included the couple's name, street address, and telephone number, all of which was unknown to both the patient and his therapist. When the number was later dialed, the woman who answered started to cry and explained that her son, Ladislav, had passed away three weeks before (1988: 108–09). A second case involves a communication between Eva Pahnke and her deceased husband, Walter N. Pahnke, during an LSD session in which Walter asked his skeptical wife to return a book that he had borrowed from a friend. He gave her the name of the friend, the name of the book, the shelf, and the sequential order of the book on this shelf. Using this information, Eva was able to find and return the book in question, which she had been completely unaware of previously (1988: 109–10).

28. In one case, a person experienced being an eagle and in that context discovered, much to his surprise, that eagles had telescopic vision and were capable of optically "zooming in" on their prey from great heights (1988: 55–56). In another case, a woman experienced becoming a lioness, and discovered that a lioness determines her need for food not by the feelings in her stomach but by rubbing her head back into the area between her raised shoulders. This unanticipated insight into animal physiology was later confirmed when she learned from a lecture that some animals have a type of fat not found in humans called "brown fat" that is stored between the

scapulae and which must be maintained at a certain level to ensure the health of the animal.

29. In *The Holotropic Mind* Grof writes: "I have witnessed, for example, a person who had no background whatsoever in ancient cultures describe details of Egyptian funeral practices, information such as the esoteric meaning and form of special amulets and sepulchral boxes, the meaning of the colors chosen for funeral cones, the technology of embalmment, and the purpose of specific ritualized practices. Having experienced himself as an embalmer in ancient Egypt, he was able to describe the size and quality of the mummy bandages, materials used in preparing the mummy cloth, and the shape and symbolism of the four Canopic jars used to hold specific organs taken from the body. Our follow-up research revealed that details he had reported about the symbolic figures on each jar, as well as the specific contents of each, were found to be accurate, though this was not knowledge that was generally available to the public" (1990: 126; for more examples see 1976: 167–71 and 1988: 81–84).

30. *The Eye of Spirit,* 1997: 90, Wilber's emphasis. See also *Eye to Eye.* Jorge Ferrer has criticized Wilber for not going far enough in distinguishing the epistemic categories of spirituality from those of science and for relying on Karl Popper's outdated assessment of the role of falsifiability in scientific practice. Drawing on the work of Habermas, Gadamer, and others, Ferrer argues that it is a mistake to import science's emphasis on verification and falsification to the extent that Wilber does to account for the validity of knowledge in other domains of human reality such as arts, literature, politics, and spirituality (Ferrer, 1998).

Chapter 2. Beyond Reincarnation

1. 1987: 50. The phrase itself is borrowed from Kierkegaard.

2. 1995: 139–40.

3. 1987: 50.

4. 1987: 50–53. In his later book, *Reincarnation,* Edwards does analyze specific cases from Stevenson.

5. Stanislav Grof, too, receives Edwards's attention in a chapter tellingly entitled "Dr. Grof, LSD, and the Amorous Snake-Woman."

6. Edwards has already defined his position on these cases. "What is fatal to . . . the general claim that wounds and illnesses may be transmitted from a dead person to a child or an embryo is that there is no conceivable way in which such a transmission could take place" (1995: 139). He is responding to earlier articles by Stevenson such as "Birthmarks and

Birth Defects Corresponding to Wounds on Deceased Persons," *Journal of Scientific Explanation,* 7.4 (1993): 403–10. For those not up to the full 2,200 page treatment, a synopsis of the larger work is available entitled *Where Reincarnation and Biology Intersect.*

7. I will not discuss the evidence for rebirth that comes from past-life therapy, though any full account of the evidence should surely do so. Winafred Lucas's excellent book *Regression Therapy: A Handbook for Professionals* testifies to the vitality and increasing sophistication of the past-life therapy movement. In concert with Stevenson's research, this volume powerfully completes the argument for rebirth by establishing beyond reasonable doubt the clinical effectiveness of this therapeutic approach.

8. Almeder sees this tension in the evidence, but he underestimates the scope of the problem. It matters less, he says, whether we say that we are the same or different persons across lives than that we recognize that everything we are now is folded into what we subsequently become. In a reincarnating universe, he writes:

> One's personality would not so much disappear from the earth as it would evolve into something very unlike what it formerly was. But this is not to suggest that people do not survive death as persons; for we often become persons very much different from the persons we were. Still, something essential to us must remain throughout the process. However, it is difficult to say what this something is. (1992: 88)

Almeder is surely correct that if reincarnation is a coherent process, "something essential to us" must remain, but given the openendedness of the process itself, it is questionable whether this something should be spoken of as a "person." And if this is the case, then the title of Almeder's book is somewhat misleading. Properly understood, reincarnation does not prove personal survival but rather invites us to surrender the concept altogether and look with openended wonder at what we might be in the process of becoming.

9. 1987: chapter 10.

10. Wambach, 1978.

11. Whitton, 1986.

12. From a transpersonal perspective, the unusual continuity of memory and affect between the lives of Stevenson's subjects suggests that these individuals underwent what might even be described as a *superficial death.* One of the functions of death is to bring our present consciousness back into contact with the more inclusive consciousness of the soul. Stevenson's children tend to give little indication that this deeper reintegration has taken place, and one suspects that the process has been short-

circuited by the traumatic circumstances surrounding their death. It is as if they bounced back into spacetime without the rest and reorientation that immersion in the more inclusive soul might have provided them.

13. 1987: 231.

Chapter 3. Expanding the Concept of the Perinatal

1. In *Realms of the Human Unconscious,* Grof states that the "natural chronological order [of birth] is never maintained" in LSD psychotherapy and that the order in which the matrices appear actually shows great variety. In summarizing the overall pattern of subjects in psycholytic therapy, he gives the general order as BPM II, III, IV, and I (1976: 149–53). This same sequence is repeated in *LSD Psychotherapy* (1980: 206, 222). That is to say, one's deepest experience of the prelabor womb often occurs *after* one has relived being delivered from the womb. The primary reason for this interesting "looping back" to the prebirth state after birth, I think, is that our memory of our biological experience is here being rescripted by a deeper psychospiritual dynamic. More recently, Grof working in conjunction with Richard Tarnas, has noted that there appears to be a correspondence between an individual's astrological transits at the time of a session and the emergence of specific perinatal archetypes during the session. If the rhythm of the deep psyche's unfolding is in some way synchronized with the changing patterns of our solar system, generalizations about the usual order of perinatal experience become problematic. Even so, I think that Grof's original observations reflects a noteworthy pattern in his clinical data.

2. 1980: 72.

3. 1976: 138–39.

4. 1976: 139.

5. While Grof's exposition has subtly changed through the years (see appendix A, n. 24), I think it is a fair assessment to say that the thrust of his published analysis of the perinatal realm to date has been to see fetal experience as forming the core of perinatal experience and to view transpersonal experiences as being drawn in through a form of thematic resonance to this core. In *Beyond the Brain,* for example, he writes, "Although the entire spectrum of experience occurring on this level cannot be reduced to a reliving of biological birth, the birth trauma seems to represent an important core of the process. For this reason, I refer to this domain of the unconscious as the *perinatal*" (1985: 99); and again, "The central element in the complex dynamics of the death-rebirth process seems to be reliving the biological birth trauma" (140). The most complete account of the relation of personal

and transpersonal elements in perinatal experience appears in *The Adventure of Self-Discovery,* where he writes:

> Connecting with the experiences of the fetus in the stages of the biological birth process functions as a selective stencil providing experiential access to specific domains of the collective unconscious involving similar states of consciousness . . . such as archetypal visions of the Great Mother or the Terrible Mother Goddess, hell, purgatory, heaven or paradise, identification with animals, and past incarnation experiences. As it is the case with the various associated COEX systems, the connecting link between these transpersonal phenomena and the BPM's is similarity of the emotions or physical sensations involved. . . .
> . . . Identification with the fetus in various stages of the birth process seems to provide selective access to themes in the transpersonal domain that involve similar emotional states and psychosomatic experiences. (1988: 10–11)

6. In asking this question, I am assuming that these experiences do have a meaningful therapeutic function, that their appearance is not simply accidental. This assumption seems warranted by the consistency with which these experiences have surfaced at approximately the same point in the therapies of hundreds of subjects. Moreover, they have proven themselves to be clinically efficacious by both the subjective accounts of the individuals involved and the clinical observation of the remission of symptoms. The problem here is trying to fit together the enormous scope of the collective experiences that can arise at the perinatal level and the life of the individual.

7. 1976: 116.

8. In *LSD Psychotherapy,* for example, Grof writes: "Activation of the destructive and self-destructive potential *in the individual* is one of the most important aspects of the death-rebirth struggle. Scenes of unbridled aggression and mass destruction, as well as sadomasochistic orgies, are standard components of the perinatal unfolding. In this context, enormous amounts of destructive energy are mobilized and discharged: the result is a dramatic reduction of aggressive feelings and tendencies" (1980: 281, my emphasis). Similarly, when he is summarizing the spiritual repercussions of experiential psychotherapy in *Beyond the Brain* and *The Adventure of Self-Discovery,* the discussion always revolves around the individual with no mention of the possibility that the larger systems encompassing the individual might be affected (1985: 366–70; 1988: 9).

I am very aware in formulating this critique that I am standing on intellectual ground that Grof has cleared, asking questions that his paradigm taught me to ask. If Grof had publically asked these questions himself twenty-five years ago, it would have quickly delegitimized his theory in the eyes of his discipline. Furthermore, it is difficult to imagine how one can provide empirical evidence that larger systems have been affected. Being the scientist that he is and given his commitment to the canons of scientific discourse, his focus on the individual was a wise choice. (On therapy's impact on one's karmic antagonist, see 1985: 47–48; 1988: 89–90.)

9. *Revision,* Summer 1996. Currently, Grof's approach to the perinatal domain is influenced by a deep appreciation of archetypal dynamics, especially as articulated in archetypal astrology. Rather than seeing these archetypal dynamics as being scripted by one's historical birth, he entertains the possibility that they may have actually influenced the original birth experience itself.

10. In a later book, I hope to address some of the methodological issues raised by working with psychedelic states as a spiritual practice. Here, I will only mention that I interrupted my work because the extreme nature of the states I was entering became too stressful for my family to endure. When one opens the door to the deep psyche, it directly and indirectly impacts one's intimate relationships. On many levels, in many ways, those we love are inevitably drawn into the work. I deeply underestimated this fact in these early years and owe more than I can say to my wife, Carol Fitzpatrick, who is a gifted clinical psychologist and Vajrayana practitioner. As a rule of thumb, the more potent the transformative practice one uses, the stronger must be the container that holds the life. The ancient wisdom traditions provide us with important models for constructing viable containers to carry out such work safely.

11. 1986:153–54. I agree with Wilber on this point. What he fails to understand, however, is that the same dynamic occurs in psychedelic contexts. Thus, his attempt to discriminate between "regressive" psychedelic states and "progressive" meditational states is completely misguided (1995: 585–88). There is no "back door" into the spiritual realm so far as I know, nor do I know what such a door would look like. In making such distinctions, Wilber is simply lobbying for his preferred form of spiritual discipline.

12. *Science, Order, and Creativity,* David Bohm and F. David Peat.

13. J. E. Lovelock, *Gaia: A New Look at Life on Earth.*

14. John D. Barrow and Frank J. Tipler, *The Anthropic Cosmological Principle.*

15. 1988: 247–48.

16. 1988: chapter 10.

17. Let me also acknowledge what may be an additional discrepancy between Sheldrake's concept of morphic resonance and my use of this notion. The idea that an individual can mediate some form of cathartic re-

lease at the species level suggests the transfer of some form of mental or psychic energy, understanding that the term "energy" is being used metaphorically in this context. By contrast, Sheldrake holds that morphic resonance is unlike other forms of resonance (such as acoustic and electromagnetic resonance) in that it does not involve a transfer of energy from one system to another, but rather a "nonenergetic transfer of information" (1988: 108). At this point, it is not clear to me whether this discrepancy can be removed by semantic clarification or whether we should propose that at least some forms of morphic resonance involve an energetic transfer of information. I note with interest that Ervin Laszlo criticizes this feature of Sheldrake's theory in his provocative book, *The Interconnected Universe* (1995: 43–44). Laszlo does not believe the evidence demands that form-creating fields be nonenergetic so much as "minutely energetic."

18. 1976: 145–49.

19. As massive organizational structures within the collective unconscious, the Meta-Matrices reflect the aggregate mental habits of humanity. They are the deep, residual etching of history on the human psyche, the patterns of the past mechanically perpetuating themselves into the present. As the vehicles of our collective memory, however, they do not explain how humanity manages to detach itself from its past and create a new and different future for itself. For this we need to look beyond memory to our collective capacity for creativity and originality. Grof seems to anticipate the possible existence of such structures when he writes in *Beyond the Brain:* "I first became aware of COEX systems as principles governing the dynamics of the individual unconscious and realized that knowledge of them was essential for understanding the inner process on this level. However, later it became obvious that the systems of condensed experience represent a general principle operating on all the levels of the psyche, rather than being limited to the biographical domain" (1985: 92).

20. Though I have here retained the convention of speaking of the perinatal as a "level" of consciousness, I have reservations about this language and have begun to think of the perinatal more as a *stage* of transformational development than a level of consciousness per se. What this term points to, I think, might be better thought of as a particular stage of inner work rather than an innate structure of consciousness. There is some usefulness to describing consciousness as having various operational "levels," but to identify the perinatal as such a level is problematic for several reasons. First, there is the fundamental fact that the perinatal level eventually disappears. Second, perinatal experience is itself inherently multidimensional or multilevel. A deep perinatal encounter may combine experiences that come from biological birth, postnatal present life, former lives, the collective unconscious, and the archetypal/mythic level, all experienced simultaneously. Because perinatal experience can draw from and integrate many levels of consciousness simultaneously, it is awkward to describe this mode

of experience as a "level" in its own right. Third, in the next chapter I will suggest that the distinctive cathartic power of perinatal experience derives precisely from the fact that different levels of consciousness are being brought together, causing the higher/larger level to work upon the lower/smaller level. Perinatal experience arises when conditioned and unconditioned consciousness collide; it is the explosive combustion that results when ego is plunged into non-egoic awareness. Finally, to use the language of "levels" suggests that this realm exists in the psyche independently of the means we have used to gain access to it. I am less certain than I once was that this is a safe assumption. How the perinatal realm manifests seems to vary according to the method used to gain access to it. We are observing something, therefore, that appears to be at least in part dependent upon our investigative instrument. What we have been calling the perinatal "level" may be a particular modality of consciousness that emerges *when the psyche is powerfully aroused*. That is, it may be a phenomenon that is more method-dependent than we have previously appreciated.

These and other considerations have led me to begin thinking of the perinatal as *a clinical category that identifies a stage of transformational engagement* rather than a category that identifies an innate structure of consciousness. To speak of the perinatal "level" of consciousness, therefore, is a shorthand for describing the distinctive experiential interface that characterizes a particular stage of inner work, and all references to "levels" or "dimensions" should be understood in this dynamic sense. Everything that is said here using the spatial metaphor of levels can be translated into the dynamic metaphor of stages of engagement.

21. Object-relations theory focuses on the most primitive disruptions of postnatal life and their impact on subsequent ego development. One of the major theoreticians of this movement, Harry Guntrip, writes that ego-splitting can occur in three different types of situations: tantalizing refusal to satisfy basic needs, rejection and neglect, and impingement. Of the three, he finds impingement to pose the most primitive trauma for the infant, whose immature and sensitive ego make him particularly vulnerable to being overwhelmed by his environment. He writes: "fear is bound to arise as the earliest disrupting factor, and remains always the deepest problem; fear, not of a hypothetical death instinct or destructive instinct working within, but fear of traumatic factors coming from without . . . 'a *reaction to impingement*'" (1969: 239). Guntrip's analysis of impingement does not extend earlier than infancy, but if the fetus is indeed conscious during delivery, it is a small step to say that the ordeal of labor represents a paradigmatic instance of severe impingement, more severe than anything the newborn is likely to face in the first few years of his or her life. Integrating Grof and Guntrip, we could describe BPM II as an *impingement-fear COEX system*. See Bache, 1981, for a further discussion of object relations theory, impingement-fear, and perinatal dynamics.

22. What may cause a person's experience to tilt toward one side or the other of this polarity depends upon many variables that I will not discuss here other than to mention the following. In addition to differences in archetypal, natal dispositions, I think a significant variable is the strength of the stimulus used to elicit these states. The clinical protocol at the Psychiatric Institute of Prague was "psycholytic" LSD-therapy, calling for a long series of relatively low dose sessions (75–300 micrograms). In this form of therapy, the unconscious is stripped layer by layer, peeling away the COEX systems and perinatal matrices in smaller increments. While the deep psyche functions holographically, making it possible for any one session to contain material from all three levels, consciousness is less mobilized in low dose sessions than in high dose sessions. Later at the Maryland Psychiatric Research Center, the clinical protocol was "psychedelic" or high dose LSD-therapy (300–500 micrograms), but treatment was restricted to a maximum of three sessions. The goal of these few sessions was to facilitate a deep mystical experience, not to work through all the issues rooted in the psychodynamic and perinatal levels. (For a description of the differences between psycholytic and psychedelic therapy, see 1980: 31–38, 119–28. For more on the Maryland program, see Grof, 1976: 23–24, and Grof and Halifax, chapter 3.)

The question of dose is significant for the following reason. I believe that a psycholytic approach to therapy will tend to emphasize the personal side of the perinatal interface while a psychedelic approach will tend to emphasize its transpersonal dynamics. Generalizations of this sort are risky because many variables influence the content of an individual session, including the personality of the subject, the experience of the therapist, the set and setting of the session, the number of previous sessions, and so on. Nevertheless, some observations on the influence of dose are possible.

A lower LSD dose generates a less amplified and less catalyzed state of awareness, which in turn results in a weaker resonance between personal and transpersonal levels during the perinatal phase of work. A weaker resonance leads to fewer transpersonal elements being drawn into the therapeutic process. As a result, perinatal sequences would naturally tend, all other things being equal, to be more saturated with personal elements, including one's biological birth. A *sustained* therapeutic regimen that uses a higher dose, on the other hand, such as 500–600 micrograms, produces a much more highly mobilized state of awareness, encouraging a stronger resonance with the surrounding transpersonal domain. In psychedelic sessions that are designed *not to bypass but to engage and resolve conflict,* transpersonal elements would tend to play a more prominent part in one's perinatal experience and could, over the course of therapy, completely overshadow the personal aspects of the death-rebirth process. (Holotropic Breathwork is, I think, closer to psycholytic therapy in this respect than psychedelic therapy.)

Grof has stated in several places that it was his work at Prague that provided him with the detailed insights into the many layers of consciousness and their interaction that we see in his paradigm (e.g., 1976: 23). During the critical years when he was developing his model, therefore, his primary data base derived from psycholytic therapy. (In *The Adventure of Self-Discovery* Grof indicates that he went through his own death-rebirth experience using 300 micrograms [1988: 27], the breakpoint between psycholytic and psychedelic work.) If my conjecture concerning the influence of dose on the slant of perinatal experience is correct, this may have encouraged a description of perinatal dynamics tilted toward the personal. In chapter 8 I will suggest another possible contributing factor.

23. There are other advantages to representing the perinatal matrices in the form of a circle. One of these is that it juxtaposes BPM I and BPM IV. When the perinatal matrices are presented in a list, BPM I and IV appear to lie at opposite ends of the perinatal spectrum, which is not how they tend to surface experientially. While not overlooking the importance of Ken Wilber's distinction between prepersonal states of undifferentiated oneness and genuinely transpersonal states of cosmic unity, these two states often arise closely juxtaposed in psychedelic states. One sometimes gets the impression that it is a single archetype manifesting in two different modalities. Inflected one way, it arises as the intimate, transparent interpenetration of two distinct life forms. Inflected another way, all traces of duality are erased and there is only the One present. (I am grateful to Richard Tarnas for this last point, as well as for numerous helpful suggestions on this chapter.)

A second advantage of the circular image is that it allows us to represent the fact that the perinatal matrices do not necessarily surface in a predetermined order. Like a compass whose needle can point in any direction, one's perinatal experience on any given day can "point" in the direction of any matrix depending on a variety of factors that we will not consider here.

Chapter 4. Solving the Riddle of Heaven's Fire

1. Atwater, 1992: 159.

2. There are three factors that make the NDE population interesting to psychologists and should be making them interesting to philosophers. First, this population is incredibly large. Estimates of the number of persons who have had an NDE are usually calculated on the basis of the 1981 Gallup poll that concluded that 8 million adult Americans had had an NDE. Even if that estimate were to turn out to be inflated, the number of persons who have had this kind of experience is staggering. Second, because

the NDE is unsolicited, this population is innocent or naive. Persons who have entered transpersonal states using Grof's methods have volunteered for the experience. They've prepared themselves intellectually and psychologically for what they might face, selected a time and place to do their work, and arranged their support system. By contrast, NDErs are not volunteers but conscripts. They did not choose to enter these regions but were suddenly snatched away from their daily routines by a heart attack or car accident and plunged into them. Finally, the NDE population is extraordinarily diversified. The experience of nearly dying catches all of us in its broad net and cuts across all our differences of race, education, age, sex, religion, intelligence, and personality type, and so on. It similarly appears not to be influenced by one's prior beliefs about the afterlife. While there are certain interpretive patterns that seem to follow broad cultural contours, the core experience keeps showing up in essentially the same form regardless of whether the subjects previously were passionate atheists, traditional religious believers, or agnostics (Grey, 1985; Ring, 1980, 1984, 1992; Sabom, 1982). There is still too little research on frightening NDEs to indicate whether any of the variables listed here may slant one's experience in a negative direction. Preliminary observations seem to indicate that they do not, but this is a tentative conclusion at this time.

3. Ring, 1991: 14–17.

4. Zaleski, 1987.

5. Ellwood, 1996.

6. In a critical review of Rawlings's latest book, *To Hell and Back* (1993), Michael Sabom demonstrated that Rawlings changed supposedly verbatim accounts of previously published FNDEs without acknowledging that he had done so, and furthermore that he modified them in such a way as to bolster his fundamentalist polemic (Sabom, 1996).

7. James Lindley et al., 1981. This survey reported the existence of a small number of negative NDEs which tended to change into positive experiences over the course of the experience.

8. Atwater, 1988; Flynn, 1986. Researchers have had a difficult time getting a handle on frightening NDEs in part because they appear to be a comparatively rare phenomenon. Many early studies of NDEs failed to turn up any frightening cases at all. A 1981 Gallup poll estimated their frequency of occurrence to be less than 1%, and this figure was later endorsed by a number of other researchers (Lindley et al., 1981; Ring, 1980). Other researchers have suggested that this figure is too low. Margot Grey found that fully 12% of her cases were negative or hellish and P. H. M. Atwater 14% (Atwater, 1994).

The early estimate of 1% should be taken with a grain of salt for three reasons. First, until recently researchers were not asking the right questions to draw out reports of frightening NDEs. In tracking the more common ecstatic near-death experience, they were simply not paying as much attention to its problematic cousin. Secondly, people who have had a frightening NDE are understandably more reluctant to talk about it than people who have had an ecstatic NDE. Kimberly Clark has worked with hundreds of NDErs and found that persons who have a frightening NDE take twice as long to open up about it to researchers as those whose experience is positive, making it likely that researchers may be missing cases and therefore underestimating the frequency of their occurrence (quoted in Flynn, 1986: 83–84). Thirdly, it is possible that frightening NDEs may be more aggressively repressed than positive NDEs. This was Rawlings' contention in 1978 when he first suggested that researchers were not finding negative NDEs because they were waiting too long to interview their subjects. He found cases in which patients had awakened in the middle of surgery terrified and begging to be saved from pursuing demons, but later in recovery could remember nothing about the incident. Accordingly, he argued that the longer after a medical crisis people are interviewed, the more likely it is that they will have repressed any frightening experiences. More frightening near-death episodes would show up, he insisted, if persons were interviewed immediately after their episode. Grey concurred with this suggestion. She found that the physicians she consulted also tended to believe that negative NDEs were more likely to be reported immediately after the medical event, before the patient has had time to mobilize his or her psychological defenses. Michael Sabom, on the other hand, interviewed many of his subjects immediately after cardiac resuscitation and he failed to find any FNDEs (Sabom, 1982, 1996). All we can say with certainty at this time is that while Rawlings's suggestion would seem to have common sense behind it, it has not yet been empirically confirmed.

The safest course at this point may be to accept the figure of 1 percent as a preliminary estimate while recognizing that many factors may be suppressing this figure and stand ready to adjust it upward as necessary. I personally expect the estimate of FNDEs to rise as research protocols improve and as people become more willing to come forward and share their distressing experiences. Ironically, I suspect that we will begin to get an accurate estimate of how often frightening NDEs actually occur only *after* we succeed in removing some of the stigma associated with having one.

9. I want to thank Ken Ring for bringing the literature on frightening NDEs to my attention and for our early conversations around this topic, which were very helpful in clarifying my understanding of this phenomenon (Ring, 1994a, 1994b, 1996; Bache, 1994, 1996).

10. Ring has successfully argued that inverted NDEs can be understood as milder versions of hellish NDEs (1994a). Therefore, if we can demonstrate that hellish and meaningless void NDEs share a common origin, we will be safe in assuming that inverted NDEs share similar ground.

11. 1992: 104–05.

12. Grey, 1985: 70. Again, this experience combines the themes of suffering and meaninglessness, for is there anything more meaningless than an unsolvable two-piece puzzle?

13. Lindley et al., 1981: 114.

14. NDE researchers are sensitive to this problem, as reflected, for example, in the attention they have paid to whether various frightening NDEs do or do not convert to positive NDEs (Irwin and Bramwell, 1988: 43). The capacity of a distressing NDE to convert to an ecstatic NDE is important because it demonstrates the organic connection between these two experiences. Once again, however, we are limited by the fact that most people only have one NDE, frightening or otherwise, and it is unrealistic to expect the full potential of these states of consciousness to reveal themselves in a single episode, however rich it may be.

15. 1976: 116–21.

16. The perinatal origins of meaningless void and hellish NDEs seems clear, but I am less certain about the status of inverted NDEs. With further research it may turn out to be the case that inverted NDEs will be able to be satisfactorily conceptualized in terms of the psychodynamic level of consciousness, and the perinatal level may need to be invoked only for its more severe cousins. We are trying to mark divisions in a continuous spectrum of consciousness, and inverted NDEs seem to me to be in a gray zone. Whatever the final determination of this matter, it will not affect the overall thrust of the interpretation of FNDEs presented here, as the perinatal is the foundation of the personal unconscious and the repository of our deepest illusions about our true identity and our deepest fears of ego-death.

17. In this context it may be significant that in three of the cases that Greyson and Bush present, the frightening phase of the NDE begins while the subject is actually in the tunnel or in the transition phase (1992: 101, 104).

18. Like Grey, P. M. H. Atwater drew upon the *Tibetan Book of the Dead* in her book *Beyond the Light* to interpret frightening NDEs as a form of inner purification, a "mechanism the psyche uses . . . for healing and for growth." She did not get beyond interpreting FNDEs as "in every case" a confrontation with one's personal shadow. Atwater deserves credit for insisting early on that unpleasant and hell-like NDEs were more common than was being recognized by most near-death researchers and for attending to the aftereffects of these darker NDEs.

19. 1994: 14.

20. Ring made an important contribution to understanding the collective dynamics of near-death experiences when he argued in *Heading Toward Omega* that the significance of NDEs only comes into focus when we

shift our perspective from the individual to the collective level and recognize the possible transformative impact of 8 million NDEs on the species-mind. He did not go the next step, however, and recognize the actual presence of the species-mind in some NDEs themselves.

21. It should be clear that I am not recommending breadth at the expense of ontological depth but rather *breadth integrated into depth*. Deep ecology and eco-psychology represent important initiatives, but they must be incorporated into a fully developed transpersonal vision of reality. Thus, I agree with much of the substance of Wilber's critique of these movements though I regret his tone and the missed opportunity to build constructive alliances with these disciplines (1995).

22. A perinatal interpretation of frightening NDEs is a hypothesis that invites further research and refinement. One avenue of research immediately suggests itself. Grof has outlined a set of clinical complications that can arise when various perinatal matrices emerge in therapy but are unresolved by the end of the session (1980:185–95). Research into the aftereffects of frightening NDEs that do not convert to positive NDEs might explore the degree to which these aftereffects parallel the clinical derivatives of unresolved BPM II material in psychedelic therapy. This is a complex assessment that must take into account the preexisting condition of both sets of subjects, but these are manageable variables if handled carefully.

A second line of inquiry has a more clinical focus. Research into the aftereffects of frightening NDEs is only just beginning, but cases being reported indicate that frightening NDEs often leave deep and long-lasting psychic wounds. One Swedish study, for example, reported the experiences of six women who had been given nitrous oxide in connection with caesarean sections. All of the women had "vivid and terrifying dreams" during anesthesia. In some cases, these "dreams" left psychic scars that lasted over a year, and one woman required psychiatric care (Bergstrom and Bernstein, 1968: 541, quoted in Ring, 1996. Ring cites these as examples of frightening experiences that arc not true NDEs but emergent reactions triggered by an anesthetic. However, I have argued that introducing the category of emergent reaction does not clarify the clinical situation. See Bache, 1994).

If severe FNDEs are in fact rooted in the perinatal level of consciousness, we would expect to find: (1) that poorly resolved FNDEs would have particularly long-lasting and pervasive negative aftereffects, and (2) that these aftereffects would be resistant to conventional therapeutic interventions. The perinatal level of consciousness is a particularly deep level of consciousness that is largely untouched by conventional verbal therapies. Situated at the border of the personal and collective unconscious, talking therapies scarcely scratch its surface. To be effective, a therapeutic intervention must be one that bypasses the verbal intellect and engages the deep psyche directly. The more we appreciate the profound depths at which these experiences take place, the more we recognize the necessity of therapeutically meeting them on their own terms. This means creating a therapeutic opportunity for experientially completing what was started and left incomplete in the original NDE.

Holotropic therapy would thus seem to be an ideal therapy for persons suffering from a poorly resolved frightening NDE. Ideally, the therapeutic strategy would be to elicit and fully engage the unresolved perinatal material, thus allowing it to resolve itself into a positive transpersonal experience. If persons showed more clinical improvement with Holotropic Breathwork than with insight-oriented talking therapy, this would strengthen the interpretation of FNDEs offered here. Conversely, less or comparable clinical improvement would count against a perinatal interpretation of these episodes.

23. *Life*: 301–02.

24. In her spiritual classic *The Interior Castle,* St. Teresa divides the spiritual path into seven stages and places the dark night in the sixth stage, coming after many lesser ordeals and immediately before the full realization of God-consciousness. Evelyn Underhill, one of the great scholars of mysticism, divides the mystic's path into five stages: Awakening, Purgation, Illumination, the Dark Night, and the Unitive State. She too places the dark night immediately before final union with God. Hence the dark night represents the final challenge the mystic must face in his or her long search for spiritual awakening. The *Vissudhimagga,* a Buddhist manual of meditation practice, calls this ordeal the "Higher Realizations."

25. This is also the thrust of Gracia Fay Ellwood's beautiful article "Distressing Near-Death Experiences as Photographic Negatives" (1996), which demonstrates the parallels between FNDEs and the mystic's dark night experience. Ellwood suggests that the FNDE might be thought of as a photographic negative of the transcendental reality, that is, the same reality is present but experienced from a reversed position. The Divine is seen but "from the back," so to speak. Ellwood does not explore as deeply as I have here exactly what is the source of this reversal.

26. Floyd, 1996: 192–93. Floyd does not have the subject's account of her experience in her own words, only as quoted in the detailed notes he made during his interview of her (personal communication).

Chapter 5. Beyond the Soul

1. For a provocative overview of the various English translations and interpretations of *The Tibetan Book of the Dead,* see Donald Lopez's *Prisoners of Shangri-La: Tibetan Buddhism and the West,* chapter 2.

2. For a clinical perspective on managing these injuries, see the discussion of releasement of entities in Lucas, 1993: vol. 2, chapter 6.

3. NDErs sometimes glimpse this realm of troubled spirits. One NDEr, for example, saw the following on her way to the Light: "It's a dusky, dark, dreary area, and you realize that the area is filled with a lot of lost souls, or beings, that could go the same way I'm going if they would just look up. The feeling I got was that they were all looking downward, and they were kind of shuffling, and there was a kind of moaning. There were hundreds of them, looking very dejected. The amount of confusion I felt coming off of it was tremendous. When I went through this, I felt there was a lot of pain, a lot of confusion, a lot of fear, all meshed into one. It was a very heavy feeling. They weren't turning toward the Light. In fact, they didn't even know the Light existed" (Flynn, 1986: 82–83). For other examples, see Grey, 1985: 68 and Rawlings, 1978: 104.

4. According to Pat Kubis and Mark Macy, a project of one of these "neighborhoods" is the attempt to communicate with human beings via electronic technology computers, telephones, and faxes. See their book, *Conversations Beyond the Light: Communication with Departed Friends and Colleagues by Electronic Means.*

5. As one reads Monroe's description of the Belief Systems Territory, one is reminded of the "cities of light" that many NDErs have reported seeing during their NDE (e.g., Ring, 1984). The buildings in these cities appear to be made of light, variously described as luminous golden bricks or translucent, plexiglass-like blocks. If the prospect of actual buildings existing in the afterlife seems ludicrous, we might pause to imagine what it would be like after we die to suddenly find ourselves in a world that lacked any familiar frame of reference at all. Such an environment would be completely alien to us, and our confusion would surely compromise our ability to function there.

6. "Inspec" is short for "Intelligent Species," which is Monroe's term for the advanced spiritual guides he meets in the out-of-body state. Late in the trilogy, we learn that the primary Inspec Monroe has been dealing with is in fact his Higher Self, the intelligence that integrates his many incarnations.

7. If we can in fact jump around time in our incarnations, we have to develop a more precise vocabulary for describing the reincarnation process, one that distinguishes causal sequence from chronological sequence. Currently, the term "former lives" conflates this distinction. Monroe's observation opens up the possibility that lives which are "future lives" from our present historical standpoint might in fact be causally "past lives" from our soul's perspective. These distinctions assume, of course, a linear model of reincarnation, which we may or may not want to adopt.

8. If one were to include a fourth point in this list, it might be the geometric increase in love in the upper rings. Love is the affective experience of oneness, and at these highly integrated levels, it profoundly transcends what we customarily think of as love.

9. By his own assessment, Monroe knew that his death-rebirth process was incomplete. In *Ultimate Journey* he said that it would take one more incarnation before his work on Earth was complete and he would be free to move on. If we use Ken Wilber's categories, we could say that Monroe's breakthroughs take place largely at the psychic and low subtle levels of transpersonal experience.

10. We have seen how such sessions might benefit the species-mind, but I have not described how rendering this service for the collective also benefits the individual who offers it. Such benefit does accrue, as it is impossible to assist "others" without being lifted up in turn. There are no conscripts here, only volunteers.

11. A "curl" is an energy life form.

12. 1994: 209–16, emphasis in the original. As this experience demonstrates, the transformative potential of the out-of-body state is open-ended, and for this reason I am reluctant to follow Wilber and Walsh and classify all out-of-body experiences as belonging to the psychic level of transpersonal experience, even though this classification is probably correct for the large majority of them (Wilber, 1995; Walsh, 1990).

13. 1988: 106–10; chapter 3.

14. When we juxtapose Monroe's soul-centered account of the *bardo* with Sheldrake's concept of a species-mind, it suggests that these are not different realities but the same reality experienced from two different perspectives or operating in two different modalities. Just as light can be viewed as being composed of either particles or waves, mind can be experienced in the atomistic mode of individual minds or the more holistic mode of a series of fields of intelligence, one nested in another. These perspectives may appear mutually exclusive, but they cohere experientially, just as light appears to experience no difficulty whatsoever being both a particle and a wave.

15. As we will see in the next chapter, to call all the conditioning that is being worked through "ego" is actually giving far too much credit to this personal structure. It is not just the personal ego that is dismantled through contact with these transpersonal dimensions but our sense of ourselves as a human being per se, that is, the species-ego.

16. 1991: 444.

Chapter 6. Beyond Personal Karma

1. This is a shortcoming of the account of karma that I gave in *Lifecycles*. It is not that what was said there is false, but I see it now as seriously incomplete because it failed to give a sufficient accounting of the collective sinews of karma.

Carl Jung raised the problem of karma in his autobiography, *Memories, Dreams, Reflections,* and saw clearly the connection between how we conceptualize karma and the question of personal identity:

> The crucial question is whether a man's karma is personal or not. If it is, then the preordained destiny with which a man enters life represents an achievement of previous lives, and a personal continuity therefore exists. If, however, this is not so, and an impersonal karma is seized upon in the act of birth, then that karma is incarnated again without there being any personal continuity. . . . I know no answer to the question of whether the karma which I live is the outcome of my past lives, or whether it is not rather the achievement of my ancestors, whose heritage comes together in me. Am I a combination of the lives of these ancestors and do I embody these lives again? Have I lived before in the past as a specific personality, and did I progress so far in that life that I am now able to seek a solution? I do not know. Buddha left the question open, and I like to assume that he himself did not know with certainty. (317–18)

Jung goes on to affirm his belief in reincarnation, but this did not solve all the questions he had about karma: "What I feel to be the resultant of my ancestors' lives, or a karma acquired in a previous personal life, might perhaps equally well be an impersonal archetype which today presses hard on everyone and has taken a particular hold upon me" (318).

2. Notwithstanding the subtlety of his multiquadrant map of inner and outer, individual and collective reality, it is the caustic edge in Wilber's writing that speaks volumes on this point. I simply do not know how to reconcile his implicit claim to speak from the experience of *nirvikalpa samādhi* or *sahaja samādhi* with the sense one gets from his writing that he experiences himself surrounded by fools or worse. All spiritual traditions teach that as the experience of the transcendental ground rises, the knife falls from our hands. Even those with whom we have to disagree are still seen as precious to us and deserving of our complete respect, a respect that I find often lacking in Wilber's writing. Robert McDermott has pressed this point with Wilber in print, but he has not retreated. Instead he has unfortunately chosen to defend the need for polemic in transpersonal discourse, which he calls "the wrathful aspect of enlightened

awareness." There is, however, polemic with compassion and polemic without compassion, and the two are seldom confused (McDermott, 1996a, 1996b; Wilber, 1996).

In the area of not recognizing the true cost, I would mention three points. First is Wilber's apparent lack of feeling for the death-rebirth experience as reflected in his failure to recognize the correspondence between perinatal experience and the dark night of the soul experience and his misguided attempt to equate the perinatal with the fetal and place it in Fulcrum 0 in his system (see appendix A). Second, I have always been struck by the relative lack of attention Wilber has paid to the messier aspects of spiritual purification, such as the actual difficulties that arise in working with former lives. The evolutionary sequence Wilber presents assumes reincarnation, and yet he underplays the nit and gritty complications that are part of the constant stopping and restarting caused by death and rebirth. And finally, the glibness with which he alludes to the magnitude of the suffering that the global awakening of the species might involve is incomprehensible to me. "Won't it be fun when society as a whole is going through *that* stage?" (1995: 627). He writes as if it were a distant event instead of an ordeal that will dominate the lives of our children and grandchildren.

3. These two vectors roughly correspond to Grof's distinction between transpersonal experiences that transcend the boundaries of linear time and those that transcend the boundaries of space. My project here, however, is different from Grof's. He is cataloging the full range of transpersonal experiences that can arise in psychedelic states, while I am trying to articulate the patterns of causal conditioning that are revealed in these experiences, conditioning that continuously impinges upon and informs our experience even after a session is over.

4. To speak of karma "reaching" us through space obviously implies some notion of time operating even here, and we may want to press beyond ordinary language to suggest that the spatial vector operates atemporally, in a holistic simultaneity analogous to the quantum simultaneity of nonlocal effects.

5. See, for example, books by Winafred Lucas, Roger Woolger, and Brian Weiss. While past-life therapists address a more restricted range of transtemporal experiences than surface in psychedelic states, they have examined these experiences in great detail and have refined the art of guiding persons to the interface where these unconscious influences are made conscious and integrated in a precise and repeatable manner. It is the detail of their insight into the characteristics of this interface that can help us here.

6. Roger Corless in *The Vision of Buddhism* translates the Buddhist concept *śūnyatā* as "transparency" instead of the more usual

"emptiness." He writes: "Reality, according to the Buddha, is not an illusion, it certainly exists, but its thing-ness, essence, or intrinsic autonomy cannot be found when it is analyzed. Reality is real, but its reality is *transparent to analysis*" (1989: 20). He notes that Lama Anagarika Govinda proposed the same translation of *śūnyatā* in *Creative Meditation and Multi-Dimensional Consciousness*.

7. Some past-life therapists have attempted to explore their clients' future-lives, with mixed results, I think. See, for example, Chet Snow, *Mass Dreams of the Future*.

8. If the idea of future lives influencing the present is unacceptable to the reader, he or she can simply let the dots above and below the center represent only past lives. Even though I have suggested leaving open the possibility of influence from future lives, I myself will continue to speak, largely out of habit, of our "former lives" when technically I should be saying our "other lives" (meaning both our past and future lives). Above the center point does not literally have to represent the future any more than when we later add a horizontal axis, left and right of center must represent persons standing literally to our left and right. The point of the image is to represent the dialogical relationship between our present awareness and our extended temporal existence, however we conceive it.

9. In this process there are moments when the duality of self and soul vanishes altogether, like a bubble popping, and for a few seconds it is as though there is no smaller self or even soul present, only Sacred Mind. In these moments all sense of dialogue disappears and it feels for a time as though there is only one voice speaking, and this voice comes from an invisible center that embraces the whole of our temporal being yet speaks to our specific circumstances. Dialogue dissolves into pure transparency, and Sacred Mind reaches out without interference or dilution and touches the world directly. In these moments it seems that it is always doing so and that it is only our distortions that make us think otherwise.

10. The parallels with the expanded sense of self-as-the-universe that deep ecology tries to awaken in us should be clear. One difference, however, is that for me the spatial vector is only one of several vectors that reveal our deeper identity. The intuition that our true body is the Earth is a stepping stone into the Sacred Body of the universe *and* the Sacred Mind that saturates this body and that gave birth to it. Wilber's critique of deep ecology as seeing just the body of the universe and not its mind is correct, I think, but once again one wishes that he could have made his points in such a way as to encourage rather than discourage further dialogue (1995).

11. 1990: 91.

12. This discussion obviously oversimplifies the relation of the individual to the species. Within the vast expanse of the species-mind at any

point in history, there are specific archetypal leitmotifs that mediate between the individual and the species as a whole. Cultures have devised different systems, such as natal astrology, to help identify these leitmotifs as they have become focused in a given incarnation and thus illumine the archetypal flavor of each individual. In this way these systems may afford us a certain insight into what our organic role is within the larger organism.

13. I do not intend the freedom of choice assumed by this analogy to undercut the teaching, strongly emphasized in the Eastern traditions, that in the *bardo* one is at the mercy of the one's conditioning and is pulled here and there by the powerful forces of one's mind. I believe that this is true, but I also believe that there are many degrees of conditioning in the *bardo* and therefore many degrees of freedom. True freedom of will is not conferred simply by the act of dying but is the result of great effort and hard work. It develops slowly through the conscientious engagement of the life process. As one's capacity to detach from one's conditioning increases on Earth, it also increases in one's subsequent *bardo* experience. Thus, I think that at each turn of the wheel of *saṃsāra*, one's interlife condition is characterized by more insight than one's prior earthly existence and therefore more *relative* freedom. Complete freedom is not present until full spiritual realization is achieved; until then, choice is always compromised to some degree.

14. 1975: 55.

15. This is essentially Sri Aurobindo's critique of much of India's teaching on karma and rebirth. See *The Problem of Rebirth*.

16. There is a debate over the reliability of recovered memories of abuse and therefore disagreement on how large the problem actually is. For different perspectives, see Ofshe and Watters (1994), Williams (1992), Wylie (1993), Herman and Schatzow (1987), and Russell (1983). So far, those who would discredit these memories as "false memory syndrome" have not made a convincing case. I am indebted to L. J. "Tess" Tessier for these references and for her insightful book on the effects of the denial of sexual identity on spiritual transformation, *Dancing after the Whirlwind*.

17. Two points. First, the species-mind is not a separate mind that exists "over and above" our individual minds but rather is a level of mind that is composed of all our individual minds. Our minds *are* the cells of the species-mind; our brains *are* its neurons. The collective unconscious dynamically integrates the personal unconscious of all human beings, both those on Earth and those in the *bardo*. Second, what is true of human suffering is also true of human kindness, as I said earlier. If we share the collective diseases of humanity, we also share its collective virtues. A balanced description of our situation must also take into account the positive collective assets hidden in our lives together with the liabilities.

18. Justice has been violated only if the individual has been co-erced at any step along the way or if he or she is not fairly compensated for the greater responsibilities assumed. I believe that consent is an essential part of the system and is never violated, though the consent we are talking about is largely hidden from us by the forgetfulness that temporarily blocks from our conscious awareness most of the bargains made in the *bardo*. As many books on spiritually oriented psychotherapy are showing us, however, this amnesia can be challenged and one's karmic contract made conscious. Furthermore, it is my belief and experience that the "compensation" earned by such an expansion of responsibility is more than generous. Anything we do for another helps liberate us from the prison of self-reference, and I am beginning to suspect that there are degrees of liberation that correspond to the degrees of responsibility we assume.

19. John Briggs and F. David Peat, 1990: 185–89. The phase lock-ing in these examples can be understood as being physically mediated. I am suggesting that something analogous also occurs at psychospiritual levels.

Chapter 7. Teaching in the Sacred Mind

1. This paper is an expanded version of a talk given at the International Transpersonal Association meeting at Santa Clara, California, in June 1995.

2. Pedagogically balancing the interests of both these groups of students is a complex issue that cannot be addressed here. It is much easier when the second group of students is the clear majority and the other stu-dents are more or less along for the ride.

3. Satprem, 1993: 286–87, 291.

4. There nothing unique about teaching in this respect, and the same phenomena would arise, I think, in any professional or personal set-ting where one is embedded in substantive relationships. A psychotherapist may spot synchronistic resonances surfacing in her patients, an office man-ager in her staff, and so on.

5. Unless it is highly standardized, the same course in the catalog will end up being a different educational experience when taught by differ-ent professors. This is why I suggest that these learning fields surround par-ticular instructors rather than courses that may be taught by more than one instructor. This is especially the case in the humanities where the nature of the discipline allows wide latitude for individual tailoring.

6. What can't get through our conscious filters often comes in through the back door of our dreams. I have found that dreams I have

shortly before the beginning of a course often contain the germ of new ideas that are especially well turned to the particular students taking the course in a given semester. The dream may suggest new ways of approaching old topics or new material altogether. When I have incorporated these gifts into the course, the results have consistently been very productive.

Chapter 8. The Great Awakening

1. 1984: 205.

2. 1984: 266. To the testimony of these involuntary visionaries we might add an observation that comes from Robert Monroe's out-of-body explorations. In the last chapter of *Far Journeys*, Monroe describes a large gathering of beings surrounding Earth that he observed during one of his sojourns. He was told by his Inspec guide that they had assembled to witness the birth of a new energy on Earth in our near-future. If this birth is successful, it will offer humanity a rare opportunity to emerge rapidly into a unified intelligent energy system that will range far beyond time-space as we know it. In the same volume Monroe reports another experience in which he was taken to a possible future for humanity somewhere beyond 3500 A.D. Never one to blunt his words for fear of overtaxing his readers, Monroe describes a future in which the conditions of life are beyond what even most science fiction writers have entertained. In this future, "mind over matter" has become a reality, and all technology is now essentially psychotechnology. Because industrial technology is no longer necessary, humanity has restored the world to its natural condition. Whether one chooses to take Monroe's vision of the future literally or as a suggestive indication of our evolutionary potential, I cite it as an example of how often the theme of an impending revolution in human consciousness impinges on those involved in the systematic exploration of nonordinary states.

3. "In the United States the average person sees more than 35,000 commercials a year, most of which are adds for a high-consumption lifestyle as well as a pitch for a product." (Elgin, 1993: 254).

4. Russell's sources for these calculations are the French economist George Anderla for the Organization for Economic Cooperation and Development for the rates up to 1973 and the French astrophysicist Dr. Jacque Vallee for the present rate. In order to handle the exponential growth of knowledge since the Renaissance, there has been a parallel growth in the number of scientific journals published to report this knowledge. The first scientific journal was published in 1665. By 1800 there were one hundred journals in print, by 1850 one thousand, by 1900 ten thousand, and by 1990 one hundred thousand scientific journals published around the world.

5. 1995: 143.

6. This is "Scenario 5" in *Beyond the Limits*. Meadow's computer model assumes just four kinds of physical and biological limits: (1) that the Earth contains a maximum of 3.2 billion hectares of cultivable land; (2) that the worldwide average yield achievable on each unit of land will be equivalent to the highest yield obtained by single countries today, approximately 6,500 kg of grain per hectare; (3) that the Earth contains 200 years of non-renewable resources at 1990 rates of extraction; and (4) that the ability of the Earth to absorb pollution erodes as pollution accumulates. If pollution rises to ten times 1990 global levels, it is estimated that this would reduce the human lifetime by only 3% and accelerate degradation of land fertility by 30%. The model does not make any provisions for the effect of wars, strikes, trade barriers, political infighting, or corruption.

7. The Final Declaration of the 1990 Vienna Conference states: "In several sectors the deterioration of the environment has reached a threshold beyond which damage is irreversible." Despite this fact, a recent study entitled *Defending the Future* states that "No government in the world has made any major change in policy designed to convert the unsustainable to the sustainable" (from J. George, 1995: 32). A devastating synopsis of our ecological predicament can be found in Ervin Laszlo's *The Choice: Evolution or Extinction*, chapter 2. For a penetrating analysis of the some of the social, political, and economic forces generating the eco-crisis, see also *The Coming Age of Scarcity*, edited by Michael Dobkowski and Isidor Walliman.

8. 1993: 120. Elgin predicts that by 2025, two powerful trends will converge to create a global crisis—unprecedented material adversity will confront equally unprecedented communications opportunity. Within a generation the world reserves of easily accessible oil will be depleted, we will add another three billion people to the planet, and the climate is expected to become more variable due to global warming. Just when we will need more food than ever before, petrochemical farming will become prohibitively expensive and the weather increasingly unreliable, making it "no longer a probability but a certainty that we will face an immensely difficult and challenging time in human affairs." On the positive side, a combination of revolutionary technologies including fiber-optics, user-friendly data base systems, communications satellites, and voice-recognition computers with translation capability will merge to "produce a global telecommunications network of stunning depth, breadth, and sophistication. In short, our 'global brain' will burst forth and 'turn on' during the first two decades of the twenty-first century" (1993: 248–49).

9. 1993: 121. Peter Russell also acknowledges the role of crisis in making this evolutionary jump when he writes, "The set of global problems that humanity is facing presently may turn out to be as important to our

continued evolution as 'the oxygen crisis' was. Never in the history of the human race have the dangers been so extreme; yet in their role as evolutionary catalysts, they may be just what is needed to push us to a higher level" (1995: 157).

10. Briggs and Peat, 1990: 130.

11. These systems were never "isolated" at their deeper levels, of course, but were relatively isolated in their functioning and thus appeared to be isolated.

12. Briggs and Peat, 1990: 139.

13. On synchronicity: Allan Combs and Mark Holland weave together the work of Arthur Koestler, Rupert Sheldrake, David Bohm, Ilya Progogine, Erich Jantsch, Teilhard de Chardin, and Ira Progroff in their excellent book *Synchronicity* (chapter 2).

14. As far as I am aware, Ken Ring was the first researcher to suggest that the species might be approaching something like a "planetary near-death experience" (1984: 205), an idea picked up and extended by Michael Grosso (1985: chapter 14). Stan Grof brings a perinatal perspective to the global crisis in *Beyond the Brain* (1985: 426–33).

15. 1990: 143.

16. Jung, "The Undiscovered Self," in *Collected Works of Carl Gustav Jung*, vol. 10, pars. 585–86, quoted in Tarnas, 1991: 413.

17. Hollywood has always had its finger on the pulse of the collective psyche of American culture. In 1997, it brought out two movies that form an interesting whole when viewed in the context of this chapter. On July 2nd, *Independence Day* was released, presenting audiences with scenes of the unthinkable—the unstoppable, wholesale destruction of life-as-we-have-known-it on this planet. Cutting closer to the truth than later films such as *Sudden Impact* and *Armageddon,* which placed the threat in value-neutral asteroids, the "alien" invaders in *Independence Day* were a thinly disguised version of the shadow-side of our industrial culture—greedy, wasteful, unfeeling destroyers of worlds, vulnerable within but protected and empowered by a veneer of high technology. On the very same weekend, *Phenomenon* was also released, telling the story of a modest auto mechanic whose life was suddenly transformed by a tumor which made him grow more intelligent at an exponential rate, collapsing thousands of years of psychological development into weeks. At first just simply smarter, he eventually opened to the spiritual side of life, experiencing the underlying wholeness hidden within life's diversity.

Taken together and cutting through all the details, the deep structure of this synchronistic coupling of movies could be seen as a striking dramatization of the basic thesis of this chapter. Under the extreme duress of the collapse of industrial society, we may collectively experience a quick-ening, a change in human nature so profound that capacities that were pre-viously beyond our reach may quickly come within reach. This quickening would be experienced both individually and collectively, eliciting new capac-ities within both individuals and the global community.

18. 1991:430–431. Grof has drawn attention to the growing themes of BPM III in our culture and their implications for our future:

> We see the unleashing of enormous aggressive impulses in wars and revolutionary upheavals throughout the world, in the rising criminality, in terrorism, and in race riots. Sexual expe-riences and behaviors are taking unprecedented forms. . . . The demonic element is also becoming increasingly manifest in the modern world. The rising interest in satanic cults and witch-craft, the increasing popularity of books and horror movies with occult themes, and satanic crimes attest to that fact. The scatological dimension is evident in the progressive industrial pollution, accumulation of waste products on a global scale, and rapidly deteriorating hygienic conditions in large cities.
>
> . . . It seems that we are all involved in a process that par-allels the psychological death and rebirth that so many people have experienced individually in nonordinary states of con-sciousness. If we continue to act out the destructive tendencies from our deep unconscious, we will undoubtedly destroy our-selves and all life on our planet. However, if we succeed in in-ternalizing this process on a large enough scale, it might result in evolutionary progress that can take us as far beyond our present condition as we now are from the primates. (1992: 220)

19. 1991: 431.

20. 1991: 440.

21. 1991: 442–43.

22. In this context, we might consider Robert Monroe's vision of a possible future for humanity as he records it in *Far Journeys*, a future ap-proximately 1,500 years away. In this future there were no longer any rings. The *bardo* had been emptied, the psychic congestion of compulsory rebirths eliminated. The collective unconscious was no longer the living repository of our ignorance but had become transparent to heaven. Persons could now in-carnate on earth without losing sight of spirit. The prison of the private mind had been shattered, and with this release new powers had arisen in humanity. Is this a mere pipedream, a fictitious illusion? Perhaps, but re-member that the condition within which we make all such assessments is the current field of the collective psyche. What we see as possible and im-possible is heavily shadowed by the karmic weight of the current state of the

collective unconscious. It is only in transcending this field of influence that one begins to glimpse the evolutionary possibilities that are opening to us.

23. John White has proposed the term *homo noeticus* for this new form of humanity we are becoming (White, 1981, quoted in Ring, 1984: 256). I prefer the term *homo spiritualis,* by which I mean a humanity that has stabilized the higher cognitive capacity of true spiritual discernment, a spiritually awakened humanity.

Chapter 9. The Fate of Individuality

1. Ouspensky, 1950: 195.

2. 1990: 154, 165. See also Ken Wilber's discussion of *holons* in *Sex, Ecology, Spirituality.* Holons are structures that are simultaneously whole in one context and part in another.

3. Quoted in Satprem, 1993: 227–28.

4. Lex Hixon, *Great Swan: Meetings with Ramakrishna,* 1992: 164.

5. Hixon, 1992: 156. An *avatara* is a fully conscious manifestation of Divine Reality in human form.

In *The Adventure of Self-Discovery,* Grof includes a report of a ketamine experience that combines profound transcendence with the persistence of a subtle, refined sense of individual identity much like I am suggesting here. He cites it as an example of Cosmic Consciousness.

> I realized that the state of consciousness I was in was that of a diamond. . . . All the other physical properties of the diamond seemed to be pointing to its metaphysical significance—beauty, transparence, luster, permanence, unchangeability, and the capacity to bring out of white light a rich spectrum of colors. I felt that I understood why the Tibetan Buddhism is called Vajrayana; the only way I could describe this state of ultimate cosmic ecstasy was to refer to it as "diamond consciousness." Here seemed to be all the creative energy and intelligence of the universe as pure consciousness existing beyond time and space. It was entirely abstract, yet containing all the forms and secrets of creation.
>
> I was floating in this energy as a dimensionless point of consciousness, *totally dissolved, yet maintaining some sense of separate identity* (1988: 146–47, my emphasis).

6. Eckhardt, 1980: 181, quoted in Wilber, 1995: 304–05.

Appendix A.
Ken Wilber and the Perinatal Features of the Dark Night

1. 1995: 585–88. See also Wilber, 1996; Grof, 1996.

2. 1960: 87. Unless otherwise indicated, all page references for Teresa are to her autobiography, *The Life of Teresa of Jesus* (1960).

3. P. 90.

4. P. 274.

5. P. 195.

6. P. 273.

7. P. 282.

8. P. 288.

9. P. 195

10. Pp. 274, 301.

11. Though Teresa in her autobiography describes the fourth degree of prayer as the "highest" mystical experience, her experiences appear to have deepened by the time she writes *Interior Castle* twelve years later. The metaphors of union given in the latter work (1961: 214–15) convey a more consummate and complete union than her earlier description (1960: Chapter 18). In addition, in *Life* she values rapture over union (1960:89), whereas in *Interior Castle* rapture ceases when union has matured (1961: 23). Thus the "final cleansing" recorded in the *Life* was a genuine final preparation for a degree of mystical attainment beyond that recorded in her autobiography.

12. P. 163.

13. 1961: 113.

14. 1961: 216.

15. 1961: 219.

16. 1976: 125.

17. 1960: 192–93, 196; 1961: 134.

18. Another way of making this point using Wilber's vocabulary is to say that it is unclear whether his fulcrums are marking the development of the frontal consciousness or the soul. If the full trajectory is realized in one lifetime, then it is the frontal consciousness; if many lifetimes, it is the soul. This ambiguity derives from the fact that Wilber tends not to address

the reincarnational facts of life. I am suggesting that the most coherent way to view his map is to see it as the developmental trajectory of the soul.

19. It is becoming increasingly important that transpersonal theorists pay more attention to the issue of comparative method. The moment of transpersonal disclosure is at least in part a reflection of the condition of the consciousness asking the questions, and this condition is deeply influenced by the particular spiritual method one has used to come to this moment. Our nature is our nature, but different spiritual methods bring our nature forward in different ways. We should not be delegitimating one method in order to champion another, but rather understanding that each method of unfolding into spirit has its own distinctive patterns. I think we will learn more from the careful comparative analysis of the plurality of these patterns than from attending to the patterns of only one method.

20. 1997: 181, Wilber's emphasis.

21. Contrary to Wilber's assertion (1997: 174), Grof never says that reliving one's biological birth is a necessary component of the death-rebirth transition but, on the contrary, has always acknowledged that persons may experience the entire perinatal transition in spiritual or philosophical terms.

22. 1997: 325, n. 16.

23. 1997: 176.

24. Grof himself did not initially do so. There is a subtle evolution in his description of the perinatal through his writings. I personally believe that his best presentation is found in *Realms of the Human Unconscious*. It is his most complete phenomenological description, and when he invokes the birth process as an interpretive hermeneutic, he is the most restrained, almost painfully aware that it is but one way to organize this complex, multidimensional material. There is no use of language like "core" or "central" and transpersonal experiences are not spoken of as being drawn in through thematic resonance. At the same time, there is the tilt toward the personal in his exposition and it is described as Rankian, though in a qualified sense. In *LSD Psychotherapy* the discussion is similarly open-ended though shorter. The transpersonal side is treated as an equal manifestation of the perinatal death-rebirth process even while the birth process is repeated as the overarching interpretive hermeneutic. It is only in *Beyond the Brain* and *The Adventure of Self-Discovery* that Grof goes one step further and begins to speak of birth being the "core" of the perinatal process and of the collective and archetypal aspects as being drawn in through thematic or affective resonance to this core.

25. 1997: 174.

26. 1960: 301–2. The same intimate correspondences show up when we compare perinatal experience with John of the Cross's classical description of the dark night in his book *Dark Night of the Soul* (Bache, 1991).

27. Wilber's suggestion that birth trauma may appear in the transition to Fulcrum 7 if there is unresolved pathology or "significant malformations" left over from earlier development is unconvincing, I think. We find birth fragments at Fulcrum 7 not because something has gone wrong, though this may happen, but because in the natural course of events the return to spiritual awareness sometimes brings forward memories of our previous departure from greater spiritual awareness (birth), and sometimes memories of our previous returns (death). Our entire history of plunging in and out of spacetime may be summoned by the act of spiritual awakening.

28. 1996: 178. Klein's book is a valuable source for understanding the spiritual significance of womb imagery in spiritual transformation. In Vajrayana Buddhism, Yeshey Tsogyel, The Great Bliss Queen, is a *dakini*, a feminine being who embodies the energy of enlightenment (literally a "Sky Woman"). Her mind is free of all dualistic illusions, and as such she is the embodiment of primordial freedom. Thus, Tsogyel's womb becomes the symbol of enlightenment: "The great expanse that is both Tsogyel's womb and wisdom is in the Great Completeness traditions synonymous with the womblike sphere in which a Sky Woman is said to move. Her womb and other female organs are emblematic of enlightened wisdom and the state of Buddhahood itself, and are among the most important symbols associated with the Great Bliss Queen" (160).

29. Klein, 1996: 177.

Appendix B. Ego-Death and the Species-Mind

1. Grof acknowledges that there are many deaths other than ego-death. He distinguishes, for example, between the death of ego and the death of matter, in which one transcends spacetime altogether. On the whole, however, his agenda has been to catalogue the broad range of transpersonal experiences that are possible rather than to mark the specific stages of transformation one goes through as the *bardo* falls away. One of the things needed at this point in time, therefore, is a description of the death-rebirth process that more carefully distinguishes its many layers. Such a description would open up new possibilities for integrating Grof and Wilber's paradigms because it would describe a sequence that could be correlated with Wilber's categories of psychic, subtle, causal, and nondual transpersonal experience.

2. Hixon, 1992: 156, 171, my emphasis.

3. I am choosing my words carefully here because it is not at all clear where this "higher order of intentionality" resides or "who" or "what" is coordinating one's experiences in these sessions. It is certainly not "me" in any conventional sense, but neither is it some "other." Rather, the levels of agency involved seem to be inherent in the very fabric of existence itself, in ways that shatter conventional descriptions of intentionality because the fundamental subject and object dichotomy itself has dissolved. The experience is one in which pure subjectivity is addressing itself within an enlarged "contact boundary."

Psychedelic states vary widely in intensity. Whether and how these particular dynamics will manifest may depend upon the intensity of the particular state one has entered (chapter 3, n. 22). As we saw in chapter 8, chaos theory tells us that when physical systems are pushed beyond their normal equilibrium, they sometimes demonstrate novel patterns of higher self-organization. It is precisely the "extra" energy present in these far-from-equilibrium conditions that allows these novel patterns to arise. This may also be true for psychological systems. The dynamics that I have described may only manifest themselves if the psychological system reaches a specific threshold of arousal. It may be the case that the more highly energized the state one has entered, the more likely it is that these higher orders of intentionality will surface.

Bibliography

Almeder, Robert. 1992. *Death and Personal Survival*. Lanham, Md.: Littlefield Adams.

Atwater, P. M. H. 1988. *Coming Back to Life*. New York: Dodd, Mead & Co.

———. 1992. "Is There a Hell? Surprising Observations about the Near-Death Experience." *Journal of Near-Death Studies* 10: 149–60.

———. 1994. *Beyond the Light*. New York: Birch Lane Press.

Aurobindo, Sri. 1983. *The Problem of Rebirth*. Pondicherry, India: Sri Aurobindo Ashram Press.

Bache, Christopher M. 1985. "A Reappraisal of Teresa of Avila's Supposed Hysteria." *Journal of Religion and Health* 24: 21–30.

———. 1990. *Lifecycles*. New York: Paragon House.

———. 1991. "Mysticism and Psychedelics: The Case of the Dark Night." *Journal of Religion and Health* 30: 215–36.

———. 1994. "A Perinatal Interpretation of Frightening Near-Death Experiences: A Dialogue with Kenneth Ring." *Journal of Near-Death Studies* 13: 25–45.

———. 1996. "Expanding Grof's Conception of the Perinatal: Deepening the Inquiry into Frightening Near-Death Experiences." *Journal of Near-Death Studies* 15: 115–39.

Barrow, John D. and Frank J. Tipler. 1996. *The Anthropic Cosmological Principle*. Oxford: Oxford University Press.

Bergstrom, H. and K. Bernstein. 1968. "Psychic Reactions After Analgesia with Nitrous Oxide for Caesarean Section." *Lancet* 2: 541–42.

Bohm, David. 1980. *Wholeness and the Implicate Order*. Boston: Routledge & Kegan Paul.

Bohm, David and E. David Peat. 1987. *Science, Order and Creativity*. New York: Bantam Books.

Borysenko, Joan. 1994. *The Power of the Mind to Heal*. New York: Nightingale-Conant.

337

Briggs, John. 1992. *Fractals*. New York: Simon & Schuster.

Briggs, John and David F. Peat. 1990. *Turbulent Mirror*. New York: Harper & Row.

Bush, Nancy E. 1994. "The Paradox of Jonah: Response to 'Solving the Riddle of Frightening Near-Death Experiences.'" *Journal of Near-Death Studies* 13: 47–54.

Capra, Fritjof. 1983. *The Turning Point*. New York: Bantam Books.

Carroll, Lewis. 1910. *Alice's Adventures in Wonderland*. New York: Norton.

Cobb, John B. and David Ray Griffin. 1976. *Process Theology*. Philadelphia: The Westminster Press.

Combs, Allan and Mark Holland. 1990. *Synchronicity*. New York: Paragon House.

Corless, Roger. 1989. *The Vision of Buddhism*. New York: Paragon House.

Dante Alighieri. 1990. *The Inferno of Dante*. London: J. M. Dent and Co.

Davies, Paul. 1992. *Mind of God*. New York: Simon & Schuster.

Davies, Paul and John Gribbin. 1992. *The Matter Myth*. New York: Simon & Schuster.

Delacour, Jean Baptiste. 1974. *Glimpses of the Beyond*. New York: Delacorte Press.

Dennett, Daniel C. 1991. *Consciousness Explained*. Boston: Little, Brown and Co.

Diamond, Irene and Gloria F. Orenstein, eds. *Reweaving the World*. San Francisco: Sierra Club Books, 1990.

Dobkowski, Michael N. and Isidor Walliman. 1998. *The Coming Age of Scarcity*. Syracuse, N.Y.: Syracuse University Press.

Doore, Gary, ed. 1990. *What Survives?* Los Angeles: J. P. Tarcher.

Dossey, Larry. 1989. *Recovering the Soul*. New York: Bantam Books.

———. 1993. *Healing Words*. New York: Harper San Francisco.

Eckhart, Meister. 1980. *Breakthrough*. Translated by M. Fox. New York: Image.

Edwards, Paul. 1986–87. "The Case against Reincarnation: Parts I–IV." *Free Inquiry* 6.4: 24–34; 7.1: 38–48; 7.2: 38–49; 7.3: 46–53.

———. ed. 1992. *Immortality*. New York: Macmillan.

———. 1996. *Reincarnation*. New York: Prometheus Books.

Elgin, Duane. 1993. *Awakening Earth*. New York: Morrow.

Ellwood, Gracia F. 1996. "Distressing Near-Death Experiences as Photographic Negatives." *Journal of Near-Death Studies* 15: 83–114.

Ferrer, Jorge N. 1998. "Beyond Absolutism and Relativism in Transpersonal Evolutionary Theory." *World Futures* 52: 239–80.

———. 1998. "Speak Now or Forever Hold Your Peace: A Review Essay of Ken Wilber's *The Marriage of Sense and Soul*." *Journal of Transpersonal Psychology* 30: 53–67.

Fields, Rick. 1996. "A High Society in Buddhism." *Tricycle* 6.1 (Fall): 45–58.

Floyd, Keith C. 1996. "ECT: TNT or TLC? A Near-Death Experience Triggered by Electroconvulsive Therapy." *Journal of Near-Death Studies* 14: 187–95.

Flynn, C. P. 1986. *After the Beyond*. Englewood Cliffs, N.J.: Prentice Hall.

Forman, Robert K. C., ed. 1990. *The Problem of Pure Consciousness*. New York: Oxford University Press.

Forte, Robert, ed. 1997. *Entheogens and the Future of Religion*. San Francisco: Council on Spiritual Practices.

George, James. 1995. *Asking for the Earth*. Rockport, Mass.: Element Inc.

Gibson, Arvin S. 1996. "Commentary on 'Frightening Near-Death Experiences.' " *Journal of Near-Death Studies* 15: 141–48.

Gleick, James. 1987. *Chaos*. New York: Penguin Books.

Goswami, Amit. 1993. *The Self-Aware Universe*. New York: Tarcher/Putnam.

Grey, Margaret. 1985. *Return from Death*. London: Arkana.

Greyson, Bruce and Nancy E. Bush. 1992. "Distressing Near-Death Experiences." *Psychiatry* 55: 95–110.

Greyson, Bruce and Ian Stevenson. 1980. "The Phenomenology of Near-Death Experiences." *American Journal of Psychiatry* 137: 1193–96.

Griffin, David Ray. 1986. *Physics and the Ultimate Significance of Time*. Albany: State University of New York Press.

———. 1989. *God and Religion in the Postmodern World*. Albany: State University of New York Press.

———. 1990. *Sacred Interconnections*. Albany: State University of New York Press.

———. 1993. *Founders of Constructive Postmodern Philosophy*. Albany: State University of New York Press.

Griffin, David Ray and Huston Smith. 1989. *Primordial Truth and Post-Modern Theology*. Albany: State University of New York Press.

Grof, Stanislav. 1976. *Realms of the Human Unconscious*. New York: Dutton.

———. 1977. *The Human Encounter with Death*. New York: Dutton.

———. 1980. *LSD Psychotherapy*. Pomonam, N.Y.: Hunter House.

———. 1985. *Beyond the Brain*. Albany: State University of New York Press.

———. 1988. *The Adventure of Self-Discovery*. Albany: State University of New York Press.

———. 1990. *The Holotropic Mind*. New York: Harper San Francisco.

———. 1996. "Ken Wilber's Spectrum Psychology: Observations from Clinical Consciousness Research." *Revision* 19.1: 11–24.

———. 1998. *The Cosmic Game*. Albany: State University of New York Press.

Grof, Stanislav and Christina Grof. 1980. *Beyond Death*. London: Thames & Hudson.

Grof, Stanislav and Joan Halifax. 1977. *The Human Encounter with Death*. New York: Dutton.

Grosso, Michael. 1985. *The Final Choice*. Walpole, N.H.: Stillpoint.

———. 1992. *Frontiers of the Soul*. Wheaton, Ill.: Theosophical Publishing House.

———. 1995. *The Millennium Myth*. Wheaton, Ill.: Quest Books.

Guntrip, Harry. 1969. *Object-Relations and the Self*. New York: International Universities Press.

———. 1971. *Psychoanalytic Theory, Therapy, and the Self*. New York: Basic Books.

Heilbroner, Robert L. 1981. *An Inquiry into the Human Prospect*. New York: W. W. Norton.

Herman, Judith L. and Emily Schatzow. 1987. "Recovery and verification of Memories of Childhood Sexual Trauma." *Psychoanalytic Psychology* 4.1: 1–14.

Heron, John. 1998. *Sacred Science*. Ross-on-Wye, Herefordshire, U.K.: PCCS Books.

Hillman, James. 1992. *Re-Visioning Psychology*. New York: HarperCollins.

Hixon, Lex. 1996. *Great Swan*. Burdett, N.Y.: Larson Publications.

Hopkins, Jeffrey and Lati Rinbochay. 1985. *Death, Intermediate State and Rebirth in Tibetan Buddhism.* Ithaca, NY: Snow Lion Press.

Hunt, Allen, eds. 1990. *Dharma Gaia.* Berkeley: Parallax Press. Snow Lion.

Irwin, Harvey J. and Barbara A. Bramwell. 1988. "The Devil in Heaven: A Near-Death Experience with Both Positive and Negative Facets." *Journal of Near-Death Studies* 7: 38–43.

James, William. 1975. *The Will to Believe.* Cambridge: Harvard University Press.

———. 1967. *The Writings of William James.* Edited by John J. McDermott. New York: Random House.

John of the Cross. 1959. *Dark Night of the Soul.* Edited by E. Allison Peers. Garden City, N.Y.: Image.

Jung, Carl Gustav. 1973. *Memories, Dreams and Reflections.* New York: Vintage Books, Random House.

———. 1973. *Synchronicity.* Princeton: Princeton University Press.

———. 1976. *Letters.* Vol. 1. Princeton: Princeton University Press.

Klein, Anne C. 1995. *Meeting the Great Bliss Queen.* Boston: Beacon Press.

Kubis, Pat and Mark Macy. 1996. *Conversations Beyond the Light.* Glendale, Calif.: Bridgeport Books.

Laszlo, Ervin, 1994. *The Choice.* New York: J. P. Tarcher/Putnam.

———. 1995. *The Interconnected Universe.* River Edge, N.J.: World Scientific.

Lindley, James H., Bryan Sethyn and Bob Conley. 1981. "Near-Death Experiences in a Pacific Norwest American Population: The Evergreen Study." *Anabiosis: The Journal of Near-Death Studies* 1: 104–24.

Lopez, Donald S. 1998. *Prisoners of Shangri-La.* Chicago: University of Chicago Press.

Lovejoy, Arthur O. 1936. *The Great Chain of Being.* Cambridge: Harvard University Press.

Lovelock, James. 1979. *Gaia.* Oxford: Oxford University Press.

Lucas, Winafred. 1993. *Regression Therapy.* 2 vols. Crest Park, Calif.: Deep Forest Press.

Macy, Joanna. 1991. *World as Lover, World as Self.* Berkeley, Calif.: Parallax Press.

McKenna, Terence K. 1991. *The Archaic Revival*. San Francisco: Harper San Francisco.

Meadows, Donella H., Dennis L. Meadows, and Jorgen Randers. 1992. *Beyond the Limits*. White River Junction, Vt.: Chelsea Green Publishing Co.

Monroe, Robert A. 1970. *Journeys Out of the Body*. Garden City, N.Y.: Anchor Press.

———. 1985. *Far Journeys*. New York: Doubleday.

———. 1994. *Ultimate Journey*. New York: Doubleday.

Moody, Raymond A. 1975. *Life after Life*. New York: Bantam Books.

Mookerjee, Ajit. 1983 *Kundalini*. 1983. New York: Destiny Books.

Narby, Jeremy. 1998. *The Cosmic Serpent*. New York: Tarcher/Putnam.

Nhât-Hanh, Thích. 1996. *Being Peace*. Edited by Arnold Kotler. Berkeley: Parallax Press.

Noyes, R., Jr. and D. J. Slymen. 1978–79. "The Subjective Response to Life-Threatening Danger." *Omega* 9: 313–21.

Osis, Karlis and Erlendur Haraldsson. 1977. *At the Hour of Death*. New York: Avon.

Ouspensky, P. D. 1950. *In Search of the Miraculous*. London: Routledge & Kegan Paul.

Rawlings, Maurice. 1978. *Beyond Death's Door*. New York: Thomas Nelson.

———. 1980. *Before Death Comes*. Nashville, Tenn.: Thomas Nelson.

———. 1993. *To Hell and Back*. Nashville, Tenn.: Thomas Nelson.

Ring, Kenneth. 1980. *Life at Death*. New York: Coward, McCann and Geoghegan.

———. 1984. *Heading toward Omega*. New York: Morrow.

———. 1988. "Guest Editorial: Paradise is Paradise: Reflections on Psychedelic Drugs, Mystical Experiences, and the Near-Death Experience." *Journal of Near-Death Studies* 6: 138–48.

———. 1991. "Amazing Grace: The Near-Death Experience as a Compensatory Gift." *Journal of Near-Death Studies* 10: 11–39.

———. 1992. *The Omega Project*. New York: Morrow.

———. 1994a. "Solving the Riddle of Frightening Near-Death Experiences: Some Testable Hypotheses and a Perspective Based on *A Course in Miracles*." *Journal of Near-Death Studies* 13: 5–23.

———. 1994b. "Frightening Near-Death Experiences Revisited: A Commentary on Responses to My Paper by Christopher Bache and Nancy Evans Bush." *Journal of Near-Death Studies* 13: 55–64.

———. 1996. "A Note on Anesthetically-Induced Frightening Near-Death Experiences." *Journal of Near-Death Studies* 15: 17–23.

Roszak, Theodore. 1993. *The Voice of the Earth.* New York: Simon & Schuster.

Rothberg, Donald. 1986. "Philosophical Foundations of Transpersonal Psychology: An Introduction to Some Basic Issues." *Journal of Transpersonal Psychology* 18: 1–34.

Russell, Diana E. H. 1983. "The Incidence and Prevalence of Intrafamilial and Extrafamilial Sexual Abuse of Female Children." *Child Abuse and Neglect* 7: 133–46.

Russell, Peter. 1992. *The White Hole in Time.* San Francisco: Harper San Francisco.

———. 1995. *The Global Brain Awakens.* Palo Alto, Calif.: Global Brain.

Sabom, Michael B. 1996. "Book Review: *To Hell and Back: Life after Death— Startling New Evidence* by Maurice Rawlings." *Journal of Near-Death Studies* 14: 197–209.

Sabom, Michael. 1982. *Recollections of Death.* New York: Harper & Row.

Satprem. 1993. *Sri Aurobindo or The Adventure of Consciousness.* Pondicherry, India: Sri Aurobindo Ashram Press.

Sessions, George, eds. 1995. *Deep Ecology for the Twenty-First Century.* Boston: Shambhala.

Sheldrake, Rupert. 1981. *A New Science of Life.* Los Angeles: J. P. Tarcher.

———. 1988. *The Presence of the Past.* New York: Vintage.

. 1991. *The Rebirth of Nature.* New York: Bantam.

Shuon, Frithjof. 1984. *The Transcendent Unity of Religions.* Wheaton, Ill.: Theosophical Publishing House.

Skolimowski, Henry. 1994. *The Participatory Mind.* London: Arkana.

Smith, Huston. 1989. *Beyond the Post-Modern Mind.* Wheaton, Ill: Theosophical Publishing House.

Snow, Chet B. 1989. *Mass Dreams of the Future.* New York: McGraw-Hill.

Stevenson, Ian. 1974. *Twenty Cases Suggestive of Reincarnation.* 2nd rev. ed., Charlottesville: University Press of Virginia.

———. 1975–83. *Cases of the Reincarnation Type,* 4 vols. Charlottesville: University Press of Virginia.

———. 1987. *Children Who Remember Previous Lives*. Charlottesville: University Press of Virginia.

———. 1993. "Birthmarks and Birth Defects Corresponding to Wounds on Deceased Persons." *Journal of Scientific Explanation* 7.4: 403–10.

———. 1997. *Reincarnation and Biology,* 2 vols. Charlottesville: University Press of Virginia.

———. 1997. *Where Reincarnation and Biology Intersect*. Charlottesville: University Press of Virginia.

Summit, Roland C. 1983. "The Child Sexual Abuse Accomodation Syndrome." *Child Abuse and Neglect* 7: 177–93.

Talbot, Michael. 1991. *The Holographic Universe*. New York: HarperCollins.

Tarnas, Richard. 1991. *The Passion of the Western Mind*. New York: Harmony Books.

———. 1995. *Prometheus the Awakener*. Woodstock, Conn.: Spring Publications.

Teresa of Avila. 1960 (1565). *The Life of Teresa of Jesus*. Trans. and ed. by E. Allison Peers. Garden City, N.Y.: Image Books.

———. 1961 (1577). *Interior Castle*. Trans. and ed. by E. Allison Peers. Garden City, N.Y: Image Books.

Tessier, L. J. "Tess." 1997. *Dancing after the Whirlwind*. Boston: Beacon Press.

Thurman, Robert A.F. 1993. *The Tibetan Book of the Dead*. New York: Bantam Books.

Van Franz, Marie Louise. 1988. *Psyche and Matter*. Boston: Shambhala Publications.

Walsh, Roger N. 1990. *The Spirit of Shamanism*. Los Angeles: J. P. Tarcher.

Wambach, Helen. 1978. *Reliving Past Lives*. New York: Bantam.

Weiss, Brian L. 1992. *Through Time into Healing*. New York: Fireside.

———. 1996. *Many Lives, Many Masters*. New York: Warner Books.

Whitton, Joel and Fisher, Joe. 1986. *Life between Life*. Garden City, N.Y.: Doubleday.

Wilber, Ken. 1977. *The Spectrum of Consciousness*. Wheaton, Ill.: Theosophical Publishing House.

———. 1980. *The Atman Project*. Wheaton, Ill.: Quest Books.

———. 1986. *A Sociable God*. Boston: Shambhala.

———. 1990. *Eye to Eye*. Boston: Shambhala.

———. 1995. *Sex, Ecology, Spirituality*. Boston, Shambhala.

———. 1996. "A More Integral Approach: A Response to *Revision* Authors." *Revision* 19.2: 10–34.

———. 1997. *The Eye of Spirit*. Boston: Shambhala.

———. 1998a. *The Marriage of Sense and Soul*. New York: Random House.

———. 1998b. "Response to Jorge Ferrer's 'Speak Now or Forever Hold Your Peace—A Review Essay of Ken Wilber's *The Marriage of Sense and Soul*." *Journal of Transpersonal Psychology* 30.1: 69–72.

Williams, Linda M. 1992. "Adult Memories of Childhood Abuse: Preliminary Findings from a Longitudinal Study." *APSAC Advisor*: 19–21.

Wylie, Mary S. 1993. "The Shadow of a Doubt." *Family Therapy Networker*, September/October.

Zaleski, C. 1987. *Otherworldly Journeys*. New York: Oxford University Press.

Index